Convergence of Big Data Technologies and Computational Intelligent Techniques

Govind P. Gupta
National Institute of Technology, Raipur, India

A volume in the Advances in
Computational Intelligence and
Robotics (ACIR) Book Series

Published in the United States of America by
  IGI Global
  Engineering Science Reference (an imprint of IGI Global)
  701 E. Chocolate Avenue
  Hershey PA, USA 17033
  Tel: 717-533-8845
  Fax: 717-533-8661
  E-mail: cust@igi-global.com
  Web site: http://www.igi-global.com

Library of Congress Cataloging-in-Publication Data

Names: Gupta, Govind P., 1979- editor.
Title: Convergence of big data technologies and computational intelligent
  techniques / Govind Gupta, editor.
Description: Hershey PA : Engineering Science Reference, [2023] | Includes
  bibliographical references and index. | Summary: "With rapid evolution
  and development of the internet-based services and applications, Big
  Data storage, processing and its analytics are getting huge attention so
  this book identifies applications of advanced computational intelligence
  techniques in various big data engineering and analytics problem"--
  Provided by publisher.
Identifiers: LCCN 2022016806 (print) | LCCN 2022016807 (ebook) | ISBN
  9781668452646 (hardcover) | ISBN 9781668452653 (paperback) | ISBN
  9781668452660 (ebook)
Subjects: LCSH: Big data. | Computational intelligence. | Quantitative
  research.
Classification: LCC QA76.9.B45 C669 2023 (print) | LCC QA76.9.B45 (ebook)
  | DDC 005.7--dc23/eng/20220726
LC record available at https://lccn.loc.gov/2022016806
LC ebook record available at https://lccn.loc.gov/2022016807

This book is published in the IGI Global book series Advances in Computational Intelligence and
Robotics (ACIR) (ISSN: 2327-0411; eISSN: 2327-042X)

British Cataloguing in Publication Data
A Cataloguing in Publication record for this book is available from the British Library.

All work contributed to this book is new, previously-unpublished material.
The views expressed in this book are those of the authors, but not necessarily of the publisher.

For electronic access to this publication, please contact: eresources@igi-global.com.

Advances in Computational Intelligence and Robotics (ACIR) Book Series

ISSN:2327-0411
EISSN:2327-042X

Editor-in-Chief: Ivan Giannoccaro, University of Salento, Italy

MISSION

While intelligence is traditionally a term applied to humans and human cognition, technology has progressed in such a way to allow for the development of intelligent systems able to simulate many human traits. With this new era of simulated and artificial intelligence, much research is needed in order to continue to advance the field and also to evaluate the ethical and societal concerns of the existence of artificial life and machine learning.

The **Advances in Computational Intelligence and Robotics (ACIR) Book Series** encourages scholarly discourse on all topics pertaining to evolutionary computing, artificial life, computational intelligence, machine learning, and robotics. ACIR presents the latest research being conducted on diverse topics in intelligence technologies with the goal of advancing knowledge and applications in this rapidly evolving field.

COVERAGE

- Intelligent Control
- Robotics
- Cognitive Informatics
- Computational Logic
- Automated Reasoning
- Neural Networks
- Brain Simulation
- Pattern Recognition
- Artificial Intelligence
- Cyborgs

IGI Global is currently accepting manuscripts for publication within this series. To submit a proposal for a volume in this series, please contact our Acquisition Editors at Acquisitions@igi-global.com or visit: http://www.igi-global.com/publish/.

Titles in this Series

For a list of additional titles in this series, please visit:
https://www.igi-global.com/book-series/advances-computational-intelligence-robotics/73674

Controlling Epidemics With Mathematical and Machine Learning Models
Abraham Varghese (Higher College of Technology, Oman) Eduardo M. Lacap, Jr. (Higher
College of Technology, Oman) Ibrahim Sajath (Higher College of Technology, Oman)
Kamal Kumar (Higher College of Technology, Oman) and Shajidmon Kolamban (Higher
College of Technology, Oman)
Engineering Science Reference • copyright 2023 • 300pp • H/C (ISBN: 9781799883432)
• US $270.00 (our price)

Handbook of Research on Computer Vision and Image Processing in the Deep Learning Era
A. Srinivasan (SASTRA University (Deemed), India)
Engineering Science Reference • copyright 2023 • 400pp • H/C (ISBN: 9781799888925)
• US $325.00 (our price)

Multidisciplinary Applications of Deep Learning-Based Artificial Emotional Intelligence
Chiranji Lal Chowdhary (Vellore Institute of Technology, India)
Engineering Science Reference • copyright 2023 • 296pp • H/C (ISBN: 9781668456736)
• US $270.00 (our price)

Principles and Applications of Socio-Cognitive and Affective Computing
S. Geetha (VIT University, Chennai, India) Karthika Renuka (PSG College of Technology,
India) Asnath Victy Phamila (VIT University, Chennai, India) and Karthikeyan N. (Syed
Ammal Engineering College, India)
Engineering Science Reference • copyright 2023 • 330pp • H/C (ISBN: 9781668438435)
• US $270.00 (our price)

*Revolutionizing Industrial Automation Through the Convergence of Artificial Intelligence
and the Internet of Things*
Divya Upadhyay Mishra (ABES Engineering College, Ghaziabad, India) and Shanu Sharma
(ABES Engineering College, Ghaziabad, India)
Engineering Science Reference • copyright 2023 • 279pp • H/C (ISBN: 9781668449912)
• US $270.00 (our price)

For an entire list of titles in this series, please visit:
https://www.igi-global.com/book-series/advances-computational-intelligence-robotics/73674

701 East Chocolate Avenue, Hershey, PA 17033, USA
Tel: 717-533-8845 x100 • Fax: 717-533-8661
E-Mail: cust@igi-global.com • www.igi-global.com

Editorial Advisory Board

Table of Contents

    Bhargav Naidu Matcha, Taylor's University, Lakeside Campus, India
    Sivakumar Sivanesan, Asia Pacific University of Technology and
        Innovation, Malaysia
    K. C. Ng, University of Nottingham, Malaysia
    Se Yong Eh Noum, Taylor's University, Malaysia
    Aman Sharma, Taylor's University, Malaysia

    Lavanya Sendhilvel, Vellore Institute of Technology, India
    Kush Diwakar Desai, Vellore Institute of Technology, India
    Simran Adake, Vellore Institute of Technology, India
    Rachit Bisaria, Vellore Institute of Technology, India
    Hemang Ghanshyambhai Vekariya, Vellore Institute of Technology,
        India

Detailed Table of Contents

    Bhargav Naidu Matcha, Taylor's University, Lakeside Campus, India
    Sivakumar Sivanesan, Asia Pacific University of Technology and
        Innovation, Malaysia
    K. C. Ng, University of Nottingham, Malaysia
    Se Yong Eh Noum, Taylor's University, Malaysia
    Aman Sharma, Taylor's University, Malaysia

The application of big data in urban transportation and development of smart cities has been attracting global interest. The overburdened transport infrastructure due to rapid urbanisation should be integrated with innovative technologies and brand-new ideas such as smart city in order to enhance its performance. Big data is now the emerging exemplar in intelligent transportation systems for effective management of all data for implementing safer, cleaner, and well-planned transport services, as well as providing personalised transport experience for road users. In this chapter, the authors lay forward the current research endeavours on big data for urban transportation infrastructure, its implementation, baseline framework, and usage on fields such as planning, routing, network configuration, and infrastructure maintenance. This chapter evaluates the contributions of big data on urban transport modelling techniques, tools, and mobility. Finally, the present trends and future challenges of big data are summarised for helping researchers to facilitate the development of smart cities.

Lavanya Sendhilvel, Vellore Institute of Technology, India
Kush Diwakar Desai, Vellore Institute of Technology, India
Simran Adake, Vellore Institute of Technology, India
Rachit Bisaria, Vellore Institute of Technology, India
Hemang Ghanshyambhai Vekariya, Vellore Institute of Technology,
India

Real-time data from social network sites like Twitter or Facebook has been a popular source for analytics and researchers in the recent years due to various factors like large amount of data, structured-ness, and popularity. Analyzing data is a very common requirement today, but such requirements become difficult when there is a bulk of data which needs to processed and analyzed in real time. Analyzing large number of tweets from Twitter to get different patterns and extract useful information is a massive challenge. Apache Spark is a platform that can be used to handle big data efficiently, and it offers faster solutions compared to Hadoop. This chapter addresses the issue of real-time analyzing and filtering the tweets as per the user's requirements from among the millions of other streaming tweets and classifies them into various categories. It creates an interactive automatic system that splits data based on important keywords and displays a graphical representation of connected tweets using Apache Spark.

Jayanthi Ganapathy, Sri Ramachandra Faculty of Engineering and
Technology, India
Purushothaman R., Siddartha Institute of Science and Technology, India
Ramya M., Sri Ramachandra Faculty of Engineering and Technology,
India
Joselyn Diana C., Sri Ramachandra Faculty of Engineering and
Technology, India

Emergency medical services (EMS) are inevitable in urban transport. The sustainable transport services during emergency situations are inevitable. These emergency services and vehicle operations are influenced by traffic flow rate on highways. The objective of this chapter is to present the use of transport data analytics in sustainable mobility and transport. Travel time is a key factor in emergency vehicle operations as the urban transport system is a time varying network. Temporal traffic information is a source for estimation of travel time on highways in emergency vehicle operations. The adverse traffic behavior during peak and non-peak hours of daily traffic profile hinders the operation of emergency vehicles during pandemic COVID-19 situations and so forth in evacuation planning when situation arises. Hence, this chapter presents the modern techniques and tools used in estimation of traffic flow rate on highways to access the connectivity of road network for emergency vehicle operations.

Chapter 4

Prince Rajak, National Institute of Technology, Raipur, India
Anjali Sagar Jangde, National Institute of Technology, Raipur, India
Govind P. Gupta, National Institute of Technology, Raipur, India

Brain tumor has surpassed all other types of cancers as it is the most diagnosed malignancy worldwide, and it is also the leading cause of death. Early detection and diagnosis of a brain tumor allow doctors to give better therapy and a higher chance for the patient's life. Recently, many strategies that leverage machine learning and deep learning models for detection and categorization have been presented. This chapter focuses on the design of a novel brain tumor detection and classification framework using well-known deep transfer learning models such as DenseNet201, DenseNet169, DenseNet121, MobileNet_v2, VGG19, VGG16, and Xception. Performance evaluation of the proposed framework is evaluated using a benchmark dataset in terms of accuracy and loss. It is observed that with DenseNet201, a training accuracy of 97.49% and a validation accuracy of 96.43% are observed. However, for MobileNet v2, Densenet169, and Xception model, 96% accuracy is observed. As a result, it is observed that the DenseNet201 model outperformed all other models in terms of accuracy.

Chapter 5

Mustafa Eren Akpınar, İstanbul Aydın University, Turkey

In today's technology age, digitalization is an important issue within the framework of the globalizing world structure, the internet's gaining momentum, and becoming a part of life also changes daily life practices. For this reason, many individuals, institutions, and organizations have to develop and transform themselves in order to keep up with the structure of the changing world. Journalism practices are some of the structures that need to adapt to the new digital world by improving themselves within the framework of this change and transformation. For this reason, in the context of this study, the perception of journalism and journalism practices, which is one of the structures that have transformed in the light of the changing world balances and perceptions, will be examined; the formation of people to become the data of the digital world and the concept of digital journalism will be examined by emphasizing the concept of big data, which is the main formation of this data. It is examined by the method of literature review through the technological determinism approach.

    Sreekantha Desai Karanam, NITTE (Deemed), India & Nitte Mahalinga
       Adyanthaya Memorial Institute of Technology, India
    Krithin M., NITTE (Deemed), India & Nitte Mahalinga Adyanthaya
       Memorial Institute of Technology, India
    R. V. Kulkarni, CSIBER, Kolhapur, India

The vaccines are developed to protect us from diseases, and these vaccines are saving millions of people every year. The acceptance of taking COVID-19 vaccinations was affected by their knowledge and opinion on COVID-19 vaccines. The ever-increasing misinformation and opposition to take COVID-19 vaccines have created a major problem for healthcare professionals in meeting the targets set for vaccine coverage. There is an urgent need to apply supportive and inclusive approaches to enhance people's self-confidence and acceptance of these vaccines by taking away their misconceptions. To control the spread of COVID-19 disease, practicing all the social operational standards and high vaccination coverage are required. Most healthcare workers in Asia are vaccinated. This chapter reviewed the papers on COVID-19 vaccination perceptions, issues, and side effects. The authors also designed a machine learning model to analyze the perceptions of the people from analysing their tweets. This analysis provides an insight into perceptions and drives-focused vaccination programmes.

    Omprakash Nayak, National Institute of Technology, Raipur, India
    Tejaswini Pallapothala, National Institute of Technology, Raipur, India
    Govind P. Gupta, National Institute of Technology, Raipur, India

Cardiovascular disease is among the leading sources of the growing rate of morbidity and mortality worldwide, affecting roughly 50% of the adult age group in the healthcare sector. Heart disease claims the lives of about one person per minute in this modern era. Accurate detection methods for the timely identification of cardiovascular disorders are essential because there is rapid growth in the number of patients with this disease. The goal is to understand risk factors by analyzing the heart monitoring dataset using exploratory data analysis. This chapter proposes a heart disease prediction framework using soft voting-based ensemble learning techniques. Performance evaluation of the proposed framework and its comparison with the state-of-the-art models are done using a benchmark dataset in terms of accuracy, precision, sensitivity, specificity, and F1-score. Heart disease is a long-term problem with a greater risk of becoming worse over time. The proposed model has achieved an accuracy of 90.21%.

Chapter 8

IoT-Based Health Risk Prediction by Collecting and Analyzing HIIT Data in
Real Time Using Edge Computing 166

Shrikrishn Bansal, The LNM Institute of Information Technology, India
Rajbir Kaur, The LNM Institute of Information Technology, India

Increased awareness of the benefits of physical exercise has motivated people to improve physical fitness by doing high-intensity interval training (HIIT). HIIT (where one needs to work at 70-85% of one's maximum heart rate) and forceful exercise sessions can lead to health risks such as cardiac arrest, heat strokes, or lung diseases because people are unaware of their body health and endurance status. It is essential that the health parameters of people who exercise outside controlled environments like the gym be acquired and analyzed during workout sessions. This chapter aims to design an IoT-based timely warning system based on edge computing responsible for identifying unusual patterns in the monitored health parameters and alerting the person involved in an exercise about any deviation from expected behavior. The authors collect real-time data from individuals during the exercise sessions. The data analysis provides an assessment of the health parameters and predicts any health risks during the HIIT session.

Chapter 9

Robust Dimensionality Reduction: A Resistant Search for the Relevant
Information in Complex Data 186

Jan Kalina, Institute of Computer Science, The Czech Academy of
*   Sciences, Czech Republic*

With the increasing availability of massive data in various fields of applications such as engineering, economics, or biomedicine, there appears an urgent need for new reliable tools for obtaining relevant knowledge from such data, which allow one to find and interpret the most relevant features (variables). Such interpretation is however infeasible for the habitually used methods of machine learning, which can be characterized as black boxes. This chapter is devoted to variable selection methods for finding the most relevant variables for the given task. After explaining general principles, attention is paid to robust approaches, which are suitable for data contaminated by outlying values (outliers). Three main approaches to variable selection (prior, intrinsic, and posterior) are explained, and their recently proposed examples are illustrated on applications related to credit risk management and molecular genetics. These examples reveal recent robust approaches to data analysis to be able to outperform non-robust tools.

Preface

With the rapid evolution and development of internet-based services and applications, big data problem is perceived recently in almost all domains like social network analysis, Healthcare informatics, Cyber security Analytics, Sentiment Analysis etc. Big Data refers to a collection of huge datasets that are very complex in structure and size and cannot be handle with help of traditional data management tools. Nowadays, application of computational intelligence (CI) techniques in big data analytics are very emerging research area among the software industry, data engineering researchers and academics community. Recent advancement in Computational Intelligent (CI) techniques by converging the mathematical modelling techniques with data engineering and optimization techniques, motivates the big data engineers and researchers to apply in various engineering domain related to big data. Advanced computational intelligence techniques are being designed and developed in recent years to cope with the various big data challenges to provide fast and efficient analytics which helps in making of the critical decision. Big data processing and Analytics have found various applications in different domain such as healthcare, intelligent transportation system, smart cities, smart grid, smart environment.

This book considers recent advancements in big data and computational intelligence across fields and disciplines and discusses the various opportunities and challenges of adoption. Covering topics such as deep learning, data mining, smart environments, and high-performance computing, this reference work is crucial for computer scientists, engineers, industry professionals, researchers, scholars, practitioners, academicians, instructors, and students. This book is designed to present and highlight the fundamental concept of big data technologies and application of computational intelligence tools for its analytics. The book focuses on several latest application area of big data and addresses the recent issues in providing the solutions.

The first chapter, titled "Advent of Big Data in Urban Transportation for Smart Cities: Current Progress, Trends, and Future Challenges," presents the current research endeavors on Big Data for urban transportation infrastructure, its implementation, baseline framework, and usage on fields such as planning, routing, network configuration and infrastructure maintenance. This chapter evaluates the contributions of Big Data on urban transport modelling techniques, tools, and mobility. Finally, the present trends and future challenges of Big Data are summarized for helping researchers to facilitate the development of smart cities.

The second chapter, titled "Twitter Data Analysis Using Apache Streaming," presents the issue of real time analyzing and filtering the tweets as per the user's requirements from among the millions of other streaming tweets and classifies them into various categories. It creates an interactive automatic system that splits data based on important keywords and displays a graphical representation of connected tweets using Apache Spark.

The third chapter, titled "Transport Data Analytics With Selection of Tools and Techniques," presents the modern techniques and tools used in estimation of traffic flow rate on highways to access the connectivity of road network for emergency vehicle operations. The fourth chapter, titled "Towards Design of Brain Tumor Detection Framework Using Deep Transfer Learning Techniques," presents design of a novel brain tumor detection and classification framework using well-known deep transfer learning models such as DenseNet201, DenseNet169, DenseNet121, MobileNet_v2, VGG19, VGG16, and Xception. The fifth chapter, titled "Big Data in the Context of Digital Journalism," presents application of big data in the domain of the perception of journalism and journalism practices. In this chapter, the concept of digital journalism will be examined by emphasizing the concept of big data, which is the main formation of this data.

The sixth chapter, titled "COVID-19 Vaccination Perceptions, Issues, and Challenges: An Analysis of Tweets Using Machine Learning Model," presents COVID-19 vaccination perceptions, issues and side effects. This chapter proposed a machine learning model to analyze the perceptions of the people from their tweets. The seventh chapter, titled "Heart Disease Prediction Framework Using Soft Voting-Based Ensemble Learning Techniques," presents a heart disease prediction model using soft voting-based ensemble learning techniques. The eighth chapter, titled "IoT-Based Health Risk Prediction by Collecting and Analyzing HIIT Data in Real-Time Using Edge Computing," presents design an IoT-based timely warning system based on edge computing responsible for identifying unusual patterns in the monitored health parameters and alerting the person involved in an exercise about any deviation from expected behavior.

The ninth chapter, titled "Robust Dimensionality Reduction: A Resistant Search for the Relevant Information in Complex Data," presents variable selection methods for finding the most relevant variables for the given task. This chapter discusses robust approaches, which are suitable for data contaminated by outlying values (outliers). Three main approaches to variable selection (prior, intrinsic, and posterior) are explained and their recently proposed examples are illustrated on applications related to credit risk management and molecular genetics.

   This book serves as a reference textbook for understanding big data concept and its application in the different domains and convergence of the computational intelligence for big data analytics. We hope that this book will draw attention of the researchers and academic professional and students for understanding the big data analytics using computational intelligence techniques.

Govind P. Gupta
National Institute of Technology, Raipur, India

Acknowledgment

We wish to acknowledge the valuable contributions of all the authors who have contributed their expertise in completion of the book. My sincere gratitude goes to all the peer reviewers regarding their valuable comments and suggestions about the chapters for improvement of quality and content for book chapters. We would also like to acknowledge IGI Publishing and its staff for their continuous support and assistant. Last but not the least, we express our heartfelt gratitude to the Almighty Krishna for bestowing over us the blessing and courage to complete this book.

Introduction

BIG DATA AND ITS CHARACTERISTICS

Big data is not only related to high volume of data that need to be stored and managed efficiently, but also about the design and development of next-generation data processing techniques and tools to handle the big data problems. The term 'Big Data' is coined for those huge datasets that are of high volume, having different variety of contents, growing with high velocity, and after applying the knowledge inference, it can be able to provide valuable information. It means that big data is mainly characterized by 5-Vs such as Volume, Velocity, variety, Value and Veracity (Sagiroglu and Sinanc, 2013; Zhou et al., 2017). Description of each Vs are discussed as follows:

- **Volume:** This characteristic of the big data refers to the size of the big dataset which is very large in its capacity, and it cannot be managed by traditional tools. Therefore, specialized big data processing framework and tools are required to manage the storage of the big data, perform efficient processing and analysis over it. There are various applications like social networking applications and 5G-enabled IoT services for Smart City and Smart Environment, generates huge volume of data (Sagiroglu and Sinanc, 2013).
- **Velocity:** It refers to high growth rate of the generated dataset. Source of the big data generally generates big dataset at a very high speed. For example, IoT, social networking applications generate high volume of datasets with high velocity. Since high velocity of the data generation results in high volume that processes many challenges in terms of storage requirement, online analytics, and its management (Zhou et al., 2017).
- **Variety:** It refers to different format of the data. Big data can belong to different formats such as text, image, discrete data such as sensing data, video, web data etc. These big datasets may be structured, unstructured, or semi-structured. Thus, big data processing tool needs to capable enough to handle these variety of big dataset.

- **Value:** This property of the big data refers to usefulness of the data in terms of value, it can provide for the particular purpose. The main goal of the big data processing and analytics is to provide valuable information after processing of the big data.
- **Veracity:** It refers to the quality of the extracted data. Since the big dataset is having different variety of data in a huge volume, thus, extracting the quality data is very challenging issue, due to its usefulness in predictive analysis.

APPLICATION OF BIG DATA TECHNOLOGIES

In recent years, due to exponential growth in digitalization and internet-based services, resulting in exponential growth in data generation and consumption by different applications such as social networking, smart cities, Industry 4.0, Smart Healthcare and Smart Grid etc. (Sagiroglu and Sinanc, 2013; Zhou et al., 2017). Thus, big data technologies find a lot of application domains that are discussed in detail as follows:

- Predictive Analysis in Healthcare
- Predictive analysis in Cyber Security and Threat Intelligence
- Predictive Analytics in Smart City and Smart Grid
- Intelligent natural resource (Oil and Gas) management
- Predictive Analytics in Smart Agriculture
- Predictive Analytics in Intelligent Vehicular Network
- Predictive analytics in COVID-19 like Epidemics
- Fraud Detection and Analytics in Financial and Banking Institutions
- Risk Analytics and Fault detection in Industry 4.0

Big Data Processing Tools

- **Hadoop and HDFS:** Hadoop (Borthakur, 2007) is a distributed computing framework, developed for cluster computing and big data processing for a big data problem. It is inspired by the Google file system and designed an open-source distributed file system known as Hadoop Distributed File System (HDFS) for management of the big data that are distributed over clustered computing system. It uses map reduce programming approach for designing compute for big data processing. There are various tools are developed for different applications over Hadoop ecosystems such as Cassandra and HBase, Hive for data aggregation and summarization, Apache Avro for data serialization, Pig, and Mahout for machine learning reference library (Borthakur, 2007).

- **Apache Spark:** It is a big data processing framework developed by AMP Lab, University of California, Berkeley. It is designed with distributed and advanced in-memory processing capability to overcome the limitation of Hadoop processing framework. Apache spark is developed to handle both batch and stream processing big data. It is having its own machine learning library. Architecture of the Apache spark is designed to overcome the limitation of map reduce engine of Hadoop ecosystem. Spark can perform processing 10 to 100 times faster than the map reduce engine of Hadoop. It supports four different API like Java, Python, Scala, and R (Zaharia et al., 2016).

- **Map Reduce Programming:** It is programming model that is designed for development of highly scalable program for Hadoop cluster. It is having mainly two components such as map and reduce. In the mapping components, a set of data is converted into key-value pair. Reduce function takes output of map function as input and combines those key-value pairs whose keys are similar. Any sequence of map reduce function can be applied over the big data problem in order to perform data analysis.

- **Splunk:** It is a time series indexer tool designed for big data problem. In this tool, Splunk processing language is used for searching, manipulation and analysis of big data.

- **MongoDB:** It is designed for high performance and scalable management of document database. It can be able to handle both structured and unstructured data. This tool is an open-source tool.

- **Apache CouchDB:** It is an open-source NoSQL database, designed and developed for handling multiple formats of data. It uses JSON data format for storing the data.

- **Apache Kudu: This tool is designed to** carry out fast data insertion and updation operations and for efficient scanning of table. This tool is designed with objective to remove the limitations of both HDFC and HBase. This tool can handle a very high velocity data and can perform real-time analytics over them.

- **Apache Impala:** It is a massively parallel processing engine for executing the SQL task over distributed big dataset. It is developed over Hadoop platform. It is a high-performance query engine designed particularly to integrate different big data storage engine like HDFS, Kudu, s3 and HBase and process the query over them.

COMPUTATIONAL INTELLIGENCE TECHNIQUES USED IN BIG DATA ANALYTICS

To perform intelligent predictive analysis over a big data, various computational intelligent tools and techniques are developed such as machine and deep learning tools. This section describes each technique in detail.

Machine Learning Techniques

For performing the big data analytics, mostly all the big data processing tools have included a Machine Learning (ML) library like MAHOUT in Hadoop framework and MLLib in Apache Spark etc. ML techniques are designed for performing different tasks like regression, classification, clustering etc. (Sarker, 2021; Zhang et al., 2021). It is generally categorized into different categories such as supervised learning, unsupervised learning, semi-supervised learning-based techniques.

- **Supervised Learning based Techniques:** In the supervised learning-based technique, machine learning model learns with help of leveled-training dataset and perform predictive analysis. Classification and regression-based task come under this category. There are various supervised learning models are available such as for regression task, linear regression, support vector regression algorithm. For supervised classification tasks, k-NN, Naïve Bayes, Logistic Regression, SVM, Decision Tree, Random Forest, XGBoost, CatBoost algorithm etc.
- **Un-supervised learning-based Techniques:** In unsupervised learning model, ML model learns hidden patterns and its structure with the help of un-leveled training dataset. Unsupervised ML algorithm is generally used for clustering task. There is some well-known clustering algorithm is available in literature such as K-means, C-means, Gaussian Mixture Model (GMM), Hierarchical Clustering etc. (Sarker, 2021).
- **Semi-supervised learning-based Techniques:** This class of learning algorithm is application to those datasets in which a very few samples of the dataset have leveled; bur a large part of the dataset is unleveled. This type of problem exists between supervised and unsupervised problem. These techniques are generally used in task like web content classification, image and speech recognition and text document classification etc. (Sarker, 2021; Zhang et al., 2021. The simplest example of this model is self-learning model in which first any supervised learning-based model is used as base classifier for training it with help of available leveled dataset. After that with help of trained base classifier, pseudo level of the unleveled dataset is obtained. Next, leveled, and pseudo-leveled dataset is used for training of a ML model for predictive analysis (Arif et al., 2021).

Deep Learning Techniques

Deep learning (DL) model generally uses the artificial neural network (*ANN*) concept for understanding the latent features of the input data that are required to pass to different layer of the network. Each layer of the *ANN* performs hierarchical learning and defined specific features of the supplied input dataset. It is generally used for pattern recognition task if different domain like image and video analytics, speech recognition etc. It is generally based on the approaches a human brain follows to learn the information and knowledge. DL basically consists of a learning model which is having different layer of representation. Each layer uses information provided by the previous layer to learn it deeply. There are different types of deep learning architecture available in literature such as convolutional neural networks (*CNNs*), recurrent neural networks (*RNN*). In *CNN*, different set of convolutional and pooling layers are used for learning the latent features of the training dataset (Guo et al., 2016). Convolutional layer is used for feature mapping task and pooling layer is used for reducing the feature map size for down sampling. In the end other two layers are used such as fully connected layer and normalization layer in *CNN* model. Issues with CNN model is that it cannot memorize previous state of the node and is generally perform computation using current state of the input. However, in the RNN model, memory elements are introduced by allow the backward connections between the nodes as a directed cycle. Thus, RNN uses current state as well as previous state of input for analytics. It can easily handle sequential data. Sometime, RNN suffers from vanishing gradient problem in which when value of the gradient turns out to very small resulting in the parameter updating turn out to be irrelevant (Guo et al., 2016).

Reinforcement Learning (RL)

In RL model, agents perform learning by interactive with environment. This model requires an environment which triggers an action that the agent is checking out. RL is an active learning technique in which agents are allowed to select an action from available action set within a controlled environment to maximize its total future reward (Guo et al., 2016).

Federated Learning (FL)

For distributed collaborative big data analytics, the concept of FL is suggested in which data analytics are performed locally at the edge node near the data source and only model parameters are transported to main server for aggregation of model parameters received from all local edge nodes. The main advantages of FL based big data analytics are that it enhances the data privacy and provide low latency by adopting parallel computation in a distributed environment (Nguyen et al., 2021). FL is generally used for scalable solutions in different domains like IoT, Healthcare, cyber security analysis, Threat intelligence, etc.

REFERENCES

Arif, A., Javaid, N., Aldegheishem, A., & Alrajeh, N. (2021). Big data analytics for identifying electricity theft using machine learning approaches in microgrids for smart communities. *Concurrency and Computation, 33*(17), e6316.

Borthakur, D. (2007). The hadoop distributed file system: Architecture and design. *Hadoop Project Website, 11*, 21.

Guo, Y., Liu, Y., Oerlemans, A., Lao, S., Wu, S., & Lew, M. S. (2016). Deep learning for visual understanding: A review. *Neurocomputing, 187*, 27–48. doi:10.1016/j.neucom.2015.09.116

Nguyen, D. C., Ding, M., Pathirana, P. N., Seneviratne, A., Li, J., & Poor, H. V. (2021). Federated learning for internet of things: A comprehensive survey. *IEEE Communications Surveys and Tutorials, 23*(3), 1622–1658. doi:10.1109/COMST.2021.3075439

Sagiroglu, S., & Sinanc, D. (2013, May). Big data: A review. In 2013 international conference on collaboration technologies and systems (CTS) (pp. 42-47). IEEE. doi:10.1109/CTS.2013.6567202

Sarker, I. H. (2021). Machine learning: Algorithms, real-world applications and research directions. *SN Computer Science, 2*(3), 1–21. doi:10.100742979-021-00592-x PMID:33778771

Zaharia, M., Xin, R. S., Wendell, P., Das, T., Armbrust, M., Dave, A., Meng, X., Rosen, J., Venkataraman, S., Franklin, M. J., Ghodsi, A., Gonzalez, J., Shenker, S., & Stoica, I. (2016). Apache spark: A unified engine for big data processing. *Communications of the ACM, 59*(11), 56–65. doi:10.1145/2934664

Zhang, J. Z., Srivastava, P. R., Sharma, D., & Eachempati, P. (2021). Big data analytics and machine learning: A retrospective overview and bibliometric analysis. *Expert Systems with Applications, 184*, 115561.

Zhou, L., Pan, S., Wang, J., & Vasilakos, A. V. (2017). Machine learning on big data: Opportunities and challenges. *Neurocomputing, 237*, 350–361. doi:10.1016/j.neucom.2017.01.026

Chapter 1
Advent of Big Data in Urban Transportation for Smart Cities:
Current Progress, Trends, and Future Challenges

Bhargav Naidu Matcha
https://orcid.org/0000-0001-8570-5920
Taylor's University, Lakeside Campus, India

Sivakumar Sivanesan
Asia Pacific University of Technology and Innovation, Malaysia

K. C. Ng
University of Nottingham, Malaysia

Se Yong Eh Noum
https://orcid.org/0000-0003-0398-2399
Taylor's University, Malaysia

Aman Sharma
Taylor's University, Malaysia

DOI: 10.4018/978-1-6684-5264-6.ch001

ABSTRACT

The application of big data in urban transportation and development of smart cities has been attracting global interest. The overburdened transport infrastructure due to rapid urbanisation should be integrated with innovative technologies and brand-new ideas such as smart city in order to enhance its performance. Big data is now the emerging exemplar in intelligent transportation systems for effective management of all data for implementing safer, cleaner, and well-planned transport services, as well as providing personalised transport experience for road users. In this chapter, the authors lay forward the current research endeavours on big data for urban transportation infrastructure, its implementation, baseline framework, and usage on fields such as planning, routing, network configuration, and infrastructure maintenance. This chapter evaluates the contributions of big data on urban transport modelling techniques, tools, and mobility. Finally, the present trends and future challenges of big data are summarised for helping researchers to facilitate the development of smart cities.

INTRODUCTION

Recently, the generation of traffic and transportation data in terms of their speed and volume have transcended at a higher scale compared to those methods that were utilised during the last few decades. The introduction of latest digital techniques like artificial intelligence, Internet of Things (IoT), data mining, social networks, the growth of smart cities (Bello-Orgaz et al., 2016) (Castellanos et al., 2021), recent improvements in wireless technologies, and the extensive usage of cost effective sensors and mobile devices has substantially upgraded humans perception on real-time traffic and transport mobility (Meekan et al., 2017) (Kaffash et al., 2021). Since Intelligent Transportation Systems (ITS) framework and execution is based on traffic mobility data which in terms of volume, diversity (source and format), and its variable nature requires data intensive techniques like querying and analysis, integration, high performance computing, visualisation of extensive real-time systems are necessary (Khattak, 2017; Andrienko et al., 2017; Amini et al., 2017; Usman et al., 2020). Traffic congestion and road accidents are the biggest challenges faced in urban cities that requires immediate attention (Matcha et al., 2020; Ng, 2021). Hence, a more distinctive and enhanced methods of transport data collection, transmission, storage, fusion, extraction and processing are necessary (Matcha et al., 2022; Stathopoulos et al., 2017). However, it is widely admitted that the present ITS implementation is limited to data monitoring and evaluation applications (Suh et al., 2017). The above-mentioned challenges were not fulfilled by current ITS applications for efficient monitoring, decision-making and realistic data management applications. Moreover, the transport facilities, projects and operations can be improved by implementation of advanced aggregation, integration and progressive learning approaches which is possible by inflow of massive amount of real-time data streaming sources for a better insight and policy making decisions. The classification of Big Data is shown in Figure 1.

In this scenario, Big Data has been suggested as an essential technology for the transportation sector (Rusitschka & Curry, 2016; Arfat et al., 2020b). This technological exemplar can adapt, administer, and analyse huge amounts of organised and unorganised data by providing solutions and tools to upgrade the transport sector and face future challenges. The solution requires developing state-of-the-art ITS and transportability services by extricating the worth and knowledge of the available bulk data established on the concepts and techniques of the Big Data. Finally, it is to make sure that the transport sector evolves to present a sustainable and well-developed transport services and experiences to its users by deriving value from its data. The harvesting and mining of data required to predict the patterns in transport mobility behaviour to improve safety and security requires predictive analytics, which is a technological equivalent to Big Data. For instance, infrastructure monitoring is an application based on Big Data in Transportation (Jeong et al., 2016), establishment of transport added-valued services (Mehmood & Graham, 2015; Fonzone et al., 2016; Su et al., 2016), better interpretation of road users' requirements (Chen et al., 2016b) and foreseeing the evolution of traffic flow in urban areas (Kitchin, 2014).

Traffic management is one of the areas in transportation sector where Big Data played a key role prior to its emergence. The vast amount of data sources enhanced

Figure 1. Big Data Classification

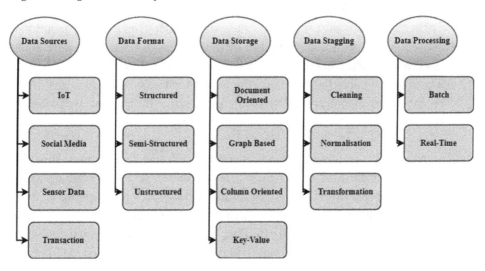

the spatial-temporal design of transport data paving way to the evolution in the area of traffic management research (Das et al., 2018). In this regard the evolution in traffic panning, forecasting, management by Big Data are diverse with unparallel results compared to traditional tools (Alsafery et al., 2018). On the whole, the key contributor for accomplishing a smarter transportation infrastructure is Big Data, despite being limited to particular applications presently (Ding et al., 2016b; Suma et al., 2017; Torre-Bastida et al., 2018).

This chapter focuses on featuring the recognition gained by Big Data for traffic and transportation sector by scrutinizing and evaluating the latest research endeavours in this innovative field. In specific this review digs into the applications and frameworks intercepted in the current literature, how the large volumes of data are analysed through Big Data features (designing, processing, evaluation, and visualisation) are determined. Moreover, the reader gets an insight into various monitoring frameworks on data collection, privacy policy, and usage focussing on the future relevance of Big Data in transport sector. This review acts as a reference source for new researchers and traffic experts for a solid overview on the impact of Big Data in transportation sector, its advantages, and future possibilities in this domain. This review contributions are summarised below:

1. This chapter lays forward the scrutinized interpretation of Big Data conceived within the field of traffic and transportation domain, with significance on data feeds, real-time requirements, and utilisation scenarios that validate the importance of Big Data techniques in this field.
2. This chapter critically evaluates the modern trends and predicts futuristic challenges in the implementation of Big Data for traffic and transportation sector. We classified literature established on the contribution of Big Data at every stage of latest research.
3. This chapter also digs into each phase of Big Data life cycle as mentioned above, laying forward a detailed study in the areas of research closely linked to each life phase, that requires further improvements.
4. The chapter finally supplements the discussed literature study by summarising the recent ITS developments and applications that utilise the Big Data technologies, resolving the gap in knowledge on Big Data in transportation sector.

The rest of the rest is organised as follows: Section 2 interprets Big Data implementation in the area of traffic and transportation sector, describing its life cycle and the aspects of data handling in this sector. Section 3 explains in detail the current technical advancements at each phase of Big Data life cycle. Section 4 discusses the implementation of Big Data for definite transport applications by classifying the Big Data related literature within the transport sector. Section 5 presents the futuristic challenges faced in the field of smart transportation, modelling, and implementations arising from Big Data technologies. Finally, Section 6 presents a list of conclusions and upcoming trends.

BIG DATA IN TRAFFIC AND TRANSPORTATION SECTOR

Definition, Characteristics, Scope, and Data Sources

The arrival of Big Data in transportation sector offered new opportunities and implementation services by resolving long-established data-based issues by means of latest data resources and techniques. There is a huge amount of overwhelming data from those transport means (e.g., motorcycle sharing scheme) where fewer studies are recorded, has opened doors for incorporation of certain aspects of these transport means unleashing latest technological offers to be seized paving way towards extraction of enhanced knowledge. At the same time, new data sources like social media (e.g., geo-tagging tweets) has exceptionally enhanced the detection of movement patterns. Moreover, the latest research into Big Data in evaluating the geo-positioning of human traces has demonstrated its worth in traffic and transportation sector. In the geospatial context the data obtained through sources is 80% geographic (Suma et al., 2017; Torre-Bastida et al., 2018; Li et al., 2016b), even though this figure is a rough assessment, it proves the importance of Big Data as a valuable source in analysing human mobility.

Definition for Big Data in the Context of Traffic and Transportation Sector

Big Data incorporates identification, collection of huge volumes of data such as traffic volume, speed, heterogeneous behaviour, their evolution over time, and utilisation of evolved models and techniques to extract, store, process and evaluate the obtained data (Beyer & Laney, 2012; Laney, 2001). In the context of transportation sector, Big Data is a collection of technologies that efficiently manage (archive, process, and retrieve) all the information necessary to build new methods to impart safer, cleaner, and conflict-free transport, in addition to providing personalised mobility services to users. That is to say, Big Data is able to solve the problems in transportation sector by utilising information at unparallel scales. This technological enhancement paved way for the development of new mobility models, facilities and implementations that stood unexplored, mostly due to the requirement of modern data that was neither been extracted nor processed.

There exist two key factors governing the selection of the Big Data in the traffic and transportation domain. The first and foremost factor is related to urbanisation of traffic infrastructure and smart cities which has provided a huge resources sources for Big Data. The second factor is due to the development of advanced communication technologies and availability of ever-growing abundant information from latest mobile technologies, IoT, and cloud technologies paving ways to latest methods of handling and processing Big Data.

The primary requirement of smart cities is the design and implementation of ITS, for the integration of diverse traffic means and movement patterns in a progressive manner in urban areas (Kitchin, 2014; Benevolo et al., 2016). The identification, extraction, and processing of movement patterns of vehicles and people throughout the cities helps in solving the transport infrastructure problems leading to safety and sustainable transport means. Hence, the ultimate objective of these technologies for sustainable transportation in smart cities is to achieve superior inter-linking and governance of urban transport, along with the improvement of smart network for a flawless multi-modal movement (Torre-Bastida et al., 2018; Okuda et al., 2012; Misra et al., 2014). In this aspect, the notion of smart mobility describes the optimisation of urban transport means by resolving the data-intensive issues like reducing traffic conflicts, congestion, and the impact on environment by transport decisions. These issues paved way for the development of sustainable transport means such as electric vehicles etc. that have minimum influence on the environment. Sadly, the optimisation techniques for the fore mentioned problems undergo internal conflicts with each other creating disruptions in the entire communities where the mode of transport opted by an individual for his/her personal reasons may not be the finest option for the community (Torre-Bastida et al., 2018; Okuda et al., 2012). This is the very reason why Big Data technologies are considered elemental in scrutinising heavy loads of new data to back up the optimisation techniques that explore numerous conflicting standards, moulding it into real-time practical knowledge paving way to advanced intelligent transport services.

The combination of compounding blocks incorporating the Information and Communications Technology (ICT) that integrates intelligent transportation and mobility services are denoted by disruptive technologies (Okuda et al., 2012; Manyika et al., 2013). The life cycle of the extracted data and services classify these technologies such that they can be implemented and deployed: data identification, collection, extraction, furnishing of infrastructure, data evaluation and security are considered as the essential protocols and approaches of each compounding technology. Recently IoT emanated as an essential technology for data collection (Gregorio et al., 2020), with specific attribute to machine-to-machine communications (Torre-Bastida et al., 2018; Tsiatsis et al., 2018). Cloud Computing plays a pivotal role in all the research activities related to infrastructure provisioning and SAAS/IAAS

Figure 2. Simplified Diagrammatic Representation of Interrelation between IoT, Big Data and Cloud Computing

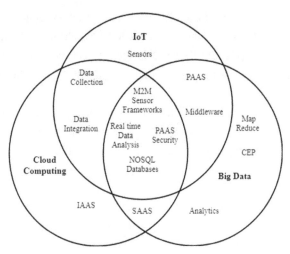

service models (Bhardwaj et al., 2010). Open Data paradigm of the research areas that are explored for the data extraction techniques (Huijboom, 2011; Janssen et al., 2012). The data evaluation stage of the data life cycle is implemented by Big Data analytical elements such as Soft Computing, Deep Learning and many more. In the end, the crucial security phase of data life cycle is taken care by cybersecurity, which is utilised to build ICT models for different sectors (Elmaghraby & Losavio, 2014), indicating an exponential rise of its relevance in digital environments. Figure 2 schematically represents the interaction between these three platforms.

Big Data Attributes and Scales in Traffic and Transportation Sector

The three important characteristics of Big Data may be described by the $3V$ model (velocity, volume, and variety) as proposed by Laney (2001). Past literature also suggested other features like visualisation, veracity, and visibility. Nevertheless, this review focuses on the former features since these factors are decisive for data collection, evaluation, storage, management, extraction, and processing. The three most important factors that distinguish Big Data from other 'ordinary' data (Beyer & Laney, 2012; Demchenko et al., 2014).

1.   **Velocity:** this factor takes into consideration of two notions: the rate at which data samples are generated and the rate at which the generated data samples are obtained and evaluated. The present ITS frameworks need instantaneous processors that deliver outputs in nanoseconds, thus enhances the modelling

ability in the computing network and development of new models for data analysis.

2. **Volume:** the total quantity of data collected, processed, and evaluated. These days, research is being conducted to handle huge volumes of data up to yottabytes (YB, 10^{34} bytes) (Kwan, 2016). The lowest volume of data for a framework to be considered as Big Data is petabytes (PB, 10^{15} bytes) (Subbu & Vasilakos, 2017).

3. **Variety:** the diversity in the collected data is the outcome of various digitalised sectors linked to different applications or services in use. The design and development of integrated systems is based on the combined extraction and evaluation of this heterogeneous data and blending of these features.

The above-mentioned factors of Big Data are not limited to any particular research domain; however, this review brings forward the significance of these features in the traffic and transportation sector.

Big Data comes into picture when the volume and size of data samples cannot be handled by conventional methods in terms of data capturing, storage, management, extraction, and analysis within the stipulated time. The size of data samples now a days have seen an exponential growth ranging in between a few terabytes to petabytes in a single data sample. In the transportation sector the datasets related to geo-location information is one of the best examples for huge data volumes, where its importance is growing in Social Media domains such as Instagram, twitter etc. where the users are encouraged to transmit and receive 60 million photos on daily basis or 500 million tweets per day. Most of the information shared in this media transfer is geotagged paving way to identify people behavioural trends from time-to-time (Boeing, 2019; Alomari et al., 2019; Suma et al., 2020).

Moreover, there is a huge inflow of movement data through various inbuilt sensors in vehicles and other devices like mobile phones, watches etc. now a days most of the urban roadways are renovated with different sensors for traffic detection which cannot be detected visually (Collier & Weiland, 1994; Semanjski & Gautama, 2015). The traffic vehicular movements, pavement conditions and other security measures are being analysed and characterised in a greater detail by expanding the density of sensor network in these sensed urban roads (Masek et al., 2016; Salim & Haque, 2015). The under developed areas in the urban limits with no resources in the past are also utilising these sensors to detect and collect data regarding crowd movement behaviour (Misra et al., 2014). On the whole, there is a huge inflow in data volume due to the growth in sensor technologies and usage.

In a similar manner, *velocity* denotes the rate at which the data is extracted and evaluated from its source to their destination. The basic advantage of Big Data techniques is that the data is analysed while being collected without utilising the storage capacity of their databases there by saving a lot of time and energy. For an instance, the extraction and analysis of diverse real-time traffic data from various sources. This diverse data provides vast opportunities by interlinking these different sources to explore the combined behaviour of people, vehicles within the urban infrastructure. There exist many diverse sources having varied features that can be interlinked such as social media, email, sensor networks, blogs, Open Data, and videos. The variations in these data sources even for a standard data such as such as radar signals for vehicle velocity and vehicle counts is due to the nature of data delivered by diverse sensors that are produced by different manufacturers. Therefore, it is important to assess the usefulness and potential of Big Data in transportation sector in collecting, extracting, analysing, and delivering the data through implementation of ITS for a sustainable and personalised transport services.

Latest Sources in Big Data for Traffic and Transportation Sector

As discussed earlier, the revolutionary changes brought by Big Data in terms of size, possibility, and variability of data. In traffic and transportation sector three essential sources of Big Data can be considered: data from social media (unstructured), data from the sensors (unstructured or semi-structured) and Open Data sources (either unstructured or semi-structured). These data sources are explained in detail in the following section and their highlighted features are outlined in Table 1.

1. **Social Media:** These days, a massive amount of data is being handled by Social Media platforms that provide crucial information for an effective data analysis. The fundamental reason behind this is the evolution of the user from a mere consumer to contributor of critical information. Hence, Social Media is considered as one of the principal contributor of critical information to Big Data which can be also denoted as Social Big Data (Kaplan & Haenlein, 2010). In transportation sector, the data tracks left by the users in their Social Media applications where they share their data which is geo-tagged providing key information on the movements of vehicles and people. The other types of data sources that fall under the same group are some of the integrated applications and resources like crowd-sourcing, i.e., the exercise of accumulating knowledge or data for development of a project by employing the services of a huge number of people. (Semanjski & Gautama, 2015) illustrated the ability of crowd-sourced data in the management of urban mobility. Three data sources namely mobile phone, geographical information system (GIS) and weather forecast data were considered in their study over a period of six months. They presented latest travel modes such as carpooling, hitchhiking etc. as sources of

data for the evaluation of crowd movements. With the recent developments in mobile technologies innovative mobile applications like Cabify, Uber etc. are introduced into the market that are linked to these new data sources to collect and extract the crowd-sourced data to evaluate the movements of vehicles and people (Komanduri et al., 2018). Transport logistics is also one of the area in which such type of data sources are being utilised (Misra et al., 2014; Paloheimo et al., 2016), paving way to the development of innovative and interlinked networks. In these type of crowd-sourcing logistics, deliveries are being made along their travel path to minimise their travel time and costs and also to limit the carbon foot print on their delivered goods (Misra et al., 2014; Rougès & Montreuil, 2014).

2. **Sensor Data:** with the rapid increase in electronic devices implanted with actuators, sensors, and software kindled by the IoT domain is drastically influencing the development of innovative techniques in transportation sector, primarily in the design and development of connected car (motor car acting as a sensor). This connected car concept assists in exchange of observed information not only with surrounding vehicles within the traffic flow and also with the infrastructure (V2V, V2I). Moreover, commercial transport logistics and supply chain operations are also benefitted by making use of these connected means of transport like autonomous vehicles (Bechtsis et al., 2017) or drones (CBS Interactive Incorporated, 2013; Scott & Scott, 2017). However, the concern towards the safety (impact of critical accidents) of these automated vehicles has further motivated researchers to look into transportation safety with reference to IoT domain. It can be seen that IoT domain has gained relevance in the field of traffic and transportation sector as an efficient technology that provides sustainable management solutions, improved safety, and user-friendly services with least environmental impacts. Past studies in urban computing also came up with similar claims by suggesting capturing, extraction, evaluation, and integration of diverse data generated by different data sources in urban areas (Kaplan & Haenlein, 2010; Zheng et al., 2014). The traffic and transportation relation issues in urban areas can be resolved in an effective manner by predominant sensing technologies like IoT in urban computing (Zheng et al., 2011; Salim & Haque, 2015; Ding et al., 2016a).

3. **Open Data:** this is the type data that is accessible to everyone for free such that they can utilise the data, modify, and share for any of their purposes. Open Data is a prospective asset for both the civilians and the public sectors of urban areas. The urban authorities should move towards an open access policy, by giving access to the open data about traffic mobility to its citizens in adaptable and machine reading formats. Most of the countries now a days are moving towards open access policies by making availability of data

Table 1. Data sources implemented in transportation sector

	Source	Category	Configuration	Application	Ref.
Conventional Data Sources	ITS	Structured	XML, CSV etc.	Vehicle Guidance, Traffic Flow Control Data	(Kong et al., 2018)
	Maps and GIS Data	Semi-Structured	GIS	Road Network Maps	(Weiss et al., 2018)
	Legacy Networks (RDBMS)	Structured	JSON, ERM, XML	Platform for Automated Toll Collection	(Y. Liu et al., 2011)
Latest Data Sources	Sensor Data	Raw Data	CSV, text, etc.	Roadway Sensors to Assess Road Conditions	(Ye et al., 2018)
	Open Data	Unstructured	CSV, text	Urban Areas Open Data	(Jara et al., 2018)
	Inter-connected Data	Semi-Structured	RDF	Urban Traffic Enhancement Data	(Jara et al., 2018)
	Social Media	Semi-Structured	CSV, RDF, XML, text	User Cellular Data, Crowd Sourcing	(Singh et al., 2017)

repositories at national transportation services level. The best example among them is United Kingdom, where they have introduced national public transport data repository (*National Public Transport Data Repository (NPTDR)*, 2018). This data repository made available of all the weekly travel information across the country through different modes like buses, trains etc. between 2004 and 2011 thereby evaluating the situation in different parts of the country that lack proper public transport services along with other issues.

Past Research Works

This section of the chapter concentrates on the past and recent research works on Big Data for traffic and transportation domain by giving significance to the diverse research studies found in the literature. This section lay forward the current trends and areas that require further study on Big Data in traffic and transportation domains. The implementation of Big Data algorithms in ITS have a large scale impact on safety of vehicles, route planning, travel time planning, and optimisation of road capacity

(Kaffash et al., 2021). The studies on Big Data technologies and its implementation on traffic and transportation sector like geospatial cloud technology has gained utmost prominence in recent years with the urban planning sector (Li et al., 2016b; Yang, 2017). There are many prominent works undertaken in geospatial cloud computing technology for urban transport industry further reinforcing the significance of Big Data in this domain (Abbasi et al., 2016; Hou et al., 2016; Arfat et al., 2020a).

Capturing Traffic and Transportation Data

Data capturing process is a combination of various tasks which focuses on (i) obtaining the captured data sets from signals, (ii) transforming the captured data sets into machine readable formats for easy accessibility on computers, (iii) driving the digitalised data towards the processing unit of the data network (Matcha et al., 2021). Hence, in traffic and transportation sector, Big Data collection is the process of organising the captured information generated by people and vehicles through various channels by utilising sensors and other electronic devices.

A good number of researchers have developed enhanced and innovative methods for capturing Big Data in traffic and transportation sector. Firstly, (Zhao et al., 2017) developed an innovative method of capturing vehicles density, volume and speed data for a continuous traffic flow over a large-scale area using a single sensor, which proves the significance of Big Data supervision of traffic features. Similarly, (Wang, 2016) in their work came up with a precise manner of capturing vehicle trajectories by analysing the images generated by automated aerial vehicles, which can be further enhances for an accurate procurement of real-time traffic data of any region. Moreover, (Liu et al., 2016) proposed usage of event graphs in development of models that identify abnormalities emerging from traffic and sensor data in Big Data repositories. With an exponential rise in sensor equipment and individual computing devices in automobile industry, challenge lies ahead in capturing the movements of vehicles through dispersed mobile sensor networks since the exchange of the real-time information between the vehicles and between vehicles and infrastructure rarely occurs. To counteract this above issue (Tiedemann et al., 2016) developed Smart Adaptive Data Aggregation (SADA). In this study, they aggregated the data generated from different dispersed mobile sensors placed on different vehicles along with other data sources by designing frameworks and techniques. This designed framework integrates the machine learning features to upgrade the perception of the driver established on the aggregate data.

In traffic and transportation sector, the procurement of data through sensors and other electronic devices requires further study on the traditional approaches and outcomes that were commonly implemented in extensive Big Data scenarios. In this regard, the work of (Zhang et al., 2018) is worth noting, which reviewed

Table 2. Big data sources and techniques for data collection in ITS

Big Data Source	Hardware	Collected Data	Reference
Connected and Autonomous Vehicles (CAVs)	Distinctive Sensors	Headway, speed, acceleration, coordinate, safety data	(Chen et al., 2017), (Montanaro et al., 2019), (Dai et al., 2021)
Floating Car Sensor	Transponders, License Plate Recognition	Origin-Destination flows, Travel Time	(Chen et al., 2016)
GPS	GPS	Vehicle Location, Traffic Density, Traffic Speed	(X. Wang et al., 2017), (Gong et al., 2012)
Passive Collection	Social Media Data	Mobile Phone, Media	(Chen et al., 2014b), (X. Zheng et al., 2016), (Zeyu et al., 2017)
Roadway Sensor	Toll Plazas, Road Tubes, LIDAR, Induction Loops, Microwave Radar, Infrared Acoustic	Classification of Vehicles, Vehicle Location, Traffic Density, Traffic Speed	(Lopes et al., 2010)
Smart Card	Smart Card	Origin-Destination flows, Travel Time	(Pelletier et al., 2011), (Nishiuchi et al., 2013)
Video	Video Camera	Classification of Vehicles, Vehicle Location, Traffic Density, Traffic Speed	(Grant et al., 2000), (Kadaieaswaran et al., 2017)
Wide Area Sensor	Airborne Sensors, GPS, Mobile trackers	Origin-Destination flows, Travel Time	(Kadaieaswaran et al., 2017), (L. Zhu et al., 2019)
Other Sources	Smart Meters, Cellular Network Devices, Smart Grid, Dedicated Tests	Electricity and Energy Consumption data, Location services, Channel Data	(Cottrill & Derrible, 2015), (L. Zhu et al., 2012)

the implementation of Big Data models regarding network sensors in smart cities development and urban informatics by focussing on significant cases. An innovative methodology developed by (Ferreira et al., 2016) which was established upon four techniques that captures and integrates information from various sources into built-in data classes. The collection of data through various Big Data sources and the tools utilised to capture required traffic and transport data is summarised in Table 2.

Presently, research works in transportation are focussing on adopting new techniques to integrate conventional database technologies and latest data sources like Big Data and Open Data. The development of new repository called SHRP2 ("Transportation Safety Meets Big Data: The SHRP 2 Naturalistic Driving Database," 2016) that captures realistic driving behaviour, traffic flow, and commercial transport logistics that accumulates 2 PB of data composed of 3500 drivers and around 50 million kilometres. Similar work by (Li et al., 2016c), that implements ITS technologies by considering words and texts as sources of information for Big Data. This work identifies and interlinks urban traffic flow to the text information uploaded by users on social media within a certain time period. Based upon the connection between the text content and the traffic flow conditions they proposed a creative word characterisation model that predicts traffic flow situations in urban areas falling under Chinese transportation sector. Big Data simulation frameworks and traffic simulators are also one of the latest trends to produce and evaluate various realistic traffic scenarios (Kamel et al., 2016) developed such naturalistic simulation scenario for Toronto (Canada) transportation system by capturing data from various electronic sources throughout the city paving way for the design and establishment of smart transport within this region.

Data Framework and Quality Assessment

The past relevant works in traffic and transportation sector focussing on data framework conceptualisation, logic, and data coherence are reviewed in this section. In this aspect, (Gonzalez, 2016) proposed new approaches and implementations to get a clear insight into the extraction methods of massive and passively captured data sources to simulate the movements of people and vehicles, along with their outcomes and applications. The end result of this work is to develop an origin-destination transport model (OD model) for the city of Boston (USA). (Faouzi & Klein, 2016) also developed new data fusion methods to obtain efficient transportation data frameworks. The work done in ("The Potential of Mobile Network Big Data as a Tool in Colombo's Transportation and Urban Planning," 2016) which demonstrates the potential of Big Data sources and its implementation in traffic management is worth acknowledging. Also, Ziliaskopoulos et al. ("The Potential of Mobile Network Big Data as a Tool in Colombo's Transportation and Urban Planning," 2016) developed an integrated framework that combines spatial-temporal data, users and models by utilising GIS and can be implemented efficiently in various transportation applications. However, (Guido et al., 2017) reviewed the significance of Big Data for the development of urban public transport infrastructure and evaluation of its quality. The assessment of Big Data sources, its quality and consistency are an important issue due to the seriousness of certain features in transport mobility such as safety, need for data accuracy, and actual accountability for their variability and dynamics.

Big Data Analytics in Traffic and Transportation Sector

The implementation of network deduction, research and optimisation approaches all fall under the category of Big Data Analytics, which is a latest technological advancement at global scale in the field of traffic and transportation sector (Wittmann, 2016; Gunturi & Shekhar, 2017; French et al., 2017). There exist two significant advantages offered by Big Data Analytics over conventional methods. (i) previous studies recommended implementation of basic models executed on large volumes of data rather than complex and advanced algorithms with inadequate data. Since, the former delivers an accurate insight into mobility behaviour (Wang, 2016; Schnoebelen, 2016). (ii) researchers are able to develop efficient and innovative models due to the sophisticated data provided by Big Data Analytics. Speed and accuracy are two main advantages of Big Data Analytics in the field of traffic and transportation sector. However, the challenges like the efficient evaluation of huge volume of real-time traffic and mobility data and the accuracy of Big Data Analytics in the predictive features of ITS need to be answered.

In this scenario, a good number of research studies have contributed to the significance of integrating Big Data Analytics in traffic and transportation domain. In this regard, we further categorise these studies based upon analytical models along with interpretation of these studies involving Big Data sources and techniques particularly implemented for traffic and transportation sector. Also, the implementation areas of Big Data Analytics are explained in detail in the areas such as public transport. An analysis is also carried out on different approaches and techniques used in integrating Big Data Analytics in Transportation sector.

As a result, Big Data Analytical models can be mainly categorised as follows:

1. **Descriptive Analytics:** In this type of analytics the features like pattern identification, use of statistics in data identification, and automated machine learning such as clustering and anomaly sensing. Basically, the functionalities like supervision, compressing and/or elaborating the captured data by spotting and scrutinising anomalies with the clusters by means of statistical applications are performed by models in these descriptive analytics. Quite a good number of research works exist in literature on implementation of descriptive analytics in traffic and transportation domain especially in automatic vehicle detection and safety approaches (Tiedemann et al., 2016; Husen et al., 2017), urban traffic flow supervision (Mdini et al., 2017), vehicle conflicts and accidents spotting (Maha Vishnu et al., 2018) or intelligent transportation (Lin et al., 2017). These are the fields in which descriptive analytics is emerging as an efficient tool for analysis of data sets.

2. **Forecasting Analytics:** In this type of analytics algorithms are executed over the monitored data to evaluate and predict the correlation between the observed elements and target variable. These models once tested and executed will be able to predict the outcome of an undisclosed target variable based on new data sources, even though these models were developed for cases based upon previously recorded data. However, there is a need for more data rich sources to forecast the heterogeneous data which is not possible with these traditional tools due to limited spatial and temporal limits (Jiang & Luo, 2022). Traffic forecasting is an important aspect in transport planning in information technology and there is need for construction of an adaptive model on the basis of historic traffic data (Xiao & Xie, 2021). In traffic and transportation sector, the applications of these models are far reached such as automated driving (real-time recognition and forecasting of traffic situation) (Bacciu et al., 2017); Uber ride-sharing concept (demand forecasting) (Laptev et al., 2017); Companies such as Optimus Ride which analyses traffic scenario using crowd-sourcing (interpretation and prediction of accidents) (Warren et al., 2019). Recent surveys by (Vlahogianni et al., 2014; Lana et al., 2018; Alsolami et al., 2020) on the growing interest on forecasting analytics for evaluating traffic scenario, demand and capacity are worth noting.

3. **Prescriptive Analytics:** In this type of analytics the approaches or methods such as optimisation methods, expert frameworks, and features from arithmetic programming, intelligent computational systems, and operations research are implemented to recommend the best course of action among other possibilities. This type of analytics takes into consideration the analysed data from descriptive and forecasting analytics and turns it to its advantage. These optimisation procedures for prescriptive analytics have systematically benefitted various fields in transportation sector especially the logistics sector (Wenyan Yuan et al., 2018), urban traffic supervision (Zedda & Pinna, 2018) or interface services between driver and passenger (Roy et al., 2017).

Before we move forward, it is worth mentioning the rapid increase in the number of research on deep learning models because of their ability to understand and solve complex data sources compared to traditional approaches. The capturing and interpreting traffic and human movement behaviours and transportation networks on a huge scale remains as the primary objective of deep learning which is almost a difficult task by other traditional machine learning techniques. Hence, in descriptive, forecasting, and prescriptive analysis of diverse and complex data sets like spotting of traffic conflicts and crashes from Social Media (Alomari et al., 2019; Zhang et al., 2018) or capturing of vehicles' license plate numbers through video processing (Yang et al., 2018), deep learning approaches such as iterative neural frameworks, explorative neural frameworks, reinforced deep learning etc. have proved to be useful in an efficient manner especially for public transport maintenance in smart cities (Zhang et al., 2018; Aqib et al., 2019).

Now we lay forward those tools and technologies in which these Big Data models are executed by summarising all those Big Data technologies specialised in traffic and transport operations. As such an ITS based air-ground Big Data Analytics platform developed by (Xiong et al., 2016a) that includes functions and operations such as sensor data collection, data interpretation, large-scale data storage, fusion of data sources, mining of data and data evaluation. This developed model is able to employ every technique listed in Big Data life cycle (data acquirement, circulation, storage, and processing) over the generated traffic and transport data (users, vehicles, and urban infrastructure). Another Big Data based model (Xiong et al., 2016b) by implementing Hadoop based applications to evaluate transportation data and validate it with field data sets from Shenzhen city (China) was developed by same author. Another instance of Big Data platform implementation in traffic and transportation sector is a cloud computing framework termed as H-TDMS proposed by (Hua et al., 2016) to collect, extract and evaluate Big Data. This framework is an adaptable tool that integrates, implements intelligent computational analysis, provides data visualisation service by implementing user-interface systems and stores huge volumes of data along with provision of secondary index for a faster data processing. (Xia et al., 2016) analysed the data produced by ITS in an efficient manner by developing a Big Data processing platform, that is built based upon HBase. One of the noteworthy research works in developing Big Data frameworks in transport sector is the one developed by (Bao et al., 2016) that is implemented on Microsoft Azure as a cloud-based trajectory data management framework to improve urban infrastructure facilities based upon the trajectories of people and vehicles.

The increasing significance of Big Data Analytics in public transportation can be denoted by two noteworthy research works. One of which by (Anwar et al., 2016), where they developed an application known as BusViz, a web-based application that utilises huge volume of public transport captured and visualised data sets to provide better user interface and efficient decision making process for public bus drivers, regulators, and transit operators. The second notable work by (Tao et al., 2014), in which focussed on huge volumes of data generated by Bus Rapid Transit (BRT) by evaluating 45 million samples of bus arrivals to understand the urban public transit system in the city of Brisbane (Australia). The development of an integrated bus route model took place based on a methodology developed by (Su et al., 2016) to assist government for building a cost effective and service oriented public transit network in the Taiwan. And also another noteworthy work by (Wei Yuan et al., 2016), in which they have proposed a model that that identifies unlicensed taxis based on Big Data Analytics.

The recent proliferation of online retail stores gave raise to complex transportation logistic problems, opening doors for Big Data Analytics to tackle these challenges in an effective manner. Big Data Analytics can be applied in designing and building of distribution networks for this commercial transport logistics. (Wang et al., 2018) identified the importance of Big Data Analytics in modelling and solving the issue of relocating distribution centres in a single sector, enabled distribution network. Also, the other area in which Big Data technologies play a prominent role is the electric vehicle, as demonstrated by (Fetene et al., 2017) in their work, where they considered the influence of real-time driving behaviour influenced by drivers' mood, weather conditions, road characteristics and other factors that affect the power-consumption rate of electric vehicles.

The findings in this subsection based on the past research works are summarised in Table 2 as per their relevant factors. Finally, we conclude this subsection by discussing some of the recent surveys on implementation of intelligent computational technologies so solve traffic and transportation problems. One of which is the review by (Vlahogianni, 2015), where they surveyed the applications of Big Data elements such as optimisation methods and computational intelligence to the field of traffic and transportation domain, while the work produced by (Wang et al., 2016) concentrated on implementing Soft Computing techniques for transport sector. Similarly, (Davidson, 2015) in their work demonstrated the importance of methodological requirement approaches from Big Data Analytics to evaluate and understand urban traffic OD patterns. Finally, the work of (Rathore et al., 2016) in which they proposed a framework based on parallel computing techniques and Big Graph processing systems to effectively analyse urban traffic Big Data by utilising large-scale graphs. All the above discussed surveys on implementation of Big Data Analytics are limited to traffic and transportation sector. However, this review explores in-depth the complete life cycle of Big Data from both tech-based and application-based standpoint.

Big Data Visualisation in Traffic and Transportation Sector

One of the important features that has gained prominence in the last few in Big Data technologies is data visualisation. As discussed in the introduction section, visualisation of data evolved from the extraction of scientific approaches to understand complicated datasets, to an imaginative area focusing on gaining insights and interpretation of data (Keim et al., 2013). As a result, there exists a void in the past research in the area of visualisation especially for transportation sector where visualisation of geo-tagged data should always correlate with geographical position of the captured information.

Table 3. Summary of literature works demonstrating the importance of big data analytics in traffic and transport sector

Objective	Approach	Horizontal/Vertical Strategy	Big Data Advantage	Real time	Reference
Descriptive	Data fusion and data mining	Horizontal (ITS)	Big Data Analytics Framework	No	(Hua et al., 2016)
	Scheduling	Vertical (logistics)	Big Data sources	No	(Wang et al., 2018)
	Data mining	Vertical (Intelligent monitoring)	Big Data Analytics Framework	No	(Xia et al., 2016)
	Fusion models	Horizontal (ITS)	Big Data integration	Yes	(Khattak, 2017)
	Massive data mining	Horizontal (real-time data)	Big Data Analytics Framework	Yes	(Xiong et al., 2016b)
	Trajectory evaluation	Horizontal (Urban trajectory data)	Big Data Analytics Framework	No	(Torre-Bastida et al., 2018) (D. Xia et al., 2021)
	Statistical functions	Horizontal (Global cities)	Smart cities	Yes	(Roy et al., 2017)
	Massive data mining	Horizontal (Ground, space, and air data)	Big Data Analytics Framework	No	(Xiong et al., 2016a)
	Econometric and statistical models	Horizontal (Driver characteristics, road data, and weather conditions)	Big Data sources	No	(Fetene et al., 2017)
Forecasting	Forecasting models	Vertical (Urban roads)	Big Data sources	No	(Zedda & Pinna, 2018) (Xiao & Xie, 2021)
	Short-term forecasting models	Horizontal (ITS)	Big Data sources	No	(Bacciu et al., 2017)
	Neural networks	Vertical (time series)	Collective applications	No	(Laptev et al., 2017)
	Classification	Vertical (Public transport)	Big Data sources	No	(Torre-Bastida et al., 2018)
	Classification and statistical models	Vertical (t-axis licences)	Big Data sources	No	(Wei Yuan et al., 2016)
	Forecasting models	Vertical (Bus and transit)	Big Data sources	Yes	(Anwar et al., 2016), (Suma et al., 2017)

continued on following page

Table 3. Continued

Objective	Approach	Horizontal/Vertical Strategy	Big Data Advantage	Real time	Reference
Prescriptive	Deep learning	Vertical (Traffic conflicts detection)	Social media data sources	No	(Zhang et al., 2018)
	Route planning and optimisation	Vertical (Transport routes)	Optimisation routing (real-time)	Yes	(Su et al., 2016)
	Heuristic algorithm	Vertical (Vehicle's routing)	Big Data sources	No	(Wenyan Yuan et al., 2018)
	Deep learning	Vertical (Vehicle's licence plate detection)	Deep learning	No	(Yang et al., 2018)

Various technical methods on visual analytics are discussed in this section. Firstly, (X. M. Wang et al., 2016) conducted a large-scale survey on visual techniques for the development and execution of processing pipelines along with necessary guidelines. (Wu et al., 2016) analysed the co-occurrence of pedestrian movement behaviour through telecommunication data by implementing visual analytics technique for Guangzhou city (China). Visual analytics contributes to major part of research on pedestrian movement in urban areas based on the variations in the data from which such movement trajectories are captured. In this aspect, (Krueger et al., 2016) analysed the travel patterns of pedestrians by reconstructing their twitter data with the help of visual analytics technique. Also, recent studies in visual analytics have paved way to the development of integrated visualisation system by combining various complex data sources. In this regard, (Wibisono et al., 2016) developed integrated Fast Incremental Tree models for traffic prediction and visualisation combined. These developed models are adaptable to fluctuations in data streams. In the end, it is worth to discuss the work of (Li et al., 2016d), where they have developed a traffic evaluation and visualisation technique based on the virtual reality GIS to manage and process traffic related Big Data.

Recently, studies in visual analytics have been focussing on the visualisation of Big Data generated by commercial taxis. (Montoya-Torres et al., 2021) in their work developed a framework that integrates data capture, processing, storage, and visualisation by means of mobile applications, web pages by setting up of Traffic Command Centres (TCC). (Ferreira et al., 2013) proposed a model that utilises urban taxi trip data to analyse the data sets to provide virtual inquiry facilities to taxi users. This proposed model takes into consideration OD data to movement of people across the city and it can analyse comprehensive spatio-temporal data consisting wide range of collections and visual descriptions. (Huang et al., 2016) utilised taxi trajectory data to evaluate the movement pattern of taxis in urban areas by means of visual analytics approach upon integrating graph networking and visual analysis. (Liu et al., 2017) also utilised similar taxi data to identify and pin-point locations using extensive GPS data by means of visual analytics by combining visualisation techniques and data mining to solve location problems on a wide scale. In the end, a new approach (Al-Dohuki et al., 2017) that efficiently manages and evaluates spatio-temporal movement patterns has been developed for analysing taxi trajectory data on a large-scale.

On the implementation of visual analytics for data retrieval, (Wang & Yang, 2016) developed an effective strategy that utilizes multi-resolution data to capture diverse traffic and transport data sets on a large-scale for visual data mining. The representation of captured complex data was efficiently performed by enhancing and integrating density-based parallel coordinates and footprint splatting techniques. (Gupta et al., 2016) focused on data representation by developing a technique to analyse and visualise movement pattern of individual actors, interactions between multiple actors and their frequently visited places. This work helped in visualising their movements on two-dimensional maps through their captured GPS footprints. Similarly, (Yu et al., 2016) developed an interactive approach to analyse and visualise traffic regions in urban cities that are not visible. A prototype was developed based on this method to evaluate vehicle trajectories through monitoring tools in relation to the hidden area under study. This developed prototype model consists of elements such as maps, matric-table views, and cloud tree map for better visualisation of these hidden traffic location. Finally, a visualisation-based urban mobility ontology has been proposed (Sobral et al., 2016) to interpret and categorise traffic and transport data by integrating visualisation approaches and sematic framework for a better visualisation.

Contributions of Open Data in Traffic and Transportation Sector

In traffic and transportation sector, Open Data is one of the main contributors of data and information for ITS, thus making it an essential source element of Big Data (Janssen et al., 2012; Zhu et al., 2018; Hounsell et al., 2016). Kaufman (2012) provided suggestions and future directions on how to extract and maintain data volumes to curb the difficulties encountered during data interpretation and to provide user-friendly frameworks. Similarly, (Wong et al., 2013) have presented the empirical findings of open transit data of Atlanta city (USA). Also, (Morris & Wier, 2016) have presented TransBASESF.org to demonstrate the contributions of Open Data in traffic and transportation sector. Basically, the public health department of San Francisco (USA) has designed and implemented geo-spatial analytics model to capture, extract, evaluate, supervise, and tackle the traffic safety problems within the metropolitan area. (Hounsell et al., 2016) have designed and implemented a project known as GOAL (Growing Old and Staying Mobile) funded by the European Commission to tackle the problems faced by elderly people while using public transport systems. This project evaluated elderly people *fitness to travel* by categorising them into five groups based on their transport needs and requirements of elderly people. Moreover, (C. An & Rockmore, 2016) broadened the scope of Open Data in transport sector by utilising open geographic data sources to search and identify public service establishments such as restaurants, hospitals, Supermarkets etc. by identifying and interlinking geographic locations of different users to their individual preferences with the help of public Yelp datasets. (Balbin et al., 2020) conducted a case study to evaluate the feasibility of open big data for public transit in the city of Toronto (Canada). The performance of public transit bus was evaluated in terms of on-time, early arrival, and late stops) through forecasting analysis by utilising real-time open big data available in Op nata Portal. Finally, (X. Zheng et al., 2016) have thoroughly reviewed the significance of Big Data in social transportation by presenting various data sources, techniques, and implementation procedures to tackle traffic issues in urban areas for a better understanding and development of next-generation ITS. The framework on Big Data implementation in ITS is shown in Figure 3.

Figure 3. Framework of Big Data Analytics Implementation in ITS

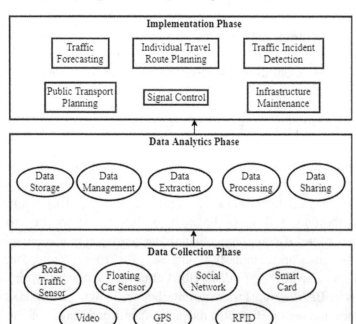

Applications of Big Data in Traffic and Transportation Sector

The development of recent technologies in ITS has helped transport planners to capture, analyse and share detailed traffic data at an exceptional rate, paving way for the development of innovative transport models and wide range opportunities to build smart cities. Big Data technologies promote wide range of applications in traffic and transportation sector by utilising the information provided by all stakeholders such as urban residents. In fact, the user involvement and application in transportation sector (upon including Big Data technologies) do not vary much significantly as compared to other conventional methods in terms of data collection, evaluation, and interpretation. Meanwhile, any changes or modifications in methodologies and techniques approved in their implementations involving each and every stakeholder will spread throughout the life cycle of Big Data, right from capturing of data to the interpretation of the captured data (paving way for new area of research interest known as edge analytics) (Satyanarayanan, 2017). The summarised overview of forthcoming analysis is presented in Table 3.

In this section we present the latest and innovative applications of Big Data technologies in ITS for traffic and transportation sector. Driver Guidance and Smart vehicles, which constantly assist the drivers and monitor their behaviours through the traffic by regularly updating them on the surrounding traffic conditions to avoid conflicts and potential crashes at the initial stage. It is one of the latest applications of Big Data technologies in transportation sector. (Yin et al., 2021) The algorithm-based sensor devices and geospatial data analytics in smart urban infrastructure helps in optimising traffic capacity thereby improving the traffic system can be achieved by smart vehicles. (Wallace & Lăzăroiu, 2021; Papu Carrone et al., 2021) The transport characteristics like mobility, driver performance, safety, roadway capacity, and parking utilities by making use of space and economical spots can be enhanced by smart vehicles. (Banerjee & Das, 2012) have developed a hybrid approach by incorporating short-term Fourier transform, sensor data fusion and support vector machines to identify and analyse defect signals to diagnose engine defects. In a similar work by (Fridman et al., 2016), they have tackled the problems encountered in integrating Big Data technologies to driving scenario due to poor synchronisation of diverse data sources that usually occurs when the data is captured by different sensors having different hardware. These works serve as examples in which Big Data Analytics is integrated with instrumented vehicles.

Big Data technologies have played a vital role in the development of Advanced Driver Assistance Systems (ADAS) (Paul et al., 2016) (Taie et al., 2016; Lee & Ahn, 2016), where the extracted information from Big Data sources are utilised to develop functionalities like navigation, assistance, and manoeuvre of a vehicle based on the behaviour of driver (perception, intellection and volition). In this regard, recent literature studies have integrated driver behaviour characteristics with Big Data Analytics. (Taie et al., 2016) have described a methodology for ADAS that can be implemented during the development phase of ADAS to remotely diagnose, forecast anomalies and maintain the ADAS data efficiently. Big Data usage has a significant role in ADAS development due to the involvement of large-scale data volumes that increase exponentially with respect to the number of vehicles, thereby increasing the number of ADAS components. Similarly, Lee & Ahn (2016) developed revolutionary algorithms to detect, classify and help in forecasting the evolved driving behaviour in ADAS. (Cui et al., 2016) developed an interactive safety analysis framework to detect and tackle situations arising due to driver behavioural changes by evaluating the risk involved due to vehicle dynamics as per ISO 26262 norm.

The work of (Urra et al., 2017) has focussed on the processing, evaluation and interpretation of traffic and transport data by presenting the outcomes of interlinked vehicle networks. Their work has evaluated the advantages in utilising mobile technologies in traffic networks and the underlying challenges. They have laid forward a questionnaire approach based on the usage of mobile technologies.

- Passenger information, which represents all the transport facilities and service information provided to the road and pedestrian users. Social Media is one of the latest technological advances that provide its user information for the development of transport facilities as demonstrated in (Kaplan & Haenlein, 2010; Zhang et al., 2018; Zheng et al., 2016). In their work, they elaborated on implementation of various techniques like crowd sourcing, visualisation, and problem tackling services, thereby proving the significance of Big Data in social transportation. (Xia et al., 2021) proposed an information framework that analyses the large volume of taxi trajectory data to identify the temporal, spatiotemporal, and spatial attributes of passenger travel characteristics by evaluating travel time, travel distance. (Fonzone et al., 2016) have laid forward a new set of directions for the public transport systems evolving from the traditional approaches to the latest innovative techniques utilising Big Data technologies.

- Roadway operations and maintenance is regarded as one of the important challenges faced by urban development planners in terms of planning, design, and construction of roadway infrastructure along with its operations, supervision, and maintenance. (Louhghalam et al., 2017) have proposed a model framework to detect and control carbon footprint during the construction, operation and maintenance of roadway. Li et al. (2016a) have developed a method to detect traffic congestion on the roadways that have restricted access by utilising crowd-sourced data obtained from the probe vehicle. Finally, (Petrovska et al., 2016) have developed enhanced web-based applications for traffic planners to monitor and control traffic operations on the roadways. (De Gennaro et al., 2016) conducted a case study in the cities of Vienna (Austria), Rome (Italy) to evaluate the potential of Big Data in road transport policies of Europe. Navigation systems were utilised to collect datasets on mobility and driving behavioural patterns by studying 28000 vehicle trips and parking events. The developed methodology and outcomes present the importance of Big Data in policy evaluation and roadway governance in European nations.

- Road traffic management is related to planning, design, development, and management of traffic flow models that assist in smooth and efficient movement of vehicles (public and private). The two important trends constituting the traffic management system are: traffic flow model development based on the data (traffic volume, density, speed etc.) obtained from sources and traffic demand assessment dealing with OD surveys and spatio-temporal movement patterns (Matcha, Sivanesan, & Ng, 2021). Regarding the forecasting of traffic variables, the potential of Deep-learning techniques has been explored (Aqib et al., 2019; Lv et al., 2015) to understand and to predict traffic flow by integrating neural architecture with traffic flow data. Finally, regarding the development of OD matrices, a model has been developed (Horn et al., 2017) by using mobile data (Tiedemann et al., 2016; "The Potential of Mobile Network Big Data as a Tool in Colombo's Transportation and Urban Planning," 2016) to tackle traffic flow problems. (Goel et al., 2018) conducted a case study to forecast travel patterns using street imagery techniques (Google Street view (GSV)) in 34 cities in Great Britain. They analysed 2000 GSV images from 1000 random locations in each city to develop regression models for four different types of travel modes such as public transport, cycling, motorcycles and cars. (Khazaei et al., 2016) conducted a case study by developing a Big Data Analytic platform (Sipresk) on urban transportation data to evaluate travel patterns in the city of Greater Toronto Area (Canada). The developed framework was utilised to analyse traffic flow characteristics such as average speed, congestion networks etc., by scrutizing huge data sets in the major freeways in Toronto city.

Another major issue in the management of urban traffic flow is traffic congestion. (S. An et al., 2016) have proposed an approach that makes use of GPS equipped with vehicle data and grid divisions to calculate the trend of urban recurrent congestion (RC).

- In the area of public transportation services, approaches such as network planning, operations planning, execution, labour policy, finance, marketing, and administration are commonly used. In this scenario, we classify research works based on two categories: 1) public transport management and 2) network planning, route modelling and simulation. In the first category, (Erhardt et al., 2017) have developed software tools to integrate and evaluate huge volumes of captured data to estimate and supervise the performance of transit systems. A case study was conducted in the city of San Francisco (USA) to evaluate the performance of the developed software tool. In the second category on route modelling, (Cerotti et al., 2017) developed an optimisation technique by interpreting the driving patterns obtained from queries or feedback from the drivers. The effectiveness of their optimisation technique to design route planning framework was modelled, analysed, and validated through a case study by the Markovian method. In the case of network planning, the studies of (Hanft et al., 2016) for public bus service planning, (Herrera-Quintero et al., 2018) for planning public transport services using IoT, and (Yin et al., 2015) for planning pedestrian movements are worth mentioning. Finally, regarding the simulation work, the significance of IoT and other Big Data sources has been demonstrated by simulating and calibrating traffic flow in order to enhance the safety of road networks (Muñoz et al., 2018). Wang et al. (2021) in their work constructed a subway-bus double-layer network using big data analytics from bus and subway network. Gephi software was utilised to analyse the complex visualisation of the network. The optimisation of the model was achieved by addition and deletion of stations in the network. Their proposed optimisation model improved the network efficiency of Beijing public transport by 2.12%. The data from public transportation is of enormous volume covering wide aspects, therefore big data framework with fast processing capability powered by supercomputing hardware is necessary (Lyu et al., 2021). Table 3 presents the summary of case studies on Big Data implementation in traffic and transportation sector of different countries. (Tavassoli et al., 2018) conducted a case study to evaluate passenger waiting time using large datasets obtained from automatic fare collection in the city of East Queensland (Australia). A total of 130000 daily rail passengers in 145 stations were considered to develop Log-logistic accelerated failure time models to forecast the public transport passenger waiting times.

- Traffic conflicts and crash management, which is a combination of multi-disciplinary tasks, should be implemented in an organised manner to identify, respond and resolving traffic incidents in a safe and spontaneous manner for smooth traffic flow (Bhargav Naidu & Chhabra, 2018). Its main objective is to minimise the impact of traffic conflicts and accidents to safe-guard the road users. In this regard, the following contributions are noteworthy: (Tien et al., 2016) have developed a model based on the Big Data analysis of social sensor to detect traffic incidents along the urban infrastructure. (Parkinson & Bamford, 2016) developed a model based on Big Data Analytics to assess transport safety risks and predict railway incidents. (Aqib et al., 2020b) in their work integrated Big Data, GPU computing and deep learning to forecast traffic incidents on road by developing a comprehensive approach for large-scale real-time incident forecasting. Finally, the behaviour and adaptability of taxi and subway trips during natural disasters have been demonstrated by analysing Big Data sources (Zhu et al., 2016). Also, (Aqib et al., 2020a) developed a cloud computing based disaster management system by integrating deep learning, In-memory computing and GPUs for smart traffic flow management. (Bao et al., 2021) investigated the impact of human activities on the spatial pattern of traffic conflicts on urban road networks using multi-source big data. Their study concluded that the multi-source big data helps in enhancing the zone level traffic crash models and the impact of human activities on traffic crashes in urban road networks. A standard traffic forecasting model used to understand and predict traffic flow features is shown in Figure 4.

Figure 4. A Typical Traffic Forecasting Model

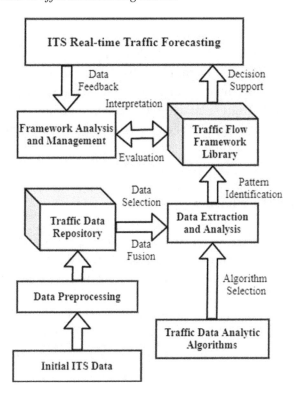

Table 4. Summary of case studies on implementation of big data analytics in logistics and transportation sector (Source: Biuk-Aghai et al., 2016)

Origin	Big Data Framework	Application	Technology
India	Vehicle monitoring network (real-time)	Upgrade operational efficiency	HDFS GPRS GPS
Ireland	Public transit network	Upgrade public transport services and mitigate road traffic congestion	Traffic Sensors CCTV GPS
Sweden	Intelligent transportation system (real-time)	Forecast traffic conditions in the future	Weather information GPS Traffic information
Tunisia	Tracking network for logistics	Cargo operations and monitoring (real-time)	GPS HBase IoT RFID SaaS cloud
UK	Customer evaluation network for Airlines	Understanding and evaluating clients' requirements	Call centre records Smart phones Social media networks
Vietnam	Traffic operations and management	Mitigate road traffic congestion and pollution	Ship sensors Traffic sensors

To the best of our knowledge, only a few studies have implemented Big Data Analytics in maritime (Kim et al., 2013) and railway (Attoh-Okine, 2015) transport services. The applications of Big Data Analytics in these transport modes are far different from its implementations in road transport. For instance, in railway transport, Big Data Analytics are implemented in condition-based maintenance (Fumeo et al., 2015) and risk management (Figueres-Esteban et al., 2015).

CURRENT CHALLENGES

The significance of Big Data Analytics in traffic and transportation sector has been demonstrated in the previous sections. However, there exists a gap in the literature that needs to be resolved along with new challenges that raise due to sharing and interpretation of information between diverse data sources across heterogeneous transport modes. In this section, we lay forward the existing and future challenges in Big Data Analytics for traffic and transportation sector that need to be resolved for the development of an efficient and advances ITS for smart cities.

Table 5. Big data stratagem in ITS implementations areas

Big Data Stratagem	Implementation	Reference
Evaluation of external forces on ship	Big data fusion and analytics	(Kim et al., 2013)
Public transport (bus) planning	Big Data Analytics	(Hanft et al., 2016) (Z. Wang et al., 2021)
Big Data frameworks in social transportation systems	Big Data social transportation	(X. Zheng et al., 2016)
Vehicle dynamics and behaviour analysis	Big Data schemes and policies	(Cui et al., 2016) (Papu Carrone et al., 2021)
Railway systems maintenance based on technical constraints	Big Data streaming analytics	(Fumeo et al., 2015)
Incident management and emergency services - Fusion of incident detections into public infrastructure	Big Data public sensor data	(Tien et al., 2016)
Method of identification of driving tendency	Big data Analytics	(J. H. Lee & Ahn, 2016)
Driving data fusion frameworks	Big Data fusion	(Fridman et al., 2016)
Driver guidance and fusion of multi-sensor data for connected and automated vehicles	Big data fusion	(Banerjee & Das, 2012) (Wallace & Lăzăroiu, 2021)
Vehicle design efficiency	Big data Analytics	(Torre-Bastida et al., 2018)
Pioneer public transport guidelines	Big Data services	(Fonzone et al., 2016)
Road traffic planning based on IoT	Big data Analytics	(Herrera-Quintero et al., 2018)
Transit system efficiency measurement and monitoring	Big data fusion and analysis	(Erhardt et al., 2017)
Management of data in vehicular networks using mobile agents	Vehicular networks	(Urra et al., 2017)
Generation of Origin-Destination matrix	Big Data Analytics	(Horn et al., 2017)
Pedestrian planning	Big Data Analytics	(L. Yin et al., 2015) (Bao et al., 2021)
RDMP stratagem for ADAS	Big Data Framework	(Taie et al., 2016)
Urban roadway planning and management Environmental footprint management and control on roadways	Big Data Analytics	(Louhghalam et al., 2017)

continued on following page

Table 5. Continued

Big Data Stratagem	Implementation	Reference
Road traffic management	Big Data	(Petrovska et al., 2016)
RC evolution patterns	Big Data real-time analysis	(S. An et al., 2016)
Management of public transit and optimisation of its route planning	Big Data Analytics	(Cerotti et al., 2017)
Flexibility of taxi and subway trips	Big Data	(Y. Zhu et al., 2016)
Analysis of risk in railway operations	Big Data visualisation	(Figueres-Esteban et al., 2015)
Simulation based methods of safety evaluation	Big Data	(Shi et al., 2016)
Traffic congestion on restricted access roadways	Big Data Analytics	(H. Li et al., 2016)
Management of traffic flow and its forecasting based on deep learning	Big Data forecasting Analytics	(Lv et al., 2015)
Forecasting safety risks using rail incident data	Big Data Analytics	(Parkinson & Bamford, 2016)

Coordinated Data Analytics

The accuracy and efficiency with which real time data can be analysed and processed determines the future role of Big Data Analytics in transportation sector. Previously, data analytics process would take days or even months, but now the time required has been reduced to minutes or even to fraction of seconds (Barlow, 2013). With these latest advancements in data analytics, users are expecting outcomes in a matter of seconds.

In traffic and transportation sector, the present ITS technologies and frameworks are not built to evaluate collected data and to perform real time data processing at a faster pace as required for potential applications like road safety management, since most of the traffic and transport problems require quick actions and solutions within a limited time frame. Therefore, based on the above required time constraints, three categories of Big Data Analytics are established:

- Batch Analytics. In this category, very lenient (hours to days) or no time constraint is applied during the processing cycle of data. In this regard, these frameworks capture, analyse and display results in different phases. The real-time scenarios such as planning of transport logistics and their supervision utilise these delay-sensitive control-panel ITS applications.

- Soft real-time analytics. In this category, the systems and data sources are subjected to limited time constraints in the order of seconds to minutes. Different online systems fall under this category to provide a quick response to the user. The best example is the feedback service provided to the users of parking lots in metropolitan cities (Tomar et al., 2018). To enhance the user-system interface, data processing and outcomes must be delivered within the limited time constraints.
- Hard real-time analytics. This category requires ultra-speed processing of data within seconds (milliseconds to nanoseconds). If this demand is not fulfilled by the developed data processing units, they would fail in supporting specific applications. Its usage in the field of transport safety regarding autonomous vehicles where traffic incidents need to be detected and processed within fraction of seconds for avoiding crashes (Du et al., 2017; Alam et al., 2020) are a good application examples in this category.

To meet with the latest advancements in various fields and to provide an efficient service to the users especially in transportation sector, real-time data processing, sharing and evaluation are considered as crucial elements. The latest enhancement and innovation in the field of intelligent transportation that requires data related to road networks, pedestrians, vehicles, and cargo, location information of vehicles and people, schedules of public transport services, transport fares data, data on user transactions or payments can be effectively implemented by an efficient real-time data processing. Therefore, for the implementation of smart transportation and intelligent vehicles, automation and optimisation of real-time services and facilities are key factors. To achieve these objectives, people need to be educated to understand the methodology and processing of these technologies in order to reap the benefits of next generation ITS rather than concentrating alone on the technological transformation of this transport domain.

Smart City

Although the complex requirements of a smart city are handled well by Big Data Analytics and their construction significantly promote the regional economic growth by improving the efficiency of public and private enterprises and standard of living of the residents (Xiao & Xie, 2021). There still exists many challenges that need to be addressed. The primary challenges faced by Big Data technologies for smart city data management criteria for urban transport sector are presented as follows:

- **Data Access:** Data collection techniques face a lot of constraints in the form of legal issues, transaction costs, and contractual misdeeds making open access to available data complex in nature. The criteria regarding what data to be collected and what data to be made open access face some privacy and confidentiality related issues that also need to be addressed (Zhu et al., 2019).

- **Quality of Data:** Quality refers to the usefulness of the data for a specific purpose, which is required for critical decision-making process. Data obtained through diverse data sources are mostly unstructured leading to decline in their quality. There is a need for quality checking of obtained data to establish quality metrics, identify and resolve erroneous data, analyse data quality and to establish a link between quality assurance gains and investments (Lee, 2017). There is a need to focus on the compound data of human behaviour, technical, institutional and regulatory features collected in live and reactive environments by abandoning the normal behaviourist orientation of data analytics (Kandt & Batty, 2021).

- **Erroneous Data:** Huge amounts of data are generated through various Big Data sources which are prone to errors and data loss making them unreliable. To rectify the errors produced from multiple datasets, the source of these datasets must be evaluated and understood. The criteria and limitations of the dataset should be established before evaluating to evade bias in data interpretation (Boyd & Crawford, 2012; Jiang & Luo, 2022).

- **Data Mop-up:** Mopping up of data is the process of clearing un-useful, inaccurate, and erroneous data from data source. This process marks the primary step in any Big Data project. To minimise the overall expenditure in a project, the data mop-up process is necessary to erase high levels of redundancy in datasets (Chen et al., 2014a; Kaffash et al., 2021).

- **Data Timeliness:** The usefulness of a given data reduces over time. In transport sector, to detect passenger movements, delay times, OD studies real-time or near real-time evaluation of flow data is required (Chen et al., 2014b; Jiang & Luo, 2022).

- **Data Heterogeneity:** Data from diverse sources like emails, social media, fax data, pdf document handlings, recorded meetings and more constitute to unstructured data. Extraction and evaluation of unstructured data is quite complex and costly too. Also, it is unfeasible to convert unstructured data to structured one. Although unstructured data is raw and cumbersome, it integrates well with database (Katal et al., 2013; Wang et al., 2021).

- **Data Visualisation:** Visualisation is a necessary criterion that assists in decision making process at every step-in data analysis. the issues arising through visualisation are still under the study of Online Analytics Processing (OLAP) research. High-dimensional traffic and transport data provides room for data visualisation tools (Chen et al., 2014; Jiang & Luo, 2022).

- **Data Lifecycle:** Traffic and transportation sector requires real-time data evaluation of Big Data Analytics. The requirement to improve the value of analysis paves way to define the life-cycle of data, the importance it exhibits and the process of computation for real-time analytics (Chen et al., 2014a; Jiang & Luo, 2022). Therefore, development of definite filtering methodologies is necessary to ensure data integrity. Since most of the available data are scattered leading to incomplete, unreliable, and misleading conclusions.

- **Data Storage and Network Problems:** The present storage techniques and hardware are not adequate enough for storing Big Data. A lot of companies are making use of cloud storage techniques for storing Big Data (Katal et al., 2013; Kaffash et al., 2021). However, when huge amount of data is involved the bandwidth of the network becomes the performance indicator.

- **Compatibility:** The integration of various Big Data Analytics with existing infrastructure systems is an arduous task and requires heavy investment. The issues relating to data visualisation tools require upgradation to provide flexibility and synchronisation for different types of data. Sometimes, it is even challenging to ingest data from upstream systems in a speedy and expected manner (Hashem et al., 2016).

- **Data Privacy and Security:** Privacy and security are primary concerns for big data implementation in smart cities since data gets transferred through integration of various networks. Important centres of smart cities provide hubs for data collection which are sensitive in nature collected without our explicit consent. Hence, high level privacy and security of confidential data of passengers, road users from unauthorised access is a primary issue in smart city applications (Mohbey, 2017).

- **Integration of Data:** Integration of Big Data involves homogenisation of social media, traditional data, data from IoT, machine-based data, web data forming a unified framework for smart city applications. Integration helps in boosting performance and reduces analysis time (Zheng et al., 2016). The integration of data from multi-vendor and multi-functional sensors, equipment and appliances is a challenge for smart city development since this deals with a vast amount of heterogeneous data (Talebkhah et al., 2021). Biggest challenge occurs when different sectors start handling Big Data in the size of terabytes or petabytes. The outline of Big Data challenges in smart cities are summarised in Figure 5.

Figure 5. Big Data Challenges in Smart City

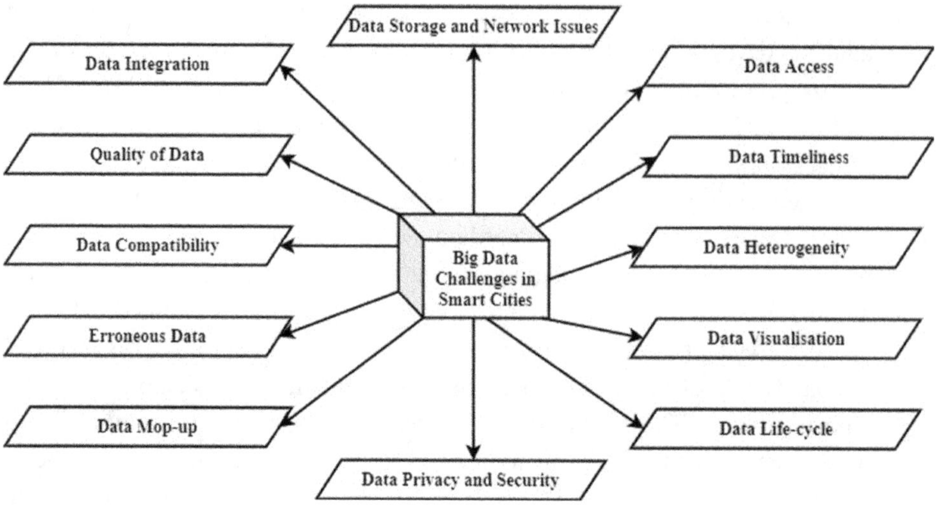

Data Privacy and Security

Data privacy and security are the widely researched issues in the field of Big Data Analytics especially in traffic and transportation domain (Hoh et al., 2006; Giannotti & Pedreschi, 2008). Privacy is one of the biggest concerns in transport applications supporting Big Data sources, since users depend on their mobile devices and computers to share and transfer their personal geo-localised information. Hence, the capture and extraction of private user data remains as a challenge for transportation sector. Unnecessary storage of data traces and location tracking as well as identity theft are some important areas in security breaches and voids. Moreover, online payment has led to several security and privacy issues corresponding to Big Data Analytics. These security risks compromise the significance of Big Data systems in modern ITS technologies. Unfortunately, we have found inadequate research studies and references on the implementation of enhanced ITS infrastructure that ensures security, integrity, enhanced data handling (personal, public, and financial data), and confidentiality. Therefore, these challenges must be tackled with enhanced technological approaches which solidify the significance of Big Data Analytics in traffic and transportation sector, guaranteeing users their rights in accordance with public laws and agreements.

Latest Data Sources

The development of latest technologies and innovations has led to the deployment of different types of sensors such as pedestrian counting equipment, obstacle spotting devices (e.g., vehicle LIDAR radars), high-definition traffic volume and speed detectors etc. for urban transportation infrastructure. The information from these diverse sensors has given rise to new sources of data to be analysed and processed thereby enhancing transport services and facilities to its users. The heterogeneity of data captured from these data sources impose complex challenges to be tackled in the following forms:

- **Data Volume and Exploration:** As a result of diverse sensor technologies usage and increase in population and number of vehicles, the number of datasets in transport analysis is becoming larger. This trend can be seen in vehicle sensing technology, even though the sensors deployed to capture traffic blind spots does not require high data volumes, whereas the other implemented services exceed the rate limits established by standard communication technologies like DSRC, in the case of high-definition LIDAR radar sensors. Present technologies and approaches are inadequate to accommodate the increase in data volume generated by diverse mobility of people and vehicles, thereby making it necessary to enhance and renovate ITS infrastructure to meet the standards of large-scale data volumes.
- **Data Diversity:** Increasing number of sensor technologies has given rise to various data sources of unique data format, accuracy level, and temporal resolution. Hence, the challenge lies in tackling this diverse transport data and break it down into machine readable language by means of interlinking, merging or fusion for combined analysis or evaluation. Here data integration is an important part of ITS data processing phase which combines the data from different data sources like automated signal control, incident detection, ramp metering, road crash analysis, pedestrian crossing, and travel time forecasting. In this context, (Faouzi & Klein, 2016) have identified the research gaps and future directions in this field. The process of decision-making based on the captured data from diverse data sources depend on the integration of this complex data. (De La Iglesia et al., 2017) have proposed an engine management system based on the captured data from sensors to enhance e-bikes battery time and energy. Based on the aggregated data, the proposed system enhances and personalises user experience by analysing and integrating the captured data.
- **Data Importance:** Generally, in Big Data life cycle, the volume of data captured as well as its smart implementation are imperative in enhancing the traffic and transportation infrastructure. Since the amount of money invested in the deployment of sensors along urban infrastructure for data collection is quite high, hence it is of primary importance to ensure the spending is efficient and effective. In this regard, (Fosso Wamba et al., 2015) have developed a

method to interlink the captured data and the processed output data to denote the amount of collected data that is put in efficient and smart usage. However, there still exists a gap in methodological interpretation between the data capturing campaign and the potential significance of Big Data Analytics.

- **Data Standards:** Generally, it refers to the quality, integrity, and trustworthiness of the captured information. With the inflow of huge volume of Big Data, homogeneity and accuracy of the data remain partially controlled. Moreover, different applications demand different levels of accuracy, certainty, and quality. For example, incident or crash analysis requires a precise and valid processed data whereas route forecasting services does not impose such requirements from processed data. Therefore, a challenging task lies ahead in developing a sound approach to assess the standards and reliability of both collection and extraction stages, as well as to identify and to assess their effects at the later stages of data processing.

CONCLUSION

Big Data Analytics is going to play a vital role in the development of next generation ITS. Accordingly, researchers and urban planners in transport sector are inclining towards developing advances methods by gaining expertise throughout the Big Data life cycle, specifically in the areas of information collection and analysis. This review has laid forward the recent advancements in traffic and transportation sector with the implementation of Big Data tools and technologies. We have reviewed the contributions of researchers in Big Data Analytics for transportation sector for the development of a smart and integrated urban community of people, vehicles, and roads.

Many researchers have contributed towards the significance of Big Data Analytics in transportation sector. (Jiang & Luo, 2022; Kaffash et al., 2021) have reviewed and demonstrated the background concepts, approaches, recent implementation, and future challenges in the area of parallel transportation management systems. Also, the works reported in (Mathew et al., 2021; Hou et al., 2016; Nkoro & Vershinin, 2014) have demonstrated the significance and latest advancements in Big Data models and ITS along with current challenges to be tackled for the development of next-generation ITS. This review focuses on two important features: (i) Classification of latest research works based on Big Data life cycle stages and their applications, enabling transport planners and researchers to equip themselves with knowledge on recent trends, technologies, and research gaps for future developments in this field; (ii) coverage of good number of research studies to provide a complete understanding of Big Data significance in traffic and transportation sector. Hence, based on our evaluation, this review has identified new research areas that are going to change the face of rapidly growing traffic and transportation sector.

- **Future Transportation Modes:** The on-going research in the transportation sector always attempts to provide safer, cleaner, more efficient, and more comfortable user experience to the end users. Sustainable and energy-efficient designs are the key factors in developing next-generation transport modes. In the near future, transportation takes a new form thanks to the innovative transportations such as hyperloop, bullet trains, jetpacks, atomic-powered vehicles, super-cavitation, magnetic levitation, non-stop trains.

- **Future Urban Transportation:** The adaptation of Big Data technologies for the development of smart cities is driven by the growing population in and around major cities and the continuous in-flow of data from these areas in various forms (structured and unstructured). In this regard, two prime factors of Big Data are highlighted – the captured data itself and the key technologies implemented in smart cities. The implemented tools and techniques must be able to capture, store, extract and process the information produced by the activities of road users and pedestrians as per the requirements established by smart cities. Moreover, the evaluation of this vast amount of data contributes to generating more information thereby enabling interlinking of different domains for the development of next-generation ITS and smart cities.

- **Mobile Services:** Nowadays, almost every mobile handset and device comes with its own sensor equipment, thereby providing location data of its users by means of multiple positioning approaches. Hence, location tracking mobile handsets are being utilised in every sector apart from transportation sector. For instance, in Industry 4.0, an accurate indoor location tracking is utilised to enhance human-machine interface and to improve the safety of workers (Yang et al., 2015).

- **Next-Generation ITS Technologies:** Enhanced real-time traffic management and smart toll-fee collection are some of the new areas being explored by the researchers, which demands development of new technologies supporting these innovative features. The design and development of next-generation ITS architecture that captures and integrates data volumes from diverse sources is essential for smart cities to gain forecasting ability and optimised techniques thereby enhancing the traffic management system (Harris et al., 2015). Big Data Analytics form the core structure of future ITS technologies due to its capabilities in integrating data from different sectors and extracting necessary information for development of efficient and sustainable cities.

- **Administrative and Economic Trends:** Various economical developmental phases in global economy have paved way for the development of latest technologies in transportation domain while administrative policies are linked to the user-captured geo-tagged data. Transportation and administrative/economic sectors are inter-dependent to one another. There are open discussions (Crawford & Schultz, 2013; Berinato, 2014) on the implementations of regulatory measures in the design and deployment of Big Data technologies in the areas of data privacy, security and governance. However, no specific conclusions have been drawn in this regard; therefore, the set-back between the technological achievements in Big Data Analytics and their applications in real-time traffic scenario for transportation sector will rise irrevocably.

The concept of Big Data Analytics deserves so much attention in the future for exploring new data sources and development of innovative frameworks in order to give rise to safe, secured, and user-friendly services for traffic and transportation sector. Last decade has seen a rise in the number of research works that focus on the significance of Big Data technologies in every domain. Meanwhile, there is an increasing concern in the community to enhance the Big Data technology in order to support real-time user services and urban facilities in a sustainable manner. The fundamental aspects of Big Data such as data collection, extraction, storage, integration, and processing of huge volumes of diverse data from various data sources (IoT, smart cities) require further exploration. The latest ground-breaking Big Data technologies implemented in the traffic and transportation sector in real-time scenario would fail unless they are modified and restructured methodologically to analyse and process data with enhanced properties (e.g., density, heterogeneity, volume, and dynamics).

ACKNOWLEDGMENT

This work was partially sponsored by Taylor's University Flagship Research Grant TUFR/2017/001/05. The author is thankful to the Taylor's University for funding scholarship during this research work. This work was sponsored by Taylor's University Post-Graduate Research Scholarship.

REFERENCES

Abbasi, A., Sarker, S., & Chiang, R. H. L. (2016). Big data research in information systems: Toward an inclusive research agenda. Journal of the Association for Information Systems. doi:10.17705/1jais.00423

Al-Dohuki, S., Wu, Y., Kamw, F., Yang, J., Li, X., Zhao, Y., Ye, X., Chen, W., Ma, C., & Wang, F. (2017). SemanticTraj: A New Approach to Interacting with Massive Taxi Trajectories. *IEEE Transactions on Visualization and Computer Graphics*, *23*(1), 11–20. Advance online publication. doi:10.1109/TVCG.2016.2598416 PMID:27514044

Alam, F., Mehmood, R., & Katib, I. (2020). Comparison of decision trees and deep learning for object classification in autonomous driving. In EAI/Springer Innovations in Communication and Computing. doi:10.1007/978-3-030-13705-2_6

Alomari, E., Mehmood, R., & Katib, I. (2019). Road traffic event detection using twitter data, machine learning, and apache spark. *Proceedings - 2019 IEEE SmartWorld, Ubiquitous Intelligence and Computing, Advanced and Trusted Computing, Scalable Computing and Communications, Internet of People and Smart City Innovation, SmartWorld/UIC/ATC/SCALCOM/IOP/SCI 2019*, 1888–1895. doi:10.1109/SmartWorld-UIC-ATC-SCALCOM-IOP-SCI.2019.00332

Alsafery, W., Alturki, B., Reiff-Marganiec, S., & Jambi, K. (2018). Smart Car Parking System Solution for the Internet of Things in Smart Cities. *1st International Conference on Computer Applications and Information Security, ICCAIS 2018*. 10.1109/CAIS.2018.8442004

Alsolami, B., Mehmood, R., & Albeshri, A. (2020). Hybrid statistical and machine learning methods for road traffic prediction: A review and tutorial. In EAI/Springer Innovations in Communication and Computing. doi:10.1007/978-3-030-13705-2_5

Amini, S., Gerostathopoulos, I., & Prehofer, C. (2017). Big data analytics architecture for real-time traffic control. *5th IEEE International Conference on Models and Technologies for Intelligent Transportation Systems, MT-ITS 2017 - Proceedings*. 10.1109/MTITS.2017.8005605

An, C., & Rockmore, D. (2016). *Improving Local Search with Open Geographic Data*. doi:10.1145/2872518.2890482

An, S., Yang, H., Wang, J., Cui, N., & Cui, J. (2016). Mining urban recurrent congestion evolution patterns from GPS-equipped vehicle mobility data. *Information Sciences*, *373*, 515–526. Advance online publication. doi:10.1016/j.ins.2016.06.033

Andrienko, G., Andrienko, N., Chen, W., Maciejewski, R., & Zhao, Y. (2017). Visual analytics of mobility and transportation: State of the art and further research directions. *IEEE Transactions on Intelligent Transportation Systems*, 18(8), 2232–2249. Advance online publication. doi:10.1109/TITS.2017.2683539

Anwar, A., Odoni, A., & Toh, N. (2016). BusViz: Big data for bus fleets. *Transportation Research Record: Journal of the Transportation Research Board*, 2544(1), 102–109. Advance online publication. doi:10.3141/2544-12

Aqib, M., Mehmood, R., Alzahrani, A., & Katib, I. (2020a). A smart disaster management system for future cities using deep learning, gpus, and in-memory computing. In EAI/Springer Innovations in Communication and Computing. doi:10.1007/978-3-030-13705-2_7

Aqib, M., Mehmood, R., Alzahrani, A., & Katib, I. (2020b). In-memory deep learning computations on gpus for prediction of road traffic incidents using big data fusion. In EAI/Springer Innovations in Communication and Computing. doi:10.1007/978-3-030-13705-2_4

Aqib, M., Mehmood, R., Alzahrani, A., Katib, I., Albeshri, A., & Altowaijri, S. M. (2019). Rapid transit systems: Smarter urban planning using big data, in-memory computing, deep learning, and GPUs. In Sustainability (Switzerland) (Vol. 11, Issue 10). doi:10.3390u11102736

Arfat, Y., Usman, S., Mehmood, R., & Katib, I. (2020a). Big data for smart infrastructure design: Opportunities and challenges. In EAI/Springer Innovations in Communication and Computing. doi:10.1007/978-3-030-13705-2_20

Arfat, Y., Usman, S., Mehmood, R., & Katib, I. (2020b). Big data tools, technologies, and applications: A survey. In EAI/Springer Innovations in Communication and Computing. doi:10.1007/978-3-030-13705-2_19

Attoh-Okine, N. (2015). Big data challenges in railway engineering. *Proceedings - 2014 IEEE International Conference on Big Data, IEEE Big Data 2014*. 10.1109/BigData.2014.7004424

Bacciu, D., Carta, A., Gnesi, S., & Semini, L. (2017). An experience in using machine learning for short-term predictions in smart transportation systems. *Journal of Logical and Algebraic Methods in Programming*. doi:10.1016/j.jlamp.2016.11.002

Balbin, P. P. F., Barker, J. C. R., Leung, C. K., Tran, M., Wall, R. P., & Cuzzocrea, A. (2020). Predictive analytics on open big data for supporting smart transportation services. *Procedia Computer Science*. Advance online publication. doi:10.1016/j.procs.2020.09.202 PMID:33042316

Banerjee, T. P., & Das, S. (2012). Multi-sensor data fusion using support vector machine for motor fault detection. *Information Sciences, 217*, 96–107. Advance online publication. doi:10.1016/j.ins.2012.06.016

Bao, J., Li, R., Yi, X., & Zheng, Y. (2016). Managing massive trajectories on the cloud. *GIS: Proceedings of the ACM International Symposium on Advances in Geographic Information Systems.* 10.1145/2996913.2996916

Bao, J., Yang, Z., Zeng, W., & Shi, X. (2021). Exploring the spatial impacts of human activities on urban traffic crashes using multi-source big data. *Journal of Transport Geography, 94*, 103118. doi:10.1016/j.jtrangeo.2021.103118

Barlow, M. (2013). Real-Time Big Data Analytics: Emerging Architecture. In Zhurnal Eksperimental'noi i Teoreticheskoi Fiziki. 1 doi:0.100713398-014-0173-7.2

Bechtsis, D., Tsolakis, N., Vlachos, D., & Iakovou, E. (2017). Sustainable supply chain management in the digitalisation era: The impact of Automated Guided Vehicles. Journal of Cleaner Production. doi:10.1016/j.jclepro.2016.10.057

Bello-Orgaz, G., Jung, J. J., & Camacho, D. (2016). Social big data: Recent achievements and new challenges. *Information Fusion, 28*, 45–59. Advance online publication. doi:10.1016/j.inffus.2015.08.005 PMID:32288689

Benevolo, C., Dameri, R. P., & D'Auria, B. (2016). *Smart Mobility in Smart City.* doi:10.1007/978-3-319-23784-8_2

Berinato, S. (2014). With big data comes big responsibility. Harvard Business Review.

Beyer, M. A., & Laney, D. (2012). *The importance of 'big data': A definition.* Gartner.

Bhardwaj, S., Jain, L., & Jain, S. (2010). Cloud Computing : A Study of Infrastructure As a Service (Iaas). *International Journal of Engineering.*

Bhargav Naidu, M., & Chhabra, R. S. (2018). Safety Indicators for Heterogeneous Non Lane Based Traffic-A Case Study at Outer Ring Road-Delhi. *Indian Journal of Science and Technology, 11*(10), 1–11. Advance online publication. doi:10.17485/ijst/2018/v11i10/103552

Biuk-Aghai, R. P., Kou, W. T., & Fong, S. (2016). Big data analytics for transportation: Problems and prospects for its application in China. *Proceedings - 2016 IEEE Region 10 Symposium, TENSYMP 2016.* 10.1109/TENCONSpring.2016.7519399

Boeing, G. (2019). Spatial information and the legibility of urban form: Big data in urban morphology. *International Journal of Information Management.* Advance online publication. doi:10.1016/j.ijinfomgt.2019.09.009

Boyd, D., & Crawford, K. (2012). Six Provocations for Big Data. SSRN *Electronic Journal*, 1–17. doi:10.2139/ssrn.1926431

Castellanos, C., Perez, B., & Correal, D. (2021). *Smart Transportation: A Reference Architecture for Big Data Analytics*. In M. A. Khan, F. Algarni, & M. T. Quasim (Eds.), *BT - Smart Cities: A Data Analytics Perspective* (pp. 161–179). Springer International Publishing. doi:10.1007/978-3-030-60922-1_8

CBS Interactive Incorporated. (2013). *Amazon Drones: Amazon Unveils Futuristic Delivery Plan*. CBS News.

Cerotti, D., Distefano, S., Merlino, G., & Puliafito, A. (2017). A Crowd-Cooperative Approach for Intelligent Transportation Systems. *IEEE Transactions on Intelligent Transportation Systems*. Advance online publication. doi:10.1109/TITS.2016.2609606

Chen, C., Luan, T. H., Guan, X., Lu, N., & Liu, Y. (2017). Connected Vehicular Transportation: Data Analytics and Traffic-Dependent Networking. *IEEE Vehicular Technology Magazine*, *12*(3), 42–54. Advance online publication. doi:10.1109/MVT.2016.2645318

Chen, C., Ma, J., Susilo, Y., Liu, Y., & Wang, M. (2016). The promises of big data and small data for travel behavior (aka human mobility) analysis. In *Transportation Research Part C*. Emerging Technologies. doi:10.1016/j.trc.2016.04.005

Chen, M., Mao, S., & Liu, Y. (2014a). Big Data: A Survey. *Mobile Networks and Applications*, *19*(2), 171–209. doi:10.100711036-013-0489-0

Chen, Y., Frei, A., & Mahmassani, H. S. (2014b). From Personal Attitudes to Public Opinion: Information Diffusion in Social Networks Toward Sustainable Transportation. *Transportation Research Record: Journal of the Transportation Research Board*, *2430*(1), 28–37. doi:10.3141/2430-04

Collier, C., & Weiland, R. J. (1994). Smart cars, smart highways. *IEEE Spectrum*, *31*(4), 27–33. Advance online publication. doi:10.1109/6.272224

Cottrill, C. D., & Derrible, S. (2015). Leveraging big data for the development of transport sustainability indicators. *Journal of Urban Technology*, *22*(1), 45–64. Advance online publication. doi:10.1080/10630732.2014.942094

Crawford, K., & Schultz, J. (2013). Big data and due processes: Toward a framework to redress predictive privacy harms. *Public Law & Legal Theory Research Paper Series*.

Cui, Y. X., Sun, L., Sui, L. H., Kang, J., & Jiang, Y. (2016). Interactive Safety Analysis Framework of Autonomous Intelligent Vehicles. *MATEC Web of Conferences*. 10.1051/matecconf/20164401029

Dai, J., Li, R., & Liu, Z. (2021). Does initial experience affect consumers' intention to use autonomous vehicles? Evidence from a field experiment in Beijing. *Accident; Analysis and Prevention, 149*, 105778. doi:10.1016/j.aap.2020.105778 PMID:33166760

Das, A., Dash, P., & Mishra, B. K. (2018). *An Innovation Model for Smart Traffic Management System Using Internet of Things (IoT)*. doi:10.1007/978-3-319-70688-7_15

Davidson, A. (2015). *Big Data Exhaust for Origin-Destination Surveys Big Data Exhaust for Origin-Destination Surveys*. Academic Press.

De Gennaro, M., Paffumi, E., & Martini, G. (2016). *Big Data for Supporting Low-Carbon Road Transport Policies in Europe: Applications, Challenges and Opportunities*. Big Data Research. doi:10.1016/j.bdr.2016.04.003

De La Iglesia, D. H., Villarubia, G., De Paz, J. F., & Bajo, J. (2017). *Multi-sensor information fusion for optimizing electric bicycle routes using a swarm intelligence algorithm*. Sensors. doi:10.339017112501

Demchenko, Y., De Laat, C., & Membrey, P. (2014). Defining architecture components of the Big Data Ecosystem. *2014 International Conference on Collaboration Technologies and Systems, CTS 2014*. 10.1109/CTS.2014.6867550

Ding, Y., Li, Y., Deng, K., Tan, H., Yuan, M., & Ni, L. M. (2016a). Detecting and Analyzing Urban Regions with High Impact of Weather Change on Transport. *IEEE Transactions on Big Data*. Advance online publication. doi:10.1109/TBDATA.2016.2623320

Ding, Z., Yang, B., Chi, Y., & Guo, L. (2016b). Enabling Smart Transportation Systems: A Parallel Spatio-Temporal Database Approach. *IEEE Transactions on Computers, 65*(5), 1377–1391. Advance online publication. doi:10.1109/TC.2015.2479596

Du, L., Jiang, W., Zhao, Z., & Su, F. (2017). Ego-Motion Classification for Driving Vehicle. *Proceedings - 2017 IEEE 3rd International Conference on Multimedia Big Data, BigMM 2017*. 10.1109/BigMM.2017.25

El Faouzi, N. E., & Klein, L. A. (2016). Data Fusion for ITS: Techniques and Research Needs. *Transportation Research Procedia*, *15*, 495–512. Advance online publication. doi:10.1016/j.trpro.2016.06.042

Elmaghraby, A. S., & Losavio, M. M. (2014). Cyber security challenges in smart cities: Safety, security and privacy. *Journal of Advanced Research*, *5*(4), 491–497. Advance online publication. doi:10.1016/j.jare.2014.02.006 PMID:25685517

Erhardt, G. D., Lock, O., Arcaute, E., & Batty, M. (2017). A big data mashing tool for measuring transit system performance. Springer Geography. doi:10.1007/978-3-319-40902-3_15

Ferreira, J. C., Monteiro, V., Afonso, J. A., & Afonso, J. L. (2016). *Methodology for knowledge extraction from mobility big data.* Advances in Intelligent Systems and Computing. doi:10.1007/978-3-319-40162-1_11

Ferreira, N., Poco, J., Vo, H. T., Freire, J., & Silva, C. T. (2013). Visual exploration of big spatio-temporal urban data: A study of New York city taxi trips. *IEEE Transactions on Visualization and Computer Graphics*, *19*(12), 2149–2158. Advance online publication. doi:10.1109/TVCG.2013.226 PMID:24051781

Fetene, G. M., Kaplan, S., Mabit, S. L., Jensen, A. F., & Prato, C. G. (2017). Harnessing big data for estimating the energy consumption and driving range of electric vehicles. *Transportation Research Part D, Transport and Environment*, *54*, 1–11. Advance online publication. doi:10.1016/j.trd.2017.04.013

Figueres-Esteban, M., Hughes, P., & Van Gulijk, C. (2015). The role of data visualization in railway Big Data Risk Analysis. *Safety and Reliability of Complex Engineered Systems - Proceedings of the 25th European Safety and Reliability Conference, ESREL 2015.* 10.1201/b19094-377

Fonzone, A., Schmöcker, J. D., & Viti, F. (2016). New services, new travelers, old models? Directions to pioneer public transport models in the era of big data. In *Journal of Intelligent Transportation Systems. Technology, Planning, and Operations.* doi:10.1080/15472450.2016.1190553

Fosso Wamba, S., Akter, S., Edwards, A., Chopin, G., & Gnanzou, D. (2015). How "big data" can make big impact: Findings from a systematic review and a longitudinal case study. *International Journal of Production Economics*, *165*, 234–246. Advance online publication. doi:10.1016/j.ijpe.2014.12.031

French, S. P., Barchers, C., & Zhang, W. (2017). How should urban planners be trained to handle big data? Springer Geography. doi:10.1007/978-3-319-40902-3_12

Fridman, L., Brown, D. E., Angell, W., Abdić, I., Reimer, B., & Noh, H. Y. (2016). Automated synchronization of driving data using vibration and steering events. *Pattern Recognition Letters*, *75*, 9–15. Advance online publication. doi:10.1016/j. patrec.2016.02.011

Fumeo, E., Oneto, L., & Anguita, D. (2015). Condition based maintenance in railway transportation systems based on big data streaming analysis. *Procedia Computer Science*, *53*, 437–446. Advance online publication. doi:10.1016/j.procs.2015.07.321

Giannotti, F., & Pedreschi, D. (2008). Mobility, data mining and privacy: Geographic knowledge discovery. In Mobility, Data Mining and Privacy: Geographic Knowledge Discovery. doi:10.1007/978-3-540-75177-9

Goel, R., Garcia, L. M. T., Goodman, A., Johnson, R., Aldred, R., Murugesan, M., Brage, S., Bhalla, K., & Woodcock, J. (2018). Estimating city-level travel patterns using street imagery: A case study of using Google Street View in Britain. *PLoS One*, *13*(5), e0196521. Advance online publication. doi:10.1371/journal.pone.0196521 PMID:29718953

Gong, H., Chen, C., Bialostozky, E., & Lawson, C. T. (2012). A GPS/GIS method for travel mode detection in New York City. *Computers, Environment and Urban Systems*, *36*(2), 131–139. Advance online publication. doi:10.1016/j. compenvurbsys.2011.05.003

Gonzalez, M. (2016). *Transportation model in the Boston metropolitan area from origin destination matrices generated with Big Data.* http://utc.mit.edu/uploads/%0AMITR24-5-FP.pd

Grant, C., Gillis, B., & Guensler, R. (2000). *Collection of Vehicle Activity Data by Video Detection for Use in Transportation Planning.* ITS Journal. doi:10.1080/10248070008903775

Gregorio, F., González, G., Schmidt, C., & Cousseau, J. (2020). Internet of Things. In Signals and Communication Technology. doi:10.1007/978-3-030-32437-7_9

Guido, G., Rogano, D., Vitale, A., Astarita, V., & Festa, D. (2017). Big data for public transportation: A DSS framework. *5th IEEE International Conference on Models and Technologies for Intelligent Transportation Systems, MT-ITS 2017 - Proceedings.* 10.1109/MTITS.2017.8005635

Gunturi, V. M. V., & Shekhar, S. (2017). Big spatio-temporal network data analytics for smart cities: Research needs. Springer Geography. doi:10.1007/978-3-319-40902-3_8

Gupta, S., Dumas, M., McGuffin, M. J., & Kapler, T. (2016). MovementSlicer: Better Gantt charts for visualizing behaviors and meetings in movement data. *IEEE Pacific Visualization Symposium*. 10.1109/PACIFICVIS.2016.7465265

Hanft, J., Iyer, S., Levine, B., & Reddy, A. V. (2016). Transforming bus service planning using integrated electronic data sources at NYC transit. *Journal of Public Transportation*, *19*(2), 89–108. Advance online publication. doi:10.5038/2375-0901.19.2.6

Harris, I., Wang, Y., & Wang, H. (2015). ICT in multimodal transport and technological trends: Unleashing potential for the future. *International Journal of Production Economics*, *159*, 88–103. Advance online publication. doi:10.1016/j.ijpe.2014.09.005

Hashem, I. A. T., Chang, V., Anuar, N. B., Adewole, K., Yaqoob, I., Gani, A., Ahmed, E., & Chiroma, H. (2016). The role of big data in smart city. *International Journal of Information Management*, *36*(5), 748–758. doi:10.1016/j.ijinfomgt.2016.05.002

Herrera-Quintero, L. F., Vega-Alfonso, J. C., Banse, K. B. A., & Carrillo Zambrano, E. (2018). *Smart ITS Sensor for the Transportation Planning Based on IoT Approaches Using Serverless and Microservices Architecture*. IEEE Intelligent Transportation Systems Magazine. doi:10.1109/MITS.2018.2806620

Hoh, B., Gruteser, M., Hui, X., & Alrabady, A. (2006). Enhancing security and privacy in traffic-monitoring systems. *IEEE Pervasive Computing*, *5*(4), 38–46. Advance online publication. doi:10.1109/MPRV.2006.69

Horn, C., Gursch, H., Kern, R., & Cik, M. (2017). *QZtool—Automatically generated origin-destination matrices from cell phone trajectories*. Advances in Intelligent Systems and Computing., doi:10.1007/978-3-319-41682-3_68

Hou, Z., Zhou, Y., & Du, R. (2016). Special issue on intelligent transportation systems, big data and intelligent technology. *Transportation Planning and Technology*, *39*(8), 747–750. Advance online publication. doi:10.1080/03081060.2016.1231893

Hounsell, N. B., Shrestha, B. P., McDonald, M., & Wong, A. (2016). Open Data and the Needs of Older People for Public Transport Information. *Transportation Research Procedia*, *14*, 4334–4343. Advance online publication. doi:10.1016/j.trpro.2016.05.355

Hua, X., Wang, J., Lei, L., Zhou, B., Zhang, X., & Liu, P. (2016). H-TDMS: A system for traffic big data management. *Communications in Computer and Information Science*, *626*, 85–96. Advance online publication. doi:10.1007/978-981-10-2209-8_8

Huang, X., Zhao, Y., Ma, C., Yang, J., Ye, X., & Zhang, C. (2016). TrajGraph: A Graph-Based Visual Analytics Approach to Studying Urban Network Centralities Using Taxi Trajectory Data. *IEEE Transactions on Visualization and Computer Graphics*, *22*(1), 160–169. Advance online publication. doi:10.1109/TVCG.2015.2467771 PMID:26529696

Huijboom, N. (2011). Open data: An International comparison of strategies. *European Journal of EPractice*.

Husen, M. N., Lee, S., & Khan, M. Q. (2017). Syntactic pattern recognition of car driving behavior detection. *Proceedings of the 11th International Conference on Ubiquitous Information Management and Communication, IMCOM 2017*. 10.1145/3022227.3022303

Janssen, M., Charalabidis, Y., & Zuiderwijk, A. (2012). Benefits, Adoption Barriers and Myths of Open Data and Open Government. *Information Systems Management*, *29*(4), 258–268. Advance online publication. doi:10.1080/10580530.2012.716740

Jara, A. J., Serrano, M., Gómez, A., Fernández, D., Molina, G., Bocchi, Y., & Alcarria, R. (2018). *Smart cities semantics and data models*. Advances in Intelligent Systems and Computing. doi:10.1007/978-3-319-73450-7_8

Jeong, S., Zhang, Y., O'Connor, S., Lynch, J. P., Sohn, H., & Law, K. H. (2016). A NoSQL data management infrastructure for bridge monitoring. *Smart Structures and Systems*, *17*(4), 669–690. Advance online publication. doi:10.12989ss.2016.17.4.669

Jiang, W., & Luo, J. (2022). Big Data for Traffic Estimation and Prediction: A Survey of Data and Tools. *Applied System Innovation*, *5*(1), 23. Advance online publication. doi:10.3390/asi5010023

Kadaieaswaran, M., Arunprasath, V., & Karthika, M. (2017). Big Data Solution for Improving Traffic Management System with Video Processing. International Journal of Engineering Science and Computing.

Kaffash, S., Nguyen, A. T., & Zhu, J. (2021). Big data algorithms and applications in intelligent transportation system: A review and bibliometric analysis. *International Journal of Production Economics*, *231*, 107868. doi:10.1016/j.ijpe.2020.107868

Kamel, I. R., Abdelgawad, H., & Abdulhai, B. (2016). *Transportation big data simulation platform for the greater Toronto Area (GTA). Lecture Notes of the Institute for Computer Sciences, Social-Informatics and Telecommunications Engineering*. LNICST. doi:10.1007/978-3-319-33681-7_37

Kandt, J., & Batty, M. (2021). Smart cities, big data and urban policy: Towards urban analytics for the long run. *Cities (London, England)*, *109*, 102992. doi:10.1016/j.cities.2020.102992

Kaplan, A. M., & Haenlein, M. (2010). Users of the world, unite! The challenges and opportunities of Social Media. *Business Horizons*, *53*(1), 59–68. Advance online publication. doi:10.1016/j.bushor.2009.09.003

Katal, A., Wazid, M., & Goudar, R. H. (2013). Big data: Issues, challenges, tools and Good practices. *2013 6th International Conference on Contemporary Computing, IC3 2013*, 404–409. 10.1109/IC3.2013.6612229

Kaufman, S. M. (2012). *Getting Started with Open Data Getting Started with Open Data*. https://wagner.nyu.edu/rudincenter/research/

Keim, D., Qu, H., & Ma, K. L. (2013). Big-data visualization. IEEE Computer Graphics and Applications. doi:10.1109/MCG.2013.54

Khattak, A. J. (2017). *Integrating big data in metropolitan regions to understand driving volatility and implications for intelligent transportation systems*. Advances in Intelligent Systems and Computing. doi:10.1007/978-3-319-38789-5_1

Khazaei, H., Zareian, S., Veleda, R., & Litoiu, M. (2016). *Sipresk: A Big Data analytic platform for smart transportation. Lecture Notes of the Institute for Computer Sciences, Social-Informatics and Telecommunications Engineering*. LNICST. doi:10.1007/978-3-319-33681-7_35

Kim, K.-I., Jeong, J. S., & Park, G.-K. (2013). Assessment of External Force Acting on Ship Using Big Data in Maritime Traffic. *Journal of Korean Institute of Intelligent Systems*. doi:10.5391/JKIIS.2013.23.5.379

Kitchin, R. (2014). The real-time city? Big data and smart urbanism. *GeoJournal*, *79*(1), 1–14. Advance online publication. doi:10.100710708-013-9516-8

Komanduri, A., Wafa, Z., Proussaloglou, K., & Jacobs, S. (2018). Assessing the Impact of App-Based Ride Share Systems in an Urban Context: Findings from Austin. *Transportation Research Record: Journal of the Transportation Research Board*, *2672*(7), 34–46. Advance online publication. doi:10.1177/0361198118796025

Kong, X., Xia, F., Ning, Z., Rahim, A., Cai, Y., Gao, Z., & Ma, J. (2018). Mobility dataset generation for vehicular social networks based on floating car data. *IEEE Transactions on Vehicular Technology*, *67*(5), 3874–3886. Advance online publication. doi:10.1109/TVT.2017.2788441

Krueger, R., Sun, G., Beck, F., Liang, R., & Ertl, T. (2016). TravelDiff: Visual comparison analytics for massive movement patterns derived from Twitter. *IEEE Pacific Visualization Symposium*. 10.1109/PACIFICVIS.2016.7465266

Kwan, M. P. (2016). Algorithmic geographies: Big data, algorithmic uncertainty, and the production of geographic knowledge. *Annals of the Association of American Geographers*. Advance online publication. doi:10.1080/00045608.2015.1117937

Lana, I., Del Ser, J., Velez, M., & Vlahogianni, E. I. (2018). Road Traffic Forecasting: Recent Advances and New Challenges. IEEE Intelligent Transportation Systems Magazine. doi:10.1109/MITS.2018.2806634

Laney, D. (2001). *3D Data Management: Controlling Data Volume, Velocity, and Variety*. Application Delivery Strategies. doi:10.1016/j.infsof.2008.09.005

Laptev, N., Yosinski, J., Li, E., Smyl, S., Li, E. L., Smyl, S., Li, L. E., & Smyl, S. (2017). Time-series Extreme Event Forecasting with Neural Networks at Uber. *International Conference on Machine Learning - Time Series Workshop*.

Lee, I. (2017). Big data: Dimensions, evolution, impacts, and challenges. *Business Horizons*, *60*(3), 293–303. doi:10.1016/j.bushor.2017.01.004

Lee, J. H., & Ahn, C. W. (2016). An Evolutionary Approach to Driving Tendency Recognition for Advanced Driver Assistance Systems. *MATEC Web of Conferences*, *56*, 0–3. 10.1051/matecconf/20165602012

Li, H., Remias, S., Taylor, A., & Bullock, D. (2016a). *Scalable Methods for Monitoring Limited Access Roadways using Crowd-Sourced Probe Data*. doi:10.5703/1288284316061

Li, S., Dragicevic, S., Castro, F. A., Sester, M., Winter, S., Coltekin, A., Pettit, C., Jiang, B., Haworth, J., Stein, A., & Cheng, T. (2016b). Geospatial big data handling theory and methods: A review and research challenges. ISPRS Journal of Photogrammetry and Remote Sensing. doi:10.1016/j.isprsjprs.2015.10.012

Li, W., Xie, X., Hu, J., Zhang, Z., & Zhang, Y. (2016c). Using big data from the web to train Chinese traffic word representation model in vector space. *Proceedings of the World Congress on Intelligent Control and Automation (WCICA)*. 10.1109/WCICA.2016.7578483

Li, X., Lv, Z., Wang, W., Zhang, B., Hu, J., Yin, L., & Feng, S. (2016d). WebVRGIS based traffic analysis and visualization system. *Advances in Engineering Software*, *93*, 1–8. Advance online publication. doi:10.1016/j.advengsoft.2015.11.003

Lin, C. T., Santoso, P. S., Chen, S. P., Lin, H. J., & Lai, S. H. (2017). Fast Vehicle Detector for Autonomous Driving. *Proceedings - 2017 IEEE International Conference on Computer Vision Workshops, ICCVW 2017.* 10.1109/ICCVW.2017.35

Liu, D., Weng, D., Li, Y., Bao, J., Zheng, Y., Qu, H., & Wu, Y. (2017). SmartAdP: Visual Analytics of Large-scale Taxi Trajectories for Selecting Billboard Locations. *IEEE Transactions on Visualization and Computer Graphics, 23*(1), 1–10. Advance online publication. doi:10.1109/TVCG.2016.2598432 PMID:27514046

Liu, M., Wang, L., Nie, L., Dai, J., & Ji, D. (2016). Event graph based contradiction recognition from big data collection. *Neurocomputing, 181,* 64–75. Advance online publication. doi:10.1016/j.neucom.2015.06.099

Liu, Y., Sourina, O., & Nguyen, M. K. (2011). *Real-time EEG-based emotion recognition and its applications.* Lecture Notes in Computer Science. doi:10.1007/978-3-642-22336-5_13

Lopes, J., Bento, J., Huang, E., Antoniou, C., & Ben-Akiva, M. (2010). Traffic and mobility data collection for real-time applications. *IEEE Conference on Intelligent Transportation Systems, Proceedings, ITSC.* 10.1109/ITSC.2010.5625282

Louhghalam, A., Akbarian, M., & Ulm, F. J. (2017). Carbon management of infrastructure performance: Integrated big data analytics and pavement-vehicle-interactions. *Journal of Cleaner Production, 142,* 956–964. Advance online publication. doi:10.1016/j.jclepro.2016.06.198

Lv, Y., Duan, Y., Kang, W., Li, Z., & Wang, F. Y. (2015). Traffic Flow Prediction with Big Data: A Deep Learning Approach. *IEEE Transactions on Intelligent Transportation Systems.* Advance online publication. doi:10.1109/TITS.2014.2345663

Lyu, T., Wang, P., Gao, Y., & Wang, Y. (2021). Research on the big data of traditional taxi and online car-hailing: A systematic review. *Journal of Traffic and Transportation Engineering, 8*(1), 1–34. doi:10.1016/j.jtte.2021.01.001

Maha Vishnu, V. C., Rajalakshmi, M., & Nedunchezhian, R. (2018). Intelligent traffic video surveillance and accident detection system with dynamic traffic signal control. *Cluster Computing, 21*(1), 135–147. Advance online publication. doi:10.100710586-017-0974-5

Manyika, J., Chui, M., & Bughin, J. (2013). *Disruptive technologies: Advances that will transform life, business, and the global economy.* McKinsey Global.

Masek, P., Masek, J., Frantik, P., Fujdiak, R., Ometov, A., Hosek, J., Andreev, S., Mlynek, P., & Misurec, J. (2016). *A harmonized perspective on transportation management in smart cities: The novel IoT-driven environment for road traffic modeling.* Sensors., doi:10.339016111872

Matcha, B. N., Namasivayam, S. N., Fouladi, M. H., Ng, K. C., Sivanesan, S., Yong, S., & Noum, E. (2020). *Simulation Strategies for Mixed Traffic Conditions : A Review of Car-Following Models and Simulation Frameworks.* doi:10.1155/2020/8231930

Matcha, B. N., Sivanesan, S., & Ng, K. C. (2021). Modelling Road Traffic Congestion at Urban Merge Section Under Mixed Traffic Conditions. *Proceedings of the Institution of Civil Engineers - Transport*, 1–49. 10.1680/jtran.20.00131

Matcha, B. N., Sivanesan, S., & Ng, K. C., & Eh Noum, S. Y. (2021). Mixed traffic driver behavioral modeling at urban merge section: An experimental study. *Transportation Letters*, 1–26. doi:10.1080/19427867.2021.1944964

Matcha, B. N., Sivanesan, S., Ng, K. C., & Eh Noum, S. Y. (2022). Modelling integrated movements of motorcycles at urban merge sections under mixed traffic conditions. *Transportmetrica B*, *10*(1), 441–467. doi:10.1080/21680566.2021.2007814

Mathew, J. K., Desai, J. C., Sakhare, R. S., Kim, W., Li, H., & Bullock, D. M. (2021). Big data applications for managing roadways. *ITE Journal*, *91*(2), 28–35.

Mdini, M., Blanc, A., Simon, G., Barotin, J., & Lecoeuvre, J. (2017). Monitoring the network monitoring system: Anomaly Detection using pattern recognition. *Proceedings of the IM 2017 - 2017 IFIP/IEEE International Symposium on Integrated Network and Service Management*. 10.23919/INM.2017.7987418

Meekan, M. G., Duarte, C. M., Fernández-Gracia, J., Thums, M., Sequeira, A. M. M., Harcourt, R., & Eguíluz, V. M. (2017). The Ecology of Human Mobility. Trends in Ecology and Evolution. doi:10.1016/j.tree.2016.12.006

Mehmood, R., & Graham, G. (2015). Big Data Logistics: A health-care Transport Capacity Sharing Model. *Procedia Computer Science*, *64*, 1107–1114. doi:10.1016/j.procs.2015.08.566

Misra, A., Gooze, A., Watkins, K., Asad, M., & Le Dantec, C. (2014). Crowdsourcing and its application to transportation data collection and management. *Transportation Research Record: Journal of the Transportation Research Board*, *2414*(1), 1–8. Advance online publication. doi:10.3141/2414-01

Mohbey, K. K. (2017). The role of big data, cloud computing and IoT to make cities smarter. *International Journal of Society Systems Science*, *9*(1), 75. doi:10.1504/IJSSS.2017.083615

Montanaro, U., Dixit, S., Fallah, S., Dianati, M., Stevens, A., Oxtoby, D., & Mouzakitis, A. (2019). Towards connected autonomous driving: Review of use-cases. *Vehicle System Dynamics*, *57*(6), 779–814. Advance online publication. doi:10.1080/0042 3114.2018.1492142

Montoya-Torres, J. R., Moreno, S., Guerrero, W. J., & Mejía, G. (2021). Big Data Analytics and Intelligent Transportation Systems. *IFAC-PapersOnLine*, *54*(2), 216–220. doi:10.1016/j.ifacol.2021.06.025

Morris, D., & Wier, M. (2016). Geospatially enabled database for analyzing traffc injuries in San Francisco, California. *Transportation Research Record: Journal of the Transportation Research Board*, *2595*(1), 40–49. Advance online publication. doi:10.3141/2595-05

Muñoz, R., Vilalta, R., Yoshikane, N., Casellas, R., Martínez, R., Tsuritani, T., & Morita, I. (2018). Integration of IoT, Transport SDN, and Edge/Cloud Computing for Dynamic Distribution of IoT Analytics and Efficient Use of Network Resources. *Journal of Lightwave Technology*, *36*(7), 1420–1428. Advance online publication. doi:10.1109/JLT.2018.2800660

Ng, B. N. M. S. S. K. (2021). Modelling Lane-changing Behaviour of Vehicles at Merge Section Under Mixed Traffic Conditions. *Journal of Transportation Engineering, Part A: Systems*, *147*(4), 04021006. Advance online publication. doi:10.1061/JTEPBS.0000502

Nishiuchi, H., King, J., & Todoroki, T. (2013). Spatial-Temporal Daily Frequent Trip Pattern of Public Transport Passengers Using Smart Card Data. *International Journal of Intelligent Transportation Systems Research*. doi:10.1007/s13177-012-0051-7

Nkoro, A. B., & Vershinin, Y. A. (2014). Current and future trends in applications of Intelligent Transport Systems on cars and infrastructure. *2014 17th IEEE International Conference on Intelligent Transportation Systems, ITSC 2014*. 10.1109/ITSC.2014.6957741

Okuda, T., Hirasawa, S., Matsukuma, N., Fukumoto, T., & Shimura, A. (2012). Smart mobility for smart cities. Hitachi Review.

Paloheimo, H., Lettenmeier, M., & Waris, H. (2016). Transport reduction by crowdsourced deliveries – a library case in Finland. *Journal of Cleaner Production*, *132*, 240–251. Advance online publication. doi:10.1016/j.jclepro.2015.04.103

Papu Carrone, A., Rich, J., Vandet, C., & An, K. (2021). Autonomous vehicles in mixed motorway traffic: Capacity utilisation, impact and policy implications. *Transportation*, *48*(6), 2907–2938. Advance online publication. doi:10.100711116-020-10154-4

Parkinson, H. J., & Bamford, G. (2016). *The potential for using big data analytics to predict safety risks by analysing rail accidents*. Civil-Comp Proceedings.

Paul, A., Chauhan, R., Srivastava, R., & Baruah, M. (2016). Advanced Driver Assistance Systems. *SAE Technical Papers*. doi:10.4271/2016-28-0223

Pelletier, M. P., Trépanier, M., & Morency, C. (2011). Smart card data use in public transit: A literature review. *Transportation Research Part C, Emerging Technologies*, *19*(4), 557–568. Advance online publication. doi:10.1016/j.trc.2010.12.003

Petrovska, N., Stevanovic, A., & Furht, B. (2016). Innovative web applications for analyzing traffic operations. In SpringerBriefs in Computer Science. doi:10.1007/978-3-319-33319-9

Rathore, M. M., Ahmad, A., Paul, A., & Thikshaja, U. K. (2016). Exploiting real-time big data to empower smart transportation using big graphs. *Proceedings - 2016 IEEE Region 10 Symposium, TENSYMP 2016*. 10.1109/TENCONSpring.2016.7519392

Rougès, J.-F., & Montreuil, B. (2014). Crowdsourcing Delivery : New Interconnected Business Models to Reinvent Delivery. *1st International Physical Internet Conference*.

Roy, S., Bose, R., & Sarddar, D. (2017). *Impaired Driving and Explosion Detection on Vehicle for Ubiquitous City. International Journal of Computational Intelligence Research ISSNArea Traffic Control System (ATCS)*.

Rusitschka, S., & Curry, E. (2016). Big data in the energy and transport sectors. In New Horizons for a Data-Driven Economy: A Roadmap for Usage and Exploitation of Big Data in Europe. doi:10.1007/978-3-319-21569-3_13

Salim, F., & Haque, U. (2015). Urban computing in the wild: A survey on large scale participation and citizen engagement with ubiquitous computing, cyber physical systems, and Internet of Things. *International Journal of Human-Computer Studies*, *81*, 31–48. Advance online publication. doi:10.1016/j.ijhcs.2015.03.003

Satyanarayanan, M. (2017). The emergence of edge computing. *Computer*, *50*(1), 30–39. Advance online publication. doi:10.1109/MC.2017.9

Schnoebelen, T. (2016). *More data beats better algorithms*. Http://Www.Datasciencecentral.Com/Profiles/Blogs/

Scott, J., & Scott, C. (2017). Drone Delivery Models for Healthcare. *Proceedings of the 50th Hawaii International Conference on System Sciences.* 10.24251/HICSS.2017.399

Semanjski, I., & Gautama, S. (2015). *Smart city mobility application—gradient boosting trees for mobility prediction and analysis based on crowdsourced data.* Sensors. doi:10.3390150715974

Shi, Q., Wu, Y., Radwan, E., & Zhang, B. (2016). *Integration of Microscopic Big Traffic Data in Simulation-Based Safety Analysis.* Final Report.

Singh, G., Bansal, D., Sofat, S., & Aggarwal, N. (2017). Smart patrolling: An efficient road surface monitoring using smartphone sensors and crowdsourcing. *Pervasive and Mobile Computing*, *40*, 71–88. Advance online publication. doi:10.1016/j.pmcj.2017.06.002

Sobral, T., Costa, V., Borges, J., Fontes, T., & Galvão, T. (2016). OBAVUM: An ontology-based approach to visualizing urban mobility data. *Proceedings of 2016 IEEE International Conference on Big Data Analysis, ICBDA 2016.* 10.1109/ICBDA.2016.7509825

Stathopoulos, A., Cirillo, C., Cherchi, E., Ben-Elia, E., Li, Y. T., & Schmöcker, J. D. (2017). Innovation adoption modeling in transportation: New models and data. *Journal of Choice Modelling.* doi:10.1016/j.jocm.2017.02.001

Su, J. M., Erdenebat, N., Ho, L. H., & Zhan, Y. T. (2016). Integration of Transit Demand and Big Data for Bus Route Design in Taiwan. *Bridging the East and West: Theories and Practices of Transportation in the Asia Pacific - Selected Papers from the Proceedings of the 11th Asia Pacific Transportation Development Conference and the 29th ICTPA Annual Conference.* 10.1061/9780784479810.003

Subbu, K. P., & Vasilakos, A. V. (2017). *Big Data for Context Aware Computing – Perspectives and Challenges.* Big Data Research. doi:10.1016/j.bdr.2017.10.002

Suh, W., Henclewood, D., Guin, A., Guensler, R., Hunter, M., & Fujimoto, R. (2017). Dynamic data driven transportation systems. *Multimedia Tools and Applications*, *76*(23), 25253–25269. Advance online publication. doi:10.100711042-016-4318-x

Suma, S., Mehmood, R., & Albeshri, A. (2020). Automatic detection and validation of smart city events using hpc and apache spark platforms. In EAI/Springer Innovations in Communication and Computing. doi:10.1007/978-3-030-13705-2_3

Suma, S., Mehmood, R., Albugami, N., Katib, I., & Albeshri, A. (2017). Enabling Next Generation Logistics and Planning for Smarter Societies. *Procedia Computer Science, 109*, 1122–1127. doi:10.1016/j.procs.2017.05.440

Taie, M. A., Moawad, E. M., Diab, M., & ElHelw, M. (2016). Remote Diagnosis, Maintenance and Prognosis for Advanced Driver Assistance Systems Using Machine Learning Algorithms. *SAE International Journal of Passenger Cars. Electronic and Electrical Systems, 9*(1), 114–122. Advance online publication. doi:10.4271/2016-01-0076

Talebkhah, M., Sali, A., Marjani, M., Gordan, M., Hashim, S. J., & Rokhani, F. Z. (2021). IoT and Big Data Applications in Smart Cities: Recent Advances, Challenges, and Critical Issues. *IEEE Access: Practical Innovations, Open Solutions, 9*, 55465–55484. doi:10.1109/ACCESS.2021.3070905

Tao, S., Corcoran, J., Mateo-Babiano, I., & Rohde, D. (2014). Exploring Bus Rapid Transit passenger travel behaviour using big data. *Applied Geography (Sevenoaks, England), 53*, 90–104. Advance online publication. doi:10.1016/j.apgeog.2014.06.008

Tavassoli, A., Mesbah, M., & Shobeirinejad, A. (2018). Modelling passenger waiting time using large-scale automatic fare collection data: An Australian case study. *Transportation Research Part F: Traffic Psychology and Behaviour, 58*, 500–510. Advance online publication. doi:10.1016/j.trf.2018.06.037

The Potential of Mobile Network Big Data as a Tool in Colombo's Transportation and Urban Planning. (2016). *Information Technologies & International Development*.

Tiedemann, T., Backe, C., Vögele, T., & Conradi, P. (2016). *An Automotive Distributed Mobile Sensor Data Collection with Machine Learning Based Data Fusion and Analysis on a Central Backend System*. Procedia Technology. doi:10.1016/j.protcy.2016.08.071

Tien, I., Musaev, A., Benas, D., Ghadi, A., Goodman, S., & Pu, C. (2016). Detection of damage and failure events of critical public infrastructure using social sensor big data. *IoTBD 2016 - Proceedings of the International Conference on Internet of Things and Big Data*. 10.5220/0005932104350440

Tomar, P., Kaur, G., & Singh, P. (2018). *A Prototype of IoT-Based Real Time Smart Street Parking System for Smart Cities*. doi:10.1007/978-3-319-60435-0_10

Torre-Bastida, A. I., Del Ser, J., Laña, I., Ilardia, M., Bilbao, M. N., & Campos-Cordobés, S. (2018). Big Data for transportation and mobility: Recent advances, trends and challenges. *IET Intelligent Transport Systems, 12*(8), 742–755. doi:10.1049/iet-its.2018.5188

Transportation Safety Meets Big Data: The SHRP 2 Naturalistic Driving Database. (2016). *Journal of The Society of Instrument and Control Engineers*. doi:10.11499/sicejl.55.415

Tsiatsis, V., Höller, J., Mulligan, C., Karnouskos, S., & Boyle, D. (2018). Internet of things: Technologies and applications for a new age of intelligence. In Internet of Things: Technologies and Applications for a New Age of Intelligence. doi:10.1016/C2017-0-00369-5

Urra, O., Ilarri, S., & Trillo-Lado, R. (2017). An approach driven by mobile agents for data management in vehicular networks. *Information Sciences*, *381*, 55–77. Advance online publication. doi:10.1016/j.ins.2016.11.007

Usman, S., Mehmood, R., & Katib, I. (2020). Big data and hpc convergence for smart infrastructures: A review and proposed architecture. In EAI/Springer Innovations in Communication and Computing. doi:10.1007/978-3-030-13705-2_23

Vlahogianni, E. I. (2015). Computational intelligence and optimization for transportation big data: Challenges and opportunities. *Computational Methods in Applied Sciences*, *38*, 107–128. Advance online publication. doi:10.1007/978-3-319-18320-6_7

Vlahogianni, E. I., Karlaftis, M. G., & Golias, J. C. (2014). Short-term traffic forecasting: Where we are and where we're going. *Transportation Research Part C, Emerging Technologies*, *43*, 3–19. Advance online publication. doi:10.1016/j.trc.2014.01.005

Wallace, S., & Lăzăroiu, G. (2021). Predictive Control Algorithms, Real-World Connected Vehicle Data, and Smart Mobility Technologies in Intelligent Transportation Planning and Engineering. *Contemporary Readings in Law and Social Justice*, *13*(2), 79–92. doi:10.22381/CRLSJ13220216

Wang, C., Li, X., Zhou, X., Wang, A., & Nedjah, N. (2016). Soft computing in big data intelligent transportation systems. *Applied Soft Computing*, *38*, 1099–1108. Advance online publication. doi:10.1016/j.asoc.2015.06.006

Wang, G., Gunasekaran, A., & Ngai, E. W. T. (2018). Distribution network design with big data: Model and analysis. *Annals of Operations Research*, *270*(1-2), 539–551. Advance online publication. doi:10.100710479-016-2263-8

Wang, L. (2016). Design, Data Collection, and Driver Behavior Simulation for the Open-Mode Integrated Transportation System (OMITS). ProQuest Dissertations and Theses.

Wang, X., Zhao, S., & Dong, L. (2017). *Research and application of traffic visualization based on vehicle GPS big data.* Smart Innovation, Systems and Technologies. doi:10.1007/978-981-10-2398-9_27

Wang, X. K., & Yang, L. (2016). Visual data mining in transportation using multiresolution data aggregation. *Frontiers in Artificial Intelligence and Applications.* doi:10.3233/978-1-61499-619-4-195

Wang, X. M., Zhang, T. Y., Ma, Y. X., Xia, J., & Chen, W. (2016). A Survey of Visual Analytic Pipelines. *Journal of Computer Science and Technology, 31*(4), 787–804. Advance online publication. doi:10.100711390-016-1663-1

Wang, Z., Li, X., Zhu, X., Li, J., Wang, F., & Wang, F. (2021). *Big data-driven public transportation network: a simulation approach.* Complex & Intelligent Systems. doi:10.100740747-021-00462-2

Warren, J., Lipkowitz, J., & Sokolov, V. (2019). *Clusters of Driving Behavior from Observational Smartphone Data.* IEEE Intelligent Transportation Systems Magazine. doi:10.1109/MITS.2019.2919516

Weiss, D. J., Nelson, A., Gibson, H. S., Temperley, W., Peedell, S., Lieber, A., Hancher, M., Poyart, E., Belchior, S., Fullman, N., Mappin, B., Dalrymple, U., Rozier, J., Lucas, T. C. D., Howes, R. E., Tusting, L. S., Kang, S. Y., Cameron, E., Bisanzio, D., ... Gething, P. W. (2018). A global map of travel time to cities to assess inequalities in accessibility in 2015. *Nature.* doi:10.1038/nature25181

Wibisono, A., Jatmiko, W., Wisesa, H. A., Hardjono, B., & Mursanto, P. (2016). Traffic big data prediction and visualization using Fast Incremental Model Trees-Drift Detection (FIMT-DD). *Knowledge-Based Systems, 93,* 33–46. Advance online publication. doi:10.1016/j.knosys.2015.10.028

Wittmann, J. (2016). Electrification and digitalization as disruptive trends: New perspectives for the automotive industry? In *Phantom Ex Machina.* Digital Disruption's Role in Business Model Transformation. doi:10.1007/978-3-319-44468-0_9

Wong, J., Reed, L., Watkins, K. E., & Hammond, R. (2013). Open Transit Data: State of the Practice and Experiences from Participating Agencies in the United States. *Transportation Research Board 92nd Annual Meeting.*

Wu, W., Xu, J., Zeng, H., Zheng, Y., Qu, H., Ni, B., Yuan, M., & Ni, L. M. (2016). TelCoVis: Visual Exploration of Co-occurrence in Urban Human Mobility Based on Telco Data. *IEEE Transactions on Visualization and Computer Graphics, 22*(1), 935–944. Advance online publication. doi:10.1109/TVCG.2015.2467194 PMID:26469282

Xia, D., Jiang, S., Yang, N., Hu, Y., Li, Y., Li, H., & Wang, L. (2021). Discovering spatiotemporal characteristics of passenger travel with mobile trajectory big data. *Physica A*, *578*, 126056. doi:10.1016/j.physa.2021.126056

Xia, Y., Chen, J., Lu, X., Wang, C., & Xu, C. (2016). Big traffic data processing framework for intelligent monitoring and recording systems. *Neurocomputing*, *181*, 139–146. Advance online publication. doi:10.1016/j.neucom.2015.07.140

Xiao, X., & Xie, C. (2021). Rational planning and urban governance based on smart cities and big data. *Environmental Technology & Innovation*, *21*, 101381. doi:10.1016/j.eti.2021.101381

Xiong, G., Zhu, F., Dong, X., Fan, H., Hu, B., Kong, Q., Kang, W., & Teng, T. (2016a). *A Kind of Novel ITS Based on Space-Air-Ground Big-Data.* IEEE Intelligent Transportation Systems Magazine. doi:10.1109/MITS.2015.2503200

Xiong, W., Yu, Z., Eeckhout, L., Bei, Z., Zhang, F., & Xu, C. (2016b). ShenZhen transportation system (SZTS): A novel big data benchmark suite. *The Journal of Supercomputing*, *72*(11), 4337–4364. Advance online publication. doi:10.100711227-016-1742-7

Yang, C. P. (2017). Geospatial cloud computing and big data. In *Computers, Environment and Urban Systems*. doi:10.1016/j.compenvurbsys.2016.05.001

Yang, Y., Li, D., & Duan, Z. (2018). Chinese vehicle license plate recognition using kernel-based extreme learning machine with deep convolutional features. *IET Intelligent Transport Systems*, *12*(3), 213–219. Advance online publication. doi:10.1049/iet-its.2017.0136

Yang, Z., Wu, C., Zhou, Z., Zhang, X., Wang, X., & Liu, Y. (2015). Mobility increases localizability: A survey on wireless indoor localization using inertial sensors. *ACM Computing Surveys*, *47*(3), 1–34. Advance online publication. doi:10.1145/2676430

Ye, X., Li, W., & Huang, Q. (2018). *A Synthesized Urban Science in the Context of Big Data and Cyberinfrastructure*. doi:10.1007/978-3-319-51929-6_22

Yin, L., Cheng, Q., Wang, Z., & Shao, Z. (2015). "Big data" for pedestrian volume: Exploring the use of Google Street View images for pedestrian counts. *Applied Geography (Sevenoaks, England)*, *63*, 337–345. Advance online publication. doi:10.1016/j.apgeog.2015.07.010

Yin, T., Li, Y., Fan, J., Wang, T., & Shi, Y. (n.d.). *A Novel Gated Recurrent Unit Network Based on SVM and Moth-Flame Optimization Algorithm for Behavior Decision-Making of Autonomous Vehicles*. doi:10.1109/ACCESS.2021.3054755

Yu, D., Wang, R., Wang, J., & Li, W. (2016). Discovering and visualizing underlying traffic regions from vehicle trajectories withmulti-features. *The Journal of Imaging Science and Technology, 60*(2), 20403-1, 20403-18. Advance online publication. doi:10.2352/J.ImagingSci.Technol.2016.60.2.020403

Yuan, W., Wang, J., Li, J., Yan, B., & Wu, J. (2018). Two-Stage Heuristic Algorithm for a New Model of Hazardous Material Multi-depot Vehicle Routing Problem. *Advances in Intelligent Systems and Computing.* doi:10.1007/978-3-319-66939-7_32

Yuan, W., Deng, P., Taleb, T., Wan, J., & Bi, C. (2016, June). An Unlicensed Taxi Identification Model Based on Big Data Analysis. *IEEE Transactions on Intelligent Transportation Systems, 17*(6), 1703–1713. Advance online publication. doi:10.1109/TITS.2015.2498180

Zedda, M., & Pinna, F. (2018). *Prediction Models for Space Mean Speed on Urban Roads.* doi:10.1007/978-981-10-6319-0_2

Zeyu, J., Shuiping, Y., Mingduan, Z., Yongqiang, C., & Yi, L. (2017). Model Study for Intelligent Transportation System with Big Data. *Procedia Computer Science, 107*, 418–426. Advance online publication. doi:10.1016/j.procs.2017.03.132

Zhang, Q., Yang, L. T., Chen, Z., & Li, P. (2018). A survey on deep learning for big data. In Information Fusion. doi:10.1016/j.inffus.2017.10.006

Zhang, Z., He, Q., Gao, J., & Ni, M. (2018). A deep learning approach for detecting traffic accidents from social media data. *Transportation Research Part C, Emerging Technologies, 86*, 580–596. Advance online publication. doi:10.1016/j.trc.2017.11.027

Zhao, X., Dawson, D., Sarasua, W. A., & Birchfield, S. T. (2017). Automated Traffic Surveillance System with Aerial Camera Arrays Imagery: Macroscopic Data Collection with Vehicle Tracking. *Journal of Computing in Civil Engineering, 31*(3), 04016072. Advance online publication. doi:10.1061/(ASCE)CP.1943-5487.0000646

Zheng, X., Chen, W., Wang, P., Shen, D., Chen, S., Wang, X., Zhang, Q., & Yang, L. (2016). Big Data for Social Transportation. *IEEE Transactions on Intelligent Transportation Systems, 17*(3), 620–630. Advance online publication. doi:10.1109/TITS.2015.2480157

Zheng, Y., Capra, L., Wolfson, O., & Yang, H. (2014). Urban computing: Concepts, methodologies, and applications. *ACM Transactions on Intelligent Systems and Technology, 5*(3), 1–55. Advance online publication. doi:10.1145/2629592

Zheng, Y., Liu, Y., Yuan, J., & Xie, X. (2011). Urban computing with taxicabs. *UbiComp'11 - Proceedings of the 2011 ACM Conference on Ubiquitous Computing.* 10.1145/2030112.2030126

Zhu, L., Yu, F. R., Ning, B., & Tang, T. (2012). Cross-layer handoff design in MIMO-enabled WLANs for Communication-Based Train Control (CBTC) systems. *IEEE Journal on Selected Areas in Communications*, *30*(4), 719–728. Advance online publication. doi:10.1109/JSAC.2012.120506

Zhu, L., Yu, F. R., Wang, Y., Ning, B., & Tang, T. (2018). *Big Data Analytics in Action.* doi:10.4018/978-1-5225-7609-9.ch009

Zhu, L., Yu, F. R., Wang, Y., Ning, B., & Tang, T. (2019). Big Data Analytics in Intelligent Transportation Systems: A Survey. IEEE Transactions on Intelligent Transportation Systems. doi:10.1109/TITS.2018.2815678

Zhu, Y., Ozbay, K., Xie, K., & Yang, H. (2016). Using big data to study resilience of taxi and subway trips for Hurricanes Sandy and Irene. *Transportation Research Record: Journal of the Transportation Research Board*, *2599*(1), 70–80. Advance online publication. doi:10.3141/2599-09

Chapter 2
Twitter Data Analysis Using Apache Streaming

Lavanya Sendhilvel
Vellore Institute of Technology, India

Kush Diwakar Desai
Vellore Institute of Technology, India

Simran Adake
Vellore Institute of Technology, India

Rachit Bisaria
Vellore Institute of Technology, India

Hemang Ghanshyambhai Vekariya
Vellore Institute of Technology, India

ABSTRACT

Real-time data from social network sites like Twitter or Facebook has been a popular source for analytics and researchers in the recent years due to various factors like large amount of data, structured-ness, and popularity. Analyzing data is a very common requirement today, but such requirements become difficult when there is a bulk of data which needs to processed and analyzed in real time. Analyzing large number of tweets from Twitter to get different patterns and extract useful information is a massive challenge. Apache Spark is a platform that can be used to handle big data efficiently, and it offers faster solutions compared to Hadoop. This chapter addresses the issue of real-time analyzing and filtering the tweets as per the user's requirements from among the millions of other streaming tweets and classifies them into various categories. It creates an interactive automatic system that splits data based on important keywords and displays a graphical representation of connected tweets using Apache Spark.

DOI: 10.4018/978-1-6684-5264-6.ch002

INTRODUCTION

Twitter is a popular social media site where people communicate abouts news, topics of interest, grievances using short messages commonly referred as tweets. Twitter users can express or share their opinions, information regarding events, products in anything in their tweets. Hashtag is the convention of prefixing a word in a tweet with the symbol '#' which indicates a keyword or topic of the tweet. It is used for categorization of tweets based on topics and helps in searching. Keeping up with users and their tweets, trending hashtags help us understand what is going around in the world and people's sentiment on it. Tweets often contains latest information, and it is frequently updated. Tweet analysis can reveal useful information which can create a practical and immediate application in the life of common man.

Due to the benefits of networking sites like twitter, users find it easy to share information or opinions regarding any event, products etc. instead of publishing them in print or online media which saves cost, time and efforts. This paper investigates the problem of real time analysis and filtering those specific tweets which a user wants without having any twitter account. Because social media material is unstructured in comparison to other sources, big data technology like Spark can manage the processing and analysis of unstructured data. The tweets will be streamed and processed in real time using Apache Streaming and TCP client socket programming. Aggregated tweets under categories such as sports, news, traffic jams, complaints etc are stored locally making it easy for users to keep a track of topic/s they are interested in.

The goal of this work is to make a Twitter Data Analysis programme available to the public as a service. We have utilised Apache Spark to use a developer API to extract live tweets from Twitter, classify the tweets, and show them on the user interface. IntelliJ, an integrated development environment has been used to run this programme. Two services have been included, one for classifying real-time tweets and the other for visualising the data from archived tweets.

LITERATURE SURVEY

Twitter trend analysis is done by 2 methods-first using normal execution environment in which latent dirich let allocation, cosine similarity, k-mean clustering and Jaccard similarity techniques and second using big data Apache spark tool implementation. ("Apache Spark", 2016). They both were compared and conclusion was made spark are better and faster than normal execution environment ("Apache Hadoop", n.d.). The twitter streamed data in Apache spark the data in clustered to achieve less computations time sparks works in 2 phase first by creating viable clustered utilization by using fuzzy c-mean clustering and it is further improved by adaptive particle swarm optimization

(PSO). In 2nd phase pre-processed Higgs data is classified utilizing the modified support vector classified. The purposed works utilize both twitter data set and Higgs dataset ("Significance of Apache Spark", 2016). Streaming twitter data analysis for effective job search. the data collected from twitter is clustered and filtered into different for categories and classifications are created. A graphical representation is also provided for most advertised or in- demand job category. This is than deployed on the cloud and. spack-ec2 script is used (Cordova and Moh, 2015). Developing real time data analysis for twitter streaming data. A system created with in-memory processing which and analyses structured and semi-structures data. The framework created include data ingestion, stream processing and data visualization using Apache Kafka (Song, Lee, and Kim, 2011). Twitter data streaming analysis using Apache Cassandra and Zeppelin. Apache flume in also used to configure and integrate with spark Stemming. The streamed data is stored into Cassandra and analysed using Apache Zeppelin. The result is displayed on dashboard created using Json (Hughes et al., 2012). Stock market analysis from twitter based on streaming data Apache Funk and Apache storm have been used. Correlation is found between stock price. The data in further visualize using data visualization techniques. A graph is also used to show difference in accuracy when single node and multi-node stream are used (Sumner et al., 2012). The big trajectory and twitter data stream using Apache Strom framework, traffic storm application is using storm topology. An online traffic situation and crowded street, with possible explanation for the traffic (Dehong et al., 2014). Tweets are gathered and a sentimental analysis in performed using big date technique. Apache fumes is used to stream ongoing Tweets data into HDFS. Pig script is used to extract raw tweet data. Dictionary based method for sentiment analysis. And tweets a classified into positive, negative, neutral ("Spark Overview", n.d.). Justified the characteristics of Apache Spark and also compared the performance of Hadoop MapReduce and Spark using sorting and showed that Apache Spark have set world record in sorting by taking lesser time than Hadoop MapReduce (Yang et al., 2013). Processed live tweets from twitter API and performed sentiment analysis. Future plan is to find a method to predict the location of a tweet on the basis of tweets information (Singh and Reddy, 2015). The author has used Possibilistic Fuzzy C-Means with SVM to achieve high levels of accuracy on movie tweets and worked on up to 3-grams. Building a domain oriented approach by considering domain independent and domain specific lexicons in the area of smartphone brands have shown rise of around 2 points on an average over the unigram baseline in (Lee et al., 2011). Makazhanov and Rafiei (2013) have proven that Spark system has rapid computational time compared to Hadoop Mapreduce while working on corpus based sentiment analysis. To calculate the sentiment of a given sentence or paragraph is broken into words which are categorised into positive and negative words using an existing database of words and based on the count of positive and negative words the polarity was analysed in (Nodarakis et al., 2016; Ahmed et al., 2020) proposes that there is a significant effect on the sentiment analysis by considering domain specific texts and hence the authors have performed analysis on electronic products. The potency of Apache spark while handling huge amounts of data for performing machine learning tasks like classification, regression and dimension reduction has been highlighted well in (Zaki et al., 2020). Even with limited computational power, typically in a standard single computer Apache spark's ability to classify expertly has experimentally proven in (Kılınç, 2019; Rajput, Grover, and Rathi, 2020) talks about the importance of how performing sentiment analysis on customer opinion in real time can tremendously affect one's decision making process for a business domain. The strong effect of taking emoticons present in the text while classifying sentiment was proven to have higher impact in (Pal, 2005). For Lee et al. (2011) while performing sentiment analysis on Greek data, have found that there is a significant effect of considering emoticons into classification to get better results

BACKGROUND STUDY

Twitter is one of the most popular social media platforms, with new tweets being generated every second. Twitter users are known for freely expressing their emotions, making it a perfect platform for gathering feedback on a variety of hot subjects, events, businesses, current events, and complaints. Many times, customers want to evaluate the most recent data on a specific issue yet gathering and processing data in real time is a time-consuming task. As a result, the goal here is to develop systems that analyze data sources from multiple microblogging and social networking sites in order to make significant long-term product design and service implementation decisions. In this paper, we use Twitter as an example of a social network to evaluate and visualize several key indicators connected to an event, product, or service.

In tweets, hashtags begin with the sign # and are followed by terms or phrases that the user wants to emphasize. Here, we've utilized hashtags to filter out tweets from a specific context that a user is interested in. To use a hashtag, insert the topic's name after the hash (#) symbol in your tweet. For example, during a major international sporting event like the World Cup, Twitter users will add the hashtag "#world cup" to the end of their tweets to indicate that it is relevant to the event. When consumers click on the "#world cup" topic in the Trends list, the tweet displays in the feed. For real-time data processing, Apache Spark Streaming has been used. Spark Streaming may ingest data from a variety of sources, including live streams from Apache Kafka, Apache Flume, Amazon Kinesis, sensors, and so on. In our case, the data source was a TCP IP socket. It provides data streaming, which divides incoming data into micro-batches for the Apache spark engine to process. This can be accomplished by using a discretized stream to represent a set of RDDs (Resilient distributed datasets). Because of in-memory caching of RDDs and improved spark abstractions, performance has increased by 10-100x.

Spark streaming uses a micro batch processing execution paradigm, which has no impact on applications because RDD creates batches as short as 0.5 seconds. Spark Stream allows one to do continuous data transformations using functions like map, join, and reduce. Once the processed data has been created, it can be saved locally. In our example, a batch size of 3 seconds was maintained, and all processed data was saved in a CSV file that was preserved locally. The data has been stored and is ready to be visualized using a variety of resources. To build multiple graphs and assess the top trending or often occurring phrases in tweets for a specific topic, we utilized Matplotlib, a Python data representation library. All of the operations are carried out in real time, making it easier for the general public to save and evaluate Twitter data relevant to their specific interests rather than having to manually search for information.

METHODOLOGY

Figure 1 shows the general model of the application which can be executed either locally or can be deployed on cloud. The application connects to Twitter through an API and collects tweets which are processed into streams of tweets specific to the user's feed in.

Twitter Authentication

In twitter, tweets are available for public through an API that allows real time access to the users. A twitter developer account needs to be registered through which various keys are generated used for authentication purpose. These are consumer key, consumer secret key, access token and access token secret key. This API fetches the tweets from twitter to the Apache Spark framework for data collection.

Server-Side Programming

After authentication, to query the tweets that are related to a specific topic, tweets are filtered using hashtag '#'. A tweet object has lots of information like ID, text data, tweet URL, sender's ID, time etc from which text data and URL are of interest. The tweet objects are thus pre-processed and sent to client side in 'UTF-8' format. A listening TCP socket in the local system (server and client) is defined before streaming the filtered tweets. The bind() method on the server attaches it to a specified IP and port, allowing it to listen for incoming requests on that IP and port.

Figure 1. System Workflow

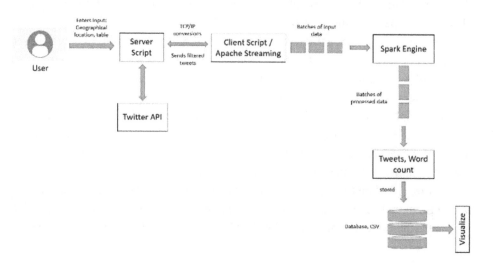

Here the application is executed locally hence the IP Address is defined as 'localhost' and port 9874 is allocated to the server. Apart from this it has a listen() method also which puts the server into the listening mode to check for incoming connections. Lastly accept() and close() methods are declared which is used for initiating a connection with the client and closing connection with client respectively.

Client-Side Programming and Data Processing using Spark Streaming

At the client side Pyspark programming is used which is the Python API for Spark. The streaming application uses Spark Structured Streaming which is a stream processing engine built on the Spark SQL engine. It provides scalability, high-throughput and fault-tolerant stream processing of live data streams. Data can be collected from many sources like Kafka, TCP sockets and can be processed using algorithms like map, reduce, join etc. Finally, processed data can be collected in databases or visualized in live dashboards.

Figure 2 shows the internal working of Spark Streaming. It receives live input data streams and divides the data into batches of some interval. These are then processed by the Spark engine to generate the final stream of results in batches. The basic abstraction provided by Spark Streaming is Discretized Stream or DStream. It depicts a continuous stream of data, either the source's input data stream or the processed data stream produced by taking some action on the input stream. Internally,

Figure 2.

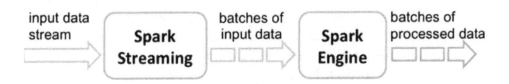

a DStream is a collection of RDDs where each RDD contains data for some unique time interval. Ex: - RDD1 will have data for time interval 0 to 1 and RDD2 will have data for time interval 1 to 2 and so on.

The DStream here is connected to the socket server created before on port 9874 and starts receiving the tweets from that port. Each record in the DStream is a tweet object. When the client side is up and running, the server starts sending out the filtered tweets on its allocated IP Address and Port. Spark Streaming receives live input data streams and divides the data into batches of 3 seconds, which are then processed by the Spark engine to generate the final stream of results in batches.

The tweets are than processed which includes separating each word of the tweet and assigning value 1 to each word. The count starts increasing as the tweets are being streamed on real time. Finally Spark's transformation function reducebyKey() is used which calculates the frequency of each word in the batch.

Tweets Categorization

The tweets are filtered as per the user's input or requirement using the hashtag '#word'. The application asks user to enter geographic location and topic-based input according to which the streaming tweets are filtered out among the other millions of tweets.

Tweets thus can be classified into various categories based upon the hashtags used in them. Table 1 clustering of tweets on the basis of various topics are:

Table 1.

Tweet Words	# Topic
#IT| Hiring| Internships | Machine Learning | Talent | #IT| Job alert | System Engineer	IT
# Sports | IPL | India vs Pakistan | Won | Tied | Wickets | Fans | Final	Sports
Chilly | Winds| Mercury Drop | Snow | Covered | Survive	Winter
#Finance | Job | Opening | Project | Specialist | Probation	#Finance

Data Preprocessing, Storage and Visualization

The words in tweets and their frequency collected from previous step are sent for further processing which involves removal of unwanted data. To remove the data which is of no use for analysis are removed using NLTK (Natural Language Toolkit) and Regex. From the NLTK library a stopwords module is used. It has a list of stopwords that are considered irrelevant and can be dropped while analyzing the data. The words are stored in 16 different languages, for our case English language is chosen. All the words in tweets are compared with the dataset in stopwords module and if there is any match found then that particular word is removed before sending it for further pre-processing. Next step is to remove the noise from the data and below have been considered as a noise:

1. HTML Links, tags and attributes (i.e., /<[^>]+>/)
2. Numeric values.

To remove the above data, Regex(re) has been used. We're also replacing all of the uppercase characters in the string with lowercase letters. Regex's re.sub() technique is used in this case. This method analyses the string for the substring we wish to remove and replaces it with whitespace. The first argument to re.sub() is a regular expression pattern, the second argument is a new string, and the third argument is the string to be processed. Finally, all the processed data is stored in a local directory in a CSV file. This file will have the data for all the tweets collected and processed and filtered as per the user's requirement. Figure 3 shows the data collected in a CSV file for the topic – Jobs selected by the user. This dataset is visualized using various plotting techniques provided in Python's data visualization library matplotlib. Matplotlib, a Python visualization package, is used to visualize the processed data saved in a CSV file. It comprises of various graphs, with the twitter data visualized using a bar plot, pie chart, and histogram. Because the saved data may contain terms that are still unusable for analysis, a threshold has been specified that a user can alter as needed. The frequency of words that exceed the chosen threshold is only picked up during the plotting process.

RESULT

Spark application was executed on the local machine with 2 threads with the hardware configuration of Intel Core I5 processor. Streaming tweets are collected in

Figure 3.

new	3
#job:	3
hr	1
advisor	1
(shared	1
services)	1
location:	3
warwick	1
salary:	3
30kpa	1
35kpa	1
https://t.co/loioenc7f2	1
#hiring	4
https://t.co/zlw5fxhks6	1
agile	1
consultants	1
experienced	1
trader	1
steel	1
procurement	1
client	1
trading	1
industry	1

Figure 4.

```
Enter the location you want tweets for : Delhi
Enter the subject of tweets : Winter
You have entered location : Delhi and subject : Winter
Waiting for Connection with Client
Connected with Client ('127.0.0.1', 59555)
```

a batch interval of 3 seconds after an initial filtering using hashtags. All the similar tweets arrived in a time interval of 10 minutes was merged and saved in a text file. Figure 4 shows users giving input as per the tweets they require. The tweets were filtered as per user's input and processed in real time, as shown in Figure 5 all the related tweets are being streamed. Figure 6,7 shows tweets collected in batches of

Figure 5.

```
The current temperature in #Delhi is 6°Celsius and I'm shive
Stupendous opening f #SpiderManNoWayHome is seen s #Welcome
Heart wrenching pic #Delhi #Winter #Donate #Blanket #Street
The residents of Delhi woke up to intense winter chills on M
#ColdWave conditions will remain intact in North India tonig
Severity to Decrease in #Rajasthan… https://t.co/2ZGRiEtw4v
```

Figure 6.

```
-------------------------------------------
Time: 2021-12-21 11:07:10
-------------------------------------------
('hungry', 1)
('but', 1)
('https://t.co/6rtOOciwTxThe', 1)
('current', 1)
('in', 5)
('is', 2)
('6°Celsius', 1)
('shivering.', 1)
('Thank', 1)
('month', 1)
...
```

Figure 7.

```
-------------------------------------------
Time: 2021-12-21 11:07:15
-------------------------------------------
('of', 2)
('AIIMS', 1)
('New', 1)
('out', 1)
('in', 1)
('protesti…', 1)
('https://t.co/A078IEY1ZDThat', 1)
('summers', 1)
('winter,', 1)
('', 1)
...
```

Figure 8.

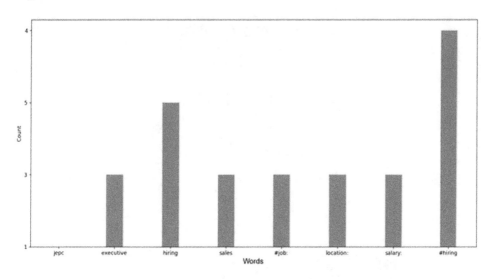

Figure 9.

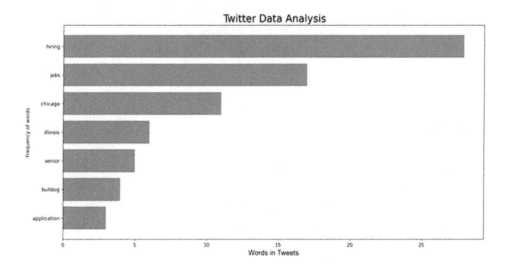

3 seconds and word count for each batch being printed on console. All the similar tweets information is getting stored locally in a CSV file continuously. The stored data is than visualized using plots like bar plot and pie chart shown in Figure 8 and Figure 9. Figure 10 depicts a Twitter study of user input for the location of Delhi and the subject of Corona.

Figure 10.

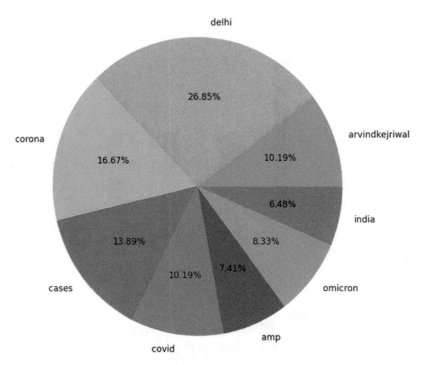

CONCLUSION

Twitter is one of the most popular social media networks, with millions of users worldwide. People, their interests, opinions, likes and dislikes, events, sporting events, politics, and movies everything is a part of it. Analyzing Twitter data can help one to figure out what's going on in the world and reveals what people are most interested in, which aids corporate organizations or brands in increasing sales, political parties in better understanding people's feelings and wants, and movie studios in receiving valid criticism for their performances, among other things. Thorough this research work we succeeded in developing and implementing a model for real time analyzing and filtering tweets as per the user's requirement without having user to create any twitter account. The streaming tweets are classified into various categories and can be stored in the user's machine thus improving the effectiveness of searching tweets manually. We evaluated the data with the matplotlib module in Python, utilizing several plots such as bar plots, piecharts, and horizontal bar graphs. In this work,

Spark Streaming and TCP Socket Programming was used to handle the streaming tweets. Spark being an open platform provides numerous features in dealing with big data analytics easily.

Future Work

Because it leverages in-memory processing, Apache Spark has shown to be an efficient framework for large data analysis. Spark can also be coupled with its other modules, such as the Spark SQL and Spark MLIB libraries, in the future. MLIB can be used to create machine learning models based on the acquired data, allowing for the prediction of future data patterns. Moreover, Spark SQL library may be used to run SQL queries on dataframes and obtain data by running queries as needed. We will attempt to depict more advanced data analysis patterns, such as sentiment analysis and decision making based upon the retrieved twitter results, in future work with more accurate results.

REFERENCES

Ahmed, H., Younis, E. M., Hendawi, A., & Ali, A. A. (2020). Heart disease identification from patients' social posts, machine learning solution on Spark. *Future Generation Computer Systems*, *111*, 714–722.

Apache Hadoop. (n.d.). *Apache Hadoop*. Retrieved from https://hadoop.apache.org/

Apache Spark. (2016). *Apache Spark*. Retrieved from https://spark.apache.org/

Cordova, I., & Moh, T. S. (2015, July). DBSCAN on resilient distributed datasets. In *2015 International Conference on High Performance Computing & Simulation (HPCS)* (pp. 531-540). IEEE. 10.1109/HPCSim.2015.7237086

Dehong, G., Wenjie, L., Xiaoyan, C., Renxian, Z., & You, O. (2014). Sequential summarization: A full view of twitter trending topics. *ACM Trans on Audio Speech Lang Process*, *22*(2), 293–302.

Hughes, D. J., Rowe, M., Batey, M., & Lee, A. (2012). A tale of two sites: Twitter vs. Facebook and the personality predictors of social media usage. *Computers in Human Behavior*, *28*(2), 561–569. doi:10.1016/j.chb.2011.11.001

Kılınç, D. (2019). A spark-based big data analysis framework for real-time sentiment prediction on streaming data. *Software, Practice & Experience*, *49*(9), 1352–1364.

Lee, K., Palsetia, D., Narayanan, R., Patwary, M. M. A., Agrawal, A., & Choudhary, A. (2011, December). Twitter trending topic classification. In *2011 IEEE 11th International Conference on Data Mining Workshops* (pp. 251-258). IEEE.

Lee, K., Palsetia, D., Narayanan, R., Patwary, M. M. A., Agrawal, A., & Choudhary, A. (2011, December). Twitter trending topic classification. In *2011 IEEE 11th International Conference on Data Mining Workshops* (pp. 251-258). IEEE.

Makazhanov, A., & Rafiei, D. (2013, August). Predicting political preference of Twitter users. In *Proceedings of the 2013 IEEE/ACM International Conference on Advances in Social Networks Analysis and Mining* (pp. 298-305). IEEE.

Nodarakis, N., Sioutas, S., Tsakalidis, A. K., & Tzimas, G. (2016, March). Large Scale Sentiment Analysis on Twitter with Spark. In EDBT/ICDT Workshops (pp. 1-8). Academic Press.

Pal, M. (2005). Random forest classifier for remote sensing classification. *International Journal of Remote Sensing, 26*(1), 217–222.

Rajput, N. K., Grover, B. A., & Rathi, V. K. (2020). *Word frequency and sentiment analysis of twitter messages during coronavirus pandemic.* arXiv preprint arXiv:2004.03925.

Significance of Apache Spark. (2016). *Hewlett Packard Enterprise.* Retrieved from https://www.mapr.com/blog/

Singh, D., & Reddy, C. K. (2015). A survey on platforms for big data analytics. *Journal of Big Data, 2*(1), 1–20. doi:10.118640537-014-0008-6 PMID:26191487

Song, J., Lee, S., & Kim, J. (2011, September). Spam filtering in twitter using sender-receiver relationship. In *International workshop on recent advances in intrusion detection* (pp. 301-317). Springer. 10.1007/978-3-642-23644-0_16

Spark Overview. (n.d.). *Apache Spark.* Retrieved from https://spark.apache.org/docs/latest/

Sumner, C., Byers, A., Boochever, R., & Park, G. J. (2012, December). Predicting dark triad personality traits from twitter usage and a linguistic analysis of tweets. In *2012 11th international conference on machine learning and applications* (Vol. 2, pp. 386-393). IEEE.

Yang, W., Liu, X., Zhang, L., & Yang, L. T. (2013, July). Big data real-time processing based on storm. In *2013 12th IEEE international conference on trust, security and privacy in computing and communications* (pp. 1784-1787). IEEE. 10.1109/TrustCom.2013.247

Zaki, N. D., Hashim, N. Y., Mohialden, Y. M., Mohammed, M. A., Sutikno, T., & Ali, A. H. (2020). A real-time big data sentiment analysis for iraqi tweets using spark streaming. *Bulletin of Electrical Engineering and Informatics*, *9*(4), 1411–1419.

Chapter 3
Transport Data Analytics With Selection of Tools and Techniques

Jayanthi Ganapathy
Sri Ramachandra Faculty of Engineering and Technology, India

Purushothaman R.
Siddartha Institute of Science and Technology, India

Ramya M.
Sri Ramachandra Faculty of Engineering and Technology, India

Joselyn Diana C.
Sri Ramachandra Faculty of Engineering and Technology, India

ABSTRACT

Emergency medical services (EMS) are inevitable in urban transport. The sustainable transport services during emergency situations are inevitable. These emergency services and vehicle operations are influenced by traffic flow rate on highways. The objective of this chapter is to present the use of transport data analytics in sustainable mobility and transport. Travel time is a key factor in emergency vehicle operations as the urban transport system is a time varying network. Temporal traffic information is a source for estimation of travel time on highways in emergency vehicle operations. The adverse traffic behavior during peak and non-peak hours of daily traffic profile hinders the operation of emergency vehicles during pandemic COVID-19 situations and so forth in evacuation planning when situation arises. Hence, this chapter presents the modern techniques and tools used in estimation of traffic flow rate on highways to access the connectivity of road network for emergency vehicle operations.

DOI: 10.4018/978-1-6684-5264-6.ch003

INTRODUCTION

Urban transport system is a time varying network. Traffic congestion induces unpredicted delay in travel time. The traffic flow rate on highways at temporal scales contributes in travel time computation in successive time instances. Formulation of Sequence Convolution based auto-encoder Long Short term Memory (SCAE-LSTM) network aims at sequencing the temporal traffic flow rate in preceding time instance to estimate the traffic flow in successive time instances. Given origin and destination (OD) pair, temporal traffic sequence helps in estimating traffic flow rate on highways. Hence, Spatial-TemporAl Reconnect (STAR) algorithm is proposed. The performance of STAR is investigated by conducting extensive experimentation on real traffic network of Chennai Metropolitan City.

The computational complexity of the algorithm is empirically analyzed. The proposed STAR algorithm is found to estimate traffic flow during peak hour traffic with reduced complexity in computation compared to other baseline methods in short term traffic flow predictions like LSTM, ConvLSTM and GRNN. Finally, conclusions on results are presented with directions for future research.

This chapter is organized to present the back ground on recent achievement followed by formulation of Sequence Convolution Auto-Encoder Long short term memory network with focus on time complexity measures. Finally, the chapter summarizes the work with directions for future research.

BACKGROUND

Recent advancements in Intelligent Transport Systems (ITS) have revolved the transport industry nationwide across the globe to serve the public in better way. Traffic flow congestion estimation and management on highways is always in demand worldwide across all nations for safe and hassle-free travel. Traffic congestion problem is inherent in travel time decisions and solving such problem is essential for travel guidance especially during peak hours of a journey. In early 1990's automated traffic controller was introduced (Bauer, 2009; Batz et al., 2010, 2013) and the two broad spectrums of research in transportation that is everlasting in infrastructure planning are (i) Shortest path computation problem and (ii) Time series traffic forecasting. In spite of technology driven traffic management using IoV (Internet of Vehicles), monitoring and control of vehicular traffic remains a serious issue in real time thus, a fully automated traffic management system is not feasible. Therefore, it is essential to manage traffic flow congestion systematically as it cannot be avoided but can be mitigated (Chen et al., 2014; Wu et al., 2016). In this view, a speedup technique is necessary to bridge the gap between traffic flow estimation and path routing of vehicular traffic between origin and destination (OD). In a spatially connected network, it is essential to analyze spatial dependency of road segment with respect to upstream and downstream traffic flow thereby, road segments (a path) that are connecting the source and destination in preceding time instances are analyzed in successive time instances for re-establishing connectivity. In this way, when traffic congestion is detected, the path is reconnected based on spatial – temporal traffic information. In the interest of reducing travel delay, Spatial-TemporAl Re-connect (STAR) algorithm is proposed in which traffic flow is estimated by sequencing spatial and temporal traffic information. The traffic information in upstream and downstream road segments represents spatial traffic information, while traffic flow at each time instance forms temporal information. The interest of this work is to formulate speedup technique by estimating traffic flow at each of arterial junctions between OD pair and re-establish path connectivity of road network based on spatial and temporal traffic sequences.

RESEARCH CHALLENGES

Temporal variation in traffic flow essentially captures the recurring and non-recurring congestion in dynamics of physical traffic flow. However, temporal traffic information alone is not sufficient in travel decisions when there is a need for reliable path on a spatially connected road network. In route guidance, a path in a travel is said to be reliable when flow rate in successive time instance is made known. This has motivated researchers to focus on influence of spatial characteristics in dynamics of traffic flow as flow rate from neighboring links contribute significant amount of traffic at current location. In this perspective, a fully automated traffic management system is not feasible. Therefore, it is essential to manage traffic flow congestion systematically as it cannot be avoided but can be mitigated. In this view, a speedup technique is necessary to bridge the gap between traffic flow estimation and path routing of vehicular traffic between origin and destination (OD). These challenges have motivated me in devising the research problem statement as discussed below:

Problem Statement

Statement 1

Given travel time-based traffic information sequence of uplink and downlink connecting the origin to destination, estimates the traffic flow at spatial intersection on highway.

In this work, both spatial and temporal information are essentially considered as they contribute significant information about traffic. In real road network, temporal variation in traffic volume has strong influence towards travel delay. Variation in travel time is the effect of congestion in time varying network. Traffic information at different time instances carry useful information about road network. Moreover, traffic information has to be analyzed at different time instances rather than arrival time and departure time alone. Edge weight augmented with temporal information would help in realizing real traffic conditions more effectively.

Identification of critical node (arterial junction) in the spatial network based on temporal variation of traffic with analysis on congestion patterns is required in real-time scenarios. Hence, temporal instances of traffic information are highly required in analyzing traffic at preceding instances. Traffic congestion incurred due to time varying travel time needs much consideration in solving path computation problem. Sequencing spatial and temporal traffic information in preceding time instance helps in estimating traffic flow in sequence in successive time instances by formalizing sequence convolution based auto-encoder Long Short-term Memory (SCAE-LSTM) network. Thus, spatial-temporal traffic characteristics extracted using convolution of upstream and downstream traffic information sequence is fed externally to auto-encoder LSTM. LSTM predicts the traffic flow at target location in successive time instances.

Statement 2

Given origin and destination pair in a travel, augment the spatially connected network to reach destination considering the spatial – temporal dependence of traffic flow.

Given source and destination with start time of journey, path connecting the arterial intersections is checked for congestion in which speed of vehicle captured by sensors in upstream and downstream is sequenced in each time instance using sequence convolution. Auto-encoder is formalized to extract the characteristics of vehicle speed in adjacent links. Auto-encoder is integrated with LSTM to estimate traffic flow rate at arterial intersection. Path to destination is re-connected considering both distance and spatial dependence of adjacent links at each time instance until destination is reached.

In a spatially connected network, it is essential to analyze spatial dependency of road segment with respect to upstream and downstream traffic flow thereby, road segments (a path) that are connecting the source and destination in preceding time instances are analyzed in successive time instances for re-establishing connectivity. In this way, when traffic congestion is detected, the path is reconnected based on spatial-temporal traffic information. In the interest of reducing travel delay, Spatial-TemporAl Re-connect (STAR) algorithm is proposed in which traffic flow is estimated by sequencing spatial and temporal traffic information. The traffic information in upstream and downstream road segments represents spatial traffic information, while traffic flow at each time instance forms temporal information. The interest of this work is to formulate speedup technique by estimating traffic flow at each of arterial junctions between OD pair and re-establish path connectivity of road network based on spatial and temporal traffic sequences.

INTELLIGENT TRANSPORT SYSTEMS FOR EMERGENCY VEHICLE OPERATIONS

The performance of Spatial-TemporAl Re-connect (STAR) algorithm is analysed on time varying road traffic network. The computational complexity of any shortest path algorithm is dependent on number of nodes and arcs. The dependency of road segments connecting arterial junctions is analysed in re-establishing connectivity by formalising SCAE-LSTM network. The significance of STAR algorithm in managing traffic is reported with extensive experimentation under different traffic conditions in three different sites. The peak hour traffic is evaluated for each site during weekdays and weekends.

Study Area and Data Collection

Estimation of traffic speed using SCAE-LSTM and dynamic path connectivity using STAR algorithm is experimented on road network covering southern region of Chennai city located in Tamil Nadu state of India. The state highway SH-49 and SH-49A is chosen for this study as this highway experiences significant traffic on all working days and weekends. The length of study area considered in experimentation on state highway SH-49 (East Coast Road) is 690 Km. The length of the state highway SH-49A is 43.7 Km. This metropolitan transport network is a highly connected road network covering major arterial junctions connecting urban streets, motorways, and expressways.

The state highway of this southern region is facilitated with centralized toll collection center. Motor vehicle passing through this state highway connects three toll plazas namely (1) Perungudi Toll Plaza, which is entry to centralized toll collection center from northern region of Chennai city, (2) East Coast Road (ECR) and (3) Egattur toll plaza, which is exit of the toll collection center.

Travel time during free flow is computed in early morning (5:00 AM – 6:00 AM), Afternoon (12:00 NOON – 02:00 PM) and post evening (10:00 PM-11:30 PM). The actual travel time is computed in morning peak hours (8:00 AM – 11:30 AM) and evening peak hours (05:00 PM – 9:00 PM) during week days while peak hour changes during weekends.

The historical data set describing the vehicle speed in mile/ hr is used as training data set. Speed of vehicle in state highway SH-49 is captured by the sensor and stored in centralized server which is high end server located in Perungudi Toll Plaza. Estimation of vehicle speed is done by training auto-encoder LSTM with historical data set and validated by testing the model with actual speed of vehicle. Vehicle miles travelled (VMT) recorded for 36 months between January 2017 and December 2020 is used for training the Auto-Encoder LSTM network, while VMT recorded for ten months between January 2021 and October 2021 is used as test data set in evaluating the system.

Performance of SCAE-LSTM

The training phase of LSTM requires computationally elaborates operational settings. The traffic data sets representing traffic speed, flow rate, and occupancy are voluminous and requires intensive computation methods. The potential issues concerned with the implementation of SCAE-LSTM in STAR are detailed as follows:

Given an origin and destination pair a matrix of LSTM nodes is formulated in which each LSTM node represents an arterial junction between origin and destination. During the training phase, the source of input to LSTM is the pre-trained auto-encoders whose primary function is to extract spatial-temporal traffic characteristics from upstream and downstream traffic flow in each hour of the day. Thus, extensive operational settings are required in initial training phase of LSTM nodes.

The core components operated in Algorithm I are extraction of spatial-temporal characteristics of physical traffic flow using frequent traffic sequences on upstream, downstream, and training auto-encoders using the extracted data sets. The training phase of LSTM requires computationally elaborates operational settings. The traffic data sets representing traffic speed, flow rate collected for 52 weeks is used in training auto-encoders with computationally intensive operational settings on arterial junctions.

However, training and validation error does not vary in different operational settings considering the morning and evening peak hours of the day. The stability of the system is ensured even with traffic data collection at a temporal resolution of 15-minutes. Table 2 shows the training and validation loss in different epochs.

The issues concerned with implementing STAR are space complexity. Augmenting spatially connected road networks as described in Algorithm II requires the storage of spatial coordinates of the location on a Google Map. The location information and retrieval of spatial coordinates during the inclusion and exclusion of LSTM nodes incurs high space and memory utilization. The experimental setup was made for a maximum distance of 350 miles on state highway SH 49 and SH 49A for testing the performance of the STAR algorithm. However, other practical constraints have to

Table 1. Training and validation loss

Epoch	Phases	AE-LSTM	ConvLSTM	LSTM	GRNN
10	Train	0.6	0.61	0.625	0.678
	Test	0.79	0.79	0.81	0.86
20	Train	0.58	0.585	0.6	0.625
	Test	0.65	0.685	0.68	0.786
30	Train	0.556	0.547	0.57	0.6
	Test	0.73	0.62	0.6	0.75
40	Train	0.556	0.54	0.57	0.58
	Test	0.71	0.619	0.61	0.62
50	Train	0.524	0.54	0.6	0.572
	Test	0.65	0.61	0.602	0.6
60	Train	0.529	0.528	0.57	0.575
	Test	0.652	0.519	0.605	0.605
70	Train	0.423	0.528	0.512	0.55
	Test	0.49	0.598	0.575	0.6
80	Train	0.35	0.519	0.565	0.54
	Test	0.42	0.599	0.577	0.585
90	Train	0.31	0.52	0.56	0.525
	Test	0.389	0.589	0.58	0.575
100	**Train**	**0.25**	**0.5002**	**0.525**	**0.5**
	Test	**0.281**	**0.51**	**0.55**	**0.575**
110	Train	0.2499	0.5	0.5	0.5
	Test	0.279	0.5	0.5	0.5
120	Train	0.251	0.5	0.53	0.5
	Test	0.255	0.5	0.5	0.5

be considered in the further investigation of routing vehicles, which is left to work in the future. The accuracy of models in the estimation of vehicle speed is evaluated both during training and testing phases. Models were trained to learn the behavior of traffic in the study area. Training accuracy best fits the model in learning the traffic behavior and it is validated using actual flow rate in the test data. The accuracy of models during training and validation is examined using mean relative error measure given in Equation (28). The error measure of base line models is compared with SCAE-LSTM. SCAE-LSTM fits well in learning the training data at epoch 100. Estimation of Vehicle miles is done at 15 minutes resolutions considering training and test accuracy at 100th epoch. The models descend with error rate gradually until epoch 100 and entropy log loss function for various epochs. The loss function is given in Equation (1),

$$Log\,loss = -\frac{1}{N}\sum_{i=1}^{N} Z_i log P + \left(1 - Z_i\right) log\left(1 - P\right)$$

where N is number of iterations; Z_i is the training data set; P is the joint probability of maximum likelihood estimates. The error rate of SCAE-LSTM is found to be less compared to ConvLSTM, while LSTM and GRNN are found to experience similar error rate. The speed of vehicle in miles per hour is estimated using Auto-Encoder LSTM. Congestion index is computed in proposed STAR using the estimated speed for managing traffic during peak hours.

$$RMSE(\lambda',\lambda) = \sqrt{\frac{\sum_{n=1}^{N}\left(-\right)^2}{N}} \qquad (2)$$

$$MRE(\lambda',\lambda) = \frac{\left(\sum_{n=1}^{N}\left|-\right|\right)}{N} \qquad (3)$$

$$MAE(\lambda',\lambda) = \frac{\sum_{n=1}^{N}\left|-\right|}{N} \qquad (4)$$

λ' is the predicted value, λ is the observed value, and N represents the amount of data. The baseline models used in this evaluation are Convolution LSTM (ConvLSTM), LSTM, and Gated Recurrent Neural Network (GRNN). Auto-Encoder LSTM is formalized and implemented in Python 3.8 using tensor flow and keras packages which is available under GNU public license. Experimental analysis is conducted on 2.5GHz, 64-bit processor, 16GB RAM in Windows 10 environment. The performance of Auto-Encoder LSTM model is evaluated using Root Mean Square Error (RMSE), Mean Relative Error (MRE), and Mean Absolute Error (MAE) metrics shown in (2) through (4) and compared with baseline models. The accuracy of models in estimation of vehicle speed is evaluated both during training and testing phases. Models were trained to learn the behavior of traffic in the study area. Training accuracy best fits the model in learning the traffic behavior and it is validated using actual vehicle speed using test data. The model fits well in learning the training data at earlier epoch 100. Estimation of Vehicle miles is done at various temporal scales say less than or equal to 10 mins, 15 mins, and 30 mins resolutions considering training and test accuracy at 100th epoch.

The models descend with error rate gradually up to epoch 100 and entropy log loss function for various epochs. It is evident from Table 2 error rate of SCAE-LSTM is found to be less compared to ConvLSTM while, LSTM and GRNN are found to experience similar error rate. The proposed sequence convolution-based Auto-Encoder LSTM is found to be stable in estimating speed of vehicle at different temporal resolutions compared to baseline models as Mean Relative Error (MRE) of the model does not vary and found to be in range in estimation of vehicle in different temporal resolutions. Thus, stability of the Auto-Encoder LSTM is ensured as spatial and temporal traffic information is sequenced at each time instance. The speed of vehicle is estimated from characteristic vehicle speed in sequence. In contrast, baseline models experiences variation in error rate which is due to inherent complexity of models in time series forecasting. Vehicles

Table 2. Error rate in estimation of vehicle miles/hr

| Deep Learners | Facility | Temporal Resolution | | | | | | | | |
| | | ≤10 mins | | | ≤ 15 mins | | | ≤ 30 mins | | |
		RMSE	MRE	MAE	RMSE	MRE	MAE	RMSE	MRE	MAE
SCAE-LSTM	Expressways	3.45	0.05	0.20	3.79	0.05	0.32	5.78	0.05	0.40
	Arterials	4.73	0.04	0.25	4.88	0.04	0.35	5.04	0.04	0.45
	Freeways	3.23	0.05	0.11	3.11	0.05	0.41	4.35	0.05	0.11
ConvLSTM	Expressways	12.85	0.66	23.76	13.74	0.73	24.11	12.81	0.66	23.75
	Arterials	11.47	0.62	22.05	12.01	0.77	23.72	13.05	0.62	30.32
	Freeways	11.75	0.67	21.85	9.87	0.79	22.05	10.86	0.67	32.09
LSTM	Expressways	11.58	0.78	33.44	13.55	0.78	35.21	13.75	0.78	33.45
	Arterials	11.44	0.67	32.87	12.23	0.67	33.85	12.89	0.67	28.18
	Freeways	11.84	0.72	32.03	8.89	0.72	30.56	9.02	0.72	30.19
Gated RNN	Expressways	13.65	0.89	40.84	13.65	0.89	40.84	13.65	0.89	40.87
	Arterials	12.91	0.77	40.05	12.94	0.77	39.25	13.25	0.77	40.17
	Freeways	12.02	0.78	36.86	11.32	0.78	38.26	12.15	0.78	41.19

miles are estimated for various temporal scales, say less than or equal to 10 minutes, 15 minutes, and 30 minutes to check the stability of SCAE-LSTM.

Time Complexity Analysis of STAR

In our previous research (Ganapathy, 2021, 2022; Ganapathy and García Márquez, 2021a, 2021b; Ganapathy, García Márquez, and Ragavendra Prasad, 2022; Ganapathy and Paramasivam, 2019) evaluation of traffic sequence patterns and rules for prediction of traffic volume on highways is reported in detail and used in upstream and downstream spatial traffic sequences, travel time based temporal traffic sequence pattern mining on this study. The evaluation of the proposed STAR algorithm targets two specific factors first, the time complexity in estimation of traffic flow using SCAE-LSTM for various distance measures. Second, the time complexity of speedup in path computation by augmenting arterial junctions between OD pair based on spatial-temporal traffic information sequence formulation during morning (MPHT) and evening peak hour traffic (EPHT).

The complexity of speedup technique STAR algorithm in path computation problem is analysed by experimenting the proposed spatial-temporal traffic information sequence formulation (SCAE-LSTM) on SH-49 and SH-49A for estimation of traffic flow in principle arterial junctions connecting OD pair. The proposed STAR algorithm is tested for (1) traffic flow estimation and (2) Augmentation of arterial junctions for OD pair based on spatial-temporal traffic information. The potential of SCAE-LSTM is compared with another baseline deep learner such as LSTM, ConvLSTM, and GRNN. Thus, the proposed speedup technique is evaluated for complexity in traffic flow estimation with SCAE-LSTM, LSTM, ConvLSTM and GRNN and results are compared. Average execution time of STAR algorithm is evaluated for various distance measures in miles. Experimental set up for evaluation of traffic flow with STAR algorithm started with minimum distance measure of 50 miles and extended to maximum distance measure of 300 miles on State Highway SH-49. The proposed STAR and baseline models are found to have the same complexity as the execution time of each model is found to be similar for less number of distance measure between 1 and 50 miles. But there is a gradual and significant reduction in complexity of STAR above 50 miles. A steep decrease in execution time is found with STAR for 50 miles and above while ConvLSTM exhibits the same behaviour only after 100 miles and LSTM and GRNN shows a gradual increase in complexity from 50 miles onward. Thus, STAR with SCAE-LSTM is found to have reduced complexity in computation time compared to STAR with other baseline models. This significance takes advantage of two principal elements (i) formulation of traffic information sequence at each time instance based on travel time (temporal traffic factor) and (ii) characteristic traffic sequence evaluated from both upstream and downstream road segments. The speedup of STAR in path computation is evaluated by the experimentation of the proposed formulation for different origin-destination (OD) pair. Experimental setup begins with the execution of STAR in augmenting arterial junction between OD pair based on traffic flow estimation using proposed SCAE-LSTM, LSTM, ConvLSTM and GRNN. A minimum number of 2 - 10 OD pair each with a distance measure of 200 miles is considered in this experimental setup. Mean execution time is evaluated for every 10 OD pair. This setup is extended to a maximum number of 200 OD pair of the same length. Each OD pair is located on the Google Map and arterial junctions connecting OD pair is extracted using Python Client library designed for Google Map API web services.

The proposed STAR exhibits identical characteristics in the evaluation of time complexity with respect to OD pair too. The significance of the proposed formulation of SCAE-LSTM is found to exhibit the same characteristics even when evaluated with respect to OD pairs. The proposed formulation is equivalently stable with baseline models too with respect to OD pairs. Hence, execution of the proposed formulation is found to be stable under different traffic conditions. However, average execution time in speedup evaluation of the proposed STAR for OD pair differs with execution time with respect to distance measure. This is due to the traffic behaviour during peak hours of day.

The speedup of the proposed STAR is evaluated during peak hours of the day both in the morning and evening. The speedup in augmenting arterial junctions for OD pair using STAR is found to be twice faster compared to ConvLSTM, 2.4 times that of LSTM, and three times faster compared to GRNN in both peak hours of the day. Nevertheless, the average execution time of STAR during peak hours in the evening is found to increase by 1.2 times compared to morning which is less significant compared to the stability of the model in different traffic conditions. The rate of execution of STAR is found to be stationary and identical with STAR (ConvLSTM) irrespective of peak hour of the day. These two models are found to be more stable beyond 100 OD pair compared to STAR (LSTM) and STAR (GRNN). However, STAR is faster compared to STAR (ConvLSTM) due to the formulation of spatial - temporal characteristic traffic sequence. Unlike the inherent complexity in the computation of hidden layers with LSTM and GRNN, STAR and STAR (ConvLSTM) are better speedup methods for path computation.

Sequence convolution-based Auto-Encoder LSTM is found to be stable in estimating speed of vehicle at 15 minutes temporal resolutions compared to baseline models as mean relative error (MRE) of the model does not vary and found to be in range in estimation of vehicle speed in different temporal resolutions. Thus, stability of the Auto-Encoder LSTM is ensured as spatial and temporal traffic information is sequenced at each time instance. In the interest of reducing delay in travel, Spatial-TemporAl Reconnect (STAR) algorithm is proposed for traffic flow assessment on highways. The functional performance of the STAR algorithm is evaluated against other baseline deep leaners. Extensive experiments conducted on state highway SH-49 and SH-49A of Chennai metropolitan city in Tamil Nadu and evaluation results are reported. STAR is found to be twice faster compared to ConvLSTM, 2.4 times that of LSTM, and three times faster compared to GRNN in both peak hours of the day. Evaluation on functional performance of STAR when operated on travel time varying network has shown reduced complexity in computation. The evaluation results of STAR thus, achieved have illustrated the significance of sequencing temporal and spatial factors and their logical analysis in augmenting arterial junction between OD pair.

FUTURE RESEARCH DIRECTIONS

In the interest of reducing travel time during peak hour, SCAE-LSTM network is formalised for estimating traffic flow in sequence in successive time instances. Accuracy and training performance of this model is compared with other baseline models LSTM, ConvLSTM, and GRNN. SCAE-LSTM is found to be stable in the estimation of vehicle speed at various temporal resolutions. Further, steps to evolve formulation of STAR for traffic management on connected vehicles have been taken to work in future.

CONCLUSION

Research on computational methods to reduce traffic congestion is the essential part of ITS infrastructure in the Urban Transportation system. Besides several speed up techniques in the computation of time dependent shortest paths found in literature, the logical analysis of spatial and temporal factors and their significance in traffic network was not the interest of transportation researchers over the past decade. This chapter presented the techniques and tools used in transport data analytics for emergency vehicle operations considering the traffic flow rate on highways. Further, the use of modern tools and techniques is illustrated with a case study on traffic flow rate estimation and augmentation of arterial junctions based on spatial-temporal traffic sequences.

REFERENCES

Batz, G. V., Geisberger, R., Neubauer, S., & Sanders, P. (2010, May). Time-dependent contraction hierarchies and approximation. In *International Symposium on Experimental Algorithms* (pp. 166-177). Springer. 10.1007/978-3-642-13193-6_15

Batz, G. V., Geisberger, R., Sanders, P., & Vetter, C. (2013). Minimum time-dependent travel times with contraction hierarchies. *Journal of Experimental Algorithmics*, *18*, 1–1. doi:10.1145/2444016.2444020

Bauer, R., & Delling, D. (2010). SHARC: Fast and robust unidirectional routing. *Journal of Experimental Algorithmics*, *14*, 2–4.

Chen, B. Y., Lam, W. H., Sumalee, A., Li, Q., & Tam, M. L. (2014). Reliable shortest path problems in stochastic time-dependent networks. *Journal of Intelligent Transport Systems*, *18*(2), 177–189. doi:10.1080/15472450.2013.806851

Ganapathy, J. (2021). Design of Algorithm for IoT-Based Application: Case Study on Intelligent Transport Systems. In *Internet of Things* (pp. 227–249). Springer. doi:10.1007/978-3-030-70478-0_11

Ganapathy, J. (2022) Multi Criteria Decision Making Analysis for sustainable Transport. Unpublished Manuscript. In *Sustainability: Cases And Studies in using Operations Research and Management Science Methods*. Springer.

Ganapathy, J., & García Márquez, F. P. (2021a, August). Travel Time Based Traffic Rerouting by Augmenting Traffic Flow Network with Temporal and Spatial Relations for Congestion Management. In *International Conference on Management Science and Engineering Management* (pp. 554-565). Springer. 10.1007/978-3-030-79203-9_43

Ganapathy, J., & García Márquez, F. P. (2021b, August). Data Mining and Information Technology in Transportation—A Review. In *International Conference on Management Science and Engineering Management* (pp. 849-855). Springer. 10.1007/978-3-030-79206-0_64

Ganapathy, J., García Márquez, F. P., & Ragavendra Prasad, M. (2022). Routing Vehicles on Highways by Augmenting Traffic Flow Network: A Review on Speed Up Techniques. *Integrated Emerging Methods of Artificial Intelligence & Cloud Computing*, 96-105.

Ganapathy, J., & Paramasivam, J. (2019). Prediction of traffic volume by mining traffic sequences using travel time based PrefixSpan. *IET Intelligent Transport Systems*, *13*(7), 1199–1210. doi:10.1049/iet-its.2018.5165

Wu, Y. J., Chen, F., Lu, C. T., & Yang, S. (2016). Urban traffic flow prediction using a spatio-temporal random effects model. *Journal of Intelligent Transport Systems*, *20*(3), 282–293. doi:10.1080/15472450.2015.1072050

ADDITIONAL READING

Ermagun, A., & Levinson, D. (2018). Spatiotemporal traffic forecasting: Review and proposed directions. *Transport Reviews*, *38*(6), 786–814. doi:10.1080/014416 47.2018.1442887

Huang, W., Song, G., Hong, H., & Xie, K. (2014). Deep architecture for traffic flow prediction: Deep belief networks with multitask learning. *IEEE Transactions on Intelligent Transportation Systems*, *15*(5), 2191–2201. doi:10.1109/ TITS.2014.2311123

Lingras, P., Sharma, S., & Zhong, M. (2002). Prediction of recreational travel using genetically designed regression and time-delay neural network models. *Transportation Research Record: Journal of the Transportation Research Board*, *1805*(1), 16–24. doi:10.3141/1805-03

Ma, X., Tao, Z., Wang, Y., Yu, H., & Wang, Y. (2015). Long short-term memory neural network for traffic speed prediction using remote microwave sensor data. *Transportation Research Part C, Emerging Technologies*, *54*, 187–197. doi:10.1016/j. trc.2015.03.014

Nejad, M. M., Mashayekhy, L., Chinnam, R. B., & Phillips, A. (2016). Hierarchical time-dependent shortest path algorithms for vehicle routing under ITS. *IIE Transactions*, *48*(2), 158–169. doi:10.1080/0740817X.2015.1078523

Wei, W., Wu, H., & Ma, H. (2019). An autoencoder and LSTM-based traffic flow prediction method. *Sensors (Basel)*, *19*(13), 2946. doi:10.339019132946 PMID:31277390

Zhao, Z., Chen, W., Wu, X., Chen, P. C., & Liu, J. (2017). LSTM network: A deep learning approach for short-term traffic forecast. *IET Intelligent Transport Systems*, *11*(2), 68–75. doi:10.1049/iet-its.2016.0208

Chapter 4

Towards Design of Brain Tumor Detection Framework Using Deep Transfer Learning Techniques

Prince Rajak
National Institute of Technology, Raipur, India

Anjali Sagar Jangde
National Institute of Technology, Raipur, India

Govind P. Gupta
(iD) https://orcid.org/0000-0002-0456-1572
National Institute of Technology, Raipur, India

ABSTRACT

Brain tumor has surpassed all other types of cancers as it is the most diagnosed malignancy worldwide, and it is also the leading cause of death. Early detection and diagnosis of a brain tumor allow doctors to give better therapy and a higher chance for the patient's life. Recently, many strategies that leverage machine learning and deep learning models for detection and categorization have been presented. This chapter focuses on the design of a novel brain tumor detection and classification framework using well-known deep transfer learning models such as DenseNet201, DenseNet169, DenseNet121, MobileNet_v2, VGG19, VGG16, and Xception. Performance evaluation of the proposed framework is evaluated using a benchmark dataset in terms of accuracy and loss. It is observed that with DenseNet201, a training accuracy of 97.49% and a validation accuracy of 96.43% are observed. However, for MobileNet v2, Densenet169, and Xception model, 96% accuracy is observed. As a result, it is observed that the DenseNet201 model outperformed all other models in terms of accuracy.

DOI: 10.4018/978-1-6684-5264-6.ch004

INTRODUCTION

Recently, Brain Tumor (BT) detection becomes a fundamental research challenge due to increase in cases worldwide and this problem has attracted researchers to find out AI-based detection tools for early diagnosis There are primary and secondary BT. In primary BT, a tumor grows in the brain, it can be described as 'high' and 'low' grade tumor. High grade tumor grows faster as compared to low grade whose growth is slower. The secondary BT are the tumor that grows in another part of body such as lung, breast, etc., and then spread through the brain, it is also called as metastatic. Figure 1. shows some of the types of BT and a healthy brain image. BT is the abnormal growth of cells in the brain. There are many methods that are used for detection of BT with high accuracy. The rise in artificial intelligence (AI) and machine learning (ML) field help in BT surgery. Brain surgery with AI is resulting safer and more efficient and precise. These methods are performing better in different field like early diagnosis of BT, surgery, optimizing the surgical plan, better prediction the prognosis and providing efficient support during the operation.

Early detection and identification of BT are crucial for the patient's efficient and prompt therapy. Our visual cortex's capacity to discern levels of MRI (Magnetic Resonance Imaging) images limits our ability to identify BT. So, the next technology, known as CAD (Computer-Aided Diagnosis), was invented to help radiologists detect different types of tumors and provide improved visualization capabilities. This technology automatically analyses photos and recognizes BT, as well as performs numerous operations such as segmentation, classification, and others that help doctors better comprehend and save their patients' lives, as well as researchers working in

Figure 1. Types of BT and No-tumor brain

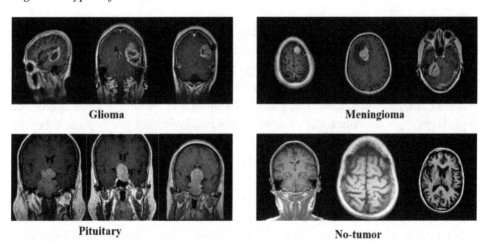

these disciplines to analyze these BT. Also, due to the improved diagnosis findings obtained by this technology, the odds of surgery are lowered. Image processing, computer vision, and image segmentation are some of the methods that may be used to determine the nature of a tumor, measure its size and depth, and better comprehend its structure. For automated detection, classification, and segmentation, these approaches have been demonstrated to be accurate and efficient.

These methods employ AI subfields that are divided into two categories: machine learning (ML) and deep learning (DL). ML employs a variety of feature selection methods, which are then used for classification and segmentation. In DL, a convolutional neural network (CNN) is utilized to extract the hidden pattern from BT images and to classify and segment BT using labelled images. SVM, KNN, Random Forest, CNN, UNET, and other ML and DL algorithms are only a few examples. This paper focuses on design of Brain Tumor framework using latest Deep transfer learning techniques. The main contribution of this work is list out as follows:

1. Design of brain tumor detection framework using latest deep transfer learning approaches such as DenseNet201, DenseNet169, DenseNet121, MobileNet_v2, VGG19, VGG16, and Xception.
2. Performance evaluation of the proposed framework is evaluated using benchmark dataset in terms of accuracy and loss.

In the later section, a related work is presented, Next, describe the description of the proposed framework using deep transfer learning models. Section 4 presents result analysis and discussion. Finally, section 5 concludes the paper.

RELATED WORK

In this section we have discuss various related study which help us to learn and build the proposed work. In this various feature extraction, pre-processing, CNN architecture, different pre-trained model and their performance and approaches are discussed.

In Das et al. (2019) they have proposed a CNN architecture to classify BT, the dataset consist of three class i.e., glioma, meningioma, pituitary. The architecture consists of three convolutional layer and two dense layers, the pre-processing of the image data is performed, the model achieves the training accuracy of 94 percent and validation accuracy 93.33 percent. In Sultan et al. (2019) the authors have proposed a CNN based framework with adding normalization layer and used regularization techniques to reduce the overfitting and optimization techniques to update the weight parameter. The dataset used contain three classes of BT i.e., meningioma, glioma, pituitary and the model achieve the accuracy of 96 for study 1 and 98 for study two.

In Abbas et al. (2021), authors have proposed a hybrid segmentation consists of threshold, watershed, cluster, region-based segmentation. This model is used with CNN framework to train the model, the dataset consists of two label tumor and non-tumor. The accuracy achieve by this whole framework is 97.32 percent. In Kumar et al. (2022), authors have proposed the hybrid deep CNN framework using transfer learning in which for pre-processing Otsu binarization method is used to enhance the image grade and remove noises, in feature extraction. This work has used GLCM method and used these data to train the proposed framework, the dataset contains three labels, benign, malignant, normal. In Swati et al. (2019), authors have used pre-trained VGG19 architecture and perform transfer learning method and perform fine tuning with different layer structure and have achieve accuracy of 94.82 percent, the dataset used contain three types of BT MRI images discuss above.

In Amin et al. (2019), authors have proposed a new procedure for BT segmentation and classification. They have used lesion enhancement for performing operations such edge enhances, smoothing, log and linear transformation, gray scale image conversion, then perform lesion segmentation method like global threshold and morphological opening to extract features used pre-trained GoogleNet and AlexNet for classification directly and new approach known as Fusion Score which generates fusion vector, used these vectors to perform multi classification. The dataset used are BRATS 2013, BRATS 2014, BRATS 2015, BRATS 2016, BRATS 2017 and ISLES. In the next study author (Pravitasari, et al., 2020) used transfer learning method used VGG16 and U-Net to build the architecture for BT segmentation and the model achieve the accuracy of 96.1 percent.

Proposed Brain Tumor Detection Framework using Deep Transfer Learning Techniques

This section presents Deep Transfer Learning (TL) model and description of the proposed framework. For BT detection, we have used TL based models in this study. It applies the knowledge obtained during training to solve a problem and to apply this knowledge to various but related problems. We used densenet201, densenet169, densenet121, mobilenet_v2, vgg19, vgg16, and Xception, among other pre-trained models. They've all been trained on millions of photos from ImageNet data. Table 1 shows the overall number of parameters employed by these pre-trained models, as well as the number of trainable and non-trainable parameters.

In this work, we have proposed the BT classification model using TL. We have used different pre-trained model which are trained on ImageNet data. In this process first we have built the hybrid BT image dataset the used pre-trained model and frozen it output layer and add proposed work layer. We have frozen the output and add a flatten layer which convert matrix in single dimension array then add two dense layers consist of 1024 neurons and 512 neurons, add on both dense layer with another layer

Table 1. Parameter used by pre-trained model

Model	Total Params	Trainable Params	Non-Trainable Params
DenseNet201	115,186,754	96,864,770	18,321,984
DenseNet169	96,662,594	84,019,714	12,642,880
DenseNet121	58,944,578	51,907,074	7,037,504
MobileNet_v2	86,670,914	84,412,930	2,257,984
VGG16	57,708,866	42,994,178	14,714,688
VGG19	63,018,562	42,994,178	20,024,384
Xception	231,103,530	210,242,050	20,861,480

Figure 2. Proposed work using Per-trained model to classify BT

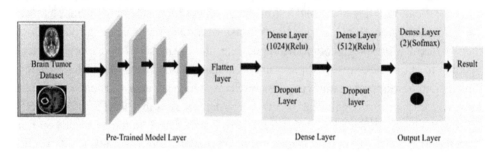

known as dropout layer with 0.2 value which stop the active neuron to take part in the training and add priority to inactive neurons to stop overfitting, both the dense layer uses the Relu activation function. Then we add the final layer also known as output layer with parameter as two neuron and used softmax activation function as classifier The model train up to 30 epoch and learning rate is 0.001, used Adam as optimizer, loss function as Binary cross entropy and the metrics parameter is binary accuracy. Figure 2. shows block diagram of the proposed framework.

DenseNet201

DenseNet201 (Jaiswal et al., 2020) is a 201-layers deep CNN with [6,12,48,32] layer pattern. We applied a pre-trained model that has trained on the ImageNet database that contains millions of images. This network can identify 1000 item categories, which is one of the criteria that indicates the network has acquired important features and patterns from these images. The size of the input image is 244 by 244. We used TensorFlow to call this pre-trained model in our study. The vanishing gradient problem had solved with DenseNets.

DenseNet169

DenseNet169 (Varshmi et al., 2019) is a CNN with layers of [6,12,32,32]. It's part of the DenseNet (Densely Connected Convolutional Networks (Huang, et al.,2017)) family, and it's termed a densely connected net since each layer is connected to every other layer. The feature maps from all previous layers are utilised as input for the subsequent layer in this method. DenseNet improves feature propagation, promotes feature reuse, and reduces the number of parameters required.

MobileNet_V2

The CNN architecture MobileNet V2 (Sandler et al., 2018) works well on mobile devices. It has 53 layers and belongs to the lightweight CNN architecture category. The MobileNet V1 design has improved, and two new features have been incorporated in MobileNet V2, including the shortcut connections between bottlenecks and linear bottlenecks between layers. The image input size is 244 by 244. This design aids in the development of mobile vision applications as well as visual recognition fields such as segmentation, classification, and object detection. In the suggested work, we used this architecture, which was pre-trained on ImageNet data.

Xception

The CNN architecture Xception (Chollet et al., 2017) has 71 layers. Extreme Inception is what it stands for. It uses the principles of Inception and a more evolved form of DSC (Depthwise Separable Convolution). The input image is 299 by 299 pixels in size. The Xception model outperforms the inception model significantly. We used Xception architecture that has been pre-trained on ImageNet data and used it with the proposed work.

DenseNet121

DeneNet121 (Zhou et al., 2022), a deep CNN model with [6,12,24,16] layers in the four dense blocks, is a deep CNN model. It's a member of the DenseNet family. The structure consists of convolutional, pooling, transition, classification layer and dense block. It uses composite function operation and works as an output of previous layers as an input of subsequent layers. It was created specifically to increase the accuracy of deep networks that has dropped due to the vanishing gradient problem.

VGG16 and VGG19

Both VGG16 (Qassim et al., 2018) and VGG19 (Carvalho et al., 2017) are VGG family members with 16 and 19 layers deep. The input image is 224 by 224 pixels in size. It has been built to improve the model's performance by increasing the depth of CNN. Visual geometry group (VGG) is a part of deep CNN architecture. The primary difference is that VGG16 has 16 layers, but VGG19 has 19 layers, implying three more convolutional layers.

PERFORMANCE ANALYSIS

Dataset Description

The dataset that we utilized was compiled from several sources to produce a hybrid dataset, and it has divided into two categories: tumor and non-tumor. The dataset includes BT photos from various perspectives, which will aid the model's training. The dataset has divided into two directories that include the names of the annotated images: training and validation. The training folder has 3010 files while the validation folder contains 914 files. We have 1510 tumor and 1500 non-tumor images for training, and 450 tumor and 460 non-tumor images for validation. Figure 3 show the two types of labels for BT.

Figure 3. Types of BT

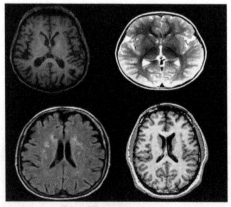 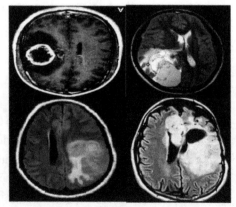

No- Tumor   **Tumor**

Result Analysis

In this work, we used a variety of pre-trained architectures, including DenseNet-201, DenseNet169, DenseNet121, Xception, MobileNet V2, VGG16 and VGG19. All the models are trained on ImageNet (Krizhevsky et al., 2012) data. To tackle our problem, we have used the weight of these pre-trained models, which were trained on very large datasets like ImageNet, we adopted a transfer learning approach. All models have thirty training epochs. To monitor the model's growth, we recorded their performance at ten, twenty, and thirty epochs. We have applied some regularization techniques, such as data argumentation and normalization, to reduce overfitting. Binary cross-entropy, the loss functions we've chosen, compares each predicted probability against the actual class labels are either 0 or 1. The optimizer we have used is Adam and to evaluate the model performance we have to use the binary accuracy metric. Then we have compiled the models for training and use the fit function to train the model in this we have passed training, validation input, epoch

Figure 4. Shown the plot between the training and validation loss and accuracy of Densenet201, the final TA is 97.49 and VA is 96.43 and loss is 0.076 and validation loss is 0.108

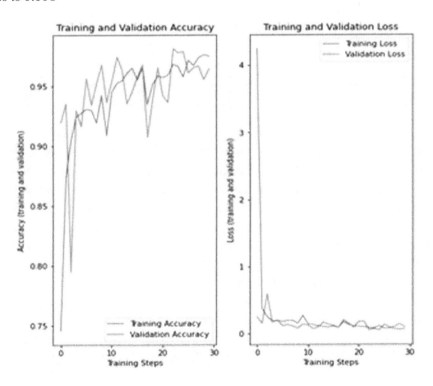

Table 2. Performance analysis of proposed work

Model	Epoch	Loss	Validation Loss	Training Accuracy (TA)	Validation Accuracy (VA)
DenseNet201	10	0.2769	0.1439	0.9087	0.9364
	20	0.1142	0.0955	0.9582	0.9654
	30	0.0768	0.1081	0.9749	0.9643
DenseNet169	10	0.2474	0.1053	0.9094	0.9542
	20	0.1185	0.1096	0.9572	0.9609
	30	0.0853	0.0843	0.9695	0.9688
DenseNet121	10	0.1897	0.0981	0.9240	0.9576
	20	0.1999	0.0968	0.9223	0.9721
	30	0.1446	0.0859	0.9406	0.9710
MobileNet_V2	10	0.1992	0.1072	0.9321	0.9665
	20	0.1003	0.0352	0.9630	0.9866
	30	0.0625	0.0265	0.9756	0.9888
VGG16	10	0.3556	0.2946	0.8418	0.8616
	20	0.2937	0.1498	0.8700	0.9509
	30	0.3137	0.1529	0.8659	0.9420
VGG19	10	0.3935	0.2776	0.8269	0.8940
	20	0.3621	0.1652	0.8103	0.9397
	30	0.3459	0.3115	0.8276	0.8326
Xception	10	0.1715	0.0982	0.9375	0.9643
	20	0.1376	0.0789	0.9525	0.9721
	30	0.0920	0.0546	0.9664	0.9733

and step taken for every epoch for training and validation. Below we have described the training performance of all the models which we have used in table 2. The table consists of the model's name, the number of epochs, training loss and validation loss reading at different epochs and also contains the training accuracy (TA) and the validation accuracy (VA) of the models. We have recorded these accuracies and loss of models at different epochs for its evaluation and selected the best performance model which is DenseNet201, DenseNet169, MobileNet_V2 and Xception. While VGG 16, VGG19 and DenseNet121 didn't perform well and showed less accuracy. The accuracy which we have achieved with the proposed work at thirty epochs for the best performance model is as follows: with DenseNet201 TA is 97.49 and VA 96.43, with DenseNet169 TA is 96.95 and VA 96.88, with MobileNet_V2 TA is 97.59 and VA 98.88 and with Xception TA is 96.66 and VA 97.33. We have presented

Figure 5. Shown the plot between the training and validation loss and accuracy of DenseNet169, the final TA is 96.95 and VA is 96.88 and loss is 0.085 and validation loss is 0.084

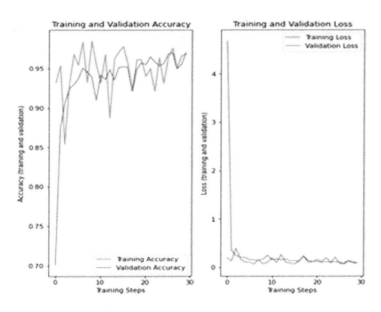

Figure 6. Shown the plot between the training and validation loss and accuracy of MobileNet¬_V2, the final TA is 97.56 and VA is 98.88 and loss is 0.062 and validation loss is 0.026

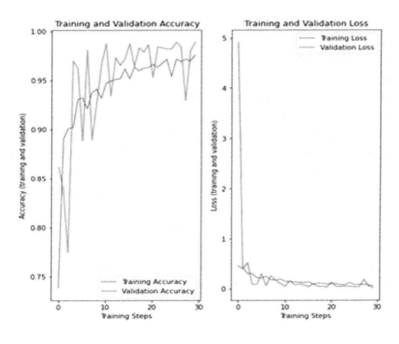

Figure 7. Shown the plot between the training and validation loss and accuracy of Xception, the final TA is 96.64 and VA is 97.33 and loss is 0.092 and validation loss is 0.054

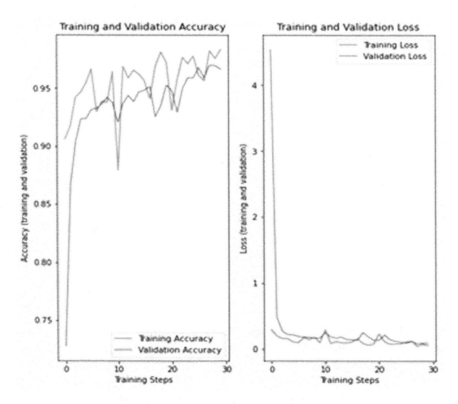

models that can aid in the diagnosis and classification of brain tumors since these four models perform better than the others. These accuracy plots and loss plots for model training and validation are also displayed below.

Below figures 4, 5, 6 and 7 represent the best model performance plots. The plot between the training accuracy and validation accuracy of the models and the plot between the training loss and validation loss at different epochs ten, twenty and thirty. The accuracy plot represents at every epoch the model learns from the input data and how it classifies the correct output and used validation input for its performance evaluation at every epoch to classify the correct output. The loss plot represents the model performance i.e., decreasing the loss shown the model performing well. Both the losses training and validation should decrease to find the best performance model. The figure 7 represent DenseNet201, 8 represent DenseNet169, 9 represent MobileNet_V2 and 10 represent Xception performance plot for training and validation of these models.

CONCLUSION

The early detection of BT lead doctor to finalize the better plan for treatment. In this study we have used the different pre-trained model and used them to build the proposed work. The accuracy which we have achieved with the proposed work at thirty epochs for the best performance model is as follows: with DenseNet201 TA is 97.49 and VA 96.43, with DenseNet169 TA is 96.95 and VA 96.88, with MobileNet_V2 TA is 97.59 and VA 98.88 and with Xception TA is 96.66 and VA 97.33. While VGG 16, VGG19 and DenseNet121 didn't perform well and showed less accuracy.

REFERENCES

Abbas, S., & Mahmoud, A. M. (2021). DiaMe: IoMT deep predictive model based on threshold aware region growing technique. *International Journal of Electrical & Computer Engineering, 11*(5).

Amin, J., Sharif, M., Yasmin, M., Saba, T., Anjum, M. A., & Fernandes, S. L. (2019). A new approach for brain tumor segmentation and classification based on score level fusion using transfer learning. *Journal of Medical Systems, 43*(11), 1–16. doi:10.100710916-019-1453-8 PMID:31643004

Carvalho, T., De Rezende, E. R., Alves, M. T., Balieiro, F. K., & Sovat, R. B. (2017, December). Exposing computer generated images by eye's region classification via transfer learning of VGG19 CNN. In *2017 16th IEEE International Conference on Machine Learning and Applications (ICMLA)* (pp. 866-870). IEEE. doi:10.1109/CCWC.2018.8301729

Chollet, F. (2017). Xception: Deep learning with depthwise separable convolutions. In *Proceedings of the IEEE conference on computer vision and pattern recognition* (pp. 1251-1258). 10.1109/CVPR.2017.195

Das, S., Aranya, O. R. R., & Labiba, N. N. (2019, May). Brain tumor classification using convolutional neural network. In *2019 1st International Conference on Advances in Science, Engineering and Robotics Technology (ICASERT)* (pp. 1-5). IEEE. 10.1109/ICASERT.2019.8934603

Huang, G., Liu, Z., Van Der Maaten, L., & Weinberger, K. Q. (2017). Densely connected convolutional networks. In *Proceedings of the IEEE conference on computer vision and pattern recognition* (pp. 4700-4708). IEEE.

Jaiswal, A., Gianchandani, N., Singh, D., Kumar, V., & Kaur, M. (2021). Classification of the COVID-19 infected patients using DenseNet201 based deep transfer learning. *Journal of Biomolecular Structure & Dynamics*, *39*(15), 5682–5689. doi:10.1080/07391102.2020.1788642 PMID:32619398

Krizhevsky, A., Sutskever, I., & Hinton, G. E. (2012). Imagenet classification with deep convolutional neural networks. *Advances in Neural Information Processing Systems*, 25.

Kumar, K. A., Prasad, A. Y., & Metan, J. (2022). A hybrid deep CNN-Cov-19-Res-Net Transfer learning architype for an enhanced Brain tumor Detection and Classification scheme in medical image processing. *Biomedical Signal Processing and Control*, *76*, 103631. doi:10.1016/j.bspc.2022.103631

Pravitasari, A. A., Iriawan, N., Almuhayar, M., Azmi, T., Irhamah, I., Fithriasari, K., Purnami, S. W., & Ferriastuti, W. (2020). UNet-VGG16 with transfer learning for MRI-based brain tumor segmentation. *TELKOMNIKA*, *18*(3), 1310–1318. doi:10.12928/telkomnika.v18i3.14753

Qassim, H., Verma, A., & Feinzimer, D. (2018, January). Compressed residual-VGG16 CNN model for big data places image recognition. In *2018 IEEE 8th Annual Computing and Communication Workshop and Conference (CCWC)* (pp. 169-175). IEEE.

Sandler, M., Howard, A., Zhu, M., Zhmoginov, A., & Chen, L. C. (2018). Mobilenetv2: Inverted residuals and linear bottlenecks. In *Proceedings of the IEEE conference on computer vision and pattern recognition* (pp. 4510-4520). IEEE.

Sultan, H. H., Salem, N. M., & Al-Atabany, W. (2019). Multi-classification of brain tumor images using deep neural network. *IEEE Access: Practical Innovations, Open Solutions*, *7*, 69215–69225. doi:10.1109/ACCESS.2019.2919122

Swati, Z. N. K., Zhao, Q., Kabir, M., Ali, F., Ali, Z., Ahmed, S., & Lu, J. (2019). Brain tumor classification for MR images using transfer learning and fine-tuning. *Computerized Medical Imaging and Graphics*, *75*, 34–46. doi:10.1016/j.compmedimag.2019.05.001 PMID:31150950

Varshni, D., Thakral, K., Agarwal, L., Nijhawan, R., & Mittal, A. (2019, February). Pneumonia detection using CNN based feature extraction. In *2019 IEEE international conference on electrical, computer and communication technologies (ICECCT)* (pp. 1-7). IEEE.

Zhou, Q., Zhu, W., Li, F., Yuan, M., Zheng, L., & Liu, X. (2022). Transfer Learning of the ResNet-18 and DenseNet-121 Model Used to Diagnose Intracranial Hemorrhage in CT Scanning. *Current Pharmaceutical Design*, 28(4), 287–295. doi:10.2174/13 8161282766621121343357 PMID:34961458

Chapter 5
Big Data in the Context
of Digital Journalism

Mustafa Eren Akpınar

https://orcid.org/0000-0002-3917-3203

İstanbul Aydın University, Turkey

ABSTRACT

In today's technology age, digitalization is an important issue within the framework of the globalizing world structure, the internet's gaining momentum, and becoming a part of life also changes daily life practices. For this reason, many individuals, institutions, and organizations have to develop and transform themselves in order to keep up with the structure of the changing world. Journalism practices are some of the structures that need to adapt to the new digital world by improving themselves within the framework of this change and transformation. For this reason, in the context of this study, the perception of journalism and journalism practices, which is one of the structures that have transformed in the light of the changing world balances and perceptions, will be examined; the formation of people to become the data of the digital world and the concept of digital journalism will be examined by emphasizing the concept of big data, which is the main formation of this data. It is examined by the method of literature review through the technological determinism approach.

INTRODUCTION

The traditional concept of journalism, which can be considered to have started with the 17th century, has to transform with today's technology world, especially because it cannot keep up with the speed provided by mobile technologies. In

DOI: 10.4018/978-1-6684-5264-6.ch005

this case, although it does not cause the complete disappearance of the traditional journalism, the written press, it causes a great loss of value. Because traditional journalism understandings and practices can no longer meet today's need for speed and cannot catch up with the transformation speed of the digital world, which is developing day by day. For this reason, the attitudes of individuals who are getting used to the opportunities offered by the internet and mobile technologies towards primitive journalism practices are changing according to the traditional or today's perception, and the traditional journalism perception is replaced by the digital journalism perception. In its simplest definition, digital journalism can be defined as journalism practices made through the internet, and it brings with it some different parameters and concepts as well as journalism.

At the beginning of these is the need of people for technological devices such as phones or computers. Almost every person in today's world feels a need for technology and technological developments are included in people's lives in such a short time that after a while technology becomes more difficult than a tool. This is due to the advancement of technology day by day. However, the fact that technology is a natural part of life brings with it some problems. The most important of these problems is the increasing use of technological tools and in the light of these uses, individuals become individuals who are used by technology rather than using technology. Because, whether people using technology realize it or not, a digital footprint is formed and when these footprints accumulate, big data emerges. In order to benefit from big data and digital footprint, every social media application or every website implements some applications called cookies for the service it offers, and most of the social media accounts require certain permissions when they are installed on your phone or computer. Although these permissions vary according to the application, they can usually be listed as accessing files, accessing the camera, accessing the microphone, and accessing messages in some applications, and individuals who know that applications or sites will not work well if these permissions are not given, often approve these permissions without reading them, and after approval, that application is no longer available. or the site starts to store your data. After this storage process, since that application or site can better analyze your interests, it starts to produce personalized content and campaigns and processes your personal information for its own benefit, using your data, often without your knowledge.

For this reason, in the first part of this study, digitalization, internet, digital journalism, technological determinism are explained with an emphasis on approach. In the second part, by interpreting what big data is and how it relates to data journalism, the study is concluded by making a discussion on how a change is experienced with digitalization, which is one of the changing journalism practices, and how they can be associated with big data.

Digitization, Digital Journalism and Technological Determinism

Digitization emerges as one of the most important concepts of today's world, and digitalization stands out with its constantly evolving and transforming structure among the accelerating technologies of social and individual life (Olcay, 2018, p. 92), which exposes not only the individual but also the societies with different normative structural transformations. becomes a concept. However, it is not correct to see the concept of digitalization only as a single concept. The concept of digitalization is the product of a process that emerges as a result of a certain process and actually occurs in the light of certain accumulations. Therefore, in order to understand digitalization, it is a better move to first understand the internet. Because the internet is one of the most striking examples of new media (Çetinkaya, 2018, p. 100) and is a phenomenon that conducive to the emergence of both the concept of new media and the concept of digitalization.

Therefore, it is not correct to define digitalization without having a brief knowledge of the internet. Perceiving and evaluating the Internet as an intricate communication platform created by new media types (Özdemir, 2019, p. 11) is the right approach. In fact, this is an indication that the internet is and has a leading structural position in today's communication technologies. In this context, digitalization is actually a product of internet-based technological determinism. An example of this is the emergence of new forms, both interpersonal and inter-communal, that is, mass-based, with digitalization (Güngör, 2020, p. 400). It can be considered as an example of the technological determinism approach, an approach pioneered by names such as Harold Adam Innis, McLuhan, and Nicolas Negroponte. The technological determinism approach believes that this situation has the power to determine social activities, based on the idea that technology has an independent mode of action (Çoban, 2013, p. 2). Although the Technological Determinism approach, which forms the basis of this belief, is basically the same, it also brings some minor differences. For example, according to Innis, communication technologies are the main determinants of both social and economic structures (Yaylagül, 2019, p. 69), and in fact, technology has a guiding structure in our lives.

In addition, McLuhan (Güngör, 2020, p. 184), influenced by Innis' views, examines technological determinism from a similar window with Innis. McLuhan, arguing that the world has turned into a global village with communication technologies and that everything is interconnected (Yaylagül, 2019, p. 70), takes Innis' views one step further and prefers to examine technology with its global dimension apart from its social and economic dimension. In this way, it analyzes today's requirements from a broader perspective, emphasizing the importance of technology and digitalization.

In the context of today's conditions and within the framework of the technological determinism approach, the importance of technology and digitalization is better understood, and it becomes a necessity to change some of today's practices. One of these requirements is the change of newspapers, which are a product of communication technology. First of all, newspapers, which serve the purpose of providing limited news flow in limited regions, become more appealing to larger masses with the presence of the printing press in the light of developing technologies. Afterwards, it further develops the audiences it addresses with radio, television, and finally the internet, one of the most important elements of today's technology world. However, considering today's technology world, it cannot be denied that there has been a great change that radio and television cannot do. The best example of this is the fact that the importance of newspapers and magazines, which were the print media, did not suffer a great loss when radio and television came out. However, with the developing technologies and the new generation born into this technology, the newspapers, which are the written press, are on the point of losing their importance to a great extent, by taking a big blow from the internet, not from radio and television. For this reason, almost all of the newspapers, which are print media, are beginning to need digitalization in order not to disappear. In this case, digital journalism, which is basically the same, reveals the concepts of internet journalism or, in other words, online journalism.

Digital journalism, or in other words, online journalism, can be defined as the fourth type of journalism that serves to gather and disseminate news alongside newspapers, radio and television (Bardoel & Deuze, 2001, p. 92). From this point of view, it is easier to realize how important digitalization is, and it would not be wrong to say that journalism practices trying to adapt to digitalization have gained a very rapid acceleration in adaptation. In addition, with the effect of digitalization, the competition of many newspapers with each other over social media and the internet adds a new type of competition to their sectoral competition and allows that competition among newspapers to be fueled. In addition, the journalism profession, which could only be done by those with a certain financial support due to the high printing, publishing, and distribution burdens of the newspapers, is experiencing a great rise with the increase of the internet and digitalization. Many journalists are now able to do internet broadcasting without spending a lot of money, and this already makes their race even tougher with the addition of new factors to the competition among the print media.

However, in this competitive environment brought about by digital journalism, it is necessary to mention two different variables. These are divided into institutions with both print and online media, and institutions with only online media (Çetinkaya, 2018, p. 106). Based on this distinction, it should be realized that although there is more competition in the online environment, that is, in the digital environment, this multi-competitive environment cannot always be protected in every medium. It should be known that media with only digital presence are relatively more disadvantageous against those with print media. Because it is observed that media channels with only digital presence may not be able to appeal to all audiences, and at the same time, it is more difficult to stand out in the complex and crowded environment of the internet and digital. For example, it should not be forgotten that there is a huge gap between the brand awareness of a newspaper with print media and the awareness of a newspaper that only exists in digital media.

DATA JOURNALISM AND BIG DATA RELATIONSHIP

Along with digital journalism, the concept of data journalism, which has entered our lives with developing technologies, is a concept that is a little more difficult to understand due to its more complicated structure than digital journalism. For this reason, it can be confused with other concepts from time to time. In order to avoid this conceptual confusion, first of all, it is necessary to know what data and journalism are, and then to examine what data journalism is. Although the concept called data has many different definitions, it is generally defined as the main element, knowledge, data muta, done (Turkish Language Institution, 2011, p. 2480), which is the basis of a research, a discussion and a reasoning based on observation and experimentation. Journalism, on the other hand, is defined as "the job of the journalist" (Turkish Language Institution, 2011, p. 909), who undertakes the task of reporting (Birsen, Oğur, & Özmen, 2018, p. 372). According to Appelgren and Nygren, data journalism, on the other hand, is about finding news in an area that no one has narrated or researched, unlike the daily work of newspapers in newsrooms where the routine news flow is dominant (Cited by Narin et al., 2017, p. 223). In this context, although data journalism is thought of as a type of journalism that creates a source for digital content production (Kazan, 2019, p. 103), it is actually a type of journalism that only deepens and complements journalism, unlike journalism practices that are completely independent of or replace traditional journalism (Narin et al., 2017, p. 223). In fact, according to some views, it is not correct to see data journalism as a different form of journalism. Because journalism has been dealing with data since its early days, and the type of journalism defined as data journalism is actually not different from the traditional journalism understanding (Narin et al., 2017, pp. 223-224).

In this context, there is no harm in comparing data journalism with investigative journalism, and in data journalism, as in investigative journalism, many data are processed and followed. In both types of journalism, research and data acquisition are basically aimed, and this shows that both journalism types are actually in a relationship to each other. The best example of this is in both investigative journalism and data journalism, the detailed investigation of all the events that have no relationship or, on the contrary, a certain relationship with each other (Aslan, Bayrakçı, & Küçükvardar, 2016, p. 58) and reveal the connections of these events with each other. analysis of the data and then transforming it into a story, news content (Aslan, Bayrakçı, & Küçükvardar, 2016, p. 58).

However, in order for the data to be processed and converted into a story or news text, this data must first be obtained, and in fact, what enables data journalism to obtain this data is that it is a type of journalism associated with big data. Big data can be defined as data sets that are beyond traditional data processing and storage systems and are too large to be managed and analyzed with traditional systems (Ohlhorst, 2013, p. 1). Big data, which was shortened as 5V in the first definitions, was updated as 7V and then 10V over time and expanded as "Volume, Velocity, Variety, Value, Veracity, Volatility, Validity, Vulnerability, Variability and Visualization" (Act. Atalay & Çelik, 2017, pp. 156- 157). Within the framework of this expansion, each concept is defined in different ways. However, it will be a very sufficient way to refer to 5V in order to understand big data. Because, basically, the output point of big data is also related to 5V.

- **Volume:** means that the data pool that grows exponentially has no upper limit (Patgiri & Ahmed, 2016: 19), that is, it basically does not have a limited volume.
- **Velocity:** It is completely related to the speed of the data (Tole, 2013, p. 32). The speed of data access is a point to be considered in this regard.
- **Variety:** Variety, which is divided into three as structured, semi-structured and unstructured, appears as the type of data analyzed (Aksu & Güzeller, 2019).
- **Value:** According to Khan et al., it is expressed as the quality of the stored data and the benefit that can be derived from this data (Act. Aksu & Güzeller, 2019).
- **Veracity:** Veracity, which is the fifth feature of big data, is defined as the probability and consistency of data (Tole, 2013, p. 33).

However, the necessary expansion studies are still continuing for the developing technologies and the requirements of the transforming digital world. Because big data is a phenomenon that covers much more than the technological structure of a phenomenon (Altunışık, 2015, p. 48). Because of this, it would be more accurate to explain big data as a term that offers a data flow and storage in itself, which cannot be examined within the framework of standard data collection steps.

What constitutes this data warehouse, called big data, is the product of individuals putting their data on the internet environment consciously or unconsciously through many channels such as social media, internet, scientific studies. Because, together with the internet, digitalization and technological developments, each individual sometimes uploads their own data to a social media platform, sometimes allows cookies on the sites they use, and sometimes makes their personal data accessible through completely different methods. They allow people to return with personalized content or advertisements, and in fact, this concept, called big data, is nothing but a data repository that can be accessed by brands or sites at any time, consisting of the permissions and information that people give themselves to social media or internet sites.

CONCLUSION

In this study, by focusing on the digitalized world in the light of developing technologies, the positive and negative benefits of technology, digitality and the internet are mentioned conceptually and contextually, and examples are given by talking about what digitalization and the internet are through a technological determinist approach. The impact of these concepts on today's society and the hegemony of individuals are mentioned, and interpretations are made about the transforming world order, and then what journalism is and how journalism's historical adventure is. Definitions have been made about the transformation of traditional journalism into digital journalism with the effect of digitalization, and in the light of these, the relationship between data journalism and big data has been dealt with, and the views on the equivalents in today's world have been emphasized through the definitions presented as a result of these correlations.

Along with these definitions and explanations, the concepts of digital world, journalism and big data were explained, and today's current situation was mentioned, and interpretations were made with the support of the definitions in order to realize how important it is to adapt to the digitalized world. Considering what could happen if one cannot adapt to today's technology world, information was given about the idea that institutions that do not exist in the digital world may face the danger of extinction. Thus, in order to better understand journalism and journalists, explanations were made with the support of literature. In the following sections, some open-ended discourses were produced in order to think about what these concepts actually evoke or mean by transferring big data through digital journalism and data journalism.

As a result, in this study titled "Big Data in the Context of Digital Journalism", the importance of digitalization was emphasized by emphasizing what journalism is, what digitality is, what the concepts of big data and data journalism connote. It has been tried to explain how everyone should follow a path in order to have a place in the flow of life, how digitality entered our lives, and it is aimed to gain an idea about the requirements and deficiencies of adapting to the digital age. For this, researches about the relationship between big data and digital journalism have been presented and it has been said that the feared big data concept is actually a necessity brought by the digital world, and it has been determined that it creates both a risk and an advantage in the framework of the new world order.

REFERENCES

Aksu, G., & Güzeller, C. O. (2019). *Büyük Veri: Sosyal Bilimler ile Eğitim Bilimlerinde Kullanımı ve Uygulama Alanları* [Big Data: Usage and Application Areas in Social Sciences and Educational Sciences]. Mediterranean Journal of Humanities.

Altunışık, R. (2015). Büyük Veri: Fırsatlar Kaynağı mı Yoksa Yeni Sorunlar Yumağı mı? [Big Data: A Source of Opportunities or a Mass of New Challenges?]. *Yıldız Social Science Review*, *1*(1), 45–76.

Aslan, A., Bayrakçı, S., & Küçükvardar, M. (2016). Bilişim Çağında Geleneksel Gazeteciliğin Dönüşümü: Veri Gazeteciliği [The Transformation of Traditional Journalism in the Information Age: Data Journalism]. *Marmara İletişim Dergisi*, (26), 55–70.

Atalay, M., & Çelik, E. (2017). Büyük Veri Analizinde Yapay Zeka ve Makine Öğrenmesi Uygulamaları [Applications of Artificial Intelligence and Machine Learning in Big Data Analytics]. *Mehmet Akif Ersoy Üniversitesi Sosyal Bilimler Enstitüsü Dergisi*, *9*(22), 155–172. doi:10.20875/makusobed.309727

Bardoel, J., & Deuze, M. (2001). Network Journalism: Converging Competences Of Old And New Media Professionals. *Australian Journalism Review*, *23*(2), 91–103.

Birsen, Ö., Oğur, O., & Özmen, Ş. Y. (2018). Alternatif Gazetecilik Örneği Olarak Yavaş Medyanın Geleneksel Gazetecilik Değerleri Üzerinden İncelenmesi [Examining Slow Media as an Example of Alternative Journalism through Traditional Journalistic Values]. *Anadolu Üniversitesi İletişim Bilimleri Fakültesi Uluslararası Hakemli Dergisi*, *26*(3), 370–384.

Çetinkaya, A. (2018). *İçerik Üretiminden Reklama Çevrimiçi Gazetecilik* [Online Journalism from Content Production to Advertising]. Nobel Akademik Yayınları.

Çoban, S. (2013). *Teknolojik Determinizm Bağlamında Bilgi Toplumu Strateji Belgesinin İncelenmesi* [Examination of the Information Society Strategy Document in the Context of Technological Determinism]. Akademik Bilişim Konferansları.

Güngör, N. (2020). *İletişim Kuramlar ve Yaklaşımlar (5. b.)* [Communication Theories and Approaches (5. b.)]. Siyasal Kitabevi.

Kazan, H. (2019). *Dijital Çağda Gazetecilikte Yeni Kavramlar: Robot Gazeteciliği, Veri Gazeteciliği, Hiperyerel Gazetecilik. In Dijital Çağda Habercilik Kuram ve Uygulamada Yeni Yönelimler.* Der Yayınları.

Narin, B., Ayaz, B., Fırat, F., & Fırat, D. (2017). Büyük Veri ve Gazetecilik İlişkisi Bağlamında Veri Gazeteciliği. [Data Journalism in the Context of the Relationship between Big Data and Journalism]. *AJIT-e. Online Academic Journal of Information Technology, 8*(30), 215–235. doi:10.5824/1309-1581.2017.5.010.x

Ohlhorst, F. (2013). *Big Data Analytics: Turning Big Data into Big Money.* Wiley Publicity.

Olcay, S. (2018). Sosyalleşmenin Dijitalleşmesi Olarak Sosyal Medya ve Resimler Arasında Kaybolma Bozukluğu: Photolurkıng [Disappearance Disorder Between Social Media and Pictures as the Digitalization of Socialization: Photolurking]. *Yeni Medya Elektronik Dergisi, 2*(2), 90–104. doi:10.17932/IAU. EJNM.25480200.2018.2/2.90-104

Özdemir, Z. (2019). *Dijitalleşme Sürecinde İletişim ve Haberciliğin Evrimi. In Dijital Çağda Habercilik Kuram ve Uygulamada Yeni Yönelimler.* Der Yayınları.

Patgiri, R., & Ahmed, A. (2016). Big Data: The V's of the Game Changer Paradigm. In *IEEE 18th International Conference on High Performance Computing and Communications; IEEE 14th International Conference on Smart City; IEEE 2nd International Conference on Data Science and Systems* (pp. 17-24). IEEE.

Tole, A. A. (2013). Big Data Challenges. *Database Systems Journal, 4*(3), 31–40.

Türk Dil Kurumu. (2011). *Türkçe Sözlük (11 b.)* [Turkish Dictionary (11 b.)]. Türk Dil Kurumu Yayınları.

Yaylagül, L. (2019). *Kitle İletişim Kuramları Egemen ve Eleştirel Yaklaşımlar (10 b.)* [Theories of Mass Communication Dominant and Critical Approaches (10 b.)]. Dipnot Yayınları.

Chapter 6

COVID–19 Vaccination Perceptions, Issues, and Challenges:
An Analysis of Tweets Using Machine Learning Models

Sreekantha Desai Karanam

(iD) https://orcid.org/0000-0002-5217-7006

NITTE (Deemed), India & Nitte Mahalinga Adyanthaya Memorial Institute of Technology, India

Krithin M.

NITTE (Deemed), India & Nitte Mahalinga Adyanthaya Memorial Institute of Technology, India

R. V. Kulkarni

(iD) https://orcid.org/0000-0002-7102-2421

CSIBER, Kolhapur, India

DOI: 10.4018/978-1-6684-5264-6.ch006

ABSTRACT

The vaccines are developed to protect us from diseases, and these vaccines are saving millions of people every year. The acceptance of taking COVID-19 vaccinations was affected by their knowledge and opinion on COVID-19 vaccines. The ever-increasing misinformation and opposition to take COVID-19 vaccines have created a major problem for healthcare professionals in meeting the targets set for vaccine coverage. There is an urgent need to apply supportive and inclusive approaches to enhance people's self-confidence and acceptance of these vaccines by taking away their misconceptions. To control the spread of COVID-19 disease, practicing all the social operational standards and high vaccination coverage are required. Most healthcare workers in Asia are vaccinated. This chapter reviewed the papers on COVID-19 vaccination perceptions, issues, and side effects. The authors also designed a machine learning model to analyze the perceptions of the people from analysing their tweets. This analysis provides an insight into perceptions and drives-focused vaccination programmes.

INTRODUCTION

All viruses including coronavirus that leads to Covid-19 disease undergoes evolution with time. The virus makes copies of itself with minor random modifications each time for its sustainability. Vaccines will strengthen the body immune by fighting against viruses. The safety and effectiveness of vaccines are tested rigorously. Billions of people have safely received Covid-19 vaccines already. All licensed Covid-19 vaccines have been cautiously undergone a multi-stage testing process, with a large number of clinical trials involving tens of thousands of people. These clinical trials are carefully developed to discover all safety concerns. The Covid-19 vaccination drive needs to be the top priority to achieve herd immunity. The resistance to the Covid-19 vaccine is much higher than other vaccines. The benefits such as trust, protection, social acceptance are realized from vaccination promote taking Covid-19 are by the people. The people below the age group of 54 have more resistance to the Covid-19 vaccine. The vaccination acceptance rate is also associated with existing healthcare system performance, available support facilities during pandemic times. The vaccination drive should concentrate on areas where poor people live in less hygienic conditions with low Socio-Economic Status (SES) having heavy disease burden to ensure equality of vaccine distribution to provide more rigorous disease mitigation. Today there are many conflicting problems related to the frequency of administration, vaccine efficacy and durability, preferred vaccine type, pregnant/lactating women, and vaccination in children (<18 years). These problems need to resolve in due time. Researchers discovered that there is a significantly higher risk of cardiac involvement from Covid-19 infection compared to Covid-19 vaccination.

COVAX: The COVID-19 Vaccines Global Access Facility

Covax is unique global cooperation for accelerating up the invention, development, manufacture and equitable distribution of Covid-19 vaccines. COVAX objective is to develop effective Covid-19 vaccines. The COVAX Advance Market Commitment (AMC) is an innovative financing instrument that will support the collaboration of 92 low- and middle-income economies in the COVAX facility - availing to donor-funded doses of safe and effective Covid-19 vaccines. A National Deployment and Vaccination Plans (NDVP) is an operational plan to implement and monitor the Covid-19 vaccination roll-out in a country. AMC92 countries must design a Covid-19 NDVPs and submit them. This NDVP serves as the "one-country plan" and main framework for a country's vaccine distribution and vaccination process.

The list of *Acronyms used in this paper used* are shown in Table 1

REVIEW OF RECENT LITERATURE

Perceptions and Issues Concerned with Covid-19 Vaccination

Wang et al. (2021a) have investigated on individuals person's Willingness to Pay (WTP) and financing mechanism options for Covid-19 vaccination in China. The authors applied a network stratified random sampling survey method during the period 1st to 18th March 2020 by involving 2058 people. The survey questions included parameters such as out-of-pocket WTP, financing option priority, risk perception and attitude towards Covid-19 perception. The authors also applied multi-variable Tobit regression to compute impact factors for people's out-of-pocket WTP. The results of this survey revealed that the individual's mean WTP expense for full Covid-19 vaccination was CNY 254 (USD 36.8) with a median of CNY 100 (USD 14.5). Most respondents believed that governments (90.9%) and health insurance (78.0%) should pay for partial or full expenses of Covid-19 vaccination, only 84.3% stated that individuals need to pay. Wang et al. (2021a) have conducted an online survey to assess a cross-sectional, population-based the willingness, hesitancy, and coverage of the Covid-19 vaccine in China. Authors collected 8742 valid samples and classified (n = 3902; 44.6%) as the vaccine-priority group and the non-priority group (n = 4840; 55.4%). The percentage of people's trust in the vaccine, delivery system, and government were 69.0%, 78.0% and 81.3%, respectively. 67.1% of the participants were reportedly willing to accept the Covid-19 vaccination, only 9.0%

Table 1. The list of Acronyms used in this paper

Acronym	Description	Acronym	Description
Covid-19	Corona Virus Disease of 2019	cMRI	Cardiac Magnetic Resonance Imaging
WHO	World Health Organization	DHVI	Duke's Human Vaccine Institute
COVAX	The COVID-19 Vaccines Global Access Facility	BERT	Bidirectional Encoder Representations from Transformers
NDVPs	National Deployment and Vaccination Plans	IPFS	Inter Planetary File System
WTP	Willingness To Pay	BCG	Bacille Calmette-Guerin, is a vaccine for tuberculosis
COVAX AMC92	92 countries entering Advance Market Commitment for Covid-19 vaccination	18F-FDG PET/ CT	Positron Emission Tomography with2-deoxy-2-[fluorine-18] Fluoro-D-Glucose
UNICEF	United Nations International Children's Emergency Fund	LDLT	Living Donor Liver Transplantation
SES	Socio Economic status.	PPARs	Peroxisome Proliferator-Activated Receptors
ICU	Intensive Care Unit	DM	Diabetes Mellitus
RTPCR	Reverse Transcription Polymerase Chain Reaction	SARS-CoV-2	Severe Acute Respiratory Syndrome CoronaVirus-2
LLPCs	Long-Lived Plasma Cells	VRV	Vaccine Record Verification
SBI	Society of Breast Imaging	DWMs	Dark Web Marketing
LAP	Lymph Adeno Pathy	CPH	Clinical Public Health
HCWs	Health Care Workers	VOC	Variants of Concern
RNA	Ribo Nucleic Acid	ACADIC	Artificial Intelligence and Data Innovation Consortium

refused it. 834 (35.5%) reported vaccine hesitancy, including acceptors with doubts (48.8%), refusers (39.4%), and delayers (11.8%).

Kessels, Luyten, and Tubeuf (2021) surveyed on Belgians representative sample of 2,060 people during October 2020. Regression analyses discovered the predictors associated with willingness and attitude towards Covid-19 vaccination. The results of this survey revealed that 34% of the participants said that they will take vaccination for Covid-19 and 39% are not sure about taking the vaccination. The factors affecting the acceptance of vaccination are associated with age, support from the government's dealing with the Covid-19 pandemic, medical risk, spoken language, gender, and to a small extent having known someone who was hospitalised because of Covid-19. Authors discovered that 17% (N = 349) of samples were not interested in getting the Covid-19 vaccination. These are young, French spoken working women, with minimum education, and do not belong to Covid-19 risk clusters. They were not happy with the government's activities and support for a pandemic, and even do not know somebody who was hospitalized due to Covid-19 infection. Caspi et al. (2021) studyed the association between people getting Covid-19 vaccination and socio-economic status (SES). Israel's Ministry of Health has provided a nationwide ecological study using open-sourced, de-identified, summarized data for this study purpose. The association between SES, vaccination percentage and active Covid-19 cases was explored during the vaccination camp using weighted Pearson correlations. The authors wanted to estimate the sufficiency of first dose vaccination completed when compared with Covid-19 disease cases. A metric for computing the vaccination need ratio was designed by dividing the total number of active cases (per 10,000 people) versus the vaccinated percentage of the people above sixty years of age. The correlation between this matrix and the SES was analysed.

A negative correlation was discovered between the Covid-19 active cases and the vaccinated people percentage of the study population in each municipality (r=-0.47, 95% confidence interval -0.59 to -0.30). The vaccination percentage considerably correlated with the municipal SES (r=0.83, 95% confidence interval 0.79 to 0.87). This same status remained over a five-week time. A negative correlation between the vaccination needs ratio and municipal SES (r=-0.80, 95% confidence interval -0.88 to -0.66) was observed. Lower Covid-19 vaccination percentage was related to lower SES and high active disease burden. Brown et al. (2021) presented a multi-modal pictorial view of axillary lymphadenopathy in patients vaccinated against Covid-19 recently. The vaccination program for large masses is in progress throughout the world to fight against Covid-19 disease. Now it has become vital for radiologists to update their knowledge about Covid-19 vaccination in the differential diagnosis of unilateral axillary lymphadenopathy. Radiologists should be aware of typical appearances across all imaging methods. The authors studied the current regulations on the management of unilateral axillary lymphadenopathy in the recent Covid-19 vaccination programme. Hyland et al. (2021) studied the hesitance and resistance problems to the Covid-19 vaccination programme which causes a serious challenge to attain the required vaccine consumption levels to reach herd immunity levels in the general population. The nationwide representative samples of the people of the Republic of Ireland (N ¼ 1041) and the United Kingdom (N ¼ 2025) were assessed. The authors traced the attitudes towards Covid-19 vaccination using longitudinal data during the pandemic. This study was designed as a quantitative, longitudinal design. The attitudes of the adult towards Covid-19 vaccination at three periods from March to August 2020 was analysed. The results have shown a statistically considerable increase in resistance to Covid-19 vaccination in Irish (from 9.5% to 18.1%) and British (from 6.2% to 10%) people.

Umasabor-Bubu et al. (2021) investigated on the high coverage of influenza vaccination and the scope to stop a proportion of Covid-19 morbidity and mortality. Authors investigated to check the flu-vaccination association with severe Covid-19 disease. The authors examined the admissions to intensive care unit (ICU), ventilator-use, mortality, hospital length of stay and total ICU days. These observations revealed that flu-vaccination was correlated with a considerably reduced likelihood of ICU admission especially among aged <65 and non-obese people. The public health drive of flu vaccination would help to control the intense requirements for critical Covid-19 care and huge stocks of unused Covid-19 vaccines. Authors reviewed the state of 588 Covid-19 hospitalized patients admitted during the peak of the pandemic's first wave, between 03/12/2020 and 06/30/2020 at SUNY Downstate Medical Center; a New York State dedicated COVID-only hospital. Patients reported on admission if they had been previously vaccinated for Influenza (Yes or No) during the last flu season (09/01/19 - 03/31/20). Results revealed the increased likelihood of a need for an ICU admission among self-reported non-flu-vaccinated relative to self-reported flu-vaccinated patients only for ages <65 (aOR: 4.16, 95%CI: 1.03-16.73), and non-obese patients (aOR: 2.61, 95% CI: 1.35-5.03. Patelarou et al. (2021) made proposed that majority of the people should be vaccinated to achieve herd immunity to fight against the Covid-19 pandemic third wave was made.

Safe and effective vaccine drives are very essential to reach the required levels of herd immunity. Vaccinating all nursing professionals and students is very vital since they are going to be the role models for educating, counselling and guiding the patients. This paper applied a multi-centre, cross-sectional design. An online survey of 2249 undergraduate nursing students was carried out in seven universities in Greece, Albania, Cyprus, Spain, Italy, the Czech Republic, and Kosovo. The data was collected from December 2020 to January 2021 in all these countries. The results revealed that 43.8% of students have accepted a safe and effective Covid-19 vaccine. The rate of accepting vaccines was higher in Italian nursing students. The factors that influenced vaccination were male gender (p = 0.008), no working experience in healthcare facilities during the pandemic (p = 0.001), vaccination for influenza in 2019 and 2020 (p < 0.001), trust in doctors (p < 0.001), governments and experts (p = 0.012), high level of knowledge (p < 0.001) and fear of Covid-19 (p < 0.001). Duke, Posch, and Green (2021) studied the side effects after the Covid-19 vaccination and one of them is axillary adenopathy. The authors discovered four patients with axillary adenopathy after vaccinating with Moderna and Pfizer-BioNTech for Covid-19 disease. These patients revealed unilateral axillary adenopathy and adenopathy continuously for two to three weeks after vaccination. A team of physicians from Harvard recommended a clinical follow-up with sonographic imaging if clinical concern continues even after six weeks. Since a large number of people are vaccinated, radiologists need to become alert on possible vaccine-introduced unilateral axillary adenopathy on screening and diagnostic breast imaging to decrease the number of extra biopsies conducted on this patient's pool.

Cucunawangsih et al. (2021) noticed that the healthcare workers (HCWs) are at enhanced exposure to Covid-19 disease because this HCW are dealing with Covid-19 patients. Indonesia has decided to vaccinate HCW first in the Covid-19 national vaccination drive. The number of new Covid-19 cases reported daily is high and also the statistics about the efficiency of the vaccine in HCW was not readily available. So HCW continues to be at risk of exposure to Covid-19 disease. The author's objective was to identify the covid-19 affected HCWs at Siloam teaching hospital, Indonesia. An online and off-line survey was carried out by the prevention and control unit of the hospital for Covid-19 infection. The results from this study revealed that those 1040 HCWs who have taken two doses of the Covid-19 vaccine, only 13 (1.25%) were tested positive in RTPCR in about 5 days after the second dose of vaccination. Therefore, the HCW with symptoms after the second dose of vaccination need not be assumed as vaccine-related symptoms, and Covid-19 testing should be carried out for HCWs on regular basis. Pal, Bhadada, and Misra (2021) summarized the existing evidence on the consumption of Covid-19 vaccines in diabetes mellitus patients was presented. The authors carried out an extensive literature survey on the side effects of Covid-19 vaccines in patients with type 1 and type 2 diabetes mellitus. The new Covid-19 variant forecasts a poor medical diagnosis in patients with diabetes mellitus (DM). Early precautions are the best ways for managing the dangers related to Covid-19 in patients with DM. The first step is to get full vaccination as early as possible. Regular vaccination for pneumonia, influenza and hepatitis B is suggested in patients with DM for good health and considerable safety. The medical data is revealing a strong neutralizing antibody effect in Covid-19 cases with DM, vaccination in individuals with DM is justified.

The people with DM are at a heavy risk of infection to Covid-19 disease so they should be given high priority for the vaccination programme. Mir et al. (2021) analyzed the people's acceptance for Covid-19 vaccination which is vital for the successful implementation of a vaccination program. The objective of this study is to discover the crucial parameters affecting Indians perceptions and intentions to consume the Covid-19 vaccine. This study revealed that perceived benefits, social norms, and trust are associated considerably with people's acceptance of Covid-19 vaccinations. The risk perceptions and social media exposure are not significantly affected people's attitudes towards Covid-19 vaccinations. Albert et al.'s (2021) study discovered that Covid-19 vaccination often causes minor side effects. These side-effects may become very critical after the second dose. The authors reported more cases of serious side effects with a case of a 24-year-old man who was admitted to the hospital with acute substernal chest pain, four days after his second dose of Covid-19 Moderna vaccination. Laboratory studies also reported elevated troponins and negative viral serologies. Cardiac magnetic resonance imaging (cMRI) demonstrated edema and delayed gadolinium enlargement of the left ventricle in a mid-myocardial and epicardial distribution. Myocarditis has been reported after taking many vaccines earlier also, so extensive research is required to support the relationship with myocarditis after taking Covid-19 vaccines.

Blanchard-Rohner et al. (2021) stated that herd immunity and mass vaccination are essential to fight against Covid-19 disease. The vaccination disbelief is increasing in many countries, estimating the acceptance to get vaccinated for Covid-19 is very important for public health across the world. The objective of this survey is to investigate the quantity of risk to individual and family Covid-19 infection and available ICU facilities during the pandemics affects the perception about Covid-19 vaccines. A two-phase study was conducted for comparing the perceptions of vaccines before and after the pandemic. The people of the UK were surveyed in October 2019 about their vaccination perceptions, and again in a second phase survey in April 2020. In the second phase also, the same questions were asked to the same people related to Covid-19 exposure and vaccine attitudes just like in the first study. This study integrated the results from both surveys one before and the other after the Covid-19 pandemic. Regression analysis of the influence of personal and public health factors on perceptions towards Covid-19 vaccination was carried out. The first phase study was in October 2019 considering a national representative sample size of 1653 UK citizens. The same citizen who was involved in the first phase were included in the second phase also in April 2020, but only 1194 (72%) participated. In total, 85% of participants (and 55% of vaccine sceptics) are going to accept the vaccination for Covid-19.

Acceptance for Covid-19 vaccination was higher amongst all groups. Khubchandani and Macias (2021) surveyed the Covid-19 vaccines which were authorized for public use in America in late 2020 and early 2021. Social and print media highlighted the hesitancy and resistance to Covid-19 vaccination in racial and ethnic minorities. The Covid-19 vaccination hesitancy association with racial and ethnic minorities, unique socio-demographic and cognitive correlates was not clear. The objective of this survey was to investigate Covid-19 vaccine hesitancy among African Americans and Hispanics (the largest minority groups in the U.S.). The authors carried out a comprehensive study of literature with a final pool of 13 studies (n ¼ 107,841 participants) who have participated in this study. The major predictors of vaccine hesitancy in African Americans and Hispanics. The socio-demographic characteristics (e.g., age, gender, income, education, and household size); medical mistrust and history of racial discrimination; exposure to myths and misinformation, perceived risk of getting infected with Covid-19; beliefs about vaccines and past vaccine compliance, and concerns about the safety, efficacy, and side effects from the Covid-19 vaccines. Unless a proactive approach is adopted,

Covid-19 vaccination rates in certain populations would continue to remain lower than what is desirable. Ala'a and Tarhini (2021) discovered the challenges in controlling the Covid-19 pandemic waves in different situations and capabilities. The recently approved vaccines have generated good hope to combat this pandemic very effectively through the widespread vaccine programs. If a large percentage of people are vaccinated, then attaining herd immunity would be possible. The range of percentage of vaccinated people changes significantly from country to country. Authors would like to identify the factors such as distribution and delivery of the vaccine to distant places is an issue or perception of the people to get vaccinated is the prime issue. Adequate Covid-19 vaccination is affected by the availability, distribution of vaccines but also by cultural and social norms in the community as well as the complexity of human behaviours. Hughes et al. (2021) studied the critical factors to improve the immunity of the public with a fewer number of vaccines against contagious diseases such as Covid-19. Although intuition provides several mitigation strategies that may be effective which remain largely untested. A genetic programming strategy was applied to identify new ways for understanding public health issues by the governments. This paper proposed a social graph-based genetic programming method for fighting against the SARS-CoV-2 virus. The authors conducted experiments and the results have given a lot of promising insight. A portal to host the system and to present results for graphs and pandemics would be created. Researchers can submit their methods to the portal for automated valuation purposes. These results will be stored in the cloud for further research.

Mertz (2020) studied Covid-19 pandemic waves which are spreading and killing millions of people across the world. In these times there is an urgent need for an effective vaccine to fight against Covid-19 disease and save lives. The researchers at Duke's Human Vaccine Institute (DHVI) are developing a pan-coronavirus vaccine. This pan coronavirus vaccine is expected to fight against all variants of coronavirus in general. Research groups at Entos Pharmaceuticals, Inc. of Edmonton, AB, Canada, are also working on a pan-coronavirus vaccine. This pan-coronavirus vaccine identifies the virus as a pathogen and starts a strong defence against the virus. The variants of coronavirus are branches of the coronavirus tree only. DHVI is expecting with this pan-coronavirus vaccine to fight at the central trunk, said Thomas Denny, chief executive of DHVI in Durham, NC. SARS-CoV-2 virus is leading to new Covid-19 disease. Khade, Yabaji, and Srivastava (2021) said that SARS-CoV-2 contains RNA as genetic material, and it is a 79% duplicate of the bat SARS-CoV genome. This disease is highly infectious from human to human and the symptoms are like to flu. The old age people and immuno-compromised people are critically affected, and doctors across the world have used various methods for its treatment such as re-purposing of drugs including antimalarial drugs, hydroxychloroquine and anti-viral drugs.

The countries with restrictions on BCG vaccination policy are troubled very badly compared to countries with BCG vaccination implementation policy. The BCG vaccination policy helped to lower the total number of Covid-19 cases or supported the increased recovery rate. Countries like the USA, Italy, where BCG vaccination policy is not very mandatory are worst affected. However, countries like India, China, Iran, etc. where the BCG vaccination policy is mandatory found to be either affected to a minimum extent or have a high recovery rate. The trained immunity prevents some viral infection. Countries like New Zealand, Australia, China and Rwanda can control the infection rate and reach a very low level of infected new cases. However, countries like India, the United States, and Brazil observed more cases after lifting locked down. Fleury et al. (2021) identified the vaccination immune response may generate false-positive 18F-FDG PET/CTuptake. An extended supraclavicular lymph nodal activation after Covid-19 vaccination revealed on 18F-FDG PET/CT mimics a Virchow nodule in a patient with a medical history of well-differentiated appendicular adenocarcinoma.

Elbaset et al. (2020) found that the current SARS-CoV-2 pandemic may negatively affect the care of liver transplant candidates and recipients. Accordingly, each country must have its national guidelines based on the current situation and according to available tools. Liver Transplantation Scientific Committee of Waiting List Project in Egypt was established on 13 April 2020. One of the major goals of this Scientific Committee is the design of a national protocol for Transplant Centers in Egypt to treat living donor liver transplantation (LDLT) during the SARS-CoV-2 pandemic. This protocol highlights basic hospital requirements for LDLT during the SARS-CoV-2 pandemic, the patient selection from the waiting list, management of patients on the waiting list, and post-transplant management. Many coronavirus vaccines have been fast-tracked to stop the pandemic; the usage of immune adjuvants that can boost immunological memory has come up to the forefront discovered by AbdelMassih et al. (2020). This is particularly significant given the rates of failure of seroconversion and re-infection after Covid-19 infection, which can make the vaccine role and outcome questionable. Peroxisome proliferator-activated receptors (PPARs) have an established immune-modulatory role, but their effects as adjuvants to vaccination have not been explored till today. It is increasingly recognized that PPAR agonists can up-regulate the levels of anti-apoptotic factors such as MCL-1. Such an effect can improve the results of vaccination by enhancing the longevity of long-lived plasma cells (LLPCs). The interaction between PPAR agonists and the immune system has not stopped here, as T cell memory is also stimulated through improved T regulatory cells, antagonizing PD-L1 and switching the metabolism of T cells to fatty acid oxidation, which has a remarkable effect on the persistence of T memory cells. The recent investigation of a few epidemiological studies found hope for a reduced impact of Covid-19 for countries that practice universal BCG vaccination policy (Mohamed Hussein et al., 2020). This report discovers a correlation between the case fatality rates of Covid-19 and the percentage of BCG vaccination coverage in 183 most affected countries. The main objective of this observational ecological report is to assess the possible effects of the previous BCG vaccination in different populations and the epidemic outcomes especially the rates of severe/ critical cases and case fatalities.

This analysis is preliminary since it is based on constantly rolling data while the Covid-19 pandemic is still unfolding. These findings seem to support the fact that an older BCG vaccine may have a protective role in avoiding severe/critical SARS-CoV2 pneumonia and relatively decrease its fatalities. Chew et al. (2021) proposed that in the fight against Covid-19, vaccination is vital in achieving herd immunity. Many Asian countries are starting to vaccinate front line workers; however, expedited vaccine development has led to hesitancy among the general population. The authors evaluated the willingness of healthcare workers to receive the Covid-19 vaccine. From the 12th to 21st of December 2020; 1,720 healthcare workers were recruited from six countries: China, India, Indonesia, Singapore, Vietnam, and Bhutan. The self-administered survey collected information on the willingness to vaccinate, perception of Covid-19, vaccine concerns, Covid-19 risk profile, stigma, pro-socialness scale, and trust in health authorities. More than 95% of the healthcare workers surveyed were willing to vaccinate. The COVID-19 pandemic has affected all over the world from the year 2020 wave after wave (Wallace, 2020). The nations across the globe are reporting ever-increasing pandemic deaths, infected people and healthcare professionals are constantly fighting. The government is driving the vaccination program and striving to get all their citizens vaccinated. People are not cooperating some are not taking vaccination and opposing this vaccination, do not wear masks and violate quarantine norms. Public health emergencies occurred in the past also, but this corona pandemic surprised even the scientists. The variants of the virus may create still more deaths and panic in public life. Keshavarz et al. (2021) discussed certain benefits and safety features of the Covid-19 vaccines used today but there are also some bad side effects observed such as lymphadenopathy (LAP). The authors have reviewed many cases of LAP after the Covid-19 vaccination. This paper explored the information from online databases, papers from Scopus, Medline, Web of Science, Elsevier, Cochrane library. The authors carried out a total of 19 studies (68 cases), including 60 (88.2%) females and eight (11.8%) males with a presentation of LAP after the Covid-19 vaccination. Most of the LAP imaging findings related to Covid-19 vaccination (n=66, 97%) were seen from the first day to four weeks after vaccination. However, LAP remained after 5 and 6 weeks of the first and second dosages of Covid-19 vaccination with decreased lymph nodes' size and residual cortical thickening in two cases. The Table <<tbc2>>2 presents the highlights from each paper

Table 2. Summary of highlights from each paper

Sl No	Authors	Study / Methodology	Results
1	Wang et al. (2021b)	Willingness To Pay for vaccination	Most respondents believed that governments (90.9%) and health insurance (78.0%) should pay for partial or full expenses of Covid-19 vaccination
2	Wang et al (2021a)	Assess the willingness, hesitancy, and coverage of the Covid-19 vaccine in China	The percentage of people's trust in the vaccine, delivery system, and government were 69.0%, 78.0% and 81.3%, respectively. 67.1% of the participants were reportedly willing to accept the Covid-19 vaccination, only 9.0% refused it.
3	Kessels, Luyten, and Tebeuf (2021)	Willingness and attitude towards Covid-19 vaccination in Belgium	Only 34% of the participants said that they will get vaccinated against Covid-19 and 39% are not sure about taking the vaccination. 17% (N = 349) samples not interested in getting Covid-19 vaccinated
4	Caspi et al. (2021)	SES, vaccination percentage, and active Covid-19 in SES, vaccination percentage, and active Covid-19 Israel	After 23 days of vaccination camp, about 56.8% of people over the age of 60 were vaccinated in Israel with the first dose of the BNT162b2 Covid-19 vaccine
5	Brown et al. (2021)	Axillary lymphadenopathy in patients vaccinated against Covid-19	Radiologists should be aware of typical appearances across all imaging methods.
6	Hyland et al. (2021)	Hesitance and resistance problems to Covid-19 vaccination in the Republic of Ireland and the UK	Increased resistance to Covid-19 vaccination were identified in Irish (from 9.5% to 18.1%) and British (from 6.2% to 10%) people
7	Umasabor-Bubu et al. (2021)	Admissions to intensive care unit (ICU), ventilator-use, mortality, hospital length of stay and total ICU days	Increased likelihood of requiring an ICU admission among self-reported non-flu-vaccinated relative to self-reported flu-vaccinated patients only for ages <65, and non-obese patients
8	Patelarou et al. (2021)	A survey of 2249 undergraduate nursing students was carried out in 7 universities in Greece, Albania, Cyprus, Spain, Italy, Czech Republic, and Kosovo through a web	The results revealed that 43.8% of students have accepted a safe and effective Covid-19 vaccine. The rate of accepting vaccines was higher in Italian nursing students.
9	Duke, Posch, and Green (2021)	Studied the side effects after Covid-19 vaccination	Radiologists should be alert on possible vaccine-introduced unilateral axillary adenopathy on screening and diagnostic breast imaging
10	Cucunawangsih et al. (2021)	HCWs enhanced exposure to Covid-19 disease	Out of 1040 HCWs who have taken two doses of the Covid-19 vaccine, only 13 (1.25%) were tested positive in RTPCR in about 5 days after the second dose of vaccination
11	Pal, Bhadada, and Misra (2021)	Side effects of Covid-19 vaccines in patients with type 1 and type 2 diabetes mellitus	The people with DM are at a heavy risk of the infection to Covid-19 disease so they should be given high priority for the vaccination programme

continued on following page

Table 2. Continued

Sl No	Authors	Study / Methodology	Results
12	Hilal Hamid Mir	Indians perceptions and intentions to consume Covid-19 vaccine	This study revealed that perceived benefits, social norms, and trust are associated considerably with people's acceptance of Covid-19 vaccinations
13	Albert et al. (2021)	Covid-19 vaccination side-effects reported elevated troponins and negative viral serologies	There are reports that there is an increased risk of cardiac engagement from Covid-19 infection in comparison to Covid-19 vaccination
14	Blanchard-Rohner et al. (2021)	Investigate how individual and family Covid-19 risk and available ICU facilities during the pandemics affect the perception about Covid-19 vaccines	In total, 85% of participants (and 55% of vaccine sceptics) are going to accept the vaccination for Covid-19
15	Khubchandani and Macias (2021)	Hesitancy and resistance to Covid-19 vaccination in racial and ethnic minorities.	Adult Americans across all studies were 26.3% contrast, the overall pooled prevalence rate of Covid-19 vaccination hesitancy for African-Americans was 41.6% and for Hispanics, it was 30.2%
16	Ala'a and Tarhini (2021)	To identify the factors such as distribution and delivery of the vaccine to distant places is the issue of perception of the people to get vaccinated	Adequate Covid-19 vaccination is affected by the availability, distribution of vaccines but also by cultural and social norms in the community as well as the complexity of human behaviours.
17	Hughes et al. (2020)	A genetic programming strategy was applied to identify new ways for understanding public health issues by the governments.	The authors conducted experiments and results have given a lot of promising insight. Authors have developed alternative strategies for a random ER graph and tested them in multiple ways.
18	Mertz (2020)	This pan coronavirus vaccine is expected to fight against all variants of coronavirus in general.	DHVI is expecting with this pan-coronavirus vaccine to go fight at the central trunk," said Thomas Denny, chief executive of DHVI in Durham, NC.
19	Khade, Yabaji, and Srivastava (2021)	Impact of BCG vaccination implementation policy	Countries like the USA, Italy, where BCG vaccination policy is not very mandatory are worst affected. However, countries like India, China, Iran, etc. where the BCG vaccination policy is mandatory found to be either affected to a minimum extent or have a high recovery rate
20	Fleury et al. (2021)	Study on axillary lymph nodal activation on 18FFDG PET/CT following influenza and Covid-19 vaccination	Nuclear physicians should be careful when cancers staging and re-staging. This is especially important for patients with breast cancer having been vaccinated on the homolateral upper limb, digestive cancer patients vaccinated on the left side, or with lung or head and neck carcinoma.

Technological Solutions for Effectively Managing Vaccination Program

Deka, Goswami, and Anand (2020) discussed maintenance of a large number of immutable vaccination records and provision for accessing the records to prove immunity has been the need of the hour. The latest spread of Covid19 disease, related resistance and lack of trust over vaccinations has been worsened the situation. Governments are looking for a reliable and secure system for keeping the track of vaccination. Many papers based on IT solutions were proposed in the past but none of them proved to be safe and reliable. This paper has suggested a blockchain-based method to keep the records of proof of vaccination and immunity for people. The objective was to design a reliable and efficient system for securely managing the vaccination records using the concept of smart contracts built over the Ethereum blockchain. The results of transaction logs derived from the system showed that this proposed system is viable and cost-effective enough to for vaccination records management. Jadidi et al. (2020) stated that vaccination is an effective method to prevent the spread of infectious diseases, but when the number of available vaccines is limited, it is not possible to vaccinate everyone in a society.

A two-step model was proposed to distribute a limited number of vaccines among the people of a society, in a way that would disrupt the transmission chain of the infectious disease most efficiently. In the first step, the vaccines are reserved for different communities in the society (e.g. cities in a country). In the second step, vaccination is allocated to the individuals that eliminate the maximum number of transmission paths for the infection is discovered according to the regulations of WHO. The coronavirus pandemic has brought in unexpected polices, enforcing lockdowns in the areas most hit by the pandemic by the authorities (Cotfas et al., 2021). Social media has enabled people to keep social contact during these embarrassing times. The first vaccine with more than 90% effectiveness was announced on 9th November 2020. People across the world in social media have expressed their resistance and hesitancy on vaccination which slowed the vaccination program across the world. The author's objective was to investigate the dynamics of people's opinions on Covid-19 vaccination after one month from the first vaccine announcement until the first vaccination was rolled out in the UK, in which the civil society has shown a higher interest during the vaccination process. The performance of the conventional machine and deep learning algorithms have been carried out to select the best algorithm. 2,349,659 tweets have been gathered, examined and they are correlated with the news reported by other media.

The results from the analysis revealed that most of the tweets have a neutral stance, while the number of favour tweets overpasses the number of against tweets. The authors noticed that the presence of tweets followed the tendency of the events. For both the neutral and in favor tweets it has been observed that some of the events in media have entrained a series of spikes, which are not encountered in the case of against tweets, where the major spike has been represented by the authorization in the UK of the Pfizer BioNTech Covid-19 vaccine. Odoom et al. (2020) said that Coronavirus pandemic will go into the annals of history, and it is an undeniable fact that it was one of the devastating plagues. The Healthcare industry is undertaking a large number of activities towards testing, tracing, and treating vaccinating and management the patients. Research communities are exploring innovational solutions. There are several solutions designed for contact tracing, test result certification, fighting against misinformation, data aggregation and data analysis in a secure way using blockchain technology. The authors also included the status of vaccination status to furnish complete information and showed a proof of concept. The complete source code of this software is made open source on GitHub. The cost-benefit analysis of this solution revealed that only the contract deployer and health care service provider incurs minimum blockchain-related expenses. This solution also meets robust security requirements and is tolerant of popular security attacks. Today mobile apps are progressively used in the healthcare industry Schwab et al. (2021). These mobile apps are capable of collecting healthcare data from a person body and communicating the data to healthcare professionals for diagnosis. Constant monitoring of person conditions enables better quality and timely medical treatment. The healthcare apps should empower the patient to avail best medical services in a cost-effective way. Patient medical data is very sensitive and valuable providing; high security to data is very crucial.

The protocols used for communicating patient data among the stakeholders in the healthcare domain should ensure high security. These methods have been applied by healthcare service providers to optimize cost-effective transfers of data in mHealth applications. Nadini et al. (2020) has carried out a detailed exploration of epidemic spreading within urban environments worldwide. The authors developed an agent-based model, in which agents travel in a two-dimensional physical space and communicate based on nearest neighbourhood criteria. The plane space consists of several locations, representing bounded regions of the urban city. Authors studied locations of different densities and place them in a core-periphery structure based on empirical evidence. The higher density is placed in the centres and lower density centres in the periphery. Every agent is allocated to a home location. The study on the growth of heterogeneous interaction patterns was carried out using numerical and simulation models. The authors carried out an intensive simulation program to study the evolution of infectious diseases spreading in urban areas. It was observed that the disease will not spread when the agent is in the home location but it spreads when an agent goes into the periphery and returns into the home location and repeats this process again and again. A simplified one-dimensional version of the model was investigated to acquire analytical insight into the disease spreading mechanism and to reinforce the numerical facts discovered. The authors examined the effectiveness of vaccination programmes promoting the belief that vaccination in central and dense areas should be prioritized. Ana Santos Rutschman (2021) explored Anti-vaccine pages in Facebook social media sites have reached more people who have not yet decided about the vaccination than pro-vaccine ones. Facebook will not remove the sources of misinformation about vaccination during the Covid-19 pandemic times. Anti-vaccine pages on Facebook increased considerably more than 300 per cent— than pro-vaccine pages during the measles outbreaks in the United States. Facebook has not controlled the spread of misinformation on the vaccine. Instagram, which has been considered as a "hotbed of vaccine misinformation." Other social media have been controlled better than Facebook's current efforts. YouTube declared that it would start removing videos spreading misinformation about the vaccine.

Twitter also has implemented a similar Covid-19 misinformation policy since March 2020. Pinterest removed misleading results for vaccine searches even before the pandemic and later redirected searches to content from credible public health organizations. The silent role of Facebook in the circulation of online vaccine misinformation is worth further interrogation. Considering the large global footprint of Facebook, managing the status quo is likely to further damage the levels of vaccine trust in the United States and abroad. This would negatively impact the process of emerging Covid-19 vaccines but also for the future of vaccine strategies and public health. The health policy community can and should engage more intensively with technologists, lawmakers, advisory bodies, and activist groups outside the public health arena, where most debates on the regulation of social media have historically occurred. Emphasizing the public health dimension of definite kinds of vaccine misinformation is first to change the current regulatory tradition of defaulting to self-regulation and placing no burden on social media to delete famous and established sources of vaccine misinformation.

Wilson (2020) discovered that WHO has designed a standard format in a paper booklet called Yellow Card to record a person's vaccinations by healthcare workers. Many innovative steps are being taken to create digital identities and vaccination records for people with minimum official documentation. Healthcare workers worldwide are using this yellow card to keep a record of vaccination. This paper is designed to support the digitization of vaccinations records. This yellow card digital version can be deployed on all smartphones today with public key certificates and other authentication. The yellow card has many practical benefits for the digital actions and privacy of low doc persons. It also reveals how traditional hierarchical public key infrastructure can be implemented without dictating identification protocols to the public, thus preventing some of the disputes that plague this technology. The PKI security module can be centralized, and certificate issuance is decentralized, which permits public organizations free to perform their business as usual. The digital Yellow Card is capable of holding many attributes required by public organizations; it can therefore be scaled up to manage many other credentials for low doc and differently abled people without relying on new digital identity frameworks. The vaccination programme for preventing the deaths and spread of COVID-19 in India has started on 16th January 2021 (Dubey, 2021). India has used Oxford-AstraZeneca's Covishield and Bharat Biotech's Covaxin vaccines. This program successfully vaccinated six million people in the first four days and the government has taken the program very seriously to achieve herd immunity to the people of the country. However, there are a set of people who are not having trust and show resistance to the COVID19 vaccination.

Authors have experimented to understand the sentiments in the tweets posted in India regarding these two vaccines. This analysis showed that the majority of the people are posting positive sentiments towards these vaccines, there are also negative sentiments with emotions such as fear and anger. This research was carried out to investigate the COVID19 vaccination drive in India. The tweets collected for this study ranged from 14th January to 18th January 2021. Authors found that Covishield related tweets are more positive sentiments as compared to Covaxin. Emotions like trust and expectations were more in the case of Covishield than of the Covaxin. Covaxin has more tweets with anger and disgust emotions. These results can be associated with the doubts related to the approval of Covaxin, as well as the politics involved in its approval. The speedy development and distribution of an efficient Covid-19 vaccine raised the hopes that the pandemic can be controlled. The policymakers are facing the challenge of keeping and verification of records of vaccination might be brought to an end (Zhang et al., 2021). Designing robust vaccine record verification (VRV) systems is very important for policymakers to reopen businesses, educational institutions, and the tourism industry. There is a lot of work in progress in developing digital record verification systems. World Economic Forum has developed a digital vaccine passport called a common pass app to store vaccine status. This VRV provides accurate verification of vaccination status and also introduces considerable security and privacy vulnerabilities. The implementation of VRV systems by public health authorities ought to align with vaccine prioritization decisions to uphold fairness and equity and be built on trustworthy technology. The present Covid-19 vaccination drive has not reached more than 10% of the global population.

Bracci et al. (2021) discovered that in many countries, the citizens have not received both doses till now. There is also broad proof that there are shortages of Covid-19 related materials and services which forced people, and shoppers to acquire them online and through dark web marketplaces. There are doubts about the vaccines business happening in dark web marketplaces also. The authors discussed their work to constantly supervise 164 dark websites. By April 20, authors found 214 list-findings offering a Covid-19 vaccine, 77 of which offered authorized vaccines and 25 fabricated proofs of vaccination. Currently, active listings is 34, including eight listings offering the Pfizer/BioNTech vaccine, six the Moderna, two the AstraZeneca/Oxford, two the Sputnik V vaccine, and nine offers fabricated proofs of vaccination. The illegal business of un-authorized Covid-19 vaccines creates a robust threat to public health and risks to reduce public confidence in vaccination. The study on how Covid-19 vaccines are sold on DWMs helps law enforcement authorities to control it by enforcing successful approaches.

Mellado et al. (2020) described that Covid-19 pandemic is leading to heavy deaths and serious health issues, huge social and economic losses. Many developed countries are driving vaccination programs. Most African nations are still waiting for allocating vaccine stocks and are applying clinical public health (CPH) ways to control the pandemic. The growth of new Variants of Concern (VOC), uneven availability of vaccine supply and some logistic and vaccine delivery attributes are making the CPH policy very complex. There is an urgent need to refine CPH policies. Advanced technologies such as Big Data and Artificial Intelligence, Machine Learning techniques and collaborations can be useful for an accurate, timely, local analysis from multiple data sources to communicate to CPH decision-making, vaccination strategies and their staged roll-out. The Africa-Canada Artificial Intelligence and Data Innovation Consortium (ACADIC) has been constituted to develop and employ machine learning techniques to develop CPH strategies in Africa, which requires continuous collaboration, testing and development to optimize the equity and effectiveness of Covid-19 related CPH interventions.

The production capacity should be aligned with global demand for approved vaccines, national staged vaccine access allocation plans and prioritization-based strategies are required. Chen, Kuo, and Chan (2021) has analysed the risk for severe illness and deaths considerably increased after COVID-19 infection for old age and people suffering from respiratory issues. Authors have designed an age-stratified dynamic epidemic modelling for COVID-19 infected people to reduce hospital admissions and deaths. This model considers contact networks which is an extension of the standard SEIR (susceptible-exposed-infectious-removed) compartmental model, named age-stratified SEAHIR (susceptible-exposed asymptomatic-hospitalized-infectious-removed) model. This model captures the spread of COVID-19 over multi-type random networks with general degree distributions. The extensive study discovered that the results of vaccination prioritization depend on the reproduction number R0. The elderly should be prioritized only when R0 is considerably high. The extensive use of face masks can reduce the R0 to lower levels. Assigning high priority to the adult age group (20-39) would be very effective to decrease both mortality and hospitalizations. Chen et al. (2021) has proposed a contagious

Table 3. Summary of highlights from each paper

Sl. No	Authors	Methodology	Results
1	Deka, Goswami, and Anand (2020)	A blockchain-based method to keep the records of proof of vaccination and immunity for people.	The results of transaction logs derived from the system showed that this proposed system is viable and cost-effective enough for vaccination and records management
2	Jadidi et al. (2020)	A two-step model was proposed to distribute a limited number of vaccines among the people of a society, in a way that would disrupt the transmission chain of the infectious disease most efficiently.	The simulation results showed that a 30% reduction in the rate of infection compared to random vaccination could be achieved.
3	Cotfas et al. (2021)	The authors objective was to investigate the dynamics of people's opinions on Covid-19 vaccination after one month from the first vaccine announcement,	This method has grouped the tweets into three main groups, namely in favour, against and neutral on Covid-19 vaccination, applying BERT with an accuracy of 78.94%.
4	Odoom et al. (2020)	Authors have designed software based on blockchain and smart contracts that permits data updates only by authorized users	The authors also included the status of vaccination to furnish complete information and showed a proof of concept. The complete source code of this software is made open-source on GitHub
5	Schwab et al. (2021)	The authors discussed two distinct methods to manage and report sensitive medical information secure transfer.	Today these two methods are used in clinical practice, and their performance is monitored regularly. These methods have been applied by healthcare service providers to optimize cost-effective transfers of data in mHealth applications.
6	Nadini et al. (2020)	Epidemic spreading within urban environments developed an agent-based model	This model was investigated to acquire analytical insight into the disease spreading mechanism and to reinforce the numerical facts discovered.
7	Rutschman (2021)	Anti-vaccine pages on Facebook increased considerably more than 300 per cent—than pro-vaccine pages during the measles outbreaks in the United States	This would negatively impact the process of emerging Covid-19 vaccines but also the future of vaccine strategies and public health. The silent role of Facebook in the circulation of online vaccine misinformation is worth further interrogation.
8	Wilson (2020)	WHO Yellow Card to record person's vaccinations by healthcare workers	The digital Yellow Card is capable of holding many attributes required by public organizations; it can therefore be scaled up to manage many other credentials for low doc and differently-abled people without relying on new digital identity frameworks.

continued on following page

Table 3. Continued

Sl. No	Authors	Methodology	Results
9	Dubey (2021)	Authors have experimented to understand the sentiments in the tweets posted in India regarding these two vaccines.	Authors found that Covishield related tweets are more positive sentiments as compared to Covaxin. Emotions like trust and expectations were more in the case of Covishield than of the Covaxin. Covaxin has more tweets with anger and disgust emotions.
10	Zhang et al. (2021)	Designing robust vaccine record verification (VRV) systems is very important for policymakers to reopen businesses, educational institutions, and the tourism industry.	This VRV provides accurate verification of vaccination status and also introduces considerable security and privacy vulnerabilities.
11	Bracci et al. (2021)	Constantly supervising 164 dark web sites for Vaccines business in dark web marketplaces	Currently, active listings is 34, including eight listings offering the Pfizer/BioNTech vaccine, six the Moderna, two the AstraZeneca/Oxford, two the Sputnik V vaccine, and nine offers fabricated proofs of vaccination.
12	Mellado et al. (2021)	Advanced technologies such as Big Data and Artificial Intelligence, Machine Learning techniques and collaborations can be useful for an accurate, timely, local analysis from multiple data sources to communicate to CPH decision-making, vaccination strategies and their staged roll-out.	The Africa-Canada Artificial Intelligence and Data Innovation Consortium (ACADIC) has been constituted to develop and employ machine learning techniques to develop CPH strategies in Africa, which requires continuous collaboration, testing and development to optimize the equity and effectiveness of Covid-19 related CPH interventions.
14	Chen et al. (2021)	Authors have designed an age-stratified dynamic epidemic modelling for COVID-19 infected people to reduce hospital admissions and deaths	The extensive study discovered that the results of vaccination prioritization depend on the reproduction number R0. The elderly should be prioritized only when R0 is considerably high.
15	Chen, Kuo, and Chan (2021)	Designed a model named SEINRVseinr stands for Susceptible-Infectious-Recovered (SIR) network model.	This model was compared with other standard models to prove that random acquaintance strategy is an efficient strategy and neighbour strategies perform better in a certain interval.
16	Antal et al. (2021)	Presented blockchain technology-based system to ensure data integrity and immutability of beneficiary registration for vaccination, preventing identity thefts and impersonations.	This blockchain system showed promising results in terms of throughput, scalability, and expected cost in terms of gas for vaccination scenarios when real data is within reasonable limits.
17	Eisenstadt et al. (2020)	A smartphone app supported in decentralized server architecture. This app provides real-time verification of tamper-proof test results.	The standard performance tests revealed that it scales linearly in the worst case, as considerable processing is done locally on each app.

disease spreading model was using probabilistic node-level time-dependency for the COVID-19 pandemic.

This model was named SEINRV stands for Susceptible-Infectious-Recovered (SIR) network model. This model proposes an exposed and asymptomatic infectious state, imperfect vaccination, reinfected possibility and weighted undirected graph for social network into the traditional probabilistic node-level. Authors experimented with five vaccination approaches (including random base, degree-target base, random acquaintance, first-neighbor and second neighbor strategies) in a random network, small-world network and scale-free network. This model was compared with other standard models to prove that random acquaintance strategy is an efficient strategy and neighbor strategies perform better in a certain interval. Conducting vaccination drives worldwide to achieve herd immunity is very critical during COVID-19 pandemic times. The success of the vaccination drive would depend on the acceptance, availability, distribution and rollout of vaccination. This entire process should be transparent and traceable by all stakeholders.

Antal et al. (2021) paper presents the application of blockchain technology to implement many of these requirements of the COVID-19 vaccination drive. The authors presented a blockchain technology-based system to ensure data integrity and immutability of beneficiary registration for vaccination, preventing identity thefts and impersonations. Smart contracts are defined to supervise and trace the proper care during vaccine distribution against the safe handling rules prescribed by vaccine producers enabling the awareness of all network peers. For vaccine administration, a transparent and tamper-proof solution for side effects self-reporting is furnished considering beneficiary and administrated vaccine association. A prototype was deployed on the Ethereum test network, Ropsten, taking the COVID-19 vaccine distribution conditions into account. The results obtained for each on-chain operation can be checked and validated on the Etherscan. This blockchain system showed promising results in terms of throughput, scalability, and expected cost in terms of gas for vaccination scenarios when real data is within reasonable limits.

Eisenstadt et al. (2020) says that immunity passport is essential to return to work during Coronavirus Pandemic times. There is research in progress about the quality of antibody testing, developing vaccines, and attaining immunity to COVID-19. Authors worked on developing certificates with tamper-proof and ensuring privacy features for test results and vaccinations. This paper proposed a model for a smartphone app supported in decentralized server architecture. This app provides real-time verification of tamper-proof test results. Personal information can be stored at the user's judgement. This app facilitates the end-user to selectively share only the specific test result with no other personal information shared. This architecture is designed for scalability based upon the 2019 World

Wide Web Consortium standard called 'Verifiable Credentials', Tim Berners-Lee's decentralized personal data platform 'Solid', and a Consortium Ethereum-based blockchain. The results from a mobile phone app and decentralized server architecture enable the mixture of verifiability and privacy in a way derivable from public/private key pairs and digital signatures, generalized to avoid restrictive ownership of sensitive digital keys and/or data. The standard performance tests revealed that it scales linearly in the worst case, as considerable processing is done locally on each app.

For the test certificate Holder, Issuer (e.g. healthcare staff, pharmacy) and Verifier (e.g. an employer), it is 'just another app' that takes only minutes to use. This app is waiting for approval for the biological and key ethical issues raised.

Table 3 shows the summary of highlights from each paper such as technology adopted and results achieved in vaccination study.

METHODOLOGY TO STUDY THE TWEETS FROM TEXT BLOB LIBRARY

Authors of this paper aimed at analyzing the opinion of the Indian public on Covid-19 vaccination. The authors collected tweets from Twitter social media site. The tweets are collected from identified and verified tagged users. The tweets are collected and segregated negative, positive and neutral, city wise, vaccine wise and month for analysis. The data points are normalized for analysis and presentation purposes. The results of the analysis are presented as visualizations in various types of charts and graphs.

Positive and Negative Opinion Tweet Type-wise Analysis

The Figure 1 shows the ratio of positive to negative tweets overall in India. The Green blocks represent 1 unit of positive tweets and the Red box represents one unit of negative tweets. There are eight of Red blocks representing negative opinion tweets compared to a total of 50 positive tweets making the ratio 50/8. Figure 1 also shows the analysis of tweets in eight major cities across India. The Figure 1 shows that Bangalore has the highest number of Positive to Negative ratios i.e highest number of Green (Positive) blocks compared to only 100 Green / 7Red. The city Gurgaon has a large number of Red blocks (Negative tweets) Positive to Negative ratios is very low 100 Green/28 Red. Bangalore and Chennai have shown very few negative tweets, the reason might be that a large number of people have been vaccinated in these cities. Figure 1 show overall India and City-wise vaccination opinions represented by these tweets analysis.

Figure 1. The ratio of positive to negative tweets in 8 major cities in India

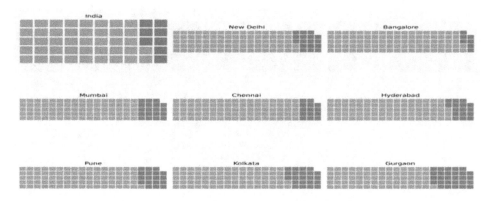

Vaccine-wise Positive and Negative Opinion Tweets Analysis

Authors have analyzed the tweets to study the opinion of people based on the effectiveness of different vaccines for Covid-19 disease. The Figure 2 represents the ratio of negative to positive tweets according to the vaccine. Each Green box represents 1 unit of positive tweets and Red represents 1 unit of negative tweets. Covaxin has a high Positive: Negative ratio of 50 (Green-Positive) /10(Red-Negative). Covishield has a Positive to Negative ratio of 50 (Green-Positive) /9(Red- Negative). Sputnik has a Positive: Negative ratio 50 (Green-Positive) / 11(Red- Negative). Overall, the vaccine has a Positive: Negative ratio of 50 (Green-Positive) /10(Red- Negative).

Month-wise Positive and Negative Opinion Tweets Analysis

The authors have analyzed trends in several positive to negative tweets month-wise from January 2021 to August 2021. The Figure 3 shows the trends month-wise. Each Green box represents 1 unit of positive tweets and Red represents 1 unit of negative tweets. The following image represents the ratio of negative to positive tweets in each month. January 2021 has shown maximum negative trends of 37 units of positive tweets and 13 units of negative tweets. February 2021 has shown 38 units of positive tweets and 12 units of negative tweets. March 2021 has shown 42 units of positive tweets and 8 units of negative tweets. April 2021 has shown 39 units of positive tweets and 11 units of negative tweets. May 2021 has shown 39 units of positive tweets and 11 units of negative tweets. June 2021 has shown 40 units of positive tweets and 10 units of negative tweets. July 2021 has shown 46 units of positive tweets and 4 units of negative tweets. August 2021 has shown

Figure 2. The ratio of positive to negative tweets for different Covid-19 vaccines

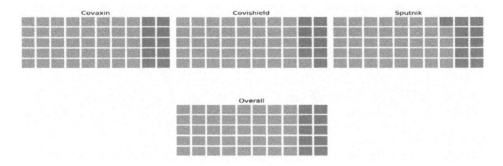

Figure 3. Month-wise Positive and Negative opinion Tweets analysis from January to August 2021

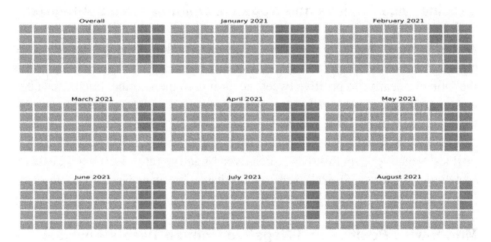

47 units of positive tweets and 3 units of negative tweets. August-2021 has a high Positive to Negative ratio whilst January-2021 has a low Positive: Negative ratio. Early Months show a trend of high negative tweets which decline as the month's pass. The month of May sees a surge in negative tweets as citizens struggled to book their slots through the app, the months of July and August show very few negative tweets as most of the citizens have received their 1st dose by then.

City-wise Visualizations of Tweets Analysis Results

Figure 4 represents Violin Plot, it shows the probability density of the data at different values. The larger the width of the orange part the higher the density of tweets in that range. The white dot between the black line represents the mean of the data.

Figure 4. The polarity of tweets in Ahmadabad

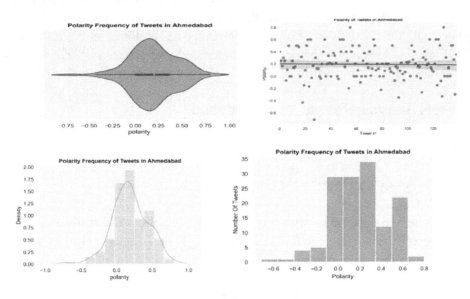

Figure 5. The polarity of tweets in Bangalore

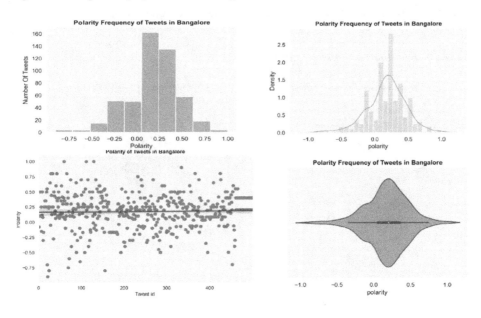

Figure 4 shows a line plot of information as a series of data points where the x-axis is the tweet id and the y-axis is the polarity. The red line represents the mean of the data. Figure 4 shows a Histogram which is a representation of the distribution of numerical data. The higher the line the higher the distribution of tweets in that range. Figure 4 also shows a kernel density estimate (KDE) plot is a method for visualizing the distribution of observations in a data set. Relative to a histogram, KDE can produce a plot that is less cluttered and more interpretable, especially when drawing multiple distributions.

Tweets Analysis Results for Ahmadabad

See Figure 4.

Tweets Analysis Results for Bangalore

See Figure 5. Bangalore shows a very high frequency of positive tweets compared to negative tweets, this might be due to the high % of vaccinated citizens and the easy availability of the vaccine doses.

Tweets Analysis Results for Bhuvaneshwar

The frequency of the positive to negative tweets is high as it was one of the very first cities where more than 90% of citizens had received their first dose.

Figure 6. The polarity of tweets in Bhuvaneshwar

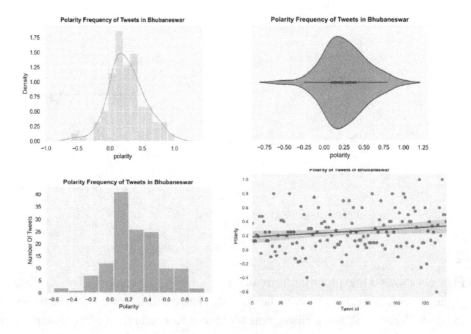

Figure 7. The polarity of tweets in Chennai

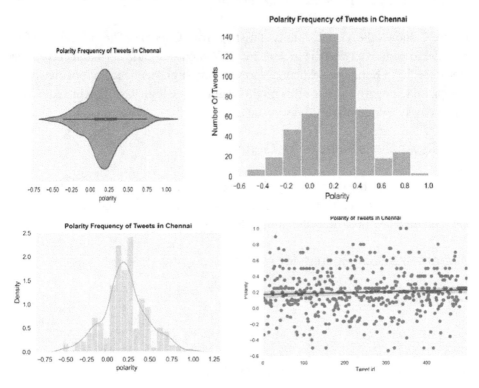

Figure 8. The polarity of tweets in Gurgaon

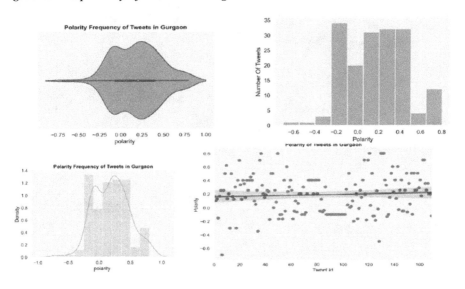

Tweets Analysis Results for Chennai

Figure 7 shows the visualizations statistics from Chennai. The frequency of the positive to negative tweets is high as more than 60% of citizens had received their first dose. Like Bangalore, Chennai shows a very high frequency of positive tweets compared to negative tweets, this might be due to the high % of vaccinated citizens and the easy availability of the vaccine doses.

Tweets Analysis Results for Gurgaon

Gurgaon has a high volume of negative tweets, which might be attributed to the low % of vaccinations and the frequent shortages in doses, Vaccination drive had to be stopped on a few occasions due to the shortages.

Tweets Analysis Results for Hyderabad

See Figure 9.

Figure 9. The polarity of tweets in Hyderabad

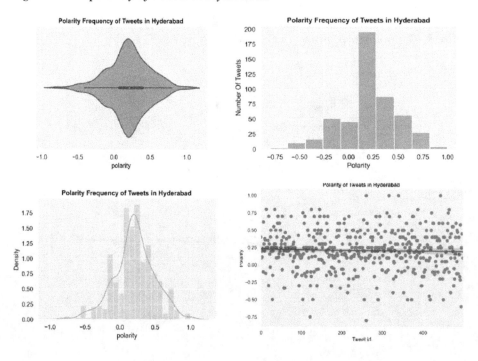

Figure 10. The polarity of tweets from verified users

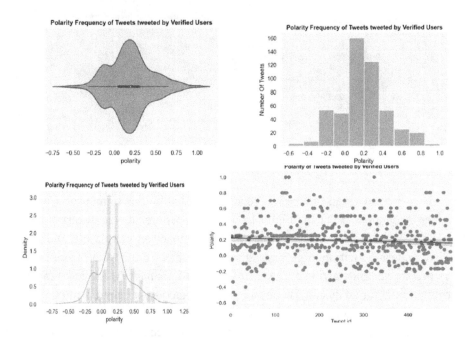

Tweets Analysis Results for Verified Users from Twitter

Data from verified users on Twitter the Verified badge on Twitter lets people know that an account of public interest is authentic. These people are usually media personalities, Journalists, Media/News outlets, Politicians, Sports Persons, etc.

Tweets Analysis Results for Most Liked Tweets

The above figure represents the stats of the top 300 most liked tweets, these are the tweets that have been liked most often of all the others and have been seen the most as shown in Figure 11

CONCLUSION

Authors have explored the people perceptions about Covid-19 vaccination by reviewing about forty selected papers from high impact journals. This review was presented in two sections. The first section covers facts on how Covid-19 vaccination affected the health of the people and their perception towords the vaccination. The

Figure 11. The polarity of tweets from most number of likes

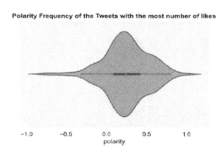
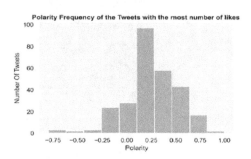

second section reviewed the various technological solutions to manage Covid-19 vaccination databases. The highlights from each paper are tabulated and compared. Social media such as Twitter has an immense impact on people life and strong media for sharing their opinion. The authors have selected the tweets from verified users of Tweeter and carried out experiments. Authors have developed a machine learning model for analysing Twitter messages related to perceptions on Covid-19 vaccination. This paper presented the data visualization of the results in graphical format for major cities in India. The results have also discussed the people opinion on various types of vaccines. This paper has provided a wholistic approach of people's responses to Covid-19 vaccinations from healthcare, technology and social media impact on perception for Covid-19 vaccination. The findings of this study gives input authorities to fine tune the vaccination programs and clear the misconceptions on covid-19 vaccinations.

REFERENCES

AbdelMassih, A. F., Menshawey, R., Ismail, J. H., Husseiny, R. J., Husseiny, Y. M., Yacoub, S., ... Castaldi, B. (2021). PPAR agonists as effective adjuvants for COVID-19 vaccines, by modifying immunogenetics: A review of literature. *Journal of Genetic Engineering and Biotechnology*, *19*(1), 1–9.

Ala'a, B., & Tarhini, Z. (2021). Beyond equity: Advocating theory-based health promotion in parallel with COVID-19 mass vaccination campaigns. *Public Health in Practice*, *2*, 100142.

Albert, E., Aurigemma, G., Saucedo, J., & Gerson, D. S. (2021). Myocarditis following COVID-19 vaccination. *Radiology Case Reports*, *16*(8), 2142–2145.

Antal, C., Cioara, T., Antal, M., & Anghel, I. (2021). Blockchain platform for COVID-19 vaccine supply management. *IEEE Open Journal of the Computer Society, 2*, 164–178.

Blanchard-Rohner, G., Caprettini, B., Rohner, D., & Voth, H. J. (2021). Impact of COVID-19 and intensive care unit capacity on vaccination support: Evidence from a two-leg representative survey in the United Kingdom. *Journal of Virus Eradication, 7*(2), 100044.

Bracci, A., Nadini, M., Aliapoulios, M., McCoy, D., Gray, I., Teytelboym, A., ... Baronchelli, A. (2021). Dark Web Marketplaces and COVID-19: Before the vaccine. *EPJ Data Science, 10*(1), 6.

Brown, A., Shah, S., Dluzewski, S., Musaddaq, B., Wagner, T., Szyszko, T., Wan, S., Groves, A., Mokbel, K., & Malhotra, A. (2021). Unilateral axillary adenopathy following COVID-19 vaccination: A multimodality pictorial illustration and review of current guidelines. *Clinical Radiology, 76*(8), 553–558. doi:10.1016/j.crad.2021.04.010 PMID:34053731

Caspi, G., Dayan, A., Eshal, Y., Liverant-Taub, S., Twig, G., Shalit, U., ... Caspi, O. (2021). Socioeconomic disparities and COVID-19 vaccination acceptance: A nationwide ecologic study. *Clinical Microbiology and Infection, 27*(10), 1502–1506.

Chen, M., Kuo, C. L., & Chan, W. K. V. (2021, April). Control of COVID-19 Pandemic: Vaccination Strategies Simulation under Probabilistic Node-Level Model. In *2021 6th International Conference on Intelligent Computing and Signal Processing (ICSP)* (pp. 119-125). IEEE.

Chen, X., Zhu, G., Zhang, L., Fang, Y., Guo, L., & Chen, X. (2021). Age-stratified COVID-19 spread analysis and vaccination: A multitype random network approach. *IEEE Transactions on Network Science and Engineering, 8*(2), 1862–1872.

Chew, N. W., Cheong, C., Kong, G., Phua, K., Ngiam, J. N., Tan, B. Y., ... Sharma, V. K. (2021). An Asia-Pacific study on healthcare workers' perceptions of, and willingness to receive, the COVID-19 vaccination. *International Journal of Infectious Diseases, 106*, 52–60.

Cotfas, L. A., Delcea, C., Roxin, I., Ioanăş, C., Gherai, D. S., & Tajariol, F. (2021). The longest month: Analyzing COVID-19 vaccination opinions dynamics from tweets in the month following the first vaccine announcement. *IEEE Access: Practical Innovations, Open Solutions, 9*, 33203–33223.

Cucunawangsih, C., Wijaya, R. S., Lugito, N. P. H., & Suriapranata, I. (2021). Post-vaccination cases of COVID-19 among healthcare workers at Siloam Teaching Hospital, Indonesia. *International Journal of Infectious Diseases*, *107*, 268–270.

Deka, S. K., Goswami, S., & Anand, A. (2020, December). A blockchain based technique for storing vaccination records. In 2020 IEEE Bombay section signature conference (IBSSC) (pp. 135-139). IEEE.

Dubey, A. D. (2021). *Public sentiment analysis of covid-19 vaccination drive in india.* Available at SSRN 3772401.

Duke, H., Posch, L., & Green, L. (2021). Axillary adenopathy following COVID-19 vaccination: A single institution case series. *Clinical Imaging*, *80*, 111–116.

Eisenstadt, M., Ramachandran, M., Chowdhury, N., Third, A., & Domingue, J. (2020). COVID-19 antibody test/vaccination certification: There's an app for that. *IEEE Open Journal of Engineering in Medicine and Biology*, *1*, 148–155.

Elbaset, A., Said, H., Sultan, A. M., Montasser, I. F., Soliman, H. E., Elayashy, M., & Makhlouf, N. A. (2021). *Egyptian protocol for living donor liver transplantation (LDLT) during SARS-CoV-2 pandemic.* Academic Press.

Fleury, V., Maucherat, B., Rusu, D., Dumont, F., & Rousseau, C. (2021). COVID-19 vaccination may cause FDG uptake beyond axillary area. *European Journal of Hybrid Imaging*, *5*(1), 1–3.

Hughes, J. A., Dubé, M., Houghten, S., & Ashlock, D. (2020, October). Vaccinating a population is a programming problem. In *2020 IEEE Conference on Computational Intelligence in Bioinformatics and Computational Biology (CIBCB)* (pp. 1-8). IEEE.

Hyland, P., Vallières, F., Shevlin, M., Bentall, R. P., McKay, R., Hartman, T. K., ... Murphy, J. (2021). Resistance to COVID-19 vaccination has increased in Ireland and the United Kingdom during the pandemic. *Public Health*, *195*, 54–56.

Jadidi, M. M., Moslemi, P., Jamshidiha, S., Masroori, I., Mohammadi, A., & Pourahmadi, V. (2020, December). Targeted vaccination for COVID-19 using mobile communication networks. In *2020 11th International Conference on Information and Knowledge Technology (IKT)* (pp. 93-97). IEEE.

Keshavarz, P., Yazdanpanah, F., Rafiee, F., & Mizandari, M. (2021). Lymphadenopathy following COVID-19 vaccination: Imaging findings review. *Academic Radiology*, *28*(8), 1058–1071.

Kessels, R., Luyten, J., & Tubeuf, S. (2021). Willingness to get vaccinated against Covid-19 and attitudes toward vaccination in general. *Vaccine*, *39*(33), 4716–4722.

Khade, S. M., Yabaji, S. M., & Srivastava, J. (2021). An update on COVID-19: SARS-CoV-2 life cycle, immunopathology, and BCG vaccination. *Preparative Biochemistry & Biotechnology, 51*(7), 650–658.

Khubchandani, J., & Macias, Y. (2021). COVID-19 vaccination hesitancy in Hispanics and African-Americans: A review and recommendations for practice. *Brain, Behavior, & Immunity-Health, 15*, 100277.

Mellado, B., Wu, J., Kong, J. D., Bragazzi, N. L., Asgary, A., Kawonga, M., ... Orbinski, J. (2021). Leveraging artificial intelligence and big data to optimize COVID-19 clinical public health and vaccination roll-out strategies in Africa. *International Journal of Environmental Research and Public Health, 18*(15), 7890.

Mertz, L. (2020). One shot wonder: A vaccine against all coronaviruses. *IEEE Pulse, 11*(6), 2–5.

Mir, H. H., Parveen, S., Mullick, N. H., & Nabi, S. (2021). Using structural equation modeling to predict Indian people's attitudes and intentions towards COVID-19 vaccination. *Diabetes & Metabolic Syndrome, 15*(3), 1017–1022.

Mohamed Hussein, A. A., Salem, M. R., Salman, S., Abdulrahim, A. F., Al Massry, N. A., Saad, M., ... Negida, A. (2020). Correlation between COVID-19 case fatality rate and percentage of BCG vaccination: Is it true the vaccine is protective? *The Egyptian Journal of Bronchology, 14*(1), 1–5.

Nadini, M., Zino, L., Rizzo, A., & Porfiri, M. (2020). A multi-agent model to study epidemic spreading and vaccination strategies in an urban-like environment. *Applied Network Science, 5*(1), 1–30.

Odoom, J., Soglo, R. S., Danso, S. A., & Xiaofang, H. (2020, December). A privacy-preserving Covid-19 updatable test result and vaccination provenance based on blockchain and smart contract. In *2019 International Conference on Mechatronics, Remote Sensing, Information Systems and Industrial Information Technologies (ICMRSISIIT)* (Vol. 1, pp. 1-6). IEEE.

Pal, R., Bhadada, S. K., & Misra, A. (2021). COVID-19 vaccination in patients with diabetes mellitus: Current concepts, uncertainties and challenges. *Diabetes & Metabolic Syndrome, 15*(2), 505–508.

Patelarou, E., Galanis, P., Mechili, E. A., Argyriadi, A., Argyriadis, A., Asimakopoulou, E., ... Patelarou, A. (2021). Factors influencing nursing students' intention to accept COVID-19 vaccination: A pooled analysis of seven European countries. *Nurse Education Today, 104*, 105010.

Rutschman, A. S. (2021). Social media self-regulation and the rise of vaccine misinformation. *Journal of Library Innovation*, *4*, 25.

Schwab, J. D., Schobel, J., Werle, S. D., Fürstberger, A., Ikonomi, N., Szekely, R., ... Kestler, H. A. (2021). Perspective on mHealth concepts to ensure users' empowerment–from adverse event tracking for COVID-19 vaccinations to oncological treatment. *IEEE Access: Practical Innovations, Open Solutions*, *9*, 83863–83875.

Umasabor-Bubu, O. Q., Bubu, O. M., Mbah, A. K., Nakeshbandi, M., & Taylor, T. N. (2021). Association between influenza vaccination and severe COVID-19 outcomes at a designated COVID-only hospital in brooklyn. *American Journal of Infection Control*, *49*(10), 1327–1330.

Wallace, J. (2021). Vaccines, Public Health, and the Law. *IEEE Technology and Society Magazine*, *40*(2), 35–39.

Wang, C., Han, B., Zhao, T., Liu, H., Liu, B., Chen, L., ... Cui, F. (2021a). Vaccination willingness, vaccine hesitancy, and estimated coverage at the first round of COVID-19 vaccination in China: A national cross-sectional study. *Vaccine*, *39*(21), 2833–2842.

Wang, J., Lyu, Y., Zhang, H., Jing, R., Lai, X., Feng, H., ... Fang, H. (2021b). Willingness to pay and financing preferences for COVID-19 vaccination in China. *Vaccine*, *39*(14), 1968–1976.

Wilson, S. (2020, November). A digital "Yellow Card" for securely recording vaccinations using Community PKI certificates. In *2020 IEEE International Symposium on Technology and Society (ISTAS)* (pp. 310-313). IEEE.

Zhang, B., Weissinger, L., Himmelreich, J., McMurry, N., Li, T. C., & Kreps, S. E. (2021). *Building robust and ethical vaccination verification systems*. Brookings TechStream.

Chapter 7

Heart Disease Prediction Framework Using Soft Voting–Based Ensemble Learning Techniques

Omprakash Nayak
National Institute of Technology, Raipur, India

Tejaswini Pallapothala
National Institute of Technology, Raipur, India

Govind P. Gupta
iD https://orcid.org/0000-0002-0456-1572
National Institute of Technology, Raipur, India

ABSTRACT

Cardiovascular disease is among the leading sources of the growing rate of morbidity and mortality worldwide, affecting roughly 50% of the adult age group in the healthcare sector. Heart disease claims the lives of about one person per minute in this modern era. Accurate detection methods for the timely identification of cardiovascular disorders are essential because there is rapid growth in the number of patients with this disease. The goal is to understand risk factors by analyzing the heart monitoring dataset using exploratory data analysis. This chapter proposes a heart disease prediction framework using soft voting-based ensemble learning techniques. Performance evaluation of the proposed framework and its comparison with the state-of-the-art models are done using a benchmark dataset in terms of accuracy, precision, sensitivity, specificity, and F1-score. Heart disease is a long-term problem with a greater risk of becoming worse over time. The proposed model has achieved an accuracy of 90.21%.

DOI: 10.4018/978-1-6684-5264-6.ch007

INTRODUCTION

The heart is the most important complex organ. In a nutshell, it controls blood circulation inside our bodies. Any cardiac abnormality might induce agony in plenty of other parts of the body (Sivabalakrishnan, 2019). Cardio Vascular Disease (CVD) is defined as any impairment in the regular beating of the heart. Coronary artery disorder is one of the leading causes of mortality in modern society. The myocardial disease can be caused by a sedentary lifestyle, smoking, drinking, and saturated calorie consumption, all of which can lead to hypertension (Dutta et al., 2020). As per the WHO survey, greater than 15 million people worldwide die each year because of heart problems. The latest WHO report published in 2020, 59.8 million fatalities worldwide transpired in 2018 because of myocardial infarction. Cardiovascular disease claimed the lives of 20.6 million individuals in 2015 (Anitha & Sridevi, 2019). Data gathering has been indicated by the WHO as having the opportunity to assist and diagnose the beginning stages of cardiac disease and deliver proper illness solutions. The key to avoiding cardio ailments is to maintain good lifestyle habits. CVDs include heart diseases, vascular diseases of the brain, and blood vessel diseases. One of the predominant sources of life-threatening impediments and fatality is cardiac disease. Heart disease treatment and therapy are highly challenging, especially in developing nations, due to a lack of effective diagnostic instruments, medical specialists, and other resources, all of which impede patient prognosis and treatment. The main contributing factors are insufficient preventive

Figure 1. Different factors affecting heart disease

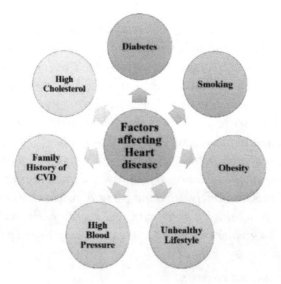

measures and a scarcity of trained or unpracticed medical personnel in the discipline (Latha & Jeeva, 2019). Although a large portion of heart disease is preventable, the number of instances continues to rise due to a shortage of preventive interventions. In today's digital era, the number of impersonal recommendations assist methods for cardiac disorder detection has been expanded by various researchers to facilitate and guarantee a good prognosis (El-Hasnony et al., 2022).

The conduction system of the heart is controlled by a set of nodes, valves, and neurotransmitters in your atrium. Each time this happens, electric impulses are transmitted through it. These signals cause individual

portions of your heart to grow and constrict. Using different machine learning models implemented with python, this study aims at predicting how well the heart is functioning (Mohan et al., 2019). The results of an electrocardiogram (ECG) test tell us how well the heart is functioning by tracing the electrical activity within the heart. The electrical pulse normally travels from the sinoatrial node (Repaka et al., 2019), represented by the P wave, across the atrium, to the atrioventricular node, and finally through the ventricular septum, indicated by the SRQ path. The curve in T will normally follow the direction of the QRS complex. When it occurs in the opposite direction, it reflects cardiac disease (Dwivedi, 2018).

Recently, many research works are studied AI-based solution for prediction of heart diseases. (Ali et al., 2019) These existing schemes suffer from poor accuracy. Thus, this paper has focused on design of an effective framework for efficient prediction of heart diseases using a novel soft voting-based ensemble learning techniques. The main contribution of this paper is pointed out as follows:

1. Design of an effective heart disease prediction framework using soft voting-based ensemble learning technique.

Figure 2. Normal QRS ST-Segment in ECG

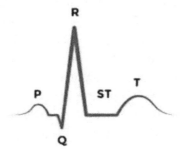

2. Performance evaluation of the proposed model and its comparison with the state-of-art models is done using a benchmark dataset in terms of accuracy, precision, sensitivity, specificity, and F1-score.

Remaining part of the paper is structured as follows: Section 2 describes review of the literature related to the heart disease prediction. Section 3 presents the proposed model with a detail working concepts. Section 4 presents description of the result analysis and comparative analysis with state-of-art techniques. In last, section 5 concludes the paper.

LITERATURE REVIEW

This section presents a brief literature review related to the heart disease prediction techniques. Apurb et al. (Sivabalakrishnan, 2019) work dealt with the forecasting of cardiac disorders employing ML techniques. The proposed approach was conducted on the cardiovascular disease UCI dataset. To forecast cardiovascular disease, they have incorporated different traditional ML approaches. The random forest classifier performed the best when it came to dataset prediction. The maximum accuracy was 90.16 percent, while the F1 score for the same was 0.909, and the precision and recall values were 0.937,0.882 respectively. In (Dutta et al., 2020), authors have discussed the imbalanced clinical data. They have gone through a variety of machine learning methods, but they are not working well to accomplish the occurrence of heart disease. A CNN model was employed to increase the network's speed and accuracy in finding and diagnosing different disease features of the heart. To grow the efficiency of the previous algorithm, they used LASSO followed by majority voting for filtering and selecting the important features.

In (Anitha & Sridevi, 2019), authors have discussed the causes and impact of cardiovascular diseases. The suggested scheme incorporates strength scores of those features which take a crucial responsibility in the classification of heart disease. They employed weighted associative rule mining to achieve a high confidence score and used an open dataset from the UCI repository and selected significant features using the WARM technique and generated 20 rules among them they are dependent on only 11 rules. In (Latha & Jeeva, 2019), for the identification and classification of heart diseases, ML techniques along with Swarm and Ant colony Optimizations is used. To acquire the most important features, the employed fast correlation technique. In the suggested research, disease detection is carried out with different ML approaches including KNN, Multilayer perceptron, Naïve Bayes,

SVM, and ANN optimized by swarm and ant colony optimization. They adopted the UCI dataset with a smaller number of features. In terms of disease diagnosis performance, the findings show that the KNN outperforms other models with the highest accuracy.

In (El-Hasnony et al., 2022), authors have explained the different active learning methods for the prediction of cardiovascular disease. The focus of this methodology is to improve categorization quality by considering feedback from users with sparsely labeled data. For feature extraction, they use hyperparameter optimization. To improve performance and provide a better outcome, the model was implemented with five active learning algorithms such as MMC, Random, Adaptive, QUIRE, and AUDI. This research aims to use multi-label active learning to reduce the costs of labeling. Among all those five learning models, QUIRE was performing in the best way with 78.4%.

In (Mohan et al., 2019), heart disease detection using different ML algorithms is studied. The collected image will be segmented, and the features extracted from it using image processing techniques. To recognize the survival of this disorder, the collected features are categorized using SVM, LR, Naïve Bayes, DT, and Hybrid Random Forest with Linear Method. Among all those approaches, HRFLM was exhibiting the highest accuracy. The proposed system accuracy was 88.4 percent, which is its best performance. In (Repaka et al., 2019), this paper detects heart disease using Naïve Bayes Classification. Alternative deep learning models and machine learning methods for visualizing heart diseases are examined in this study. Machine learning techniques like the Bayes Net, sequential minimum optimization, multi-layer perceptron, and Naïve Bayes. Author accustomed the UCI dataset and applied dimensionality reduction for feature extraction, and they performed all the classifications on 11 features. Among all the ML approaches used, Naive Bayes worked with the highest accuracy and less training time.

In (Dwivedi, 2018), this article mainly focuses on the identification of heart diseases. To detect disease, it employs XGBoost on the Statlog dataset. The simulation results suggest whichever implemented solution is both expedient and worthwhile. One of the backdrops about this study is that they used less data for training. ML techniques were used to describe the steps involved in the classification of cardiovascular disease. XGBoost was carried out to detect the disease with high accuracy.

The following section includes a tabular column that gives a quick overview of the recent works related to cardiovascular disease detection. The various ML algorithms and Neural networks were used for identifying this condition, which we will look at in the next section.

Table 1. A quick summary of studied research methodologies on the classification of heart disease using different classifiers

Article	No. of features used	Dataset	Classifier	Performance	Advantages	Drawbacks
(Sivabalakrishnan, 2019)	14	UCI repository dataset	Decision Tree Logistic Regression Naïve Bayer Random Forest	90.16%	Best prediction performance	The training dataset was small with a smaller number of features.
(Dutta et al., 2020)	10	National Health and Nutritional Examination survey data	CNN	79.5%	Low-cost diagnosis	Low performance
(Anitha & Sridevi, 2019)	8	UCI	WARM	95% (confidence score)	Exhibits best performance with a smaller number of features	Doesn't perform well if more features are used
(Latha & Jeeva, 2019)	7	UCI	KNN, FCBO, PSO, ACO	99%	Best Performance	Need more for feature selection as it is employing three feature optimization techniques
(El-Hasnony et al., 2022)	12	UCI	MMC, Random, Adaptive, QUIRE, AUDI	78.4%	The proposed solution is both feasible and effective for sparsely labeled data	Accuracy was not that much up to the mark
(Mohan et al., 2019)	11	UCI	Hybrid Random Forest with Linear model	88.4%	Best prediction performance	Need to reduce the probability of false classification
(Repaka et al., 2019)	11	UCI	Naïve Bayes	89%	Training time was very less	Low accuracy when compared to KNN and Random Forest

PROPOSED METHOD

In this section, we have discussed working of our proposed model. The proposed method follows fundamentals such as Data Preprocessing, Outlier detection and removal, splitting datasets, etc. In this paper, we are predicting heart disease by using Ensemble Learning Classifiers. We have given the same input dataset to three different ML classifiers such as CAT, EXT, and BGG Classifiers for comparing their performance based on the accuracy of the algorithms. Fig.3. illustrates the block diagram of the proposed framework.

Figure 3. Proposed Architecture

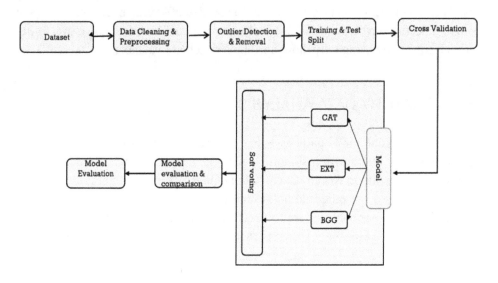

DATASET DESCRIPTION

In our present world scenario (Shah et al., 2020), input data involves a lot of noise, has missing values, and outliers, and is inconsistent. Data preprocessing involves the removal of the noise, and missing data, and organizing data in a proper format so that accuracy is increased. It enhances the quality of the data. It involves four key phases. They are Input data cleaning, Integration of the data, Transformation of the data, and Reduction of the data.

Data cleaning involves cleaning the data. It removes the noise present in the data. It handles missing values either by ignoring them or by filling the missing values by prediction manually or by certain numerical methods. Noise is removed by techniques like binning, regression, and clustering. Outliers are removed by applying certain knowledge tools (Gárate-Escamila et al., 2020). Data integration is the second step in data preprocessing. It merges the data present at multiple locations so that accuracy is increased. It is done by schema integration or object matching, removing redundant attributes from all data sources, and detection and resolution of data. Data transformation is transforming high-level data into low-level data for easier calculations. It uses generalization, attribute selection, and aggregation. Data reduction involves reducing the data dimensions so that the data is not high dimensional, but the quality of data remains the same. Data cube aggregation which is summarizing the data. Data compression is reducing the size of the data which may be lossy or lossless (Singh et al., 2018). Data discretization is used to divide the continuous data attributes into data intervals. Numerosity reduction is representing the data in a model format which reduces the burden of storing huge data. Attribute subset selection involves specifically selecting the attributes to resolve overfitting or underfitting by using only those attributes which are valuable.

EXPLORATORY DATA ANALYSIS

EDA is a technique for visually assessing information. It is used to detect trends, and patterns, or to confirm assumptions with the use of statistical summaries and graphical representations. Our data is ordinal, interval, and monotonic since as one variable increases the other variables tend to increase or decrease (Khourdifi & Bahaj, 2019). In our analysis, we focused on columns that have a higher absolute correlation value, especially columns that have a higher absolute value with the

Figure 4. Partition of the input dataset

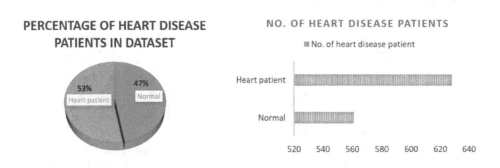

Figure 5. Checking Gender & Age-wise Distribution

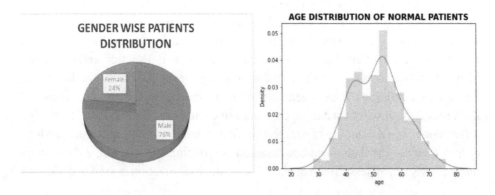

target column. So, there is a total of 1189 annals and 11 attributes with 1 response parameter. Now we will explore the outline of integer and binary variables. Here we may distribute our dataset based on different features like target variable, age, sex, and chest pain type which are shown below graphs. Bulleted lists may be included and should look like this:

In Figures 4 and 5, we can see in this dataset the male heart patient is higher than the females heart patient. And the average age of the patient is 55.

As shown in the graph in Figure 6, 76 percent of heart disease patients with chest discomfort had asymptomatic chest pain. Asymptomatic heart disorders, also called coronary thrombosis, description for 50-60 percent of cardiac morbidity and even premature mortality in India each year. Males are twice as likely as females to acquire SMI when they are in their middle years. SMI has very minor symptoms compared to cardiopulmonary arrest, and it is known as the "belligerent killer." Contrary to the signs of a typical myocardial infarction, whichever include angina

Table 2. Patients with heart disease depending on chest pain type

target	0	1
chest_pain_type		
asymptomatic	25.310000	76.910000
atypical angina	32.980000	4.940000
non-anginal pain	34.400000	14.170000
typical angina	7.310000	3.980000

Figure 6. Distribution of chest pain type

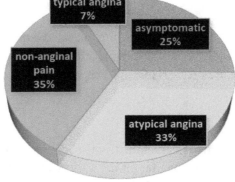

CHAIST PAIN OF HEART PATIENTS

Figure 7. Distribution of rest ECG

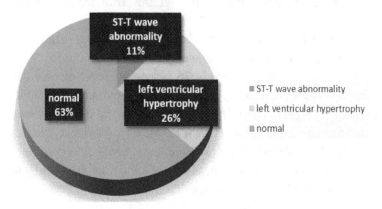

Table 3. Heart disease patient based on ECG

target	0	1
rest_ecg		
ST-T wave abnormality	11.050000	18.950000
left ventricular hypertrophy	26.020000	28.500000
normal	62.920000	52.550000

pectoris, acute pain in the jaw, dyspneic, perspiration, and vertiginous, the indicators of the myocardial disorder are transient and are frequently misdiagnosed as ordinary discomfort.

Split Dataset

We will split our dataset in two-part training part and a testing part. The training part consist of the target variable of 491 herat patient, and 446 normal patient and the testing set consists of the target variable of 123 heart patient and 112 normal patients.

Cross Validation

A set of data is acclimated to instruct the framework, but we won't predict whether our model is working well or not after training. So, to check the model we are using a cross-validation technique in this we infuse the unencountered data sample into the model and see how much it correctly (Sekar et al., 2022) classifies the data. In the methodology, we use the cross-validation technique to do that we divide the testing set into k subsets and train the model through each subset.

MACHINE LEARNING METHOD AND ALGORITHM

Soft Voting Based Ensemble Learning

Ensemble learning is a machine learning hypothesis that encompasses the findings of classification techniques to increase forecasting ability. Because we know that each ml model produces its accuracy and performance. So, some model has good performance (Rajamhoana et al., 2018) and some model has weak performance so to balance this performance mismatch we use the ensemble learning technique the voting technique to provide the best accuracy of the model. Soft voting is one of the ensembles voting methods that combine the different models to improve the model's performance. soft voting predicts the class with the largest summed probability from the model. And it also predicts the class membership probabilities (Gavhane et al., 2018).

CatBoost Classifier

Managing categorical variables can be time-consuming, especially if you have a big number of them. When your categorical variables have a lot of labels (i.e., they're highly cardinal), one-hot-encoding them raises the dimensionality enormously, making it harder to work with the data (Kavitha et al., 2021). CatBoost can cope with categorical variables automatically, and unlike other machine learning methods, it does not require considerable data pre-processing. (Tarawneh & Embarak, 2019)

Bagging Classifier

The Bagging meta-estimator is another name for it. It's an ensemble algorithm that is possibly employed to resolve both prediction and clustering difficulties (Bagging Classifier and Bagging Regressor). To make predictions, it employs the standard bagging technique (Haq et al., 2018). The steps for the bagging meta-estimator method are as follows:

1. Out of the original dataset, arbitrary subsets are constructed (Bootstrapping).
2. All features are included in the subgroup of the dataset.

3.   Each one of these smaller sets is fitted with a user-specified base estimator.

4.   To reach the e, the predictions from each model are integrated (Almustafa, 2020).

Extratree Classifier

The extract Trees approach is a form of ensemble classification algorithm that combines the outcomes of a "forest" of de-correlated decision trees. And then come up with a classification performance. It is quite similar to a Random Forest technique and differs mostly in the manner the forest's decision trees are constructed. The Extra Trees method (Al-Makhadmeh & Tolba, 2019) leverages the instruction data to construct many extremely randomized decision trees. In analysis, estimates are created by aggregating the decision tree forecasts, although a simple majority is employed in categorization.

RESULT AND ANALYSIS

Dataset Description

The lack of datasets on cardiovascular disease in the health domain is the main hindrance to the prediction of heart diseases. Increased availability of datasets on heart disease may give more research scope towards heart disease detection (Aleem et al., 2021). Machine learning/deep learning algorithms require the identification of different heart diseases and image datasets. In this section, we give a brief description of statlog and Cleveland (Khan, 2020) heart disease datasets developed by UCI. There are 11 attributes and one target attribute. It consists of 6 binary attributes and 5 integer parameters. The sample size contains 1189 patients with 53% having remarkable heart disease indicators. The remaining47% do not meet the indicators of heart disease and thus are considered healthy. Below is given the sample variables described in this dataset. Table 4 shows a checklist of all 12 parameters along with their specifications.

PERFORMANCE METRIC

Here we'll start by deciding which assessment criteria we'll use to evaluate our model performance. Sensitivity, specificity, Precision, F1-measure, Geometric mean, Mathew correlation coefficient, and ultimately the ROC AUC curve are the most relevant evaluation metrics for this problem domain.

Table 4. Information about the division of the dataset

Variables	Description
Age	Age of patient in years (Integer)
Sex	Gender of patient ($1 =$ male, $0 =$ female)
Chest pain	Chest pain type
resting bp s	Resting blood pressure (in mm/Hg on admission to hospital)
cholesterol	Serum cholesterol level
Fasting blood sugar	Fasting blood sugar $> 120mg / dl(1 =$ true, $0 =$ false)
Resting ECG	Resting electrocardiographic results
Max_heart rate	This is determined by calculating 220 maximum heart rate
Exercise angina	Exercise-Induced Angina (1 - yes, $0 =$ no)
oldpeak	ST depression induced by exercise relative to rest
ST slope	The slope of the peak exercise ST segment
target	Diagnosis of Heart Disease (Angiographic Disease Status) Value 0 : Healthy Value $1, 2, 3, 4$: heart disease stages

Matthew Correlation Coefficient (MCC*)*

The Matthews correlation coefficient (MCC) is a more appropriate analytical percentage which only really shows a high ranking if the estimation did well in all 4 confusion matrix classes (correctly predicted, false negative, incorrectly classified, and false-positive rate), correspondingly (Maji & Arora, 2019) to the magnitude of desirable and undesirable aspects in the data source.

$$MCC = (TP*TN – FP*FN) / \sqrt{(TP+FP)(TP+FN)(TN+FP)(TN+FN)} \tag{1}$$

Log Loss

The reliability of a learning approach having a confidence range from 0 to 1 as an estimation parameter is tested through logarithmic loss. The goal of our ML strategies is to diminish this score to the lowest achievable level. In a successful model, the log loss might be negligible. Log loss increases as the expected likelihood exceed mostly from real frequency. Therefore, project a chance of .012 only when consideration of identifier is 1 yields an ineffective response accompanying a large log loss.

Figure 8. Graph showing log loss for Predicted probabilities

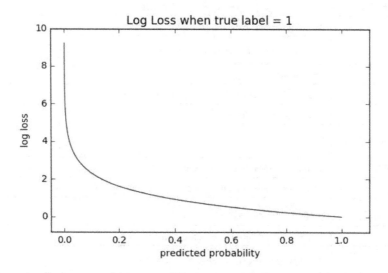

Given a true observation (isDog = 1), the graph above represents the scope of realizable log loss results. It falls as the finding likelihood method 1. Loss results in log values, on the other hand, growing fast when the expected probability drops (Saleh et al., 2020). Both sorts of errors are penalized by log loss, but notably confident and incorrect forecasts!

Table 5. Performance of all ML methods

	Model	Accuracy	Precision	Sensitivity	Specificity	F1 Score	ROC	Log Loss	MCC
0	RF	0.923404	0.92	0.934959	0.910714	0.927419	0.922837	2.645557	0.846473
1	MLP	0.859574	0.857143	0.878049	0.839286	0.86747	0.858667	4.850187	0.71843
2	KNN	0.846809	0.827068	0.894309	0.794643	0.859375	0.844476	5.291125	0.694264
3	EXT	0.914894	0.92562	0.910569	0.919643	0.918033	0.915106	2.939501	0.82967
4	XGB	0.910638	0.918033	0.910569	0.910714	0.914286	0.910642	3.086478	0.820985
5	cat	0.906383	0.917355	0.902439	0.910714	0.909836	0.906577	3.233451	0.812623
6	bgg	0.906383	0.917355	0.902439	0.910714	0.909836	0.906577	3.233451	0.812623
7	Adaboost	0.829787	0.837398	0.837398	0.821429	0.837398	0.829413	5.879009	0.658827
8	GBM	0.876596	0.885246	0.878049	0.875	0.881633	0.876524	4.26228	0.752776
9	**Proposed Model**	0.902128	0.909836	0.902439	0.901786	0.906122	0.902112	3.380428	0.803933

F1 Score

The composite index of objective functions seems to be the F1 Score. As a corollary, this metric takes into account both false negatives and false positives. Although it is sometimes obvious, F1 is occasionally highly beneficial than exactness (Dutta et al., 2020). It is certainly relevant if the dispersion of social classes is asymmetrical. Efficiency works best whenever the costs of false negatives and positives are equivalent. It is indeed essential to examine both Precision and Recall unless the value of false positives and false negatives varies considerably. The F1 score in our methodology proposed is 0.701.s.

F1 Score = 2*(Precision * Recall) / (Recall + Precision)   (2)

RESULT ANALYSIS

In our proposed method we have used 10 different ml methods to build a baseline model out of them Extra tree classifier, Bagging Classifier and Cat Boost method are our proposed methods, and the other 7 methods are used for comparison purposes. In Table 4 we will see the performance of each model. There is the various parameter that contributes to deciding the performance of the model based on these parameter value we can say that Random Forest, Extra tree classifier, and XG boost performed well as compared to other methods. We will see the performance of each ML method

Figure 9. Confusion Matrix for Ensemble Voting

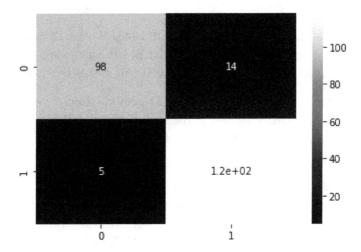

in Table 5. And Figure 9 represents the histogram representation of the performance of all models.

All three model has different accuracy and performance so here we apply the ensemble approach with a soft voting classifier. So, after applying that we get the overall accuracy of 0.902. in table 6 we will see the performance of our model. And figure 12 represents the confusion matrix or performance matrix of our model that describes the association between true negative, false positive, true positive, and false negative.

CONCLUSION

This paper has proposed a heart disease prediction framework using soft voting-based ensemble learning techniques. This research work helps to detect cardiovascular disease using the State log and Cleveland dataset's entire characteristics and key attributes. Different ensemble learning techniques including Catboost and bagging were trained in furthermore the Extra Trees Classifier, and 7 other ML approaches. The outcome of these classifiers is given as input to soft voting in the away to choose the best performance approach. The accuracy of this model was 90.21%. The Random Forest model produces excellent results when compared to the remaining other techniques. The Adaboost model's efficiency in this situation is regarded as poor, and it is no longer used to forecast the new occurrence of cardiovascular disorders. The RF classifier showed that it could learn to detect illness symptoms and then use that information to diagnose future occurrences.

REFERENCES

Al-Makhadmeh, Z., & Tolba, A. (2019). Utilizing IoT wearable medical device for heart disease prediction using higher order Boltzmannmodel: A classification approach. *Measurement, 147*, 106815. doi:10.1016/j.measurement.2019.07.043

Aleem, A., Prateek, G., & Kumar, N. (2021, December). Improving Heart Disease Prediction Using Feature Selection Through GeneticAlgorithm. In *International Conference on Advanced Network Technologies and Intelligent Computing* (pp. 765-776). Springer.

Ali, L., Rahman, A., Khan, A., Zhou, M., Javeed, A., & Khan, J. A. (2019). An automated diagnostic system for heart disease prediction based on statistical model and optimally configured deep neural network. *IEEE Access: Practical Innovations, Open Solutions, 7*, 34938–34945. doi:10.1109/ACCESS.2019.2904800

Almustafa, K. M. (2020). Prediction of heart disease and classifiers' sensitivity analysis. *BMC Bioinformatics*, *21*(1), 1–18. doi:10.118612859-020-03626-y PMID:32615980

Anitha, S., & Sridevi, N. (2019). Heart disease prediction using data mining techniques. *Journal of Analysis and Computation*.

Dutta, A., Batabyal, T., Basu, M., & Acton, S. T. (2020). An efficient convolutional neural network for coronary heart disease prediction. *Expert Systems with Applications*, *159*, 113408. doi:10.1016/j.eswa.2020.113408

Dwivedi, A. K. (2018). Performance evaluation of different machine learning techniques for prediction of heart disease. *Neural Computing & Applications*, *29*(10), 685–693. doi:10.100700521-016-2604-1

El-Hasnony, I. M., Elzeki, O. M., Alshehri, A., & Salem, H. (2022). Multi-label active learning-based machine learning model for heart disease prediction. *Sensors (Basel)*, *22*(3), 1184. doi:10.339022031184 PMID:35161928

Gárate-Escamila, A. K., El Hassani, A. H., & Andrès, E. (2020). Classification models for heart disease prediction using feature selection and PCA. *Informatics in Medicine Unlocked*, *19*, 100330. doi:10.1016/j.imu.2020.100330

Gavhane, A., Kokkula, G., Pandya, I., & Devadkar, K. (2018, March). Prediction of heart disease using machine learning. In *2018 second international conference on electronics, communication and aerospace technology (ICECA)* (pp. 1275-1278). IEEE. 10.1109/ICECA.2018.8474922

Haq, A. U., Li, J. P., Memon, M. H., Nazir, S., & Sun, R. (2018). A hybrid intelligent system framework for the prediction of heart disease using machine learning algorithms. *Mobile Information Systems*.

Kavitha, M., Gnaneswar, G., Dinesh, R., Sai, Y. R., & Suraj, R. S. (2021, January). Heart disease prediction using hybrid machine learning model. In *2021 6th International Conference on Inventive Computation Technologies (ICICT)* (pp. 1329-1333). IEEE. 10.1109/ICICT50816.2021.9358597

Khan, M. A. (2020). An IoT framework for heart disease prediction based on MDCNN classifier. *IEEE Access, 8*, 34717-34727.

Khourdifi, Y., & Bahaj, M. (2019). Heart disease prediction and classification using machine learning algorithms optimized by particle swarm optimization and ant colony optimization. *International Journal of Intelligent Engineering and Systems*, *12*(1), 242–252. doi:10.22266/ijies2019.0228.24

Latha, C. B. C., & Jeeva, S. C. (2019). Improving the accuracy of prediction of heart disease risk based on ensemble classification techniques. *Informatics in Medicine Unlocked*, *16*, 100203. doi:10.1016/j.imu.2019.100203

Maji, S., & Arora, S. (2019). Decision tree algorithms for prediction of heart disease. In *Information and communication technology forcompetitive strategies* (pp. 447–454). Springer. doi:10.1007/978-981-13-0586-3_45

Mohan, S., Thirumalai, C., & Srivastava, G. (2019). Effective heart disease prediction using hybrid machine learning techniques. *IEEE Access: Practical Innovations, Open Solutions*, *7*, 81542–81554. doi:10.1109/ACCESS.2019.2923707

Rajamhoana, S. P., Devi, C. A., Umamaheswari, K., Kiruba, R., Karunya, K., & Deepika, R. (2018, July). Analysis of neural networks based heart disease prediction system. In *2018 11th international conference on human system interaction (HSI)* (pp. 233-239). IEEE. 10.1109/HSI.2018.8431153

Repaka, A. N., Ravikanti, S. D., & Franklin, R. G. (2019, April). Design and implementing heart disease prediction using naives Bayesian. In *2019 3rd International conference on trends in electronics and informatics (ICOEI)* (pp. 292-297). IEEE. 10.1109/ICOEI.2019.8862604

Saleh, B., Saedi, A., Al-Aqbi, A., & Salman, L. (2020). Analysis of Weka Data Mining Techniques for Heart Disease Prediction System. *International Journal of Medical Reviews, 7*(1), 15-24.

Sekar, J., Aruchamy, P., Sulaima Lebbe Abdul, H., Mohammed, A. S., & Khamuruddeen, S. (2022). An efficient clinical support system for heart disease prediction using TANFIS classifier. *Computational Intelligence*, *38*(2), 610–640. doi:10.1111/coin.12487

Shah, D., Patel, S., & Bharti, S. K. (2020). Heart disease prediction using machine learning techniques. *SN Computer Science*, *1*(6), 1–6. doi:10.100742979-020-00365-y

Singh, P., Singh, S., & Pandi-Jain, G. S. (2018). Effective heart disease prediction system using data mining techniques. *International Journal-p of Nanomedicine*, *13*, 121.

Sivabalakrishnan, M. (2019). An enhanced weighted associative classification algorithm without preassigned weight based on ranking hubs. *International Journal of Advanced Computer Science and Applications*, *10*(10).

Tarawneh, M., & Embarak, O. (2019, February). Hybrid approach for heart disease prediction using data mining techniques. In *International Conference on Emerging Internetworking, Data & Web Technologies* (pp. 447-454). Springer. 10.1007/978-3-030-12839-5_41

Chapter 8

IoT–Based Health Risk Prediction by Collecting and Analyzing HIIT Data in Real Time Using Edge Computing

Shrikrishn Bansal
The LNM Institute of Information Technology, India

Rajbir Kaur
The LNM Institute of Information Technology, India

ABSTRACT

Increased awareness of the benefits of physical exercise has motivated people to improve physical fitness by doing high-intensity interval training (HIIT). HIIT (where one needs to work at 70-85% of one's maximum heart rate) and forceful exercise sessions can lead to health risks such as cardiac arrest, heat strokes, or lung diseases because people are unaware of their body health and endurance status. It is essential that the health parameters of people who exercise outside controlled environments like the gym be acquired and analyzed during workout sessions. This chapter aims to design an IoT-based timely warning system based on edge computing responsible for identifying unusual patterns in the monitored health parameters and alerting the person involved in an exercise about any deviation from expected behavior. The authors collect real-time data from individuals during the exercise sessions. The data analysis provides an assessment of the health parameters and predicts any health risks during the HIIT session.

DOI: 10.4018/978-1-6684-5264-6.ch008

INTRODUCTION

It is essential to exercise to stay healthy and fit. It is observed that people who exercise regularly have lower mental stress and anxiety levels, increased immunity, and good bone and muscle strength. In addition, the requirement of at least 150 minutes of high-intensity physical exercise a day for safe and disease-free living by the World Health Organization (WHO) has driven people to devote time and wealth to this important physical activity (Pate et al., 2006).

Several recent studies have suggested that High-intensity interval training (HIIT) may result in improvement in physical fitness and cardiovascular health as compared to continuous moderate exercise (CME) (Kessler et al., 2012). HIIT involves short, intense workouts, alternating with recovery periods. Although high-intensity exercise provides many health benefits including building muscle power, improving oxygen and blood flow, reducing blood sugar, it also carries some risks. There is a high probability that physical health is significantly affected during high-intensity exercise sessions, particularly due to the prevalence of complex ambient environments (Kemmler & Stengel, 2013). High-intensity exercise can increase the risk of sudden heart attacks and cardiac deaths in people (Eijsvogels, Thompson, and Franklin, 2018). Many health conditions can be caused while exercising at hot temperatures, people are susceptible to heat exhaustion and heatstroke.

It is recommended that people go to the gym and perform such exercises under the guidance of experienced trainers in a controlled environment. However, it is not possible for everyone to go to the gym or train under experienced trainers due to constraints of time and cost.

It is essential that the health parameters of people who exercise outside controlled environments like the gym be acquired and analyzed during the workout sessions. The analysis can provide an assessment of the health parameters in real-time during an exercise session to determine and predict any health risks. Therefore, there is a need to develop an IoT-based system that can determine physical fitness and continuously monitor exercise intensity and provide early warning of a health risk so that the user can respond accordingly.

The objective of this work is to design a real-time IoT-based early warning system with the purpose of saving lives through timely analysis of the health parameters of a person while one is exercising. The proposed system monitors the well-being of the person and displays the sensed data to the person. It predicts the risk using a machine learning model to alert the person if needed.

BACKGROUND

During the HIIT workout session, the health parameters of a person change rapidly. If a person doing HIIT is unaware of their body health and endurance status— dizziness, cardiac arrest, and other health-related problems might increase. Therefore, there must be some real-time system that can alert a person during the HIIT workout session if their health parameters deviate from the expected behavior. If the health parameters of the people are not analyzed during their workout session, health-related problems may occur, which may also result in the death of a person.

There have been several works for monitoring the health of a person. Some of these works have analyzed the data in the cloud, which leads to an increase in the latency of the response time. There are other works that are monitoring the body parameters to optimize the performance of the sportsperson.

Smeaton et al. (2008) performs real-time monitoring of the health of sportsperson during their training and sporting activity. The authors use on-body sensors to monitor the motion, breathing, heart rate, heat flux, location, and galvanic skin response (GSR). The objective of this work is to maximize the performance of a sportsperson in their event. A web-based tool was used to visualize the aggregated sensor data. The authors optimize a sportsperson's performance by alerting the coach or user when the sportsperson reaches an excessive level of physiological response.

Santosh Kumar et al. (2014) have collected data like heart rate, weight, human BP, and movements from the athlete's body. The authors provided an optimal solution using Wi-Fi to monitor the human BP and movements changing the human body with the help of sensors and displayed these values to LCD display. The objective of this work is to monitor the Blood pressure of the user during their sports activity to enable them to compare the abnormal performance of health indicators.

Cheng et al. (2017) has designed a wearable heat stroke detection device with early notification ability. The authors have collected data like GSR, heart rate, body temp, and surrounding temp and have applied the Fuzzy theory to detect the features of heatstroke for users. The suggested architecture includes sensors, microcontrollers, LoRa modules, a risk evaluation module, and an alarm module. The objective of this work is to alert the user when the system gets a high rating for the heatstroke level of the user.

The works (Smeaton et al., 2008; Kumar, 2014; Chen et al., 2017) monitor several health parameters in real-time of an athlete during training or sporting events. Athletes or sportspeople are trained under supervision. These works are not a good fit for users who exercise on their own and may be oblivious to the hazards of excessive training to their health. Moreover, these works do not predict health risk levels in real-time.

Huifeng et al. (2020) proposed a wearable IoT-based device that enables to track the performance of the sportsperson. The authors have used machine learning techniques to analyze the data in the cloud.

Bhatia and Sood (2017) have offered an intelligent IoT technology-based healthcare system to provide individuals with ubiquitous healthcare during their fitness sessions. The intelligence of the presented system lies in its capacity to assess health problems in real-time during workouts and forecast the instability of a probabilistic health state. The objective of this work is to predict the health of a person during fitness exercise as vulnerable or non-vulnerable using a machine learning model in real-time. For predictive purposes, the proposed system uses an Artificial Neural Network (ANN) model.

The authors have developed the predicting machine learning model and performed the data analysis on the cloud. This work is done for gym-based workouts where we have experienced trainers for guidance during the fitness session.

The two papers (Wang et al., 2020; Bhatia & Sood, 2017) have successfully predicted the risk level using machine learning and they performed this prediction on the cloud. Cloud analytics has a limitation of providing faster decision-making, lower cost of central data storage and management, and lower cost of data transmission as compared to edge analytics.

Majumder et al. (2019) have developed a smart IoT system to collect data for heart rate and body temperature. The authors use signal processing and machine learning to predict sudden cardiac arrests. The work (Majumder et al., 2019) has successfully implemented the machine learning model on the local mobile application instead of the cloud. The authors have trained and deployed their machine learning model on mobile applications. Mobile applications are susceptible to privacy breaches.

MAIN FOCUS OF THE CHAPTER

Different researchers have successfully implemented the solution for collecting various health parameters. Some of the works have also used machine learning models to predict the risk in real-time. These pieces of research are either for the sportspersons, athletes, or the person exercising in the gym. But this research is not implemented for the persons doing HIIT workouts outside the controlled environment. Some of the studies analyze and predict the risk using cloud computing, whereas using edge computing can lead to faster decision-making and lower the cost of data transmission. All the studies monitor different health parameters, whereas combining all the parameters in one research and adding other health parameters such as body temperature, systolic and diastolic blood pressure, and heat stroke level affected during the workout can lead to more accurate predictions for the risk during the exercise.

In this chapter, the author's primary focus is to analyze the various health parameters in real-time to predict the risk level for an individual during the HIIT workout session using a machine learning algorithm. A dataset containing different health parameters is required to train the ML model. But due to confidentiality and privacy concerns, IoT data related to health parameters that the authors are interested in is difficult to find in the public domains. As a result, the authors created their dataset by collecting the data in real-time using on-body sensors for an individual during the HIIT workout session. Age, Gender, HR, SBP, DBP, SpO2, the surrounding temperature, and body temperature are parameters that the authors have monitored during the HIIT sessions. The dataset is labeled into three classes based on the threshold values for each parameter. The authors trained various ML models: NB, KNN, ANN, Decision tree, SVM on the final dataset to find the best suitable model for the health-related data. Once the authors found the best-suited model for the dataset, the model was trained on Google Colab and deployed on the micro-controller to predict the risk level in real-time when the new set of data is collected from the individual during the workout session.

SOLUTIONS AND RECOMMENDATIONS

In this chapter, the authors propose the design of an IoT-based timely warning system based on edge computing. The system monitors the health parameters of an individual involved in some strenuous exercise. The system identifies unusual patterns in the monitored health parameters and alerts the person involved in an exercise in case there is a deviation from expected behavior in the monitored health parameter.

The authors collect real-time data related to health parameters like heart rate, systolic blood pressure, diastolic blood pressure, heat stroke, body temperature, surrounding temperature, blood saturation level (SpO2) for different age groups and genders. These health parameters are analyzed in real-time to predict any health risk. This helps the person who is at risk to timely manage the situation. To identify the model with the highest predictive efficiency, the authors train and test different machine learning models. The authors measure the performance of the model on quantity metrics like accuracy, precision, recall, and F1 score.

A person involved in strenuous exercise is prone to cardiac arrest and heat stroke (Kemmler & Stengel, 2013; Eijsvogels, Thompson, and Franklin, 2018). Parameters like Heart Rate, Blood Pressure, Stroke level, SpO2 level, Blood Sugar level, Blood Cholesterol level are monitored to determine if a person is susceptible to cardiac arrest (Smeaton et al., 2008; Kumar, 2014; Chen et al., 2017; Wang et al., 2020; Bhatia & Sood, 2018; Majumder et al., 2019; "Heart Information Center: Heart Disease Risk Factors", n.d.; "Understand Your Risks to Prevent a Heart Attack", 2016;

Table 1. Comparison of the proposed system with the other state-of-art applications

Author	Is ML Used?	Edge/Cloud	Data Transfer Protocol Used	Application Domain	Number of Health Parameters Used
Alan F. Smeaton (2008)	No	----	Not Mentioned	Sportsperson based healthcare	4
P. Santhosh Kumar (2014)	No	----	WIFI	Sportsperson based healthcare	1
Sheng-Tao Chen (2017)	No	----	LoRa	General Purpose healthcare	5
Wang Huifeng (2020)	Yes (Bayesian Classifier)	Cloud	WIFI	Sportsperson based healthcare	
Munish Bhatia (2018)	Yes (ANN)	Cloud	WIFI	GYM workout-based healthcare	6
Majumder (2019)	Yes (Decision Tree)	Local System	Bluetooth	General-purpose healthcare	2
Our Approach	Yes (ANN)	Edge	Bluetooth	Home-based HIIT workout	7

Kulick, n.d.). For this work, the author chooses parameters that are easy to measure by placing some sensors on an individual body. Hence, the authors monitored the heart rate, blood pressure, stroke level, SpO2 level of the person by using wearable body sensors and biosensors.

Heat exhaustion is a syndrome that occurs when your body overheats, resulting in excessive perspiration and a fast pulse. It's one of three heat-related disorders, the mildest of which is heat cramps and the most serious of which is heatstroke. Heat exhaustion is caused by prolonged exposure to high temperatures, especially when paired with high humidity. It can also be caused by excessive physical exercise. Heat exhaustion can quickly progress to heatstroke, a life-threatening illness that can result in death if not treated promptly. The author measured body temperature and surrounding temperature to calculate the heatstroke level as defined in (Javed et al., 2020).

Table 1 shows the comparison of works by various authors with our work.

Figure 1 shows the architecture of our work. The proposed system records in real-time, the health parameters of the person who is exercising.

Figure 1. Proposed architecture

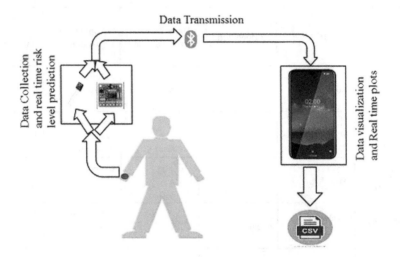

The architecture consists of the following main components:

1. **Wearable device:** The wearable device is composed of various sensors like temperature sensor, BP sensor, Pulse rate, and SpO2 sensor. The sensors are attached to Arduino nano 33 ble sense. The wearable sensors collect data about body temperature, heart rate, SpO2 level, blood pressure from the individual during HIIT sessions. The authors used Bluetooth to transfer the data to the mobile application.
2. **Machine learning model on edge device:** The authors train the machine learning model used to predict the risk level in real-time on Google colab. This model is then deployed to the micro-controller. The authors classify the risk zones as Normal, Warning, and Danger.
3. **Mobile Application:** This provides real-time visualization of the health parameters of the person during exercise. It also displays the warning if the high risk to a person's health is predicted.
4. **Data Store:** The data collected from the sensors is stored in the CSV files. The data can also be stored in the cloud.

Figure 2 shows the flow of the work. Data is acquired in real-time from the wearable body sensors of an exercising person. The data is passed to the machine learning model which analyzes the data to predict the risk level of a person. The data and the predicted risk level are communicated to the mobile application for visualization and warning if the risk to the person is high. The data along with the predicted risk level is also stored in the CSV file.

Figure 2. Proposed workflow

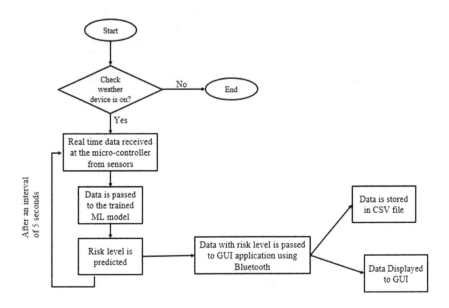

Hardware Details and Data acquisition

IoT data, especially related to health applications, are difficult to find. A few datasets that are available in public domains (*Heart Attack Prediction*, 2018; *BIDMC PPG and Respiration Dataset V1.0.0*, 2018; *Heart Disease Prediction*, 2020) did not contain data for all the parameters that the authors were interested in. As a result, the authors collect real-time data for the solution.

Figure 3 shows the block diagram of the hardware used in the proposed architecture for monitoring the health parameters of a person while they are exercising.

This Task used a variety of sensors to perform data collection tasks. The list is below:

1. **DHT11 Temperature and Humidity sensor:** The DHT11 is a low-cost temperature and humidity sensor. The sensor is attached to the Arduino board and measures the surrounding temperature in degrees Celsius of the area/room where a person is exercising. The data is directly sent as an input to the ML model.
2. **MAX30100:** The MAX30100 is a sensor arrangement that consolidates a heartbeat oximeter and a pulse screen. This sensor is used to measure heart rate in beats per min and blood oxygen level in percentage.
3. **LM35 temperature sensor:** The LM35 is a temperature sensor that is used to measure body temperature in degrees Celsius of the person involved in HIIT.

Figure 3. Block diagram of the hardware

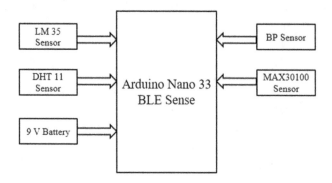

4. **Sunrom Blood pressure Sensor:** A blood pressure sensor by sunrom shows the systolic and diastolic blood pressure of an individual during HIIT in mmHg. It is easy to operate and can be fitted over your wrist like a watch.

5. **Arduino nano 33 ble:** The Nano 33 BLE Sense is Arduino's 3.3V AI-empowered board in the smallest accessible structure. It accompanies the in-fabricated Bluetooth module. It has the capacity to run Edge Computing applications (AI) utilizing TinyML. It enables the making of AI models and transfers them to the board using Arduino IDE. The Arduino Nano 33 BLE Sense has an nRF52840 microcontroller.

Figure 4. Required hardware. (a)LM35 (b)MAX30100 (c)BP sensor (d)DHT11 (e) Arduino nano 33 ble sense

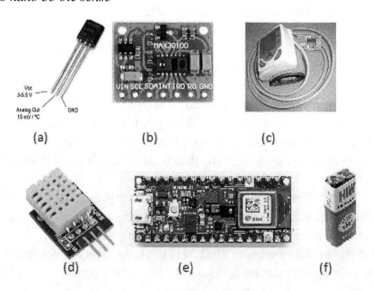

Figure 4 shows the sensors and other hardware used in our implementation. The sensors are connected to Arduino Nano 33 BLE sense. A wearable device assembled using sensors and other hardware is shown in Figure 5.

The authors used Arduino IDE to write and compile the code for the Arduino Nano 33 BLE sense micro-controller. The code consists of the following modules:

1. **Data Collection:** The data from the sensors is processed. The following libraries were used in the Arduino programming to work with the sensors:
    a. MAX30100_PulseOximeter.h
    b. Wire.h
    c. ArduinoBLE.h
    d. ArduinoJson.h
    e. DHT.h
2. **Data Communication:** The data collected from the sensors is communicated to the mobile application using Bluetooth. The BLE is integrated on the Arduino board. The values collected from the individual are sent as a JsonObject to the inbuilt Bluetooth of the Arduino.
3. **Mobile Application:** This is used to visualize the real-time data of an exercising person during their HIIT session. The application displays data and saves it in a CSV file.

Figure 6 shows how our IoT device is attached to the body to collect the real-time health parameters of the person during the HIIT workout session.

Figure 5. IoT device

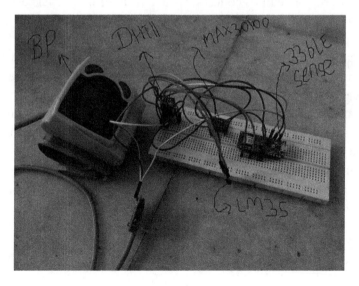

Figure 6. Device connected to the body during HIIT session

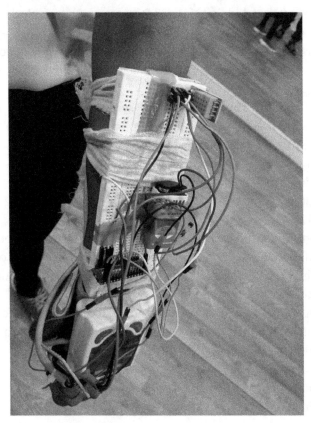

For this work, the authors collect real-time data for individuals using on-body sensor devices during their HIIT sessions. Persons from different age groups and different genders are considered. The authors collect data from 30 people. The authors collected data of each person for 5-7 days. Parameters of 18 males and 12 females are monitored. 21 persons are aged less than 45 years and 9 persons are aged more than 45 years. Every individual was asked to perform exercises for a minimum of 15 minutes. The readings of different parameters were recorded simultaneously. Table 2 and Table 3 lists HIIT sessions for people in age groups less than 45 years and people in age groups more than 45 years respectively.

DateTime, Age, Gender, HR, SBP, DBP, SpO2, the surrounding temperature, and body temperature are among the parameters that the authors have monitored while the person is doing HIIT sessions. The total number of entries in our dataset is 21931.

Figure 7 shows the sample data. It contains sensor values of different parameters in the interval of 5 seconds.

Figure 7. Sample data collected in real-time during the HIIT session

DateTime	AGE	Gender	HR	SBP	DBP	BT	ST	SpO2
2021-07-02 11:35:52	18	1	71	123	77	36.9	30	99
2021-07-02 11:35:52	18	1	74	124	77	36.9	30	97
2021-07-02 11:35:57	18	1	78	125	77	36.9	30	94
2021-07-02 11:36:02	18	1	83	126	77	37	30	92
2021-07-02 11:36:07	18	1	87	127	77	37.1	30	91
2021-07-02 11:36:12	18	1	90	128	77	37.1	30	89
2021-07-02 11:36:17	18	1	93	129	77	37.2	30	87
2021-07-02 11:36:22	18	1	98	130	77	37.2	30	84
2021-07-02 11:36:27	18	1	106	132	78	37.4	30	80
2021-07-02 11:36:32	18	1	114	134	79	37.5	30	78
2021-07-02 11:36:37	18	1	123	135	80	37.6	30	75
2021-07-02 11:36:43	18	1	130	136	82	37.7	30	71

Table 2. HIIT session for less than 45 years old

Set of Exercises
Three sets of Arm Swing for 30 sec each with 10-sec of interval
Three sets of Running for 30 sec each with 10-sec of interval
Three sets of But Kick for 30 sec each with 10-sec of interval
Three sets of Squats for 30 sec each with 10-sec of interval
Three sets of Jumping Jack for 30 sec each with 10-sec of interval
Three sets of Jump for 30 sec each with 10-sec of interval
Three sets of Side bend for 30 sec each with 10-sec of interval
Three sets of High knees for 30 sec each with 10-sec of interval

Table 3. HIIT session for greater than 45 years old

Set of Exercises
Two sets of Arm Swing for 30 sec each with 20-sec of interval
Two sets of Running for 30 sec each with 20-sec of interval
Two sets of But Kick for 30 sec each with 20-sec of interval
Two sets of Squats for 30 sec each with 20-sec of interval
Two sets of Jumping Jack for 30 sec each with 20-sec of interval
Two sets of Jump for 30 sec each with 20-sec of interval
Two sets of High knees for 30 sec each with 20-sec of interval

Here, HR represents the Heart Rate, SBP and DBP represent the Systolic and Diastolic Blood Pressure respectively, BT is the body temperature, ST is the surrounding temperature and SpO2 is the level of blood oxygen.

This data is sent as an input to the ML model so that the risk level can be predicted. The data is also stored in a CSV file as displayed in the flowchart in Figure 2.

Next, the authors trained different ML algorithms on our data. The authors compared the performance of these algorithms for usage in health risk prediction.

Comparative Analysis of Machine Learning Algorithms for Risk Level Prediction

The authors evaluated several ML algorithms to pick the most effective predictive algorithm for our dataset. Figure 8 is the block diagram of the process authors have followed for evaluation. The process is described in the following subsections.

Data Classification

The authors labeled their dataset into three classes based on the threshold values of each parameter. The class labels used are Normal zone, Warning zone, and Danger zone. Table 4 shows the threshold values for HR, SpO2, and heat stroke levels. Maximum heart rate is prescribed as 220-age by the Centers for Disease Control

Figure 8. Data analysis process

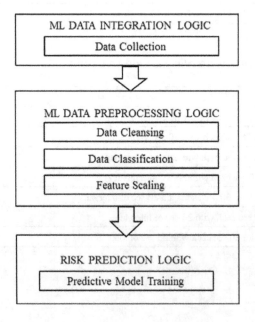

Table 4. Threshold values

Parameters	Normal Zone	Warning Zone	Danger Zone
HR	60 to HRlimit	HRlimit to HRmax	>=HRmax
SpO2 Level	92 to 100	85 to 91	<85
Heat Stroke Level	Normal	Caution	Danger

Here, HRmax = 220-age
Here, HRlimit is 80% of HRmax

Table 5. Calculation of heatstroke level

Heat Index [⁰C]	Body Temperature [⁰C]	Oxygen Level	Observation
27-32	37-38	75-73	Caution
32-41	39-40	72-70	Extreme Caution
41-54	41-42	69-65	Danger
Over 54	Above 52	Less than 65	Extreme Danger

and Prevention. The target heart rate for the HIIT session is specified as 80% of the maximum heart rate of a person (*Target Heart Rate and Estimated Maximum Heart Rate | Physical Activity*, n.d.). SpO2 level threshold values are prescribed according to BTS Guidelines (O'Driscoll et al., 2017). They suggest the SpO2 level above 92% for the healthy person.

The authors calculate Heatstroke levels using surrounding temperature, body temperature, and SpO2 level as defined in (Javed et al., 2020). Table 5 shows the formula used to get the Heat Stroke level (Javed et al., 2020).

Table 6 shows the permissible values for SBP and DBP based on age and gender. Systolic and Diastolic blood pressure threshold values are based on a study by (Sabbahi et al., 2017). They have suggested the ranges at maximal physical exertion. Their suggestions are based on the research conducted on 1605 healthy men and 1312 healthy women aged 20-79 years without cardiovascular disease.

The authors used Stratified K Fold cross-validation to split the dataset into different folds of training and testing dataset. The k-fold technique separates a dataset into k non-overlapping folds and performs cross-validation on each of them. A test set for each of the k folds is held back, while the rest of the folds are utilized as a training dataset. For each holdout set, a total of k models is fitted and assessed, and the mean performance is provided. Stratified K Fold is a K Fold variant that produces stratified folds. The folds are created by keeping track of the percentage of samples in each class. Here the authors have used k=10 for their dataset and trained the ML model on different combinations of train and test data using 10-fold cross-validation.

Table 6. Threshold values for systolic and diastolic blood pressure

	20-29	30-39	40-49	50-59	60-69
Male					
Resting SBP	124 ± 12	123±14	123±13	126±15	132±14
Resting DBP	78±9	80±10	81±10	81±9	80±9
Peak SBP	175±19	179±20	184±22	192±23	191±25
Peak DBP	78±12	80±11	83±11	85±12	85±13
Female					
Resting SBP	110±10	112±11	117±14	122±15	130±16
Resting DBP	70±9	72±10	75±10	76±10	76±10
Peak SBP	155±19	160±19	167±22	174±24	86±28
Peak DBP	74±10	78±10	80±11	82±11	83±15

The authors prepared the dataset by collecting the data in real-time during the HIIT session of an individual which led to the imbalanced dataset. This further leads to bias in training dataset which can influence the machine learning algorithms, leading to ignoring the minority class entirely. Random oversampling is used for rebalancing the class distribution to balance the dataset. It duplicates the examples from the minority class.

Feature Scaling

Feature scaling is a strategy to normalize the scope of autonomous factors. It limits the range of variables so that there is not much difference between values, and they can be compared on common ground.

The authors used Standardization to do feature scaling. Standardization is a change that focuses the information by eliminating the mean estimation of each component and afterward scale it by partitioning highlights by their standard deviation. In the wake of normalizing information, the mean will be zero and the standard deviation one.

Predictive Model Training

The authors trained the dataset on the following machine learning algorithms: Naive Bayes, KNN, ANN, Decision tree, and Support Vector Machine (SVM) to find the best suitable predictive model for health data.

Figure 9. Accuracy comparison of different ML algorithms

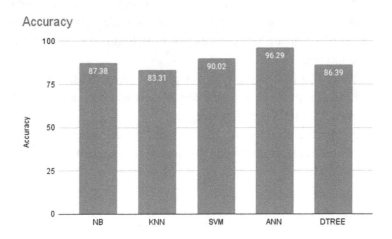

Figure 10. Precision, Recall, and F1 Score comparison of different ML algorithms

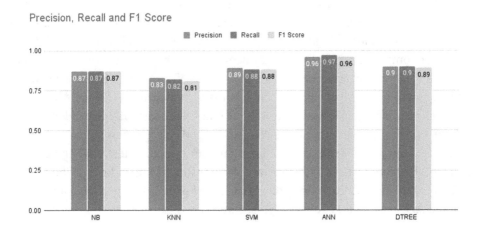

Figure 9 shows the accuracy and Figure 10 shows the precision, recall, F1 score for different machine learning models which were trained on the same dataset.

The first graph shows the accuracy level of all the algorithms when compared, the chart clearly depicts that KNN has 83.31% accuracy which is the least accuracy level as compared to other algorithms, this clearly states that this method of prediction is the least reliable, On the other hand, ANN has 96.29% accuracy highest among its corresponding methods, making it one of the most accurate methods of prediction analysis. The second graph provides an insight into three factors on which all the algorithms are mapped, these factors are precision, recall, and F1 score. The chart shows that ANN has the highest level of Precision 0.96, Recall 0.97, and F1 Score 0.96, which makes ANN the best method for prediction analysis, While KNN has the lowest level of Precision 0.83, Recall 0.82, F1 Score 0.81 as compared to its corresponding methods.

(Bansal, 2021) is a link to the code for predictive model training of different machine learning algorithms and their comparisons based on accuracy, Precision, Recall, F1 measure with the real-time dataset.

So, after comparing all the performance metrics parameters the authors found that ANN is the best performing predictive model for our dataset.

Discussion

The dataset contains 21931 records and 9 features. While training different machine learning models on a similar dataset the authors found that ANN has the highest level of accuracy. SVM outperforms KNN when there are large training data. KNN is better than SVM when the number of features is more as compared to training data. Since the data is sufficiently large it led to the high accuracy of SVM as compared to KNN. NB and DTree both are much faster than KNN due to KNN's real-time execution which leads to high accuracy compared to KNN. DTree is more flexible and easier compared to NB. DTree may neglect some key features in training data, which can lead to low accuracy when compared to NB. DTree is better when there is a large set of categorical values in data, but ANN outperforms DTree when there is enough training data. Some features in the dataset are mutually dependent which is the reason that SVM outperforms NB. ANN needs large training data to achieve sufficient accuracy. When there is a large number of parameters ANN gives high accuracy. The authors have 21931 records and 9 features in their dataset which gives 197379 parameters while training the ANN model which is quite a large number to train the ANN model and get the high accuracy.

FUTURE RESEARCH DIRECTIONS

In the future, the authors can use the person's historical health to tune the threshold values of various health metrics. Also, in this work, the authors record the data is recorded for healthy and fit persons with no history of heart problems. In the future, the work will be extended by collecting the data from unhealthy persons in clinical settings to fine-tune the machine learning model. These changes will enhance the accuracy of the prediction of our system.

CONCLUSION

The authors collect real-time health data of a person performing high-intensity activities. The parameters include age, gender, heart rate, blood pressure, body temperature, surrounding temperature, blood saturation level, and heat stroke level. The collected data is analyzed in real-time to predict and alert the person in case of health risk. The authors used ANN as a predictive machine learning model for real-time prediction of health risk during HIIT sessions. The data is analyzed locally to minimize latency in communication. The person can be alerted even in the absence of an internet connection.

REFERENCES

Bansal, S. (2021). *IoT Assisted Health Risk Monitoring*. Github. https://github.com/shrikrishnbansal/IoT-Assisted-Health-risk-monitoring

Bhatia, M., & Sood, S. (2017). A comprehensive health assessment framework to facilitate IoT-assisted smart workouts: A predictive healthcare perspective. *Computers in Industry*, *92-93*, 50–66. Advance online publication. doi:10.1016/j.compind.2017.06.009

BIDMC PPG and Respiration Dataset v1.0.0. (2018, June 20). *PhysioNet*. Retrieved February 27, 2022, from https://physionet.org/content/bidmc/1.0.0/

Chen, S. T., Lin, S. S., Lan, C. W., & Hsu, H. Y. (2017). Design and Development of a Wearable Device for Heat Stroke Detection. *Sensors (Basel)*, *18*(1), 17. doi:10.339018010017 PMID:29271893

Eijsvogels, T., Thompson, P. D., & Franklin, B. A. (2018). The "Extreme Exercise Hypothesis": Recent Findings and Cardiovascular Health Implications. *Current Treatment Options in Cardiovascular Medicine*, *20*(10), 84. doi:10.100711936-018-0674-3 PMID:30155804

Heart Attack Prediction. (2018, April 25). *Kaggle*. Retrieved February 27, 2022, from https://www.kaggle.com/imnikhilanand/heart-attack-prediction

Heart Disease Prediction. (2020, August 22). *Kaggle*. Retrieved February 27, 2022, from https://www.kaggle.com/rishidamarla/heart-disease-prediction

Heart Information Center. Heart Disease Risk Factors. (n.d.). *Texas Heart Institute*. Retrieved February 27, 2022, from https://www.texasheart.org/heart-health/heart-information-center/topics/heart-disease-risk-factors

Javed, S., Ghazala, S., & Faseeha, U. (2020). Perspectives of Heat Stroke Shield: An IoT based Solution for the Detection and Preliminary Treatment of Heat Stroke. Engineering, Technology &. *Applied Scientific Research*, *10*(2), 5576–5580. doi:10.48084/etasr.3274

Kemmler, W., & Stengel, S. (2013). Exercise Frequency, Health Risk Factors, and Diseases of the Elderly. *Archives of Physical Medicine and Rehabilitation*, *94*(11), 2046–2053. Advance online publication. doi:10.1016/j.apmr.2013.05.013 PMID:23748185

Kessler, H. S., Sisson, S. B., & Short, K. R. (2012). The potential for high-intensity interval training to reduce cardiometabolic disease risk. *Sports Medicine (Auckland, N.Z.)*, *42*(6), 489–509. doi:10.2165/11630910-000000000-00000 PMID:22587821

Kulick, D. L. (n.d.). *Heart Attack Causes, Symptoms, Causes, Treatment & How to Prevent*. MedicineNet. Retrieved February 27, 2022, from https://www.medicinenet.com/heart_attack/article.htm

Kumar, P. S. (2014). An Efficient Monitoring System For Sports Person Using Wi-Fi Communication. *International Journal of Research in Engineering and Technology*, *3*, 20–23. doi:10.15623/ijret.2014.0311003

Majumder, A. K. M., ElSaadany, Y. A., Young, R., & Ucci, D. R. (2019). An energy efficient wearable smart IoT system to predict cardiac arrest. *Advances in Human-Computer Interaction*, *2019*, 2019. doi:10.1155/2019/1507465

O'Driscoll, B. R., Howard, L. S., Earis, J., & Mark, V. (2017). British Thoracic Society Guideline for oxygen use in adults in healthcare and emergency settings. *BMJ Open Respiratory Research*, *4*(1), e000170. Advance online publication. doi:10.1136/bmjresp-2016-000170 PMID:28883921

Pate, R. R., Davis, M. G., Robinson, T. N., Stone, E. J., McKenzie, T. L., & Young, J. C.American Heart Association Council on Nutrition, Physical Activity, and Metabolism. (2006). Promoting physical activity in children and youth: a leadership role for schools: a scientific statement from the American Heart Association Council on Nutrition, Physical Activity, and Metabolism (Physical Activity Committee) in collaboration with the Councils on Cardiovascular Disease in the Young and Cardiovascular Nursing. *Circulation*, *114*(11), 1214–1224. doi:10.1161/CIRCULATIONAHA.106.177052 PMID:16908770

Sabbahi, A., Arena, R., Kaminsky, L. A., Myers, J., & Phillips, S. A. (2017). Peak Blood Pressure Responses During Maximum Cardiopulmonary Exercise Testing. American Heart Association. *Inc.*, *17*(2). Advance online publication. doi:10.1161/HYPERTENSIONAHA.117.10116 PMID:29255072

Smeaton, A. F., Diamond, D., Kelly, P., Moran, K., Lau, K.-T., Morris, D., Moyna, N., O'Connor, N. E., & Zhang, K. (2008). Aggregating Multiple Body Sensors for Analysis in Sports. *pHealth 2008 - 5th International Workshop on Wearable Micro and Nanosystems for Personalised Health.*

Target Heart Rate and Estimated Maximum Heart Rate | Physical Activity. (n.d.). *CDC*. Retrieved February 27, 2022, from https://www.cdc.gov/physicalactivity/basics/measuring/heartrate.htm

Understand Your Risks to Prevent a Heart Attack. (2016, June 30). *American Heart Association*. Retrieved February 27, 2022, from https://www.heart.org/en/health-topics/heart-attack/understand-your-risks-to-prevent-a-heart-attack

Wang, H., Kadry, S. N., & Raj, E. D. (2020). Continuous health monitoring of sportsperson using IoT devices based wearable technology. *Computer Communications*, *160*, 588–595. doi:10.1016/j.comcom.2020.04.025

KEY TERMS AND DEFINITIONS

Artificial Neural Network (ANN): Artificial neural networks (ANNs) use learning algorithms that can modify or learn on their own when new information is received. As a result, they're an excellent tool for non-linear statistical data modeling.

Data Analytics: Analyzing, refining, manipulating, and modeling data to identify useful information, informing conclusions, and assisting in decision-making is data analysis.

Edge Computing: Edge computing is a paradigm where data processing and storage are brought closer to data sources. This should increase response times while saving bandwidth.

Internet of Things (IoT): IoT refers to physical items equipped with sensors, computing power, software, and other technologies. It may communicate with other devices and systems over the Internet or other networks.

IoT Analytics: Analytics for the Internet of Things (IoT) is a data analysis tool that evaluates the vast amount of data produced by IoT devices. IoT analytics analyses large amounts of data and generates relevant insights.

Machine Learning: A machine's capacity to reproduce intelligent human behavior is machine learning.

Sensors: Sensors are the devices used to collect data from things.

Chapter 9
Robust Dimensionality Reduction:
A Resistant Search for the Relevant Information in Complex Data

Jan Kalina

iD https://orcid.org/0000-0002-8491-0364

Institute of Computer Science, The Czech Academy of Sciences, Czech Republic

ABSTRACT

With the increasing availability of massive data in various fields of applications such as engineering, economics, or biomedicine, there appears an urgent need for new reliable tools for obtaining relevant knowledge from such data, which allow one to find and interpret the most relevant features (variables). Such interpretation is however infeasible for the habitually used methods of machine learning, which can be characterized as black boxes. This chapter is devoted to variable selection methods for finding the most relevant variables for the given task. After explaining general principles, attention is paid to robust approaches, which are suitable for data contaminated by outlying values (outliers). Three main approaches to variable selection (prior, intrinsic, and posterior) are explained, and their recently proposed examples are illustrated on applications related to credit risk management and molecular genetics. These examples reveal recent robust approaches to data analysis to be able to outperform non-robust tools.

DOI: 10.4018/978-1-6684-5264-6.ch009

INTRODUCTION

As the current society is without any doubt oversupplied with data (information), it belongs to crucial tasks of informatics to contribute to a transform of the vast amount information to a small amount of relevant knowledge. In other words, the fight against redundant (useless) information belongs to key tasks of informatics, or the whole current science in general. Only with the help of tools for transforming information to knowledge, the society can expect its shift towards the ideas of the knowledge society (Tegmark, 2017). Artificial intelligence (AI) tools can be expected to contribute to such complexity reduction of the omnipresent information. Tools of computational intelligence (CI), which represents a subset of artificial intelligence, can be especially helpful in this respect. When computational intelligence needs to obtain practically useful knowledge from available information while accounting for uncertainty, machine learning with its statistical algorithms comes into play.

A plethora of innovative tools is nowadays available for obtaining relevant knowledge from (possibly big) data in a variety of tasks. To give only a single application, a number of promising artificial intelligence tools has been engaged in the fight against the COVID-19 pandemic (Lalmuanawma et al., 2020). The role of scientific computations has acquired increasing attention of practitioners as well as among statisticians (Quarteroni, 2018) and the quickly growing field of scientific computations, exploiting advanced computing for analyzing scientific problems, has been denoted as computational science (Holder & Eichholz, 2019). The key pillars of computational intelligence are generally acknowledged to include neural networks, fuzzy logic methods, or evolutionary computation algorithms; still, probabilistic methods allowing to evaluate results under randomness (uncertainty) have their irreplaceable role within computational intelligence as well.

While habitually used methods of machine learning applicable within scientific computations can be characterized as black boxes, practical applications often require to understand why a particular conclusion (e.g. decision) was made, or which are the most relevant variables contributing to explaining a given response variable. If the methods allow such clear interpretation, we speak about explainable artificial intelligence or explainable machine learning. Naturally, understanding limitations of artificial intelligence belongs to ethical issues and the impossibility to explain rigorously why given algorithms yield particular results represents an important ethical issue as such (Jacobson et al., 2020). Two approaches (or in fact aims) for improving the explainability of machine learning tools, which may be used at the same time, are dimensionality reduction and robustness to outlying values (outliers), where the latter allows to reduce the influence of individual outliers and to evaluate (quantify) the influence of individual observations.

Various types and formats of available (possibly massive) data require a broad spectrum of sophisticated methods for their analysis. A correct analysis of data with a large number of available variables (features) therefore becomes an emerging issue. Together with an increasing complexity of available data, data analysts begin to realize the importance of methods of complexity reduction for their reliable and effective analysis (Fordellone, 2019). The amount of data observed in various fields grows very rapidly, while complex data are commonly agreed to have a big potential to influence research or everyday routine activities (López-Robles et al., 2019). Complexity reduction is a general concept including any approach to simplifying data analysis and may include finding suitable relevant features from images (e.g. using imags of the brain as in Bučková et al. (2020)), voice records, narrative text (e.g. in health reports) etc. We understand **dimensionality reduction** (dimension reduction) to represent a special case of complexity reduction for the situation with numerical data, i.e. when dealing with data in the form of numbers. Naturally, dimensionality reduction methods are suitable also for Big Data, which represent a valuable capital with an underutilized opportunity for decision making and relevance for the society (cf. Bradlow et al., 2017), but definitely not only for them. In biomedical research, dimensionality reduction methods are irreplaceable in the most complex research tasks, which include the study of the brain (Tang et al., 2021), gut microbiome (Martino et al., 2021) with a key role within the immunity system, genomics or epigenetics (Damgacioglu et al., 2019).

The objective of this chapter is to explain principles of robust dimensionality reduction, to recall some promising methods, and to present illustrations of real data revealing the methods to work reliably. Robust approaches to reducing the dimensionality are explained here to represent a unique methodology for an explainable (comprehensible) data analysis. Particularly, reducing the dimensionality improves the interpretation of the knowledge acquired from the data by reducing the focus on the most important variables. While outliers can be too influential and thus misleading for standard data analysis, robust statistical tools can eliminate their influence.

This chapter has the following structure. It starts with explaining that dimensionality reduction aims at finding the most relevant information from the given data. Principles of robust statistical estimation are then explained. Further, the most important types of dimensionality reduction methods are recalled. Dimensionality reduction in the context of neural networks is discussed afterwards. As an example, a robust version of a variable selection denoted as MRMR is presented. Robust approaches suitable for contaminated data will be illustrated on classification and regression tasks in real datasets related to keystroke dynamics, credit risk management, and gene expressions.

THE CONCEPT OF INFORMATION

Statistical analysis of data in engineering, economics, biomedicine, or other fields aims at extracting such knowledge, which is useful for practical steps. We thus make a clear distinction between information (as acquired by means of observations or randomized experiments) and knowledge, where only the latter is useful for practical applications. Methods of (multivariate) statistics or machine learning may transform the information into knowledge, which may be subsequently applied e.g. in clinical decision making, financial investments, adopting strategies for reducing business costs and increasing profit, etc. Various popular tools of statistical estimation or classification (supervised learning) are however vulnerable to the presence of outlying values (outliers) in the data (Jurečková et al., 2019), while real data are often (or typically) contaminated by outliers not fulfilling the considered statistical or econometric models. As alternative tools, robust statistical procedures have been proposed for a variety of tasks including estimation, classification, or dimensionality reduction. Highly robust statistical methods with a high value of the breakdown point (as a measure of global robustness against a large percentage of severe outliers) have been tailor-made for separating data points corresponding to the desirable signal and those corresponding to noise. These robust methods aim at analyzing real data with an unknown contamination level, ignoring observations which represent only redundant measurements (ballast) and do not bring any relevant information by increasing the knowledge of the users.

Parametric statistics is related to information theory, where the latter represents an established discipline focused on evaluating and investigating information, information entropy (as a measure of uncertainty), and distance measures between random variables such as mutual information (Csiszár and Shields, 2004). Fisher information, a fundamental statistical concept, can be (if simplified) interpreted as a measure of information contained in data about an unknown parameter within a parametric family of distributions (Taylor, 2019). However, we are not aware of any discussion of the relationship between robust statistics and the concept of information. We can say that some methods of robust statistics, such as the least weighted squares regression estimator (Víšek, 2011), are based on searching for the most relevant subset of observations, while trimming away the remaining data points, which are interpreted as outliers (false information, disinformation).

Dimensionality reduction methods, which are available within the fields of statistics or machine learning, are also centered around the concept of information (Hidalgo, 2021). In general, reducing the dimensionality of data should be aimed at finding the most relevant variables (or their combination) for a particular task in a particular context. Thus, the maximal possible information for the given task should be retained from the original data. For example, principal component analysis

(PCA) searches for combinations of variables with the largest variability; in other words, an inverse of the total variance explained by the components plays the role of the information of the original data. Robust methods aimed at robust capturing of the information hidden in multivariate data are highly desirable also if (but not only if) the data contain a large number of variables (Filzmoser and Todorov, 2011).

ROBUST STATISTICAL ESTIMATION

Robust statistical estimators are well developed for the fundamental models, which include the location model and linear regression. The motivation for studying robust estimators is the vulnerability of the arithmetic mean or of the least squares estimator with respect to outlying values (outliers) in the data. This section recalls robust estimates in linear regression model (and the location model, which is its special case), which will serve as inspiration for the robust versions of neural networks used later. The standard linear regression model considers n observations, for which a continuous response is explained by p regressors (independent variables, features) under the presence of random errors. As the most common least squares estimator of regression parameters is vulnerable to the presence of outliers in the data, various robust alternatives have been proposed (Jurečková et al., 2013).

An important focus of robust statistics is to combine high robustness and high efficiency of estimators (Maronna et al., 2019). A variety of estimation tools, which are resistant to the presence of outliers in the data, has been established. Such estimators are considered highly robust with respect to outliers, which have a high value of the breakdown point, i.e. a high resistance against outliers in the data (Hubert et al., 2008). Formally, the finite-sample breakdown point is defined as the minimal fraction of data that can drive an estimator beyond all bounds when set to arbitrary values (Davies and Gather, 2005). Because robust statistics evolved as a methodology suitable for a contaminated normal distribution, efficiency is considered as a key characteristic as well. Efficiency of a linear regression estimator evaluates its performance in the model with normal errors without outliers; more formally, it evaluates the asymptotic variability of an estimator relatively to the optimal (smallest) variability, which is achieved by maximum likelihood estimates. Keeping in mind the high robustness, we decide for replacing the sum of squared residuals by loss functions of the least trimmed squares and least weighted squares estimators, which are known to yield reliable and resistant results over real data (Kalina and Schlenker, 2015).

The least trimmed squares (LTS) estimator (Rousseeuw and Leroy, 1987) represents a popular regression estimator with a high breakdown point (Jurečková et al., 2019). Formally, the LTS estimate of regression parameters is obtained as the sum of squared residuals over the total number of h observations, for which these squared residuals are the smallest. The user must choose a fixed h fulfilling $n/2 \leq h < n$ here; the most typical choice is $h=3n/4$. Squared values of residuals are arranged in ascending order. The LTS estimator may attain a high robustness but cannot achieve a high efficiency.

The least weighted squares (LWS) estimator (Víšek, 2011) for the linear regression model, motivated by the idea to down-weight potential outliers, remains much less known compared to the LTS, although it has more appealing statistical properties. The definition of the LWS exploits the concept of a given weight function. The LWS estimator with given weights is able to much exceed the LTS in terms of efficiency; the estimator is defined as the weighted sum of squared residuals, where the smallest weights are assigned to the largest squared residuals, and the largest weights to the smallest squared residuals. We may refer to (Víšek, 2011) and references cited therein for properties of the LWS; it may achieve a high breakdown point (with properly selected weights), robustness to hetero-scedasticity, and efficiency for non-contaminated samples. There is a very good experience with the performance of the LWS on real data (Kalina et al., 2019). Extension of the LWS estimator to multivariate data (i.e. to estimation of the expectation and covariance matrix) was studied in Kalina & Tichavský (2022) for high-dimensional data.

MAIN APPROCHES TO REDUCING THE DIMENSION OF COMPLEX DATA

Dimensionality reduction in the analysis of complex (possibly big) data may bring several important advantages. It is especially recommendable and in fact unavoidable for Big Data (Blazques and Domenech, 2018) or high-dimensional data, where the latter are defined as data with the number of variables exceeding (perhaps largely) the value of n. Dimensionality reduction eliminates or down-weights redundant variables (Wilson, 2018), and simplifies the subsequent data analysis by means of tools of statistics or machine learning. If the data are big and dimensionality reduction is not performed at all, one would have to resort to computationally very demanding methods. We stress however that dimensionality reduction may be beneficial also for other data, with a relatively small number of variables (Martinez et al., 2017). While standard tools of dimensionality reduction are vulnerable to the presence of outliers in the data, robust dimensionality reduction exploiting the above-described principles of robust statistical estimation are more resistant and thus suitable for the analysis of real data (Kalina & Rensová, 2015), which may be acquired by different means and from diverse sources (Kalina, 2019).

Dimensionality reduction may be beneficial also from the point of view of interpretation of the results of the data analysis. Often, it is desirable to search for parsimonious models, which are understood as simple models with a small set of relevant variables. Dimensionality reduction may e.g. divide multivariate data to a small set of quite homogeneous clusters; in an analogous way, the variables (instead of the observations) may be clustered. Some of the dimensionality reduction methods reduce or remove correlation among variables. It may be surprising for non-experts that dimensionality reduction may even improve the results of the subsequent analysis (e.g. decision making) compared to those obtained with full data. On the other hand, dimensionality reduction may lead to a loss of some relevant information if the set of variables is reduced to a too small number of relevant ones, and the results may be severaly biased.

Supervised dimensionality reduction methods are tailor-made for data coming from two or more groups, while the information about the group membership is taken into account. Ono the other hand, unsupervised dimensionality reduction methods consider data only in one group. If the data are in groups but the group labeling is not known even for the training dataset, unsupervised methods must be used. It is suboptimal to use an unsupervised approach for data coming from several known groups.

It is also important to distinguish between feature extraction and variable selection. Feature extraction methods reduce the dimensionality of data by replacing the actual observations by combinations of variables, while variable selection (also feature selection) methods reduce the dimensionality by selecting a smaller set of important variables and ignores all remaining ones.

Feature Extraction

Feature extraction methods search for the most relevant combinations of the measurements and replace the original data with a small number of such combinations, which may be linear or nonlinear. Feature extraction is performed always as a prior step, i.e. before the actual data analysis. Popular methods include principal component analysis (PCA), factor analysis, correspondence analysis, independent component analysis, partial least squares regression, multivariate scaling (Greene, 2017), or methods based on information theory. Usually, feature extraction (unlike variable selection) ensures decorrelation, yields reliable predictions (at least if there are not contaminated by outliers), and its results have a good local robustness (stability). It deserves to be recalled that PCA as the most common dimensionality reduction method is an unsupervised method and thus is not suitable for data coming from two or more different groups (i.e. for a mixture of populations). In fact, although PCA is commonly appraised for finding decorrelated components, numerous machine learning method do not need the data to be uncorrelated.

Variable Selection

Variable selection procedures can be classified as:

- Prior (a priori, preliminary), i.e. before the data analysis of interest (regression, classification, clustering, instrumental variables estimation, etc.),
- Intrinsic (sparse), using a suitable regularization within the data analysis of interest,
- Posterior (post hoc analysis), i.e. after the data analysis of interest.

Some methods may be performed as a prior or as posterior variable section. This is true e.g. for hypothesis testing and various methods of backward elimination, which may be used either before the analysis of interest or after it. Nevertheless, hypothesis testing for reducing the dimensionality cannot be used directly, because a repeated using of the same procedure contributes to an increase of the probability of type I error.

1. **Prior variable selection** represents a preliminary or assistive step prior to the particular analysis task (e.g. regression modeling or learning a classification rule). Prior variable selection allows to analyze only a small set of relevant variables and to give comprehensible answers to various questions, e.g. how to interpret values of individual parameters or which variables are the most important ones for predicting the response. If the relevant variables are selected before the data analysis as such, future measurements in the same situation can be performed on a smaller set of variables, which may reduce financial or organizational demands of the experiments (or measurements). Numerous variable selection methods with the ability to ignore redundant variables include wrappers, filters, embedded methods, the minimum redundancy maximum relevance approach, or information-theory based methods. An important class of tools includes hypothesis testing; this either requires distributional assumptions (such as in specific regression models) or may be performed without them (e.g. by nonparametric bootstrap).

2. **Intrinsic variable selection** (sparse variable selection) may be performed within regression or classification tasks by means of regularization (Fan et al., 2020). Methods of this type, which are the most recently proposed, typically yield sparse solutions, exploiting information only from some variables while ignoring the remaining observations. Although regularization may ensure local robustness to small changes of the data, we can say that regularized methods may suffer from the presence of outliers in the data. Such tools are important e.g. within regression models; robust methods of intrinsic variable selection based on regularization were overviewed in Filzmoser and Nordhausen (2020).

In general, it is not possible to give a general answer to the question which dimensionality reduction approach is the best for a given dataset. The recent paper of Heinze et al. (2017) attempted to perform at least some systematic comparisons of various dimensionality reduction methods and to formulate some practical recommendations related to this problem. Choosing the appropriate method for Big Data nevertheless remains to contain a number of open problems (Zhao et al., 2018). Of course, each method has its own set of assumptions. In addition, some methods are more suitable for economic data, others would be often exploited in biomedicine etc. We can thus say that dimensionality reduction should be tailored for the particular task/problem within the given field of expertise (medicine, economics, engineering etc.) as well as the statistical task of the analysis (regression or classification). The authors of this chapter hold the same opinion as Olson (2017) that if the data analysis require a clear interpretation, a prior or sparse variable selection should be preferable to feature extraction.

Some Recent Applications

It is perhaps surprising that feature extraction methods remain so popular in biomedicine. Examples of real-world biomedical applications, where dimensionality reduction represented an important part of the methodology, include:

- The study of spontaneous and induced neuronal oscillations in brains in schizophrenia patients and healthy controls of Haufe et al. (2014), where unsupervised feature extraction was performed by means of spatio-spectral decomposition;
- The study searching for predictors of age of a tissue based on DNA methylation products of Lee et al. (2018), where supervised principal component regression was performed;
- Automated segmentation procedure for infrared images of the iris proposed by Tan and Kumar (2012), combined with a search for the most discriminative features with a good human identification ability.
- The analysis of massive EEG data (Sadiq et al., 2021) of healthy individuals during right-hand or right-food movements; the task was to find features allowing to discriminate between the hand movement and foot movement, and this was solved by means of neighborhood components analysis, which is a supervised feature extraction method.
- The study of chest pain patients in the emergency department (Liu et al., 2021), where heart rate parameters obtained from electrocardiograms (ECG) were used to predict the risk of individual patients; different dimensionality reduction methods were used for finding the best heart rate parameters, and multidimensional scaling (a nonlinear and unsupervised feature extraction method) turned out to yield the best results.

MINIMUM REDUNDANCY MAXIMUM RELEVANCE

The minimum redundancy maximum relevance (MRMR) approach to dimensionality reduction can be described as a well known class of tools for supervised variable selection for data observed in two or more groups (Ding and Peng, 2005). We describe the principles for analyzing p-dimensional data coming from two groups. The advantage of the approach is that it does not incline to selecting strongly correlated variables. The method requires to measure relevance of a set of variables for the classification task, i.e. to evaluate the contribution of a given variable to the classification task. Also it is necessary to use a measure of redundancy of a set of variables. We use here the mutual information as the measure of both relevance and redundancy. This however requires all variables in the given dataset to be categorical. If these are continuous, they must be first transformed to categorical variables. An alternative approach would be to use other measures based on information theory, specific test statistics or p-values, or some (possibly very simple) ad hoc criteria.

The group label (indicator variable corresponding to the group label) in the context of MRMR approaches usually plays the role of a response variable Y. The MRMR procedure in its habitually used form selects gradually one variable after another and these form a set denoted as S. First, we need to evaluate for each variable (say Z) its relevance for the classification task, which will be denoted as Relevance ($\{Y, Z\}$). The very first selected variable maximizes this relevance among all variables. Further, we need to evaluate for each variable Z, which is not present in S yet, the value of

$$\text{Relevance} (\{Y, Z\}) - \alpha \cdot \text{Redundancy} (S \cup Z). \tag{1}$$

Here, $\alpha \in (0, 1]$ is a chosen parameter and $S \cup Z$ denotes the set of variables included so far in S together with the variable Z. Such variable is selected to the set S, which maximizes (1). We can interpret (1) as a penalized version of the relevance. The selection of variables according to (1) is repeated and new variables are added to the set of selected variables until a given stopping rule is fulfilled. The user may either choose a fixed number of relevant variables, or require that the selected variables contribute to explaining more than a given percentage (e.g. 90%) of the inter-class variability of the observed data.

The value of the parameter α is usually chosen to yield the maximal classification accuracy. It is popular to use leave-k-out (and especially leave-one-out) cross validation to find the best α in the following way. For a fixed α, there are k randomly chosen observations left out, the classifier is computed and the observation left out are classified. This is repeated sufficiently many times and the overall classification accuracy is eveluted. The whole procedure is repeated for various α and such its value is selected as the optimal one, which yields the maximal classification accuracy.

APPLICATION 1: KEYSTROKE DYNAMICS

The MRMR supervised variable selection will be now illustrated on the biometric authentication task. Here, a group of 32 probands was asked to type the word "*kladruby*" 5-times at the habitual speed; such analysis goes beyond the preliminary results presented in Kalina and Schlenker (2015). In the practical application, one of the 32 individuals identifies himself/herself (say as XY) and types the password. It would be possible to consider a classification task to 32 groups. Nevertheless, the task within the practical problem is different. An individual claims to be a given person (say XY) and the system has the aim to verify if this is true. Such authentication (rather than recognition) task is a classification problem to assign the individual to one of the $K = 2$ groups performed with p=15 and n=$32*5=160$.

The classification accuracy of a linear support vector machine (SVM) classifier with all the variables is equal to 0.93. The following analysis is peformed with the LDA classifier, which is much simpler than the SVM approach. If the dimensionality of the data is reduced, the SVM classifier has a tendency to overfitting, because it is not designed for data with a small n. If only 4 variables selected by MRMR are used, the classification accuracy of the LDA is 0.93 in a LOOCV study. Keystroke latencies again turn out to be more important than keystroke durations by the MRMR criterion. The most important variables according to the MRMR criterion are ad, ru, dr, and ub. If only the variable ad *is* used, the classification accuracy of the LDA linear SVM in the LOOCV is 0.57. If ad *a*nd ru *a*re used together, it increases to 0.82. The first three of these variables yield 0.90 and all four yield already 0.93. On the whole, MRMR does not improve classification but loses only a little and allows to find the most relevant variables for the classification task.

An alternative unsupervised approach based on selecting only variables with the largest variability leads to selecting u*b* and b*y*. Nevertheless, constructing a classification rule based on them would be quite misleading, because LDA using these two variables gives the classification accuracy equal only to 0.55 in a LOOCV.

APPLICATION 2: CREDIT RISK MANAGEMENT

This section is devoted to an example of decision making in the field of credit risk. The study presented here reveals the advantage of dimensionality reduction. In the recent monograph by Witzany (2017) on credit risk management, credit scoring was characterized as an important methodology for modeling and predicting the credit of individual bank customers. A careful detection of individuals or companies not able to repay a mortgage will be even more important in the unstable post-COVID-19 economies (Wakode, 2020) with a fractal structure. The banks must evaluate all individual clients (loan applicants) in order to decide to which of the two groups they belong:

1. Clients able to repay (redeem) the loan in time,
2. Clients likely to fail to repay the loan.

The models for the decision making are learned over a database of available data from the past, while the model must be only (e.g. once per two years) re-validated and/or updated.

Specific decision support systems have been implemeneted and successfully applied also to tasks of credit risk management as overviewed e.g. by Ignatius et al. (2018). Particularly, the system of Luo (2020) aims at assessing creditworthiness of private companies before they lend money (if their request for a loan is approved). The system used e.g. the logistic regression, which is currently the most common method in credit risk. The classification methods however suffer here from the fact that the two groups of clients are imbalanced (unequal). Therefore, we decided for including a trick allowing to improve the classification performance; we used an oversampling technique based on random generation of new observations as combinations of the available ones. Although Big Data have been many times applied in corporate credit scoring and prediction (Witzany, 2017), we are not aware of a publicly available credit risk dataset with a large number of variables. Therefore, we analyze now a well known and rather small dataset and present original results of recently proposed methods for such data.

We present our analysis of the Australian credit risk dataset now. This dataset is publicly available in the UCI repository (Dua & Graff, 2017), for which preliminary results (especially studying the effect of dimensionality reduction) were presented by Kalina (2017), however without a cross validation. Our particular application considers $n = 690$ observations and $p = 14$ variables, where there are 6 continuous and 8 categorical variables. There are 383 clients (observations) in class I and the remaining 307 clients belong to class II. We use several standard as well as recently proposed classifiers, including robust neural networks. The results are evaluated in a 5-fold cross validation. We use R software for the computations.

We use several well known classifiers. Methods proposed only recently contain interquantile robust versions of multilayer perceptrons and radial basis function (RBF) networks and their robust versions based on the loss function of the least

Table 1. Results of the credit risk management example. The table presents classification accuracies of individual methods, the parametrs of which are given in the last column. The classification accuracies are evaluated for an autovalidation study and for a 5-fold cross validation study

Method	Auto-validation	5-fold cross validation	Note (parameters of the method)
Logistic regression (LR)	0.88	0.72	-
L_1 -regularized LR	0.90	0.74	-
L_2 -regularized LR	0.90	0.75	-
Linear discriminant analysis	0.86	0.71	-
Support vector machines	0.90	0.73	Gaussian kernel
Classification tree	0.83	0.67	-
Multilayer perceptron (MLP)	0.85	0.70	2 hidden layers with16 and 8 neurons
Interquantile MLP	0.85	0.73	
LWS-based MLP	0.84	0.72	
RBF network	0.87	0.73	70 radial units
Interquantile RBF network	0.86	0.76	
LWS-based RBF network	0.85	0.75	

weighted squares (LWS) estimator (see Kalina (2015)); these were proposed and investigated by Kalina & Vidnerová (2020) and we use our own implementation for them. Fixed parameters $\tau = 0.15$ and $\tau = 0.85$ were used for the interquantile approaches, while linear weights were used for the LWS-based approaches. Optimal values of regularization parameters (i.e. for regularized versions of logistic regression and for support vector machines) were determined in a 5-fold cross validation.

Table 1 evaluates the results in the form of the classification accuracy, which is defined as the ratio of the number of correctly classified cases to the total number of observations. This is presented either in an autovalidation (autoverification) study, where the classification accuracy is evaluated over the entire (training) dataset, or in a 5-fold cross validation performed in a standard way. Autovalidation is however known to usually lead to (possibly severely) biased results, while cross validation represents an attempt for an independent validation.

To interpret the results in Table 1, there is a remarkable difference between the results of the (biased) autovalidation and the cross validation. In fact, methods performing the best in the autovalidation are not necessarily the best in the cross validation. The classification tree, so popular in management applications, turns out to be outperformed by all other methods presented here; the tree was used with such settings of parameters, which are default in R software. The best classification results are obtained with LWS-based RBF network, i.e. a version of RBF networks with a robust loss function proposed only very recently. This method is based on assigning weights to individual observations, while the most reliable (least outlying) obtain the largest weights. Indeed, neural networks are without any surprise more flexible tools compared to others (e.g. compared to logistic regression, as it represents only their special case). Regularization brings benefits in this dataset and it is worth mentioning that it improves the result of logistic regression compared to its plain (i.e. the most popular) version.

To conclude the example, reliable decision making requires to use very recent data analysis tools. Because the data are multicollinear, i.e. the correlations of the regressors are significant, the example shows the advantage of the sparsity ensured by intrinsic variable selection. We can also see here the benefit of robust analysis of data compared to standard (non-robust) procedures, which remain vulnerable to the presence of outliers in the data. We believe that the importance of these robust tools will be increasing together with an increasing contamination and uncertainty in the economics data worldwide, reflecting the instability and non-stationarity of the world economy as a consequence of the COVID-19 pandemic.

APPLICATION 3: CLASSIFICATION OF HIGH-DIMENSIONAL GENE EXPRESSIONS

The next application has the aim to analyze high-dimensional gene expression (GE) measurements coming from the cerebrovascular stroke study of the Center of Biomedical Informatics, Prague. The dataset contains 38 950 GE values measured as continuous variables in a paired design on 24 pairs of individuals. These include 24 individuals after a cerebrovascular stroke and 24 control persons without a manifested cardiovascular disease; measurements in patients with stroke was performed very shortly (as soon as possible) after the stroke. Each GE measurement corresponds to a particular gene transcript. To reduce the computational demands, we consider only the first $p=3000$ genes from the available dataset. The task is to learn a classification method to 2 groups, allowing to assign a set of GE measurement of a new (possibly independent) individual to the group of patients or to the group of control persons. This dataset was previously analyzed by different methods (hypothesis testing based on interpoint distances) by Marozzi et al. (2020). Here, we used R software for the computations; the optimization of the centroid and the weights was performed in C++.

The centroid-based classifier is used here in various forms, while the initial centroid is obtained as the average of the measurements of the 24 patients (i.e. without the control persons). Equal weights are considered as the initial ones, i.e. each variable obtains the same weight 1/3000, so that their sum is naturally equal to 1. The optimization of the centroids and weights exploits parameters, for which we use the same values as in Kalina & Matonoha (2020). We use here two improvements of available centroid-based classification approaches, which are motivated by a need for explainability of the results; these tools denoted as thresholded optimal centroid and binarized optimal weights have not been considered before in the context of centroid-based classification.

Thresholded Optimal Centroid

Starting with the initial centroid (say c), a new centroid is constructed. If the value of c for a particular gene is below a given threshold, the value of the new centroid for such gene is enforced to be 0. For all remaining genes, the new centroid coincides with the initial centroid. Particularly, when normalizing the centroid to have the sum of all values equal to 1, we use the threshold equal to 0.000 05. This thresholded optimal centroid is used together with equal weights.

Binarized Optimal Weights

When the optimal centroid with optimal weights is computed, it is natural to ask the question how much information would be lost by a binarization of the optimal weights. Thus, we modify the optimal weights (say w) to be binary. This is done in a simple way as follows. If the value of w for a particular gene is below a given threshold (in our case 0.0001), the weight is enforced to be 0. For all remaining genes, the new weights are equal to a constant (the same for all genes); this constant is determined so that the sum of all the weights is equal to 1.

For comparisons, we also use PCA over the whole dataset (i.e. combining data of both groups. The classification rule is constructed by means of linear discriminant analysis (LDA) only over the first 10 principal components. Using PCA allows to compute LDA in a standard form, without the need for using one of numerous available regularized versions (Kalina & Duintjer Tebbens, 2015).

Apart from the raw data, we also consider 3 contaminated versions in order to investigate the robustness of the methods. Three different contamination levels are considered, namely we contaminate 4%, 8%, or 12% of the values for every observation (every individual) by severe outliers. For each particular individual, the variables (genes) to be contaminated are randomly chosen and independent random variables from the normal distribution with expectation 0 and standard deviation 1 are generated and added to the true values. When working with the contaminated data, the centroids and weights use only contaminated data, so the methods do not have access to raw (non-contaminated) data at all.

Table 2. Results of the classification methods for the high-dimensional gene expression dataset. The raw data as well their contaminated versions are considered

Centroid	Weights	Classification accuracy	Number of used genes
Raw data (no contamination)			
Initial	Initial	0.73	3000
Optimal	Initial	0.81	3000
Thresholded optimal	Initial	0.77	986
Optimal	Optimal	0.85	247
Optimal	Binarized optimal	0.85	196
Initial centroid using r-LWS		0.77	3000
PCA $\Rightarrow$ LDA		0.69	3000
Contamination level 0.04			
Initial	Initial	0.69	3000
Optimal	Initial	0.81	3000
Thresholded optimal	Initial	0.77	1034
Optimal	Optimal	0.85	261
Optimal	Binarized optimal	0.85	213
Initial centroid using r-LWS		0.77	3000
PCA $\Rightarrow$ LDA		0.65	3000
Contamination level 0.08			
Initial	Initial	0.67	3000
Optimal	Initial	0.79	3000
Thresholded optimal	Initial	0.75	1095
Optimal	Optimal	0.83	259
Optimal	Binarized optimal	0.83	202
Initial centroid using r-LWS		0.73	3000
PCA $\Rightarrow$ LDA		0.63	3000
Contamination level 0.12			
Initial	Initial	0.63	3000
Optimal	Initial	0.77	3000
Thresholded optimal	Initial	0.73	1215
Optimal	Optimal	0.81	283
Optimal	Binarized optimal	0.81	220
Initial centroid using r-LWS		0.69	3000
PCA $\Rightarrow$ LDA		0.58	3000

The results of the analysis of the GE measurements presented in Table 1 have the form of classification accuracies, defined as the ratios of the properly classified samples divided by the total number of samples. The table also shows the number of genes used within the classification rule of every particular method. Comparisons with standard machine learning are not presented here, because these were already thoroughly studied by Kalina & Matonoha (2020). Results of the optimized centroid with optimized weights much outperform those obtained with the initial centroid on the raw data. The approach exploiting the robust correlation coefficient *r-LWS* (Kalina and Schlenker, 2015) yields better results compared to the standard Pearson correlation coefficient, but is outperformed by the method based on the optimized centroid.

The binarized optimal weights, which were proposed here as a novel extension of the approach based on optimal centroids, yield the same result here as the optimal (and much more complex) weights. Thus, we can say that binary weights carry practically the same information as the optimal weights, at least with respect to the classification task. In other words, although the optimization is delicate and focuses on subtle nuances of the weights, the binarization as a quite rough transformation does not lose much of the classification ability of the centroid. The thresholded optimal centroid loses the classification ability and cannot be recommended.

It follows from these computations that optimizing the centroid yields very promising results. In addition, simplifying the optimal centroid (and improving its explainability) is possible, but cannot be achieved from the centroid itself, but can be achieved by additional optimization of the weights. Such method can be characterized as a posterior variable selection. In fact, the weights carry the information about the reliability of individual variables for the classification task. A small set of variables turns out to carry the majority of the information relevant for the classification and it is possible to use suitable classification methods in terms of comprehensibility only at the price of a negligible reduction of the classification performance and (at least for some methods) to improve the interpretation of subsequent data analysis.

Further, let us interpret the results of Table 1 obtained for contaminated data. Centroid-based approaches with initial (non-optimal) choices are influenced by outliers to a large extent. On the other hand, centroid-based classification using the optimal centroid with optimal weights turns out to be more robust, able to outperform all other approaches used in this study.

PCA turns out not to be suitable here, which follows from the fact that it represents an unsupervised dimensionality reduction method. We already explained that PCA is not intended to be used for data in two different groups (from two different populations), as it attempts namely to explain the variability of the response, but not the separation between the groups. The vulnerability of PCA with respect to outliers is revealed here as another its disadvantage.

On the whole, the presented analysis reveals the ability of centroid-based classifers to solve the classification task for the GE dataset well. The classification based on centroids (with or without weights assigned to the centroid) can be perceived as an explainable method yielding much improved results compared to those obtained with a simple (initial, naïve) centroid. The optimization of the weights performs a posterior variable selection. The optimal centroid with optimal weights can be interpreted as a classifier with a sparse (intrinsic) variable selection, which is based on about 1000 genes and the classification rule of the optimal centroid with binarized weights is based on about 200 relevant genes. In this context, forgetting the information much improves the explainability and does not lead to any loss of classification performance.

APPLICATION 4: A CLINICAL DECISION SUPPORT SYSTEM BASED ON GENE EXPRESSION MEASUREMENTS

Clinical decision support systems represent tools of artificial intelligence allowing to assist physicians in the task of clinical decision making. The authors of this chapter participated on proposing and implementing a prototype of a clinical decision support system denoted as SIR (System for selecting relevant Information for decision suppoRt). While decision support systems require to analyze complex data, it appears that most of the currently available decision support systems do not have a sophisticated statistical component with a reliable tool for dimensionality reduction. Such advanced statistical methodology was incorporated to the system SIR. Thus, the system SIR is reliable also for data with a large number of variables. The system was evaluated on data in the field of molecular genetics and on brain activity data of patients with schizophrenia. The system SIR can be described as an easy-to-use web-based generic service devoted to data collection and decision support. It is mainly proposed for being used by physicians (general practitioners) in the primary care, but it is able to handle data from any area of medicine.

A full clinical trial may be uploaded to the system SIR together with a data model. If the clinical trial is sufficiently large, the end-user may exploit SIR to analyze it and use the acquired knowledge within clinical decision support for real patients. The data import can be performed through the automatically generated interface from an electronic health record (EHR) or health information system (HIS), although a manual input of data is also possible. The input numerical variables may be continuous as well categorized. The system cleans the input data e.g. by checking if the values of the imported quantitative variables do not exceed given bounds required by the data model. The data are used as training data to construct the optimal classification rule for the decision making problem.

The system SIR exploits the Minium Redundance Maximum Relevance (MRMR) variable selection, which was described above. The system SIR is also able to determine the best classification method for constructing the given classification rule. Particularly, the system has the ability to decide automatically for one of several different methods:

- Linear discriminant analysis (LDA),
- Support vector machines (SVM),
- Empirical Bayes classifier,
- Classification tree.

Let us recall that the empirical Bayes classifier (inference mechanism) minimizes the aposterior Bayes risk across all groups of samples. LDA is a multivariate statistical method for separating groups by means of a linear function. The same covariance structure is assumed in each group within LDA; the method (and a covariance matrix itself) may be unsuitable in situations, when diverse (incomparable) variables are measured. To choose the most suitable classifier from the given list, a criterion of optimality is adaptively chosen to minimize the risk of a wrong classification result, taking into account special properties of the data and the sample sizes. This risk is minimized within a leave-one-out cross validation study, based on evaluating each classifier on the data after removing (repeatedly) one observation and aggregating the results; such cross validation is acknowledged as a reliable attempt to perform a validation over independent data (which are often not available).

It is required in the system SIR that the user (physician) specifies the prior diagnosis already before entering the data to SIR, because it is only the physician who carries the legal responsibility for the final clinical decision. Then, SIR can be used through the web service to obtain a diagnosis support. Finally, the clinician is asked to manually select his/her final decision and only if it is not in accordance with SIR, the clinician is required to write a short text justifying the decision. Technical details of the system SIR can be found elsewhere (Kalina, 2019), where numerical results presenting the accuracy of the clinical decision support were presented as very reliable.

CONCLUSION

This chapter is focused on recently proposed robust methods for dimensionality reduction, which may have find applications in the analysis of complex data by means of multivariate statistics and mainly machine learning. The chapter does not (and cannot) bring an overview of a plethora of available variable selection methods.

While feature extraction methods seem to be already well developed, new methods have been recently proposed, which belong to prior, intrinsic, or posterior methods of variable selection. The chapter is devoted to methods based on probabilistic thinking and robust statistical estimation. In this context, it deserves to be stressed that statistically robust methods focus primarily on robustness (resistance) against the presence of outliers in the data. The chapter follows the idea that reducing the dimensionality of data always requires to solve the trade-off between simplicity and retaining relevant information; this is true on the level of variables (removing the redundant variables from the analysis) as well as on the level of observations (trimming away outliers). Thus, robust variable selection methods turn out to separate signal from noise, i.e. to find order in chaotically arranged multivariate information.

The real-life examples of this chapter are motivated by our attempt to persuade the reader about the potential of reducing the dimensionality of multivariate data. In the applications presented here related to classification or regression tasks, robust variable selection methods yield the best results. When appropriately performed in a robust way, i.e. not being misled by outliers in the data, variable selection should be also appealing for practitioners as it is able to ensure explainability in a better way compared to feature extraction methods.

In the future, the authors of this chapter would like to perform basic research related to approximate neurocomputing and methods for decreasing the energetic complexity of neural networks, especially for training convolutional neural networks. New methods of computational intelligence also require discussions about ethical aspects, which also remain to contain many open problems.

ACKNOWLEDGMENT

The work was supported by the grants GA22-02067S of the Czech Science Foundation.

REFERENCES

Blazques, D., & Domenech, J. (2018). Big Data sources and methods for social and economic analyses. *Technological Forecasting and Social Change, 130*, 99–113. doi:10.1016/j.techfore.2017.07.027

Bradlow, E. T., Gangwar, M., Kopalle, P., & Voleti, S. (2017). The role of Big Data and predictive analytics in retailing. *Journal of Retailing, 93*(1), 79–95. doi:10.1016/j.jretai.2016.12.004

Bučková, B., Brunovský, M., Bareš, M., & Hlinka, J. (2020). Predicting sex from EEG: Validity and generalizability of deep-learning-based interpretable classifier. *Frontiers in Neuroscience*, *14*, 589303. doi:10.3389/fnins.2020.589303 PMID:33192274

Csiszár, I., & Shields, P. C. (2004). Information Theory and Statistics: A Tutorial. *Foundations and Trends in Communications and Information Theory*, *1*(4), 417–528. doi:10.1561/0100000004

Damgacioglu, H., Celik, E., & Celik, N. (2019). Estimating gene expression from high-dimensional DNA methylation levels in cancer data: A bimodal unsupervised dimension reduction algorithm. *Computers & Industrial Engineering*, *130*, 348–357. doi:10.1016/j.cie.2019.02.038

Davies, P. L., & Gather, U. (2005). Breakdown and groups. *Annals of Statistics*, *33*(3), 977–1035. doi:10.1214/009053604000001138

Ding, C., & Peng, H. (2005). Minimum redundancy feature selection from microarray gene expression data. *Journal of Bioinformatics and Computational Biology*, *3*(02), 185–205. doi:10.1142/S0219720005001004 PMID:15852500

Dua, D. & Graff, C. (2017). *UCI machine learning repository*. Available at http://archive.ics.uci.edu/ml

Fan, J., Ke, Y., & Wang, K. (2020). Factor-adjusted regularized model selection. *Journal of Econometrics*, *216*(1), 71–85. doi:10.1016/j.jeconom.2020.01.006 PMID:32269406

Filzmoser, P., & Nordhausen, K. (2020). Robust linear regression for high-dimensional data: An overview. *Wiley Interdisciplinary Reviews: Computational Statistics*, *13*, e1524.

Filzmoser, P., & Todorov, V. (2011). Review of robust multivariate statistical methods in high dimension. *Analytica Chimica Acta*, *705*(1-2), 2–14. doi:10.1016/j.aca.2011.03.055 PMID:21962341

Fordellone, M. (2019). *Statistical analysis of complex data. Dimensionality reduction and classification methods*. LAP LAMBERT Academic Publishing.

Greene, W. H. (2017). *Econometric analysis* (8th ed.). Pearson.

Haufe, S., Dähne, S., & Nikulin, V. V. (2014). Dimensionality reduction for the analysis of brain oscillations. *NeuroImage*, *101*, 583–597. doi:10.1016/j.neuroimage.2014.06.073 PMID:25003816

Heinze, G., Wallisch, C., & Dunkler, D. (2017). Variable selection–A review and recommendations for the practicing statistician. *Biometrical Journal. Biometrische Zeitschrift*, *60*(3), 431–449. doi:10.1002/bimj.201700067 PMID:29292533

Hidalgo, C. A. (2021). Economic complexity theory and applications. *Nature Reviews Physics*, *3*(2), 92–113. doi:10.103842254-020-00275-1

Holder, A., & Eichholz, J. (2019). *An introduction to computational science*. Springer. doi:10.1007/978-3-030-15679-4

Hubert, M., Rousseeuw, P. J., & Van Aelst, S. (2008). High-breakdown robust multivariate methods. *Statistical Science*, *23*(1), 92–119. doi:10.1214/088342307000000087

Ignatius, J., Hatami-Marbini, A., Rahman, A., Dhamotharan, L., & Khoshnevis, P. (2018). A fuzzy decision support system for credit scoring. *Neural Computing & Applications*, *29*(10), 921–937. doi:10.100700521-016-2592-1

Jacobson, N. J., Bentley, K. H., Walton, A., Wang, S. B., Fortgang, R. G., Millner, A. J., Coombs, G. III, Rodman, A. M., & Coppersmith, D. D. L. (2020). Ethical dilemmas posed by mobile health and machine learning in psychiatry research. *Bulletin of the World Health Organization*, *98*(4), 270–276. doi:10.2471/BLT.19.237107 PMID:32284651

Jurečková, J., Picek, J., & Schindler, M. (2019). *Robust statistical methods with R* (2nd ed.). CRC Press. doi:10.1201/b21993

Jurečková, J., Sen, P. K., & Picek, J. (2013). *Methodology in robust and nonparametric statistics*. CRC Press.

Kalina, J. (2015). Three contributions to robust regression diagnostics. Journal of Applied Mathematics. *Statistics and Informatics*, *11*(2), 69–78.

Kalina, J. (2017). High-dimensional data in economics and their (robust) analysis. *Serbian Journal of Management*, *12*(1), 157–169. doi:10.5937jm12-10778

Kalina, J. (2019). Mental health clinical decision support exploiting Big Data. In K. T. Chui & M. D. Lytras (Eds.), *Computational Methods and Algorithms for Medicine and Optimized Clinical Practice* (pp. 160–184). IGI Global. doi:10.4018/978-1-5225-8244-1.ch008

Kalina, J., & Duintjer Tebbens, J. (2015). Algorithms for regularized linear discriminant analysis. *Proceedings of the 6th International Conference on Bioinformatics Models Methods, and Algorithms (BIOINFORMATICS '15)*, 128-133. 10.5220/0005234901280133

Kalina, J., & Matonoha, C. (2020). A sparse pair-preserving centroid-based supervised learning method for high-dimensional biomedical data or images. *Biocybernetics and Biomedical Engineering*, *40*(2), 774–786. doi:10.1016/j.bbe.2020.03.008

Kalina, J., & Rensová, D. (2015). How to reduce dimensionality of data: Robustness point of view. *Serbian Journal of Management*, *10*(1), 131–140. doi:10.5937jm10-6531

Kalina, J., & Schlenker, A. (2015). A robust supervised variable selection for noisy high-dimensional data. *BioMed Research International*, *2015*, 320385. doi:10.1155/2015/320385 PMID:26137474

Kalina, J., & Tichavský, J. (2022). (in press). The minimum weighted covariance determinant estimator for high-dimensional data. *Advances in Data Analysis and Classification*. Advance online publication. doi:10.100711634-021-00471-6

Kalina, J., Vašaničová, P., & Litavcová, E. (2019). Regression quantiles under heteroscedasticity and multicollinearity: Analysis of travel and tourism competitiveness. Ekonomický časopis. *Journal of Economics*, *67*(1), 69–85.

Kalina, J., & Vidnerová, P. (2020). Robust multilayer perceptrons: Robust loss functions and their derivatives. *Proceedings of the 21ˢᵗ EANN (Engineering Applications of Neural Networks) 2020 Conference*, 546–557.

Lalmuanawma, S., Hussain, J., & Chhaakchhuak, L. (2020). Applications of machine learning and artificial intelligence for Covid-19 (SARS-CoV-2) pandemic: A review. *Chaos, Solitons, and Fractals*, *139*, 110059. doi:10.1016/j.chaos.2020.110059 PMID:32834612

Lee, J., Ciccarello, S., Acharjee, M., & Das, K. (2018). Dimension reduction of gene expression data. *Journal of Statistical Theory and Practice*, *12*(2), 450–461. doi:10.1080/15598608.2017.1413456

Liu, N., Chee, M. L., Koh, Z. X., Leow, S. L., Ho, A. F. W., Guo, D., & Ong, M. E. H. (2021). Utilizing machine learning dimensionality reduction for risk stratification of chest pain patients in the emergency department. *BMC Medical Research Methodology*, *21*(1), 74. doi:10.118612874-021-01265-2 PMID:33865317

López-Robles, J. R., Rodríguez-Salvador, M., Gamboa-Rosales, N. K., Ramirez-Rosales, S., & Cobo, M. J. (2019). The last five years of Big Data Research in economics, econometrics and finance: Identification and conceptual analysis. *Procedia Computer Science*, *162*, 729–736. doi:10.1016/j.procs.2019.12.044

Luo, C. (2020). A comprehensive decision support approach for credit scoring. *Industrial Management & Data Systems*, *120*(2), 280–290. doi:10.1108/IMDS-03-2019-0182

Maronna, R. A., Martin, R. D., Yohai, V. J., & Salibián-Barrera, M. (2019). *Robust statistics. Theory and methods (with R)* (2nd ed.). Wiley.

Marozzi, M., Mukherjee, A., & Kalina, J. (2020). Interpoint distance tests for high-dimensional comparison studies. *Journal of Applied Statistics*, *47*(4), 653–665. doi:10.1080/02664763.2019.1649374 PMID:35707487

Martinez, W. L., Martinez, A. R., & Solka, J. L. (2017). *Exploratory data analysis with MATLAB* (3rd ed.). Chapman & Hall/CRC.

Martino, C., Shenhav, L., Marotz, C. A., Armstrong, G., McDonald, D., Vázquez-Baeza, Y., Morton, J. T., Jiang, L., Dominguez-Bello, M. G., Swafford, A. D., Halperin, E., & Knight, R. (2021). Context-aware dimensionality reduction deconvolutes gut microbial community dynamics. *Nature Biotechnology*, *39*(2), 165–168. doi:10.103841587-020-0660-7 PMID:32868914

Olson, D. L. (2017). *Descriptive data mining*. Springer. doi:10.1007/978-981-10-3340-7

Quarteroni, A. (2018). The role of statistics in the era of big data: A computational scientist' perspective. *Statistics & Probability Letters*, *136*, 63–67. doi:10.1016/j.spl.2018.02.047

Rousseeuw, P. J., & Leroy, A. M. (1987). *Robust regression and outlier detection*. Wiley. doi:10.1002/0471725382

Sadiq, M. T., Yu, X., & Yuan, Z. (2021). Exploiting dimensionality reduction and neural network techniques for the development of expert brain-computer interfaces. *Expert Systems with Applications*, *164*, 114031. doi:10.1016/j.eswa.2020.114031

Tan, C. W., & Kumar, A. (2012). Unified framework for automated iris segmentation using distantly acquired face images. *IEEE Transactions on Image Processing*, *21*(9), 4068–4079. doi:10.1109/TIP.2012.2199125 PMID:22614641

Tang, Y., Chen, D., & Li, X. (2021). Dimensionality reduction methods for brain imaging data analysis. *ACM Computing Surveys*, *54*, 87.

Taylor, S. (2019). Clustering financial return distributions using the Fisher information metric. *Entropy (Basel, Switzerland)*, *21*(2), 110. doi:10.3390/e21020110 PMID:33266826

Tegmark, M. (2017). *Life 3.0: Being human in the age of artificial intelligence.* Alfred A. Knopf.

Víšek, J. Á. (2011). Consistency of the least weighted squares under heteroscedasticity. *Kybernetika, 47,* 179–206.

Wakode, S. (2020). Efficacious scrutinizing of COVID-19 impact on banking using credit risk metrics. *International Journal of Finance & Economics, 6*(3), 51–56.

Wilson, P. W. (2018). Dimension reduction in nonparametric models of production. *European Journal of Operational Research, 267*(1), 349–367. doi:10.1016/j.ejor.2017.11.020

Witzany, J. (2017). *Credit risk management. Pricing, Measurement, and Modeling.* Springer. doi:10.1007/978-3-319-49800-3

Zhao, L., Chen, Z., Hu, Y., Min, G., & Jiang, Z. (2018). Distributed feature selection for efficient economic big data analysis. *IEEE Transactions on Big Data, 5*(2), 164–176. doi:10.1109/TBDATA.2016.2601934

Compilation of References

Abbas, S., & Mahmoud, A. M. (2021). DiaMe: IoMT deep predictive model based on threshold aware region growing technique. *International Journal of Electrical & Computer Engineering, 11*(5).

AbdelMassih, A. F., Menshawey, R., Ismail, J. H., Husseiny, R. J., Husseiny, Y. M., Yacoub, S., ... Castaldi, B. (2021). PPAR agonists as effective adjuvants for COVID-19 vaccines, by modifying immunogenetics: A review of literature. *Journal of Genetic Engineering and Biotechnology, 19*(1), 1–9.

Ahmed, H., Younis, E. M., Hendawi, A., & Ali, A. A. (2020). Heart disease identification from patients' social posts, machine learning solution on Spark. *Future Generation Computer Systems, 111*, 714–722.

Aksu, G., & Güzeller, C. O. (2019). *Büyük Veri: Sosyal Bilimler ile Eğitim Bilimlerinde Kullanımı ve Uygulama Alanları* [Big Data: Usage and Application Areas in Social Sciences and Educational Sciences]. Mediterranean Journal of Humanities.

Ala'a, B., & Tarhini, Z. (2021). Beyond equity: Advocating theory-based health promotion in parallel with COVID-19 mass vaccination campaigns. *Public Health in Practice, 2*, 100142.

Albert, E., Aurigemma, G., Saucedo, J., & Gerson, D. S. (2021). Myocarditis following COVID-19 vaccination. *Radiology Case Reports, 16*(8), 2142–2145.

Aleem, A., Prateek, G., & Kumar, N. (2021, December). Improving Heart Disease Prediction Using Feature Selection Through Genetic Algorithm. In *International Conference on Advanced Network Technologies and Intelligent Computing* (pp. 765-776). Springer.

Ali, L., Rahman, A., Khan, A., Zhou, M., Javeed, A., & Khan, J. A. (2019). An automated diagnostic system for heart disease prediction based on statistical model and optimally configured deep neural network. *IEEE Access: Practical Innovations, Open Solutions, 7*, 34938–34945. doi:10.1109/ACCESS.2019.2904800

Al-Makhadmeh, Z., & Tolba, A. (2019). Utilizing IoT wearable medical device for heart disease prediction using higher order Boltzmann model: A classification approach. *Measurement, 147*, 106815. doi:10.1016/j.measurement.2019.07.043

Almustafa, K. M. (2020). Prediction of heart disease and classifiers' sensitivity analysis. *BMC Bioinformatics*, *21*(1), 1–18. doi:10.118612859-020-03626-y PMID:32615980

Altunışık, R. (2015). Büyük Veri: Fırsatlar Kaynağı mı Yoksa Yeni Sorunlar Yumağı mı? [Big Data: A Source of Opportunities or a Mass of New Challenges?]. *Yıldız Social Science Review*, *1*(1), 45–76.

Amin, J., Sharif, M., Yasmin, M., Saba, T., Anjum, M. A., & Fernandes, S. L. (2019). A new approach for brain tumor segmentation and classification based on score level fusion using transfer learning. *Journal of Medical Systems*, *43*(11), 1–16. doi:10.100710916-019-1453-8 PMID:31643004

Anitha, S., & Sridevi, N. (2019). Heart disease prediction using data mining techniques. *Journal of Analysis and Computation*.

Antal, C., Cioara, T., Antal, M., & Anghel, I. (2021). Blockchain platform for COVID-19 vaccine supply management. *IEEE Open Journal of the Computer Society*, *2*, 164–178.

Apache Hadoop. (n.d.). *Apache Hadoop.* Retrieved from https://hadoop.apache.org/

Apache Spark. (2016). *Apache Spark.* Retrieved from https://spark.apache.org/

Aslan, A., Bayrakçı, S., & Küçükvardar, M. (2016). Bilişim Çağında Geleneksel Gazeteciliğin Dönüşümü: Veri Gazeteciliği [The Transformation of Traditional Journalism in the Information Age: Data Journalism]. *Marmara İletişim Dergisi*, (26), 55–70.

Atalay, M., & Çelik, E. (2017). Büyük Veri Analizinde Yapay Zeka ve Makine Öğrenmesi Uygulamaları [Applications of Artificial Intelligence and Machine Learning in Big Data Analytics]. *Mehmet Akif Ersoy Üniversitesi Sosyal Bilimler Enstitüsü Dergisi*, *9*(22), 155–172. doi:10.20875/makusobed.309727

Bansal, S. (2021). *IoT Assisted Health Risk Monitoring.* Github. https://github.com/shrikrishnbansal/IoT-Assisted-Health-risk-monitoring

Bardoel, J., & Deuze, M. (2001). Network Journalism: Converging Competences Of Old And New Media Professionals. *Australian Journalism Review*, *23*(2), 91–103.

Batz, G. V., Geisberger, R., Neubauer, S., & Sanders, P. (2010, May). Time-dependent contraction hierarchies and approximation. In *International Symposium on Experimental Algorithms* (pp. 166-177). Springer. 10.1007/978-3-642-13193-6_15

Batz, G. V., Geisberger, R., Sanders, P., & Vetter, C. (2013). Minimum time-dependent travel times with contraction hierarchies. *Journal of Experimental Algorithmics*, *18*, 1–1. doi:10.1145/2444016.2444020

Bauer, R., & Delling, D. (2010). SHARC: Fast and robust unidirectional routing. *Journal of Experimental Algorithmics*, *14*, 2–4.

Bhatia, M., & Sood, S. (2017). A comprehensive health assessment framework to facilitate IoT-assisted smart workouts: A predictive healthcare perspective. *Computers in Industry*, *92-93*, 50–66. Advance online publication. doi:10.1016/j.compind.2017.06.009

BIDMC PPG and Respiration Dataset v1.0.0. (2018, June 20). *PhysioNet*. Retrieved February 27, 2022, from https://physionet.org/content/bidmc/1.0.0/

Birsen, Ö., Oğur, O., & Özmen, Ş. Y. (2018). Alternatif Gazetecilik Örneği Olarak Yavaş Medyanın Geleneksel Gazetecilik Değerleri Üzerinden İncelenmesi [Examining Slow Media as an Example of Alternative Journalism through Traditional Journalistic Values]. *Anadolu Üniversitesi İletişim Bilimleri Fakültesi Uluslararası Hakemli Dergisi*, *26*(3), 370–384.

Blanchard-Rohner, G., Caprettini, B., Rohner, D., & Voth, H. J. (2021). Impact of COVID-19 and intensive care unit capacity on vaccination support: Evidence from a two-leg representative survey in the United Kingdom. *Journal of Virus Eradication*, *7*(2), 100044.

Blazques, D., & Domenech, J. (2018). Big Data sources and methods for social and economic analyses. *Technological Forecasting and Social Change*, *130*, 99–113. doi:10.1016/j.techfore.2017.07.027

Bracci, A., Nadini, M., Aliapoulios, M., McCoy, D., Gray, I., Teytelboym, A., ... Baronchelli, A. (2021). Dark Web Marketplaces and COVID-19: Before the vaccine. *EPJ Data Science*, *10*(1), 6.

Bradlow, E. T., Gangwar, M., Kopalle, P., & Voleti, S. (2017). The role of Big Data and predictive analytics in retailing. *Journal of Retailing*, *93*(1), 79–95. doi:10.1016/j.jretai.2016.12.004

Brown, A., Shah, S., Dluzewski, S., Musaddaq, B., Wagner, T., Szyszko, T., Wan, S., Groves, A., Mokbel, K., & Malhotra, A. (2021). Unilateral axillary adenopathy following COVID-19 vaccination: A multimodality pictorial illustration and review of current guidelines. *Clinical Radiology*, *76*(8), 553–558. doi:10.1016/j.crad.2021.04.010 PMID:34053731

Bučková, B., Brunovský, M., Bareš, M., & Hlinka, J. (2020). Predicting sex from EEG: Validity and generalizability of deep-learning-based interpretable classifier. *Frontiers in Neuroscience*, *14*, 589303. doi:10.3389/fnins.2020.589303 PMID:33192274

Carvalho, T., De Rezende, E. R., Alves, M. T., Balieiro, F. K., & Sovat, R. B. (2017, December). Exposing computer generated images by eye's region classification via transfer learning of VGG19 CNN. In *2017 16th IEEE International Conference on Machine Learning and Applications (ICMLA)* (pp. 866-870). IEEE. doi:10.1109/CCWC.2018.8301729

Caspi, G., Dayan, A., Eshal, Y., Liverant-Taub, S., Twig, G., Shalit, U., ... Caspi, O. (2021). Socioeconomic disparities and COVID-19 vaccination acceptance: A nationwide ecologic study. *Clinical Microbiology and Infection*, *27*(10), 1502–1506.

Çetinkaya, A. (2018). *İçerik Üretiminden Reklama Çevrimiçi Gazetecilik* [Online Journalism from Content Production to Advertising]. Nobel Akademik Yayınları.

Chen, M., Kuo, C. L., & Chan, W. K. V. (2021, April). Control of COVID-19 Pandemic: Vaccination Strategies Simulation under Probabilistic Node-Level Model. In *2021 6th International Conference on Intelligent Computing and Signal Processing (ICSP)* (pp. 119-125). IEEE.

Chen, B. Y., Lam, W. H., Sumalee, A., Li, Q., & Tam, M. L. (2014). Reliable shortest path problems in stochastic time-dependent networks. *Journal of Intelligent Transport Systems*, *18*(2), 177–189. doi:10.1080/15472450.2013.806851

Chen, S. T., Lin, S. S., Lan, C. W., & Hsu, H. Y. (2017). Design and Development of a Wearable Device for Heat Stroke Detection. *Sensors (Basel)*, *18*(1), 17. doi:10.339018010017 PMID:29271893

Chen, X., Zhu, G., Zhang, L., Fang, Y., Guo, L., & Chen, X. (2021). Age-stratified COVID-19 spread analysis and vaccination: A multitype random network approach. *IEEE Transactions on Network Science and Engineering*, *8*(2), 1862–1872.

Chew, N. W., Cheong, C., Kong, G., Phua, K., Ngiam, J. N., Tan, B. Y., ... Sharma, V. K. (2021). An Asia-Pacific study on healthcare workers' perceptions of, and willingness to receive, the COVID-19 vaccination. *International Journal of Infectious Diseases*, *106*, 52–60.

Chollet, F. (2017). Xception: Deep learning with depthwise separable convolutions. In *Proceedings of the IEEE conference on computer vision and pattern recognition* (pp. 1251-1258). 10.1109/CVPR.2017.195

Çoban, S. (2013). *Teknolojik Determinizm Bağlamında Bilgi Toplumu Strateji Belgesinin İncelenmesi* [Examination of the Information Society Strategy Document in the Context of Technological Determinism]. Akademik Bilişim Konferansları.

Cordova, I., & Moh, T. S. (2015, July). DBSCAN on resilient distributed datasets. In *2015 International Conference on High Performance Computing & Simulation (HPCS)* (pp. 531-540). IEEE. 10.1109/HPCSim.2015.7237086

Cotfas, L. A., Delcea, C., Roxin, I., Ioanăş, C., Gherai, D. S., & Tajariol, F. (2021). The longest month: Analyzing COVID-19 vaccination opinions dynamics from tweets in the month following the first vaccine announcement. *IEEE Access: Practical Innovations, Open Solutions*, *9*, 33203–33223.

Csiszár, I., & Shields, P. C. (2004). Information Theory and Statistics: A Tutorial. *Foundations and Trends in Communications and Information Theory*, *1*(4), 417–528. doi:10.1561/0100000004

Cucunawangsih, C., Wijaya, R. S., Lugito, N. P. H., & Suriapranata, I. (2021). Post-vaccination cases of COVID-19 among healthcare workers at Siloam Teaching Hospital, Indonesia. *International Journal of Infectious Diseases*, *107*, 268–270.

Damgacioglu, H., Celik, E., & Celik, N. (2019). Estimating gene expression from high-dimensional DNA methylation levels in cancer data: A bimodal unsupervised dimension reduction algorithm. *Computers & Industrial Engineering*, *130*, 348–357. doi:10.1016/j.cie.2019.02.038

Das, S., Aranya, O. R. R., & Labiba, N. N. (2019, May). Brain tumor classification using convolutional neural network. In *2019 1st International Conference on Advances in Science, Engineering and Robotics Technology (ICASERT)* (pp. 1-5). IEEE. 10.1109/ICASERT.2019.8934603

Davies, P. L., & Gather, U. (2005). Breakdown and groups. *Annals of Statistics*, *33*(3), 977–1035. doi:10.1214/009053604000001138

Dehong, G., Wenjie, L., Xiaoyan, C., Renxian, Z., & You, O. (2014). Sequential summarization: A full view of twitter trending topics. *ACM Trans on Audio Speech Lang Process*, *22*(2), 293–302.

Deka, S. K., Goswami, S., & Anand, A. (2020, December). A blockchain based technique for storing vaccination records. In 2020 IEEE Bombay section signature conference (IBSSC) (pp. 135-139). IEEE.

Ding, C., & Peng, H. (2005). Minimum redundancy feature selection from microarray gene expression data. *Journal of Bioinformatics and Computational Biology*, *3*(02), 185–205. doi:10.1142/S0219720005001004 PMID:15852500

Dua, D. & Graff, C. (2017). *UCI machine learning repository*. Available at http://archive.ics.uci.edu/ml

Dubey, A. D. (2021). *Public sentiment analysis of covid-19 vaccination drive in india*. Available at SSRN 3772401.

Duke, H., Posch, L., & Green, L. (2021). Axillary adenopathy following COVID-19 vaccination: A single institution case series. *Clinical Imaging*, *80*, 111–116.

Dutta, A., Batabyal, T., Basu, M., & Acton, S. T. (2020). An efficient convolutional neural network for coronary heart disease prediction. *Expert Systems with Applications*, *159*, 113408. doi:10.1016/j.eswa.2020.113408

Dwivedi, A. K. (2018). Performance evaluation of different machine learning techniques for prediction of heart disease. *Neural Computing & Applications*, *29*(10), 685–693. doi:10.100700521-016-2604-1

Eijsvogels, T., Thompson, P. D., & Franklin, B. A. (2018). The "Extreme Exercise Hypothesis": Recent Findings and Cardiovascular Health Implications. *Current Treatment Options in Cardiovascular Medicine*, *20*(10), 84. doi:10.100711936-018-0674-3 PMID:30155804

Eisenstadt, M., Ramachandran, M., Chowdhury, N., Third, A., & Domingue, J. (2020). COVID-19 antibody test/vaccination certification: There's an app for that. *IEEE Open Journal of Engineering in Medicine and Biology*, *1*, 148–155.

Elbaset, A., Said, H., Sultan, A. M., Montasser, I. F., Soliman, H. E., Elayashy, M., & Makhlouf, N. A. (2021). *Egyptian protocol for living donor liver transplantation (LDLT) during SARS-CoV-2 pandemic*. Academic Press.

El-Hasnony, I. M., Elzeki, O. M., Alshehri, A., & Salem, H. (2022). Multi-label active learning-based machine learning model for heart disease prediction. *Sensors (Basel)*, *22*(3), 1184. doi:10.339022031184 PMID:35161928

Fan, J., Ke, Y., & Wang, K. (2020). Factor-adjusted regularized model selection. *Journal of Econometrics*, *216*(1), 71–85. doi:10.1016/j.jeconom.2020.01.006 PMID:32269406

Filzmoser, P., & Nordhausen, K. (2020). Robust linear regression for high-dimensional data: An overview. *Wiley Interdisciplinary Reviews: Computational Statistics*, *13*, e1524.

Filzmoser, P., & Todorov, V. (2011). Review of robust multivariate statistical methods in high dimension. *Analytica Chimica Acta*, *705*(1-2), 2–14. doi:10.1016/j.aca.2011.03.055 PMID:21962341

Fleury, V., Maucherat, B., Rusu, D., Dumont, F., & Rousseau, C. (2021). COVID-19 vaccination may cause FDG uptake beyond axillary area. *European Journal of Hybrid Imaging*, *5*(1), 1–3.

Fordellone, M. (2019). *Statistical analysis of complex data. Dimensionality reduction and classification methods*. LAP LAMBERT Academic Publishing.

Ganapathy, J. (2022) Multi Criteria Decision Making Analysis for sustainable Transport. Unpublished Manuscript. In *Sustainability: Cases And Studies in using Operations Research and Management Science Methods*. Springer.

Ganapathy, J., García Márquez, F. P., & Ragavendra Prasad, M. (2022). Routing Vehicles on Highways by Augmenting Traffic Flow Network: A Review on Speed Up Techniques. *Integrated Emerging Methods of Artificial Intelligence & Cloud Computing*, 96-105.

Ganapathy, J. (2021). Design of Algorithm for IoT-Based Application: Case Study on Intelligent Transport Systems. In *Internet of Things* (pp. 227–249). Springer. doi:10.1007/978-3-030-70478-0_11

Ganapathy, J., & García Márquez, F. P. (2021a, August). Travel Time Based Traffic Rerouting by Augmenting Traffic Flow Network with Temporal and Spatial Relations for Congestion Management. In *International Conference on Management Science and Engineering Management* (pp. 554-565). Springer. 10.1007/978-3-030-79203-9_43

Ganapathy, J., & García Márquez, F. P. (2021b, August). Data Mining and Information Technology in Transportation—A Review. In *International Conference on Management Science and Engineering Management* (pp. 849-855). Springer. 10.1007/978-3-030-79206-0_64

Ganapathy, J., & Paramasivam, J. (2019). Prediction of traffic volume by mining traffic sequences using travel time based PrefixSpan. *IET Intelligent Transport Systems*, *13*(7), 1199–1210. doi:10.1049/iet-its.2018.5165

Gárate-Escamila, A. K., El Hassani, A. H., & Andrès, E. (2020). Classification models for heart disease prediction using feature selection and PCA. *Informatics in Medicine Unlocked*, *19*, 100330. doi:10.1016/j.imu.2020.100330

Gavhane, A., Kokkula, G., Pandya, I., & Devadkar, K. (2018, March). Prediction of heart disease using machine learning. In *2018 second international conference on electronics, communication and aerospace technology (ICECA)* (pp. 1275-1278). IEEE. 10.1109/ICECA.2018.8474922

Greene, W. H. (2017). *Econometric analysis* (8th ed.). Pearson.

Güngör, N. (2020). *İletişim Kuramlar ve Yaklaşımlar (5. b.)* [Communication Theories and Approaches (5. b.)]. Siyasal Kitabevi.

Haq, A. U., Li, J. P., Memon, M. H., Nazir, S., & Sun, R. (2018). A hybrid intelligent system framework for the prediction of heart disease using machine learning algorithms. *Mobile Information Systems*.

Haufe, S., Dähne, S., & Nikulin, V. V. (2014). Dimensionality reduction for the analysis of brain oscillations. *NeuroImage*, *101*, 583–597. doi:10.1016/j.neuroimage.2014.06.073 PMID:25003816

Heart Attack Prediction. (2018, April 25). *Kaggle*. Retrieved February 27, 2022, from https://www.kaggle.com/imnikhilanand/heart-attack-prediction

Heart Disease Prediction. (2020, August 22). *Kaggle*. Retrieved February 27, 2022, from https://www.kaggle.com/rishidamarla/heart-disease-prediction

Heart Information Center. Heart Disease Risk Factors. (n.d.). *Texas Heart Institute*. Retrieved February 27, 2022, from https://www.texasheart.org/heart-health/heart-information-center/topics/heart-disease-risk-factors

Heinze, G., Wallisch, C., & Dunkler, D. (2017). Variable selection–A review and recommendations for the practicing statistician. *Biometrical Journal. Biometrische Zeitschrift*, *60*(3), 431–449. doi:10.1002/bimj.201700067 PMID:29292533

Hidalgo, C. A. (2021). Economic complexity theory and applications. *Nature Reviews Physics*, *3*(2), 92–113. doi:10.103842254-020-00275-1

Holder, A., & Eichholz, J. (2019). *An introduction to computational science*. Springer. doi:10.1007/978-3-030-15679-4

Huang, G., Liu, Z., Van Der Maaten, L., & Weinberger, K. Q. (2017). Densely connected convolutional networks. In *Proceedings of the IEEE conference on computer vision and pattern recognition* (pp. 4700-4708). IEEE.

Hubert, M., Rousseeuw, P. J., & Van Aelst, S. (2008). High-breakdown robust multivariate methods. *Statistical Science*, *23*(1), 92–119. doi:10.1214/088342307000000087

Hughes, D. J., Rowe, M., Batey, M., & Lee, A. (2012). A tale of two sites: Twitter vs. Facebook and the personality predictors of social media usage. *Computers in Human Behavior*, *28*(2), 561–569. doi:10.1016/j.chb.2011.11.001

Hughes, J. A., Dubé, M., Houghten, S., & Ashlock, D. (2020, October). Vaccinating a population is a programming problem. In *2020 IEEE Conference on Computational Intelligence in Bioinformatics and Computational Biology (CIBCB)* (pp. 1-8). IEEE.

Hyland, P., Vallières, F., Shevlin, M., Bentall, R. P., McKay, R., Hartman, T. K., ... Murphy, J. (2021). Resistance to COVID-19 vaccination has increased in Ireland and the United Kingdom during the pandemic. *Public Health*, *195*, 54–56.

Ignatius, J., Hatami-Marbini, A., Rahman, A., Dhamotharan, L., & Khoshnevis, P. (2018). A fuzzy decision support system for credit scoring. *Neural Computing & Applications*, *29*(10), 921–937. doi:10.100700521-016-2592-1

Jacobson, N. J., Bentley, K. H., Walton, A., Wang, S. B., Fortgang, R. G., Millner, A. J., Coombs, G. III, Rodman, A. M., & Coppersmith, D. D. L. (2020). Ethical dilemmas posed by mobile health and machine learning in psychiatry research. *Bulletin of the World Health Organization*, *98*(4), 270–276. doi:10.2471/BLT.19.237107 PMID:32284651

Jadidi, M. M., Moslemi, P., Jamshidiha, S., Masroori, I., Mohammadi, A., & Pourahmadi, V. (2020, December). Targeted vaccination for COVID-19 using mobile communication networks. In *2020 11th International Conference on Information and Knowledge Technology (IKT)* (pp. 93-97). IEEE.

Jaiswal, A., Gianchandani, N., Singh, D., Kumar, V., & Kaur, M. (2021). Classification of the COVID-19 infected patients using DenseNet201 based deep transfer learning. *Journal of Biomolecular Structure & Dynamics*, *39*(15), 5682–5689. doi:10.1080/07391102.2020.17886 42 PMID:32619398

Javed, S., Ghazala, S., & Faseeha, U. (2020). Perspectives of Heat Stroke Shield: An IoT based Solution for the Detection and Preliminary Treatment of Heat Stroke. Engineering, Technology &. *Applied Scientific Research*, *10*(2), 5576–5580. doi:10.48084/etasr.3274

Jurečková, J., Picek, J., & Schindler, M. (2019). *Robust statistical methods with R* (2nd ed.). CRC Press. doi:10.1201/b21993

Jurečková, J., Sen, P. K., & Picek, J. (2013). *Methodology in robust and nonparametric statistics*. CRC Press.

Kalina, J., & Vidnerová, P. (2020). Robust multilayer perceptrons: Robust loss functions and their derivatives. *Proceedings of the 21st EANN (Engineering Applications of Neural Networks) 2020 Conference*, 546–557.

Kalina, J. (2015). Three contributions to robust regression diagnostics. Journal of Applied Mathematics. *Statistics and Informatics*, *11*(2), 69–78.

Kalina, J. (2017). High-dimensional data in economics and their (robust) analysis. *Serbian Journal of Management*, *12*(1), 157–169. doi:10.5937jm12-10778

Kalina, J. (2019). Mental health clinical decision support exploiting Big Data. In K. T. Chui & M. D. Lytras (Eds.), *Computational Methods and Algorithms for Medicine and Optimized Clinical Practice* (pp. 160–184). IGI Global. doi:10.4018/978-1-5225-8244-1.ch008

Kalina, J., & Duintjer Tebbens, J. (2015). Algorithms for regularized linear discriminant analysis. *Proceedings of the 6th International Conference on Bioinformatics Models Methods, and Algorithms (BIOINFORMATICS '15)*, 128-133. 10.5220/0005234901280133

Kalina, J., & Matonoha, C. (2020). A sparse pair-preserving centroid-based supervised learning method for high-dimensional biomedical data or images. *Biocybernetics and Biomedical Engineering*, *40*(2), 774–786. doi:10.1016/j.bbe.2020.03.008

Kalina, J., & Rensová, D. (2015). How to reduce dimensionality of data: Robustness point of view. *Serbian Journal of Management*, *10*(1), 131–140. doi:10.5937jm10-6531

Kalina, J., & Schlenker, A. (2015). A robust supervised variable selection for noisy high-dimensional data. *BioMed Research International*, *2015*, 320385. doi:10.1155/2015/320385 PMID:26137474

Kalina, J., & Tichavský, J. (2022). (in press). The minimum weighted covariance determinant estimator for high-dimensional data. *Advances in Data Analysis and Classification*. Advance online publication. doi:10.100711634-021-00471-6

Kalina, J., Vašaničová, P., & Litavcová, E. (2019). Regression quantiles under heteroscedasticity and multicollinearity: Analysis of travel and tourism competitiveness. Ekonomický časopis. *Journal of Economics*, *67*(1), 69–85.

Kavitha, M., Gnaneswar, G., Dinesh, R., Sai, Y. R., & Suraj, R. S. (2021, January). Heart disease prediction using hybrid machine learning model. In *2021 6th International Conference on Inventive Computation Technologies (ICICT)* (pp. 1329-1333). IEEE. 10.1109/ICICT50816.2021.9358597

Kazan, H. (2019). *Dijital Çağda Gazetecilikte Yeni Kavramlar: Robot Gazeteciliği, Veri Gazeteciliği, Hiperyerel Gazetecilik. In Dijital Çağda Habercilik Kuram ve Uygulamada Yeni Yönelimler*. Der Yayınları.

Kemmler, W., & Stengel, S. (2013). Exercise Frequency, Health Risk Factors, and Diseases of the Elderly. *Archives of Physical Medicine and Rehabilitation*, *94*(11), 2046–2053. Advance online publication. doi:10.1016/j.apmr.2013.05.013 PMID:23748185

Keshavarz, P., Yazdanpanah, F., Rafiee, F., & Mizandari, M. (2021). Lymphadenopathy following COVID-19 vaccination: Imaging findings review. *Academic Radiology*, *28*(8), 1058–1071.

Kessels, R., Luyten, J., & Tubeuf, S. (2021). Willingness to get vaccinated against Covid-19 and attitudes toward vaccination in general. *Vaccine*, *39*(33), 4716–4722.

Kessler, H. S., Sisson, S. B., & Short, K. R. (2012). The potential for high-intensity interval training to reduce cardiometabolic disease risk. *Sports Medicine (Auckland, N.Z.)*, *42*(6), 489–509. doi:10.2165/11630910-000000000-00000 PMID:22587821

Khade, S. M., Yabaji, S. M., & Srivastava, J. (2021). An update on COVID-19: SARS-CoV-2 life cycle, immunopathology, and BCG vaccination. *Preparative Biochemistry & Biotechnology, 51*(7), 650–658.

Khan, M. A. (2020). An IoT framework for heart disease prediction based on MDCNN classifier. *IEEE Access, 8*, 34717-34727.

Khourdifi, Y., & Bahaj, M. (2019). Heart disease prediction and classification using machine learning algorithms optimized by particle swarm optimization and ant colony optimization. *International Journal of Intelligent Engineering and Systems, 12*(1), 242–252. doi:10.22266/ijies2019.0228.24

Khubchandani, J., & Macias, Y. (2021). COVID-19 vaccination hesitancy in Hispanics and African-Americans: A review and recommendations for practice. *Brain, Behavior, & Immunity-Health, 15*, 100277.

Kılınç, D. (2019). A spark-based big data analysis framework for real-time sentiment prediction on streaming data. *Software, Practice & Experience, 49*(9), 1352–1364.

Krizhevsky, A., Sutskever, I., & Hinton, G. E. (2012). Imagenet classification with deep convolutional neural networks. *Advances in Neural Information Processing Systems*, 25.

Kulick, D. L. (n.d.). *Heart Attack Causes, Symptoms, Causes, Treatment & How to Prevent.* MedicineNet. Retrieved February 27, 2022, from https://www.medicinenet.com/heart_attack/article.htm

Kumar, P. S. (2014). An Efficient Monitoring System For Sports Person Using Wi-Fi Communication. *International Journal of Research in Engineering and Technology, 3*, 20–23. doi:10.15623/ijret.2014.0311003

Kumar, K. A., Prasad, A. Y., & Metan, J. (2022). A hybrid deep CNN-Cov-19-Res-Net Transfer learning architype for an enhanced Brain tumor Detection and Classification scheme in medical image processing. *Biomedical Signal Processing and Control, 76*, 103631. doi:10.1016/j.bspc.2022.103631

Lalmuanawma, S., Hussain, J., & Chhaakchhuak, L. (2020). Applications of machine learning and artificial intelligence for Covid-19 (SARS-CoV-2) pandemic: A review. *Chaos, Solitons, and Fractals, 139*, 110059. doi:10.1016/j.chaos.2020.110059 PMID:32834612

Latha, C. B. C., & Jeeva, S. C. (2019). Improving the accuracy of prediction of heart disease risk based on ensemble classification techniques. *Informatics in Medicine Unlocked, 16*, 100203. doi:10.1016/j.imu.2019.100203

Lee, K., Palsetia, D., Narayanan, R., Patwary, M. M. A., Agrawal, A., & Choudhary, A. (2011, December). Twitter trending topic classification. In *2011 IEEE 11th International Conference on Data Mining Workshops* (pp. 251-258). IEEE.

Lee, J., Ciccarello, S., Acharjee, M., & Das, K. (2018). Dimension reduction of gene expression data. *Journal of Statistical Theory and Practice*, *12*(2), 450–461. doi:10.1080/15598608.2017.1413456

Liu, N., Chee, M. L., Koh, Z. X., Leow, S. L., Ho, A. F. W., Guo, D., & Ong, M. E. H. (2021). Utilizing machine learning dimensionality reduction for risk stratification of chest pain patients in the emergency department. *BMC Medical Research Methodology*, *21*(1), 74. doi:10.118612874-021-01265-2 PMID:33865317

López-Robles, J. R., Rodríguez-Salvador, M., Gamboa-Rosales, N. K., Ramirez-Rosales, S., & Cobo, M. J. (2019). The last five years of Big Data Research in economics, econometrics and finance: Identification and conceptual analysis. *Procedia Computer Science*, *162*, 729–736. doi:10.1016/j.procs.2019.12.044

Luo, C. (2020). A comprehensive decision support approach for credit scoring. *Industrial Management & Data Systems*, *120*(2), 280–290. doi:10.1108/IMDS-03-2019-0182

Maji, S., & Arora, S. (2019). Decision tree algorithms for prediction of heart disease. In *Information and communication technology forcompetitive strategies* (pp. 447–454). Springer. doi:10.1007/978-981-13-0586-3_45

Majumder, A. K. M., ElSaadany, Y. A., Young, R., & Ucci, D. R. (2019). An energy efficient wearable smart IoT system to predict cardiac arrest. *Advances in Human-Computer Interaction*, *2019*, 2019. doi:10.1155/2019/1507465

Makazhanov, A., & Rafiei, D. (2013, August). Predicting political preference of Twitter users. In *Proceedings of the 2013 IEEE/ACM International Conference on Advances in Social Networks Analysis and Mining* (pp. 298-305). IEEE.

Maronna, R. A., Martin, R. D., Yohai, V. J., & Salibián-Barrera, M. (2019). *Robust statistics. Theory and methods (with R)* (2nd ed.). Wiley.

Marozzi, M., Mukherjee, A., & Kalina, J. (2020). Interpoint distance tests for high-dimensional comparison studies. *Journal of Applied Statistics*, *47*(4), 653–665. doi:10.1080/02664763.2019.1649374 PMID:35707487

Martinez, W. L., Martinez, A. R., & Solka, J. L. (2017). *Exploratory data analysis with MATLAB* (3rd ed.). Chapman & Hall/CRC.

Martino, C., Shenhav, L., Marotz, C. A., Armstrong, G., McDonald, D., Vázquez-Baeza, Y., Morton, J. T., Jiang, L., Dominguez-Bello, M. G., Swafford, A. D., Halperin, E., & Knight, R. (2021). Context-aware dimensionality reduction deconvolutes gut microbial community dynamics. *Nature Biotechnology*, *39*(2), 165–168. doi:10.103841587-020-0660-7 PMID:32868914

Mellado, B., Wu, J., Kong, J. D., Bragazzi, N. L., Asgary, A., Kawonga, M., ... Orbinski, J. (2021). Leveraging artificial intelligence and big data to optimize COVID-19 clinical public health and vaccination roll-out strategies in Africa. *International Journal of Environmental Research and Public Health*, *18*(15), 7890.

Mertz, L. (2020). One shot wonder: A vaccine against all coronaviruses. *IEEE Pulse*, *11*(6), 2–5.

Mir, H. H., Parveen, S., Mullick, N. H., & Nabi, S. (2021). Using structural equation modeling to predict Indian people's attitudes and intentions towards COVID-19 vaccination. *Diabetes & Metabolic Syndrome*, *15*(3), 1017–1022.

Mohamed Hussein, A. A., Salem, M. R., Salman, S., Abdulrahim, A. F., Al Massry, N. A., Saad, M., ... Negida, A. (2020). Correlation between COVID-19 case fatality rate and percentage of BCG vaccination: Is it true the vaccine is protective? *The Egyptian Journal of Bronchology*, *14*(1), 1–5.

Mohan, S., Thirumalai, C., & Srivastava, G. (2019). Effective heart disease prediction using hybrid machine learning techniques. *IEEE Access: Practical Innovations, Open Solutions*, *7*, 81542–81554. doi:10.1109/ACCESS.2019.2923707

Nadini, M., Zino, L., Rizzo, A., & Porfiri, M. (2020). A multi-agent model to study epidemic spreading and vaccination strategies in an urban-like environment. *Applied Network Science*, *5*(1), 1–30.

Narin, B., Ayaz, B., Fırat, F., & Fırat, D. (2017). Büyük Veri ve Gazetecilik İlişkisi Bağlamında Veri Gazeteciliği. [Data Journalism in the Context of the Relationship between Big Data and Journalism]. *AJIT-e. Online Academic Journal of Information Technology*, *8*(30), 215–235. doi:10.5824/1309-1581.2017.5.010.x

Nodarakis, N., Sioutas, S., Tsakalidis, A. K., & Tzimas, G. (2016, March). Large Scale Sentiment Analysis on Twitter with Spark. In EDBT/ICDT Workshops (pp. 1-8). Academic Press.

O'Driscoll, B. R., Howard, L. S., Earis, J., & Mark, V. (2017). British Thoracic Society Guideline for oxygen use in adults in healthcare and emergency settings. *BMJ Open Respiratory Research*, *4*(1), e000170. Advance online publication. doi:10.1136/bmjresp-2016-000170 PMID:28883921

Odoom, J., Soglo, R. S., Danso, S. A., & Xiaofang, H. (2020, December). A privacy-preserving Covid-19 updatable test result and vaccination provenance based on blockchain and smart contract. In *2019 International Conference on Mechatronics, Remote Sensing, Information Systems and Industrial Information Technologies (ICMRSISIIT)* (Vol. 1, pp. 1-6). IEEE.

Ohlhorst, F. (2013). *Big Data Analytics: Turning Big Data into Big Money*. Wiley Publicity.

Olcay, S. (2018). Sosyalleşmenin Dijitalleşmesi Olarak Sosyal Medya ve Resimler Arasında Kaybolma Bozukluğu: Photolurkıng [Disappearance Disorder Between Social Media and Pictures as the Digitalization of Socialization: Photolurking]. *Yeni Medya Elektronik Dergisi*, *2*(2), 90–104. doi:10.17932/IAU.EJNM.25480200.2018.2/2.90-104

Olson, D. L. (2017). *Descriptive data mining*. Springer. doi:10.1007/978-981-10-3340-7

Özdemir, Z. (2019). *Dijitalleşme Sürecinde İletişim ve Haberciliğin Evrimi. In Dijital Çağda Habercilik Kuram ve Uygulamada Yeni Yönelimler*. Der Yayınları.

Pal, M. (2005). Random forest classifier for remote sensing classification. *International Journal of Remote Sensing*, *26*(1), 217–222.

Pal, R., Bhadada, S. K., & Misra, A. (2021). COVID-19 vaccination in patients with diabetes mellitus: Current concepts, uncertainties and challenges. *Diabetes & Metabolic Syndrome*, *15*(2), 505–508.

Patelarou, E., Galanis, P., Mechili, E. A., Argyriadi, A., Argyriadis, A., Asimakopoulou, E., ... Patelarou, A. (2021). Factors influencing nursing students' intention to accept COVID-19 vaccination: A pooled analysis of seven European countries. *Nurse Education Today*, *104*, 105010.

Pate, R. R., Davis, M. G., Robinson, T. N., Stone, E. J., McKenzie, T. L., & Young, J. C.American Heart Association Council on Nutrition, Physical Activity, and Metabolism. (2006). Promoting physical activity in children and youth: a leadership role for schools: a scientific statement from the American Heart Association Council on Nutrition, Physical Activity, and Metabolism (Physical Activity Committee) in collaboration with the Councils on Cardiovascular Disease in the Young and Cardiovascular Nursing. *Circulation*, *114*(11), 1214–1224. doi:10.1161/CIRCULATIONAHA.106.177052 PMID:16908770

Patgiri, R., & Ahmed, A. (2016). Big Data: The V's of the Game Changer Paradigm. In *IEEE 18th International Conference on High Performance Computing and Communications; IEEE 14th International Conference on Smart City; IEEE 2nd International Conference on Data Science and Systems* (pp. 17-24). IEEE.

Pravitasari, A. A., Iriawan, N., Almuhayar, M., Azmi, T., Irhamah, I., Fithriasari, K., Purnami, S. W., & Ferriastuti, W. (2020). UNet-VGG16 with transfer learning for MRI-based brain tumor segmentation. *TELKOMNIKA*, *18*(3), 1310–1318. doi:10.12928/telkomnika.v18i3.14753

Qassim, H., Verma, A., & Feinzimer, D. (2018, January). Compressed residual-VGG16 CNN model for big data places image recognition. In *2018 IEEE 8th Annual Computing and Communication Workshop and Conference (CCWC)* (pp. 169-175). IEEE.

Quarteroni, A. (2018). The role of statistics in the era of big data: A computational scientist' perspective. *Statistics & Probability Letters*, *136*, 63–67. doi:10.1016/j.spl.2018.02.047

Rajamhoana, S. P., Devi, C. A., Umamaheswari, K., Kiruba, R., Karunya, K., & Deepika, R. (2018, July). Analysis of neural networks based heart disease prediction system. In *2018 11th international conference on human system interaction (HSI)* (pp. 233-239). IEEE. 10.1109/HSI.2018.8431153

Rajput, N. K., Grover, B. A., & Rathi, V. K. (2020). *Word frequency and sentiment analysis of twitter messages during coronavirus pandemic*. arXiv preprint arXiv:2004.03925.

Repaka, A. N., Ravikanti, S. D., & Franklin, R. G. (2019, April). Design and implementing heart disease prediction using naives Bayesian. In *2019 3rd International conference on trends in electronics and informatics (ICOEI)* (pp. 292-297). IEEE. 10.1109/ICOEI.2019.8862604

Rousseeuw, P. J., & Leroy, A. M. (1987). *Robust regression and outlier detection*. Wiley. doi:10.1002/0471725382

Rutschman, A. S. (2021). Social media self-regulation and the rise of vaccine misinformation. *Journal of Library Innovation*, *4*, 25.

Sabbahi, A., Arena, R., Kaminsky, L. A., Myers, J., & Phillips, S. A. (2017). Peak Blood Pressure Responses During Maximum Cardiopulmonary Exercise Testing. American Heart Association. *Inc.*, *17*(2). Advance online publication. doi:10.1161/HYPERTENSIONAHA.117.10116 PMID:29255072

Sadiq, M. T., Yu, X., & Yuan, Z. (2021). Exploiting dimensionality reduction and neural network techniques for the development of expert brain-computer interfaces. *Expert Systems with Applications*, *164*, 114031. doi:10.1016/j.eswa.2020.114031

Saleh, B., Saedi, A., Al-Aqbi, A., & Salman, L. (2020). Analysis of Weka Data Mining Techniques for Heart Disease Prediction System. *International Journal of Medical Reviews, 7*(1), 15-24.

Sandler, M., Howard, A., Zhu, M., Zhmoginov, A., & Chen, L. C. (2018). Mobilenetv2: Inverted residuals and linear bottlenecks. In *Proceedings of the IEEE conference on computer vision and pattern recognition* (pp. 4510-4520). IEEE.

Schwab, J. D., Schobel, J., Werle, S. D., Fürstberger, A., Ikonomi, N., Szekely, R., ... Kestler, H. A. (2021). Perspective on mHealth concepts to ensure users' empowerment–from adverse event tracking for COVID-19 vaccinations to oncological treatment. *IEEE Access: Practical Innovations, Open Solutions*, *9*, 83863–83875.

Sekar, J., Aruchamy, P., Sulaima Lebbe Abdul, H., Mohammed, A. S., & Khamuruddeen, S. (2022). An efficient clinical support system for heart disease prediction using TANFIS classifier. *Computational Intelligence*, *38*(2), 610–640. doi:10.1111/coin.12487

Shah, D., Patel, S., & Bharti, S. K. (2020). Heart disease prediction using machine learning techniques. *SN Computer Science*, *1*(6), 1–6. doi:10.100742979-020-00365-y

Significance of Apache Spark. (2016). *Hewlett Packard Enterprise*. Retrieved from https://www.mapr.com/blog/

Singh, P., Singh, S., & Pandi-Jain, G. S. (2018). Effective heart disease prediction system using data mining techniques. *International Journal-p of Nanomedicine*, *13*, 121.

Singh, D., & Reddy, C. K. (2015). A survey on platforms for big data analytics. *Journal of Big Data*, *2*(1), 1–20. doi:10.118640537-014-0008-6 PMID:26191487

Sivabalakrishnan, M. (2019). An enhanced weighted associative classification algorithm without preassigned weight based on ranking hubs. *International Journal of Advanced Computer Science and Applications*, *10*(10).

Smeaton, A. F., Diamond, D., Kelly, P., Moran, K., Lau, K.-T., Morris, D., Moyna, N., O'Connor, N. E., & Zhang, K. (2008). Aggregating Multiple Body Sensors for Analysis in Sports. *pHealth 2008 - 5th International Workshop on Wearable Micro and Nanosystems for Personalised Health*.

Song, J., Lee, S., & Kim, J. (2011, September). Spam filtering in twitter using sender-receiver relationship. In *International workshop on recent advances in intrusion detection* (pp. 301-317). Springer. 10.1007/978-3-642-23644-0_16

Spark Overview. (n.d.). *Apache Spark*. Retrieved from https://spark.apache.org/docs/latest/

Sultan, H. H., Salem, N. M., & Al-Atabany, W. (2019). Multi-classification of brain tumor images using deep neural network. *IEEE Access: Practical Innovations, Open Solutions, 7*, 69215–69225. doi:10.1109/ACCESS.2019.2919122

Sumner, C., Byers, A., Boochever, R., & Park, G. J. (2012, December). Predicting dark triad personality traits from twitter usage and a linguistic analysis of tweets. In *2012 11th international conference on machine learning and applications* (Vol. 2, pp. 386-393). IEEE.

Swati, Z. N. K., Zhao, Q., Kabir, M., Ali, F., Ali, Z., Ahmed, S., & Lu, J. (2019). Brain tumor classification for MR images using transfer learning and fine-tuning. *Computerized Medical Imaging and Graphics, 75*, 34–46. doi:10.1016/j.compmedimag.2019.05.001 PMID:31150950

Tan, C. W., & Kumar, A. (2012). Unified framework for automated iris segmentation using distantly acquired face images. *IEEE Transactions on Image Processing, 21*(9), 4068–4079. doi:10.1109/TIP.2012.2199125 PMID:22614641

Tang, Y., Chen, D., & Li, X. (2021). Dimensionality reduction methods for brain imaging data analysis. *ACM Computing Surveys, 54*, 87.

Tarawneh, M., & Embarak, O. (2019, February). Hybrid approach for heart disease prediction using data mining techniques. In *International Conference on Emerging Internetworking, Data & Web Technologies* (pp. 447-454). Springer. 10.1007/978-3-030-12839-5_41

Target Heart Rate and Estimated Maximum Heart Rate | Physical Activity. (n.d.). *CDC*. Retrieved February 27, 2022, from https://www.cdc.gov/physicalactivity/basics/measuring/heartrate.htm

Taylor, S. (2019). Clustering financial return distributions using the Fisher information metric. *Entropy (Basel, Switzerland), 21*(2), 110. doi:10.3390/e21020110 PMID:33266826

Tegmark, M. (2017). *Life 3.0: Being human in the age of artificial intelligence.* Alfred A. Knopf.

Tole, A. A. (2013). Big Data Challenges. *Database Systems Journal, 4*(3), 31–40.

Türk Dil Kurumu. (2011). *Türkçe Sözlük (11 b.)* [Turkish Dictionary (11 b.)]. Türk Dil Kurumu Yayınları.

Umasabor-Bubu, O. Q., Bubu, O. M., Mbah, A. K., Nakeshbandi, M., & Taylor, T. N. (2021). Association between influenza vaccination and severe COVID-19 outcomes at a designated COVID-only hospital in brooklyn. *American Journal of Infection Control, 49*(10), 1327–1330.

Understand Your Risks to Prevent a Heart Attack. (2016, June 30). *American Heart Association*. Retrieved February 27, 2022, from https://www.heart.org/en/health-topics/heart-attack/understand-your-risks-to-prevent-a-heart-attack

Varshni, D., Thakral, K., Agarwal, L., Nijhawan, R., & Mittal, A. (2019, February). Pneumonia detection using CNN based feature extraction. In *2019 IEEE international conference on electrical, computer and communication technologies (ICECCT)* (pp. 1-7). IEEE.

Víšek, J. Á. (2011). Consistency of the least weighted squares under heteroscedasticity. *Kybernetika, 47*, 179–206.

Wakode, S. (2020). Efficacious scrutinizing of COVID-19 impact on banking using credit risk metrics. *International Journal of Finance & Economics, 6*(3), 51–56.

Wallace, J. (2021). Vaccines, Public Health, and the Law. *IEEE Technology and Society Magazine, 40*(2), 35–39.

Wang, C., Han, B., Zhao, T., Liu, H., Liu, B., Chen, L., ... Cui, F. (2021a). Vaccination willingness, vaccine hesitancy, and estimated coverage at the first round of COVID-19 vaccination in China: A national cross-sectional study. *Vaccine, 39*(21), 2833–2842.

Wang, H., Kadry, S. N., & Raj, E. D. (2020). Continuous health monitoring of sportsperson using IoT devices based wearable technology. *Computer Communications, 160*, 588–595. doi:10.1016/j.comcom.2020.04.025

Wang, J., Lyu, Y., Zhang, H., Jing, R., Lai, X., Feng, H., ... Fang, H. (2021b). Willingness to pay and financing preferences for COVID-19 vaccination in China. *Vaccine, 39*(14), 1968–1976.

Wilson, P. W. (2018). Dimension reduction in nonparametric models of production. *European Journal of Operational Research, 267*(1), 349–367. doi:10.1016/j.ejor.2017.11.020

Wilson, S. (2020, November). A digital "Yellow Card" for securely recording vaccinations using Community PKI certificates. In *2020 IEEE International Symposium on Technology and Society (ISTAS)* (pp. 310-313). IEEE.

Witzany, J. (2017). *Credit risk management. Pricing, Measurement, and Modeling*. Springer. doi:10.1007/978-3-319-49800-3

Wu, Y. J., Chen, F., Lu, C. T., & Yang, S. (2016). Urban traffic flow prediction using a spatio-temporal random effects model. *Journal of Intelligent Transport Systems, 20*(3), 282–293. doi:10.1080/15472450.2015.1072050

Yang, W., Liu, X., Zhang, L., & Yang, L. T. (2013, July). Big data real-time processing based on storm. In *2013 12th IEEE international conference on trust, security and privacy in computing and communications* (pp. 1784-1787). IEEE. 10.1109/TrustCom.2013.247

Yaylagül, L. (2019). *Kitle İletişim Kuramları Egemen ve Eleştirel Yaklaşımlar (10 b.)* [Theories of Mass Communication Dominant and Critical Approaches (10 b.)]. Dipnot Yayınları.

Zaki, N. D., Hashim, N. Y., Mohialden, Y. M., Mohammed, M. A., Sutikno, T., & Ali, A. H. (2020). A real-time big data sentiment analysis for iraqi tweets using spark streaming. *Bulletin of Electrical Engineering and Informatics, 9*(4), 1411–1419.

Compilation of References

Zhang, B., Weissinger, L., Himmelreich, J., McMurry, N., Li, T. C., & Kreps, S. E. (2021). *Building robust and ethical vaccination verification systems*. Brookings TechStream.

Zhao, L., Chen, Z., Hu, Y., Min, G., & Jiang, Z. (2018). Distributed feature selection for efficient economic big data analysis. *IEEE Transactions on Big Data*, *5*(2), 164–176. doi:10.1109/TBDATA.2016.2601934

Zhou, Q., Zhu, W., Li, F., Yuan, M., Zheng, L., & Liu, X. (2022). Transfer Learning of the ResNet-18 and DenseNet-121 Model Used to Diagnose Intracranial Hemorrhage in CT Scanning. *Current Pharmaceutical Design*, *28*(4), 287–295. doi:10.2174/1381612827666211213143357 PMID:34961458

About the Contributors

Govind P. Gupta is currently working as Assistant Professor in National Institute of Technology, Raipur. He has done PhD from IIT, Roorkee. His area of interests are Computer Networking, Distributed Algorithms design for Wireless Sensor Networks, Performance Analysis, Big Data Processing, Parallel and Distributed Computing, Design & Analysis of Algorithms.

* * *

Simran Adake is an M.Tech Computer Science Big Data Analytics Student at VIT University.

Mustafa Eren Akpınar, born on October 27, 1998, graduated from Kocaeli University, Faculty of Communication, Department of Journalism in 2020. In the same year, he received a master's degree from Istanbul Aydın University Graduate Education Institute, Department of Journalism. He completed his master's degree in the same department in June 2022 and received a master's degree. Mustafa Eren Akpınar currently conducts research mainly in the fields of Social Media Studies, Gender Studies, Digital Communication, Communication Studies and Journalism and Media Studies.

Shrikrishn Bansal has received his Bachelor of Technology (CSE) in 2018 from Galgotias University, Greater Noida and Master of Technology (CSE) in 2021 from The LNM Institute of Information Technology, Jaipur. His research interests include IoT, IoT Analytics, Data Analysis and Data Science.

Rachit Bisaria is an M.Tech Computer Science Big Data Analytics Student at VIT University.

Kush Desai is an M.Tech Computer Science Big Data Analytics Student at VIT University.

Sreekantha Desai Karanam is serving as Professor in the Dept. of Information Science & Engineering NMAM Institute of Technology, NITTE since Nov. 2014. He received Best Research Publications Award from VGST. Govt. of Karnataka for the year 2020-21. He has visited Paris city, France to present two research papers in international Conference, and also visited Belgium, Germany, Switzerland, Austria and Italy in Europe in Jan 2016. Published two Indian patents. Currently guiding four Ph. D students. Recognized research paper reviewer for four international journals and editorial member of one international journal. Member of professional bodies like ISTE, Research Gate, IFERP, IRJC and Online Risk library. He has successful implemented two funded research projects one from UGC and another from VGST Rs 20 Lakhs, Govt. of Karnataka. Authored one books, 13 book chapters, published 25 papers in international journals and presented 30 research papers in international/national conferences. He has 21 years of teaching experience and 6 years of industry experience in TATA group. Awarded Ph.D from Symbiosis International University, Pune in 2014. Secured Second Rank to Gulbarga University in B.Sc(Electronics) degree examinations and National Merit Scholarship. Member of Rotary Club, Nitte since July 2016. Participated in and organized many national workshops and conferences.

Se Yong Eh Noum obtained his Ph.D. in Materials Science (Polymer Nano-composites) in 2011. He started his career as Senior Research and Engineering Engineer in Fuji Electric (Malaysia) and continue to serve them for 3 years, focusing his research and development of plasma-enhanced chemical vapor deposition (PECVD) of a nanometers-thin layer of carbon overcoat on magnetic memory disc. Since 2014, he has joined the academia to focus more teaching and learning and as well as research. His research background centers around nano-composites materials and deposition of carbon thin film technology.

Jayanthi G. is working as Assistant Professor at Faculty of Engineering and Technology, SRIHER, Tamil Nadu. She has 15 years of teaching experience and 5 years of research experience in the field of Data Science, Artificial Intelligence and Machine Learning. She has published research papers in SCI indexed journal and international journals.

Rajbir Kaur received her Bachelors in Science (Electronics) in 1994, Masters in Computer Application in 1999 from JNVU, Jodhpur and Ph.D. in Computer Science from NIT, Jaipur, Raj, India in 2012. She is presently an Assistant Professor in the Department of Computer Science and Engineering at The LNMIIT, Jaipur, India. Her research interests include Internet of things - architectures and data analysis, mobile ad hoc networks and wireless sensor networks.

R. V. Kulkarni is a professor of computer studies at Chhatrapathi Shahu Institute of Business Education and Research in Kolhapur, India.

Krithin M. is a Project Intern at Council of Scientific and Industrial Research. Event Lead, Codechef College Chapter NMAMIT.

Ramya M. is Experienced Faculty and Ex-Program Analyst with demonstrated history of working in various industry projects. Strong operational professional with a Master's degree focused in Information Technology.

Bhargav Naidu Matcha obtained his PhD in Engineering (Traffic Simulations) from Taylor's university in the school of computer science and engineering, Malaysia. His research interests include microscopic driver behavior modelling under mixed traffic conditions, traffic data collection and analysis, congestion analysis, crowd dynamics, and road safety analysis.

Omprakash Nayak is an M. Tech Scholar at NIT Raipur.

K. C. Ng obtained his Ph.D. in Mechanical Engineering (solution-adaptive Computational Fluid Dynamics) in 2006. Soon after his graduation, he worked as a CFD software developer in Daikin Malaysia for 5 years, developing an in-house CFD software for simulating indoor/outdoor airflow problems. In 2008, he worked as a post-doctoral researcher in National University of Singapore (NUS), performing Direct Numerical Simulation (DNS) for simulating turbulent flow. He was trained in Altair India (Bangalore) by a group of professional CAE software developers. His current interest includes developing particle-based CFD methods for simulating complex engineering problems such as Fluid-Structure Interaction and multi-physics problem.

Purushothaman R. received Doctor of Philosophy in Computer Science and Engineering from the Anna University, Tamil Nadu, India and has over 14 years' experience. He is working as Associate Professor in Department of CSE, Siddartha Institute of Science and Technology, Andhra Pradesh, India. His teaching and research interests includes AI/ML, Data Mining, Cyber Security. He has published over 23 papers in various SCI, WoS & Scopus Indexed Journals and Conferences.

Prince Rajak is an M.Tech student at the National Institute of Technology, Raipur, who is passionate about computer vision, deep learning, and machine learning.

Lavanya Sendhilvel is an Associate Professor at VIT University.

Aman Sharma is currently pursuing the Ph.D. in computer science from School of Computer Science and Engineering, Taylor's University, Subang Jaya, Malaysia. He is an Active Member of the Center of Data Science and Analytics (C4DSA), Taylor's University. He has completed his M. Tech in Computer science and engineering from Vellore Institute of Technology (VIT) University, Vellore, Tamil Nadu, India. He carried out his final project thesis from, Supercomputer education and research Centre under Indian Institute of Science (IISc), Bengaluru, Karnataka, India. His research areas are big data analytics, machine learning and travel behavior modeling development.

Sivakumar Sivanesan is a professional engineer with over 18 years of experience having begun his career in industry with brands like Panasonic and is currently the Head of the School of Engineering at Asia Pacific University of Technology & Innovation, Malaysia. His enthusiasm to seek new knowledge, coupled with a compelling vision to produce engineers capable of addressing global challenges through effective enhancement of knowledge, nurturing of skills and an emphasis on emotional intelligence had propelled him towards the academic field for the past 15 years. He is a firm believer in continual quality improvement and in imparting his knowledge to all.

Hemang Vekariya is an M.Tech Big Data Computer Science Big Data Analytics student at VIT University.

Index

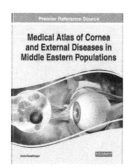
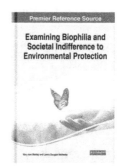
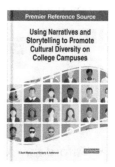

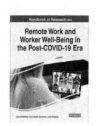

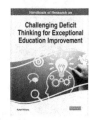

Printed in the USA
CPSIA information can be obtained
at www.ICGtesting.com
LVHW080003051224
798213LV00006B/747

That was the very word he used, and what a filthy one it is. She said she knew in that instant they would be the best of fuck-buddies. She said it was probably the rudest thing she had ever heard. It was *definitely* the rudest thing I had ever heard. It made me quake. It made the thoughts pour through my head and the blood fizz in my veins. Imagine a guy actually saying such a thing to you! Imagine having to do it! With that in my head, after maybe an hour of being tied up, she shuffled down upon me, grasped the flesh of my hood between thumb and forefinger, and squeezed it hard to trap my little bud. It instantly gave me another enormous climax to match my birthday gift. That was all it took: mere seconds of concerted attention at my most sensitive place.

In essence it was a whole hour of foreplay but the actual physical stimulation was minimal. It was all down to her being so beautiful and free with her sexuality, to her rude words and the images they produced. To show how turned on she had got me she used her fingers inside me and made me come again before the last climax had even died down. That would be the blueprint for all our couplings for a while. I yearned for every next visit. It would be embellished over time. Her words would get ruder – things I cannot begin to tell you about. The dirtier she got, the more it turned me on, the harder I came – when she finally allowed me to do so. It never took more than a single hard pinch, or a few sucks, to have me howling.

Oftentimes she would masturbate right above my face, so the droplets of her lovely cream would splash my lips and cheeks. She would tell me about all the filthy acts she had committed with her boyfriends and girlfriends, of the threesomes and orgies she had instigated. Porn stars would have blushed at her antics. In my head I had done a million disgusting things, stuff so rude I could barely think about it unless my pussy was hot and naked – and if it wasn't, it certainly would be, the second such thoughts arose. That beautiful girl whispered things to me that you would not hear on any internet site, sometimes while kissing me tenderly, or gently nibbling my earlobes or my engorged nipples, sometimes whilst blowing on my hot, desperate clit. However, no matter how much she drove me to distraction with cock-hunger, I never resorted to getting one for myself. I left myself entirely in her hands.

That is the thing, you see. In my head I was the most depraved of harlots but in reality I had barely seen a stiff prick in the flesh, let alone had one inside me. Between us, through her words and my insatiable imagination, we had committed acts so unspeakable that you might think we both needed locking up. Yet in truth I had licked and fingered one single beautiful, delicious pussy, no more. I had sucked one pair of wonderful soft tits. I had been gagged a few times – with my knickers, my tights and also with a shop-bought ball gag. I had had vibrators pressed to my clit or slid inside me. That was the true extent of my kinkiness, nothing compared with most girls I knew.

My one true claim to kinkiness was that I had been tied. I had done *bondage*. Mainly it was to her headboard but it had also been to radiators and stair posts, to her oven door and, just once, to a railing on her balcony overlooking the city. One time she left me bound naked to her bed whilst a party raged downstairs. Before the guests arrived she had spent half an hour telling me who she was going to send up and what she was going to have them do to me. For over three hours I writhed around, awaiting a visit, with the pictures she had conjured in my head. She never sent anyone. When she finally came up she wordlessly slipped three fingers right up my dripping hole, sucked upon my little clit and made me scream. Then she untied me and sent me home. Ten minutes after she had walked back in I was dressed and going out the door, on legs that could barely hold me up.

For my nineteenth birthday I was promised a treat. I thought I was finally going to get what I constantly dreamed of. She told me to show up in a bikini. She cuffed me behind my back and had me lie across the back seat of her car. She drove me around for ages in daylight, telling me she was going to find me some lovely cocks to suck. I remember my face was aflame, half from embarrassment at my state of undress if anyone should see me there, half from the heat of her dirty talk.

She told me all about the truck drivers who stopped at the various lay-bys and how fat and hard their pricks were. She said the first time she had ever taken two hard cocks at once was in the very lay-by she was heading for. She didn't let me have what I was inwardly begging for. She pulled up, sure enough, but she didn't drag me out as I had hoped. Instead she just climbed in beside me and pressed a vibrator to my crotch, not even bothering to pull my bikini bottoms aside. I came so hard that day I wet myself. It would be another whole year before she finally relented and let me lose my virginity.

So you see I am not the wanton fuck-bitch my head keeps telling me I am. I was tame by today's standards, practically angelic. It is not what I *did* when I was tied up and restrained, but the *potential* of what could be done. Very little happens other than the fantasies Madeleine and I build together, but I promise you, the orgasms it gives me are earth-shattering and utterly addictive, all because I am bound. Even if I could cure my little wanky problem I would still wish to be restrained because of that naughty *potential* for anything to happen. Outside of my own fantasies I was practically chaste, certainly a vanilla girl in practice, although after the lay-by incident Madeleine did start to up the ante.

A few weeks later she blindfolded me after tying my wrists. She left me in my underwear and told me Pierson was coming round. He never spoke so I don't know if it was him. I do know that *someone* fucked my beautiful Madeleine right next to me. I could hear his grunts. I could hear his cock slapping against her soft bottom and wet flesh. All the while she told me what was happening, what the cock felt like inside her and how it would feel in me. I didn't get it that time. Pierson left shortly after I heard him finish in Madeleine's mouth.

The next time I was summoned another visitor called – 'a punk with a fat cock', to use Madeleine's words. I never saw this one either. He fucked her noisily and she gave me a commentary. This time she was above me on her hands and knees, whispering the words at my ear, her hand down the front of my knickers. This time I was given the cock to finish, and she talked me through it, telling me exactly what to do and how fabulous it looked in my mouth.

Similar episodes followed over my next visits. I would be blindfolded and she would have sex beside me with anonymous men, or sometimes with girls armed with strap-on cocks. Sometimes she would chain me in the corner to the radiator, if she needed the whole bed for her filthy games. I would get myself all het up with wanting.

'If it's Pierson, please let him fuck me,' I used to plead as they went about their noisy business. 'Please let me have that beautiful cock.'

'It isn't Pierson,' she would say, although sometimes I am sure that it was.

On later visits I would be stripped during their games, to be naked for the benefit of the visitor I couldn't see. I would beg to suck Pierson's cock, and would occasionally have one stuffed in my mouth to gorge upon, only to be subsequently informed that it wasn't his after all. I don't know whose they were. Some would empty into my mouth, others onto my belly and breasts. I was obsessed with having him. I was clearly in love with her, but all my fantasies involved him, because of the things she said and did to me when I was tied and at her mercy.

She promised me the ultimate treat for my twentieth birthday. I couldn't wait. A hundred or more frustrating orgasms were wrenched from my body in the build-up to that visit. I knew what she was going to give to me. She tied me and blindfolded me and then stripped me bare.

'Pierson is coming to fuck you,' she said.

I almost came just from her next kiss. This time there would be no jealous bitch to steal him away. I lay with my legs open and with her gently stroking me wet, and then I felt his weight upon the bed. He didn't speak. He didn't do anything to me except hold my legs apart as he pushed his way in. Two years after the promise was first made to me he slid inside me and fucked my virginity clean away, making me wail and shudder. I couldn't even put my arms around him and hold him. In all honesty, to this day I cannot hand on heart say that it was him for sure who took my cherry, since I never actually saw him. It had to be him, though, because it was a beautiful, beautiful cock inside me that day, giving me perhaps the biggest climax of my life so far.

In the last year since losing my virginity I have been entered a further ten times. Three times it has been by an unknown woman with a toy at her waist. The other seven times it has been Pierson, or so Madeleine says. Each time has been similarly wonderful although doubts have crept in. One time he was definitely bigger than the last. The grunts are different, the smells too. The power of his climax varies. If I could free my hands I could whip off the blindfold and be sure. It could be that he has never visited me even once, that eight different unidentified men have been inside me, including the one who took my virginity. I couldn't see why Madeleine would lie to me, as she and he were such good friends and it was something she *could* bring about. I got to thinking that after my eighteenth, when he saw me partially naked, he decided he wouldn't make a return visit.

So, when Madeleine decided to offer me anything I wanted for my twenty-first birthday, there really was only one option.

'I want Pierson,' I declared. 'Just me and him, and without the blindfold for once.'

'Why change?' she asked. 'You think the reality so much better than the fantasy? He has a very particular way with girls that you may not like. He doesn't do the build-up or the dirty talk like I do. Perhaps you should let me pick your treat?'

I stuck to my guns and so now, this very hour, I am to live my fantasy in full at last. It is still to be in Madeleine's bed, not my own. She is still to prepare me, although she will leave straight after to give me the privacy I require. She holds me briefly because I am shaking with the anticipation. She asks me if I want to be tied. For the first time, if I choose, I can embrace a man while he is on me, hold him to me and feel his heart against mine. I can make love without restriction, take half the responsibility, impose myself, defend myself if need be. However, I refuse all this and tell her yes, I still want her to tie me.

'It will be his way, not mine,' she warns.

I smile and say that is what I want. I have to know for sure, to see him and *it* with my own eyes. She looks a little disappointed but shrugs and sets to work. She oils me first, all over my naked body, saying it will prevent the bands from chafing. I don't yet know what she means, but the thought of these bands keeps my heart racing. They prove to be thick belts in shiny PVC, fastened tight with a buckle. She secures one at my ankles first and then another just below my knees, then upwards, up to my shoulders, eight in all.

My legs are squeezed together and I can feel the warm throb of excitement between my constricted thighs. My arms are tight by my sides, my hands flat against the outside of my legs. There is one right across my chest, squashing my breasts, practically stopping my racing heart from beating at all. It's like when you are zipped into a sleeping bag, except this time I am naked and thus completely vulnerable between the bands. I can be got at. Suddenly I realise this is not about the *potential* for things to happen, but what actually *will* happen. My breath falters and I feel a cold sweep through my body.

I squeal as Madeleine sends a sudden final gush of oil between my buttocks. There is a touch of animosity about it. I shiver, suddenly feeling very exposed. I begin to regret shunning the blindfold. The darkness always made me more secure, it made everything surreal. I wonder if it is too late to opt for the safety of Madeleine after all, but she is going, without so much as a goodbye kiss, leaving me to him and his ways that I know nothing about. *Show me your anus.* He wouldn't say anything so dirty to me, would he? He wouldn't actually *make* me do it?

Downstairs the door opens and closes to signal his arrival. I hear the two of them exchange quiet words, and then he is coming up the stairs to me. I am on my back on the bed, trussed like a turkey, awaiting his beautiful cock in the flesh. Then he is there, sneering at my bound body, a glint in his eye. He is in black as always, bigger and even more assured now than he was on this very day three years ago. I doubt he remembers that day, or that he left me there tied. He is still as mute and impersonal. He doesn't look like he cares that it's my birthday. I am to be his treat, not he mine. He opens his shirt fully and I see the hard muscles of his stomach, and the tattoo on his chest. Then his black jeans are coming undone and I can already see he is hard inside his Calvin Kleins.

'You are going to suck my cock and balls, you dirty bitch,' he declares.

It is an abrupt start, but one that has my mouth watering. His pants are off and I watch his cock spring from its constriction and fill out until it is hard and bobbing. It is not huge, just sleek and lovely. I don't care how many girls have been blessed with it over the years. Now it is for me alone. He climbs on the bed and straddles me. More than ever I feel my constriction. If he bent forward now and kissed me I would come. But there is to be no kissing. Instead he shuffles up the bed on his knees, clutching his lovely manhood, still straddling me. He moves right up until his thighs are at my ears, then he frees his heavy balls to land splat on my lips. I open up to take them. I have never sucked on balls before. The sack is shaved smooth. He feels warm and silky in my mouth.

His prick is hard but he is leaning forward and holding it, wiping the tip across my forehead and eyes. I can feel the faint trail of pre-come left on my skin: Pierson's pre-come from his glorious pole. He pulls his balls free and my saliva is smeared rudely all over my cheeks as he drags his sack across my face in wiping his prick all over me. He must know of my worship. Finger me now. Stick two or three of them up my raging cunt and feel my years of aching passion bathe you. He is still slapping my face with his erection so I picture his fingers inside me instead. Then I realise he couldn't actually get them in me, because of the bands fastening me so tight.

There is little time to dwell on this as he is placing pillows in the middle of the bed and hauling me sideways and over, so that I am on my front with my hips raised by the pillows. *He has a particular way with girls.* That's what Madeleine had said, not half an hour ago. I feel nervy, perhaps because I have always been so safe before. He has me by the hair, pulling my head back and calling me a filthy bitch. Once he is inside me I will be fine. Give me your beautiful cock, I'm thinking, but I know I cannot part my legs to take him. His big hands are at my bottom, pinching and squeezing, pulling the cheeks apart.

'You have a nice tight little shit-hole,' he says.

I can only gasp and whimper. Then he is smacking me, each undefended, totally bare cheek at a time. Madeleine never mentioned him doing this in her fantasy tales. He cares nothing for my dislike of pain. Luckily I am well upholstered enough there to absorb the smacks without it becoming agony. Madeleine has told me a million times that she was about to spank me but she never has. He has just gone and done it, and it hurts. He lets up just moments before I have to beg him to stop. He straddles me again, his hips outside of mine, his cock-head now slapping my sore bum cheeks. He wipes the tip of his prick across the expanse and I feel another wet trail laid down – proof of his continued desire.

He is grasping his prick and rubbing it in the slipperiness of my bum crack. I remember the rude squirt of oil just before she left me. I can feel the head of his cock forcing its way in to run up and down my deep cleft. He prods and I feel it at my anus, which tightens against him. His face is at my ear, his fist still clutching my hair to hold my head back.

'You want me to fuck you, don't you? You want me to stick my big cock all the way up your tight arse.'

'Yes,' I breathe. I am shaking, but yes, I do want it.

He presses forward and my bottom tries to hold out, but it can't. His weight is too much and I begin to open up for him. I try to relax as best I can, pushing out against him, doing all the things Madeleine used to describe to me while she lay at my side and spoke of this very cock. I feel white pain, then a fizzle of joy. His glans is within me and I close up around it. Then he presses more and his shaft starts its remorseless slide into my rudest place. On it goes as he gasps and calls me a bitch and a filthy cunt. His dirty words keep me going. I wish I could grip the bed but I cannot. He fills me; searing pain with electric pleasure. I can feel him almost in my stomach. It is a unique sensation, so different to being done in the usual place.

I want to ask him if he has indeed ever fucked me before as Madeleine claims, but what if he says no? It doesn't matter; one way or another this beautiful cock has taken my virginity and I will treasure that fact always. He grips my shoulders and fucks me, pulling back to the tip then driving his sleek meat forward. I would explode if he pinched my clit as Madeleine likes to do. I would scream the house down. His weight is on my back. He is slapping hard against me and my bum cheeks are dancing. Now my passage is all relaxed and slippery, it is divine. There is no resistance, so he fucks me relentlessly for maybe ten hot, hard minutes, and then he spurts his seed deep into my behind.

He draws out and I feel my bottom hole clench up, then relax again. I want to cover the dirty sight with my hand, but that is impossible. I stay face pressed to bed with my eyes closed, waiting for his next move. My orgasm would be instant, if he would only touch me. It isn't going to happen, because I can hear his belt being done up. He leaves me without a word. My addled brain tries to sum it all up. It was an incredible fucking, but I've been left short. For all the beautiful contact, the fullness in my behind, the thrill of him, he couldn't do what Madeleine can do with the slightest of kisses. It will surely be one of the most memorable times of my life, but think what it would have been with some patience and thought beforehand.

Half an hour it must be that I remain here stranded, trying to work out whether I'm over him now or not. Finally Madeleine returns. She gently rolls me onto my back and begins to unbuckle the straps around my legs. She unleashes me up to my middle, keeping the straps at my waist and above so that I cannot yet free my hands. For half an hour I have been desperate to give myself what he did not. I'm still throbbing there. I think of telling her but she already knows. She gets close and blows gently upon me, and then, without warning, she puts her soft mouth around my hot clit and sucks as hard as she can. I scream.

I'm so glad I didn't drive her away. Sometimes the reality is not quite the same as the fantasy or anticipation. Sometimes sex is about the potential rather than what does happen. In my head I am the filthiest girl imaginable and I will always get off on you telling me that. The ruder you are, the longer you go on telling me, the better. In truth I am now just a little dirtier than I was before, which isn't that much. One day I might give all this up, go for normal relationships with the kissing and the hand-holding, the embraces during love-making. But not quite yet, not while Madeleine can keep my hands off my pussy and make me scream with just her slightest touch.

Taming Maria
Kathleen Tudor

As he read, Miles slowly became aware of Maria standing in front of him. He finished the page he was on, and then methodically placed the bookmark, closed the book and set it on his lap before he looked up to address her. Her eyes were properly lowered, focused on his hands, which he'd folded over the cover. 'Yes?'

'Master, I'm ready to prepare supper.'

'What do you need?'

'The potatoes need to be diced and the asparagus cut,' she said. As part of their master/slave relationship, he'd forbidden her to handle weapons, including the kitchen knives. The simple act of preparing a meal became an exercise in submission when she was forced to request his assistance any time she needed a sharp edge.

He rose and set the book down on the coffee table. 'Is everything laid out?'

'Yes, Master.' She preceded him to the kitchen, and he smiled as he admired the way her naked body moved. Her long legs were shapely and toned, and no less sexy for the lack of heels. She'd been wearing a cute little dress earlier in the day, but had taken it off, perhaps in the hope of catching his attention. He smiled at her cheekiness and leaned forward to swat her on the ass.

In the kitchen, she gestured politely to the cutting board, where the washed vegetables were gleaming freshly, awaiting his attention. He pulled his favourite knife from the block and started in on the asparagus while Maria went to the spice rack and started mixing spices for the chicken.

He'd made quick work of the asparagus and had begun to dice the potatoes when he felt a small finger dig into his lower ribs. He jerked the knife up from the board, clenching his elbows to his sides in automatic reaction, and slowly turned around. Maria was sprinkling her spices over the chicken. He cleared his throat.

'Yes, Master?'

He glared, but when she maintained the façade of wide-eyed innocence, he turned back to the potatoes, shaking his head. He'd cut two more of the small reds when her little fingers dug into his other side. He jerked again, resisting the un-domly urge to giggle, and spun. She was still attending to the chicken. 'Are you all right, sir?' she asked, still maintaining her innocence.

He sighed and said, 'Maria' with a warning in his tone. She blinked over her shoulder at him, the picture of puzzlement, and he had to bite his cheek to keep from smiling. The brat. He pulled the Saran Wrap out of a nearby drawer and used it to cover the bowl where he'd placed the asparagus, then went back to dicing.

He was nearly finished with his chopping, the third time he felt her tickling hands. This time he dropped the knife and snatched up the Saran Wrap. He spun as he pulled out the plastic film and wrapped it around her, spinning her as he went, so as to bind her arms firmly to her sides. Her eyes were wide with surprise rather than false innocence, now, and he smiled wickedly as he captured her.

'Will you excuse me for a moment?' He took her by the shoulders and moved her to one side, then wrapped the chicken and put it back in the fridge. Maria was starting to look worried. Good, she deserved to worry. Honestly – tickling!

Her wrapping covered her from shoulder to waist, leaving her ass and legs free. He wrapped the plastic around her a couple more times for good measure, and then examined his handiwork. Maria remained obediently silent, waiting to see what he would do with her. He smiled, pleased to let her wonder. Satisfied that she wouldn't escape her cocoon, he left the kitchen and gestured for her to follow. 'Come, dear.'

163

Her footsteps fell in obediently behind him. She was a very good slave, obedient and trusting, but not afraid to speak her own mind. And the little sparks of defiance and brattiness just made her submission all the sweeter. He wouldn't punish her, but he did have to show her who was boss.

He'd start with a taste of her own medicine. She followed him into their bedroom and squeaked when he grabbed her and pushed her hard towards the bed. She hit the edge and toppled onto it, her face ploughing into the mattress. He hefted her the rest of the way onto it, straddled her legs so that she couldn't move them more than a few inches, and applied his fingertips and nails gently to the bottoms of her feet and that special spot on her calves.

Maria screamed as his intentions became clear, and then giggled madly, thrashing as much as she was able within her limited range of motion. Miles was glad she couldn't see his face, because his gleeful grin was anything but dignified. He felt a boyish pleasure in making her laugh until she was gasping for breath, and it was this pleasure that reminded him why she'd probably done the tickling herself. Well, pleasure wasn't hers to *take* any more, particularly not from him.

Her thrashing beneath him made his cock rise eagerly, and his tickling became faster and even less merciful until she was gasping and begging in between the uncontrollable laughter. When he finally moved off of her, tears streaked her face from laughing so hard, and his cock throbbed with pleasure as she struggled against the intensity.

'If you would wait here, my darling, I'll be right back,' he said.

She was still gathering her breath, so he didn't wait for an answer. Instead he went straight to the kitchen and poured a large glass of water from the pitcher in the fridge. Then he went to the bathroom and grabbed a towel and her robe. He returned to the bedroom and put everything down, unlocked the toy cabinet, pulled out a beautiful hand-carved wooden paddle and added it to the tools and toys. Then he went to their dresser, where he struck a match and lit a candle.

'We're going to play a game, my love,' he said. She was watching him intently when he turned back towards the bed. He smiled at her, then moved to her side and picked up her sleeping mask from the bedside table. He showed it to her before he slipped it over her eyes. Then he picked up a silk scarf and tied it over the mask, making sure there was no way for it to slide up and offer her a small view of what was about to happen.

'The game we're going to play is called Hot or Cold. The rules are very simple.' He moved the candle and the glass of water to within easy reach on the bedside table, and then picked up the paddle in his right hand. 'I am going to drip something onto your back. All you have to do is tell me whether it is hot or cold.'

He saw her sigh with relief and relax, and his grin reappeared. The human body is a funny thing. Cold can burn and burns can feel freezing – the feeling is more of an intensity level than a specific temperature gauge – and he'd learned through experience that hot wax and iced water feel almost exactly the same on the skin. Particularly if you're blindfolded.

The Saran Wrap was his favourite special touch in temperature play like this. It would transfer the sensations perfectly to her skin, while keeping her immobile and making it much simpler to clean everything up afterward.

'What do I get if I win?' she asked. Leave it to Maria to think of that.

'Hmm …' He went back to the toy cabinet and dug out a small vibrator. 'How about pleasure? Every time you guess correctly, I'll turn the vibrator on for five seconds. But wrong guesses must be punished. I have my paddle here.' He swished it in the air over her ass so that she would hear the sound and feel the breeze. 'Every wrong guess will earn you a swat. Are you ready?'

She nodded eagerly, and he grinned and dipped his fingers silently into the cold water. He held them over her back and the water dripped onto her shoulder blade. She shuddered. 'Hot.'

Smack! She jumped and screamed as the paddle came

down on her ass. Her mouth was open in a stunned expression, and he struggled not to laugh. She was realising ...

He would make the next one easy. He lifted the candle and allowed a single drop of wax to land on her other shoulder blade. She paused, considering what she knew of him, probably, and guessed 'hot'.

He purred approval and reached between her legs to activate the vibrator, making sure it was on her clit. He counted slowly to five, and shut it off again, and she whimpered. 'Patience,' he teased, and dripped the candle on her lower back. She jumped and shivered at the pinpoint of intensity, and guessed. 'Cold?' He smiled. She was probably guessing based on what she thought he would do, rather than trying to tell the difference in the sensations.

Smack! This time he dipped his fingers into the water as quickly as possible and let the drops fall on her lower back. 'Hot!'

Smack! She cried out, her ass already turning a lovely shade of cherry red, and he switched back to the candle. 'Hot,' she said, whimpering the word, her body already flinching for the next blow of the paddle. She screamed again when he activated the vibrator without a word, and then moaned and ground into it a second before it shut off.

By now she would be overwhelmed by the sensory

input, desperate to separate hot from cold and pleasure from pain, all of them mixing within her, indistinguishable. His own body was responding eagerly to her plight, and he paused to stroke the length of his cock before continuing the game. She moaned when he dripped the candle across her back again, this time pouring a little more wax than before. 'Hot?'

He activated the vibrator, and she ground into it immediately, her body churning with sensations. She'd always come easily, his little pet, and he'd trained her to come even more so. With the spankings and the teasing and especially with the vibrator straight against her clit, she would be very close already. He grinned and decided to do whatever he could to make things hard for her.

She missed the next three guesses, and the paddle fell, *smack! Smack! SMACK!* She breathed heavily, writhing as if to escape, and thrashed hard when the next drops of water fell. 'Hot! No, cold! Cold!' He stopped the paddle in mid-swing and reached for the vibrator instead, and this time the pleasure was enough. She screamed and thrashed wildly in her bonds as she came, and Miles left it on long enough to draw her orgasm out, and then longer. His cock throbbed and he cupped his erection in his free hand, rubbing gently as Maria shook and cried, and then finally turned her head and screamed into the mattress as he forced a second orgasm out of her.

He hadn't had a forced-orgasm scene with her in a long while, and he made a mental note to remedy that as soon as possible. In the meantime, his dear pet was quivering with exhaustion and sensory overload, and her plastic wrapping was damp and covered with drips of wax. He pulled the vibrator away from her and turned it off, then pulled her mask up and stroked her face, gently.

'Maria. Come back to me, sweetheart.' She was deep in subspace, her eyes vague and unfocused. 'I need you to stand. Can you do that?' She nodded as if in a trance and got up unsteadily, but she stood unsupported once he'd helped her to her feet. He grabbed a pair of scissors and cut the plastic cleanly up the front of her body. As soon as it fell away, he wrapped her in the large towel and scrubbed at her skin, drying the sweat that had gathered beneath the plastic. She might not realise it, but the plastic had been trapping heat that her body was desperate to release. Removing the wrap would feel like a dunk into cold water.

Sure enough, she started to shiver. He tossed the towel away, got her into her robe with careful efficiency, tossed back the covers and slid her into bed. When he climbed in beside her, she curled against his side. He smiled as he pulled her close. Definitely worth missing dinner.

* * *

169

Maria cuddled close and sighed, her mind still lost in the fog of subspace. She'd gone from warm to freezing, but she was quickly warming up again, and there was no better place to get cosy than against Miles's hard body, when she was tucked beneath his protective arm.

She pressed even closer, feeling almost drunk with the experience, and slid one leg over his. Her thigh brushed against a raging erection, and Maria smiled, delighted that she had pleased him. She nudged her leg harder against his erection and listened happily as he took a deep breath, enjoying her touch.

She slid her hand down his chest, reached for the bulge in his trousers and, when she found it, teased her fingers over the fabric, squeezing and rubbing. Miles gave a lazy moan. 'What are you up to?' he asked.

In answer, she tilted her head back and kissed him, opening her mouth beneath his to invite him deeper into the embrace. He sighed into her mouth and shifted onto his side to take a more active role in kissing her, and she whimpered, happy to have enticed him. He reached around and dragged the robe up enough to dig his short nails into her sensitive, reddened ass, and the pleasure of the pain was like a drug. She captured his leg between her thighs and rubbed up against him.

Miles chuckled and pulled away and she released him, mindful of her obedience, as she usually tried to be. He pulled off his shirt and then got out of bed to kick off his trousers and underwear as well, and Maria drank in the sight of him, filled with her usual lust at the sight of his naked body.

She was expecting him to continue to take charge, so it surprised her when he only slid into the bed beside her again. She curled up against him, purring in pleasure at the feel of his naked skin against hers. He put his arms behind his head, relaxed, and she climbed half on top of him, rubbing herself against him as she moved.

Miles chuckled. 'You just came,' he reminded her.

'You feel so good.' Maria kissed his neck and jaw as she continued to grind her clit against his thigh. So close ... so good ...

He exploded into movement, rolling her over onto her back and putting one hand over her mouth and nose. She instinctively tried to gasp, but he'd cut her air off completely. Her pussy throbbed with the delayed orgasm and with arousal at this particular form of torture – one that she loved almost as much as she hated. She lay still for a moment but, before the urge to struggle could overtake her, Miles gave her that sexy smile and sent his other hand between her legs.

He didn't bother with finesse, just ground the base of his hand into her clit. It was all she needed. Thrilled and excited by the breath play, aroused and so close to orgasm already, as sensitive as he had trained her to be, Maria felt her body obey his unspoken command, releasing a

171

rush of ecstasy that was all the sweeter as she fought to cry out or to inhale. The spicy with the sweet – the cinnamon and sugar of their life.

She trembled with the after-effects of the orgasm but, instead of calming, her thrashing grew even wilder as her body willed her to find a way to breathe. Her chest burned even as her cunt throbbed, and her eyes watered with the need for air. Air!

And then she had it. He pulled his hand away and she gasped it down like it was the first time, sucking it deep inside her. She was almost afraid to exhale, but for the next breath she had to. The breath came spilling out of her, and then her greatest fear and desire came upon her as he clapped his hand over her face again. This time she fought him immediately, but he shifted onto her, pinning her with his weight and pressing his hand into her face.

Then he took a deep breath, moved his hand to uncover her mouth without unpinching her nose, and immediately sealed her lips with his. She opened her mouth beneath his, and his breath rushed into her, hot and moist and sweet. He let up when she had taken it all, and she lay gasping beneath him, her body hotter and readier than ever, rising yet again to desire. He knew how to push every single one of her buttons.

She whimpered as soon as she had the air to do it, and arched her back to press into him, raising her hips in an attempt to rub against him. 'You're like a cat in heat,' he said, but she could see that he was pleased. And that he would reward her desire.

'I want you, Master,' she said. She reached for him, pulled him tight against her and dared to take hold of his cock, trying to direct it to the fire that burned between her legs.

'That's not your decision to make,' he said, his voice stern.

'Yes, Master.' She let go even as he drew away, realising she'd gone too far but still too aroused to care much, though she knew she'd feel bad about it later.

He got up and rooted around on the floor. She nearly started to cry with frustration – was he going to just get dressed and leave her there? – but when he straightened up he was holding not a pair of pants but a strip of the plastic wrap.

She gasped, not sure what he planned to do with it. Miles just smiled at her discomfiture and moved back onto the bed. 'Hands up,' he said, and she raised her hands over her head almost before she'd processed the words. He wrapped the plastic around them, not so tightly as to cut off her circulation but enough to be sure she wouldn't just slip out of it. Then he put her arms over the bedpost, grabbed her hips and pulled her down the bed until her arms were stretched tight.

Maria moaned as her arms were pulled high over her head. Her triceps were stretched and her wrists pinched by the plastic, and she felt her shoulders warm in what she knew would turn into a burning sensation in a surprisingly short time. She could get out of the bond by herself, but only if she scooted up towards the headboard.

Miles grinned down at her as she arched her back and sighed. She was already falling into the sensation. The feeling of being bound sent her mind swirling into a place of submission and desire, where pleasure and pain mingled and exchanged places. Her breathing became shallow and fast, and she spread her legs wide, pleased when the robe fell open to reveal her pussy to the open air.

She rocked her hips as if fucking the air, and indeed every stray movement of the air currents against her skin seemed charged. Miles laughed, and his cock twitched as he knelt over her and watched her writhe. It was almost as if she could feel his eyes on her skin.

'What am I going to do with you?' he asked her. 'My beautiful slave who doesn't seem to know her place.'

'Fuck me. Oh, please, *please* fuck me!'

'Somehow I don't think rewarding you is going to solve the problem,' he said dryly. He moved like a cobra, his hand shooting out faster than she could think, and he slapped her breast, hard. The sting travelled straight to her pussy and she moaned with the pleasure of it. 'But that's the problem, isn't it? Even punishment is a reward. I could whip your pussy and you'd still probably beg for more.'

She whimpered at the thought, terrified at the idea of a whip that close to the most sensitive part of her body, but she left her legs spread wide, inviting him in. She was almost completely sure that he wouldn't actually do that.

'How –' he punctuated the word with a slap across her breast '– to punish –' *slap* '– a masochist?' This time he grabbed her nipples, pinched them hard and pulled on them until her breasts stood up like two cones. The pain was searing, and she cried out, her hips still rolling. All she needed was a touch, just one little touch on her clit, and she knew she could come. She moved to squeeze her legs together, but he caught her and shifted to plant his leg between her knees. 'You see what I mean?' he asked her, releasing her nipples.

Of course, punishing her was really quite easy. All he ever had to do was tell her that she had failed him – had failed in the submission to which she had dedicated herself – but this wasn't really about punishment. If it was, he never would have reached between her legs and pressed his thumb against her clit. He ground it against her like he was grinding out a cigarette, but it didn't matter. She screamed in gratitude, thanking him in a choked voice even as she came. The pleasure rushed through her, shaking her from her head to her toes and back again, and she let herself be lost to it for a long time.

He waited until she was done before he picked her up and rolled her over, forcing her to cross her arms at the wrists, the bonds stretching uncomfortably tight. He lay on top of her and spread her legs with one hand, his touch hot and hard the way that she knew he got when he wanted her more than anything else.

She spread her legs for him, her face pressed tight into one arm as she opened desperately for his cock. A moment later he speared her, forcing her clit into the sheets and making her cry out, not quite coming yet, but ... there, when he thrust again, the pressure was enough. Too much, even! She cried out in pleasure and pain as her overwhelmed body let loose yet another flood of endorphins, but each time he pounded into her it drove her into the mattress again and again. Her body cried out under the onslaught and she sobbed and bucked beneath him until it was as if she had been possessed by the spirit of Orgasm. The pleasure rode her instead of the other way around, and all she could do was dig her fingers desperately into the sheets and pray she survived.

His cock slammed into her again and again, and she had resigned herself to dying of sheer pleasure when he finally buried himself inside of her and grabbed her by the shoulder blades, his fingers digging painfully into her flesh as he came, growling fiercely with the pleasure of it.

He moved away from her more quickly than he usually did, and pulled and pushed her limp, panting form until she was on her back, her hands released from the headboard though still tied together. He considered her that way, and she watched him through glazed eyes, her mind still swimming in the after-effects of the intense pleasure.

'Can you cook like that?' he asked.

She wiggled her hands and considered her bonds. 'If you take things out of the oven for me,' she said, dreading the idea of finishing her cooking with her hands tied together.

'Good. Then do it. I think *someone* needs a little reminder of her place.' She got up off the bed, her body flushed and raw and still tingling delightfully, and Miles slapped her on the ass as she moved past him. 'Nice appetiser, though.'

The Demands of Mistress Miranda
Michael Hemmingson

I knocked on the Beverly Hills mansion door, nervous about my return to Mistress Miranda because I had failed her before. The door was answered by a maid dressed in a typical French maid's uniform, black with a white apron; she was quite pretty, five foot three with short black hair and a pale complexion.

'Mr Morton?' she asked in a soft voice.

'Yes.'

'Mistress is downstairs. I will show you to her.'

I followed the maid to the recreation room that I had failed Miranda in. She was sitting on the same sofa, dressed this time in a totally black, form-fitting dress that almost took my breath away. She seemed more beautiful than I remembered her.

'Thank you, Jennifer,' she said.

Jennifer turned and went back upstairs.

178

Miranda looked me up and down like I was mud on her heels. 'Mr Morton. I trust this time things will be different.'

'I hope so,' I replied.

'Mr *Morton*, you were *dismissed* last week because you felt a need to disobey me. You must understand that when I tell you to do something ... *anything* ... anything at all, it will be done *without* question, *without* hesitation. The second I feel you are incapable of that requirement, you will once more be asked to leave, and you will never be welcome here again. Is that *understood*?'

I said, 'Yes.'

'Good. Now come closer to me.'

I moved towards her. She was like a magnet. I was drawn to her as I had never been drawn to any woman. Had she cast some kind of spell on me? It was almost uncanny.

She looked at my crotch.

'Take it out,' she said with a firm voice.

My mind raced for a fleeting moment, wondering why she would do this with her maid in another room.

I lowered my fly. I said, 'It's not hard yet, Mistress Miranda.'

'That is fine. I like to watch a cock get hard. I am sure we can achieve that state in just a few moments. *And*, Mr Morton, until you are told otherwise, you are to address me as "Mistress".'

'Yes, Mistress.'

I took my cock out. She watched as it hung limply.

She said, 'You have a gorgeous cock, Mr Morton.'

She stared at it while my face turned a thousand shades of red.

'You may make it hard now, Mr Morton.'

I reached down and slowly stroked myself into an erection. It was surprisingly easy. I stood in front of her, stroking myself, while she watched intently.

'Very nice,' she said with approval. 'I like your cock very much. I think we can find some interesting things to do with it. Bring it closer and take your hand away.'

I stepped towards her as she leaned forward, my penis only inches from her face.

She reached inside my underpants and gathered my testicles. Gently, she extracted them from their confines and drew them outside into the night air. Her touch was electric and my cock gained in stature.

'There is too much hair on your balls, Mr Morton. We will have to shave them, sooner rather than later.'

She grasped my cock and squeezed it, lightly at first, and then quite firmly. Almost too tightly. But I endured, taking a deep breath. She ran her thumb alongside the urethra, pressing inwards and upwards, forcing clear pre-come to emerge like a moist worm from the ground.

'Very nice texture,' she said with her Beverly Hills accent. 'Except for the balls, I think everything is quite in order.'

I wanted to thank her, but thought better of it. She began to stroke me lightly for a few moments and I tilted my head back, enjoying the feeling. I could feel the urge building inside me.

'One of my rules, Mr Morton, is that you are not permitted to come unless I give you permission. Is that understood?'

'Yes, Mistress.'

'Have you ever been whipped?' she asked out of the blue.

The word 'whipped' buzzed around my head for a moment like a bee in a bottle. I bit my lower lip.

'No, Mistress.'

'You *shall* be, of course. Turn around and let me examine the target area.'

She released my cock and I turned away from her.

'Drop your trousers,' she ordered.

I opened my belt, undid the button and let my trousers drop to a circle around my feet.

'The underpants too.'

The underpants followed.

'Bend over, hands on your knees.'

I bent over and she pushed my shirt halfway up my back to give herself an unobstructed view of my naked ass. I felt her eyes on me, yet, despite the obvious embarrassment, I somehow liked the feeling of being under this woman's power.

Her fingertips searched the surface of my skin and then, without warning, she used her thumbs to pry the cheeks apart, exposing my most private of places.

She said, 'Very nice anus, too. Very *fuckable*.'

I couldn't believe what I had just heard. I had never thought of my asshole as fuckable.

'The first evening, Mr Morton, is always the easiest. Kind of a test to determine your predisposition to events that will follow. If you have potential for growth, then I am sure we will have many pleasant evenings together.'

Still prying my ass cheeks apart, she ran the nail of her index finger across my anus. It actually felt good. Surprisingly good.

'But, as I said, the hairs on your genitals must be removed. Jennifer will take care of that in a few moments and then prepare you.'

She called Jennifer. There I was, my backside exposed to the wind, and a maid I had barely met was standing next to me.

'Yes, Mistress?'

So she called her 'Mistress' too.

'Mr Morton requires his genitals to be shaved. When you are done, bring him to the Pleasure Room and prepare him for a little whipping.'

'At your service, ma'am. Mr Morton, please follow me.'

I pulled up my clothes and followed Jennifer to a

rather large, beautifully tiled bathroom, large enough to accommodate an eight-foot table that had bath towels lying across it.

'You will get completely undressed and lie down on the table,' the maid told me in a soft yet firm voice.

'Completely?' I asked.

She didn't answer me. Her stern look was all that was necessary. And I didn't want word to get back to Miranda that I had hesitated even in the slightest.

I disrobed down to my birthday suit, my cock now limp as a noodle, and eased my back onto the table. Jennifer seemed unaware of my predicament as she moved about the bathroom, basically ignoring me.

I closed my eyes and thought deeply about how far all this would go. I opened my eyes once more when I felt the maid's hands on my balls.

'I am going to lather you up a little,' she said, half-whispering. 'Please don't move.'

I saw the straight-edged razor in her hand and knew I dare not move. Nonchalantly, she coated my testicles with a thick lather of shaving cream. It was quite cold to the touch and I felt my cock shrivel slightly at the first touch. She then lathered the area around the base of my cock.

I closed my eyes again at the first touch of the blade to my privates. I was leaving my most worldly possessions in what I hoped were the capable hands of a young maid.

183

I felt the blade contact the sensitive surface of the testicles. I clenched my hands tightly.

'Relax, Mr Morton, I have done this many times before.'

Somehow I assumed she had. As she removed the hairs around my balls, she applied more lather and soothingly warm water as needed to accomplish her mission. The rest of my pubic hairs were next.

I was almost petrified, but kept perfectly still and came through the procedure unscathed.

Jennifer dried me with a soft cotton towel. Her touch urged my manhood slightly, but I maintained my dignity long enough for her to help me from the table.

'Come with me, please,' she said politely.

'My clothes?'

'You won't be needing them where you are going, Mr Morton. Not for the rest of the evening anyway.'

Totally naked, my cock swinging freely, I walked next to Jennifer to a room at the far end of the corridor. She used a key to open the door and held it for me to enter. There was only one item of furniture in the room, if you could call it furniture: a black sawhorse with a thick red velvet pad on top of the crossbar. And leather cuffs at the bottom of each of the four legs.

'You will lean over the sawhorse, Mr Morton,' Jennifer said, 'your tummy on top of the cushion.'

With more than a little trepidation I moved across the thick carpet to the ominous-looking contraption that stood in the centre of the room. Hardly had I bent over it when the maid moved to kneel behind me.

Quickly she pulled my left leg to the side, affixed the leather cuff around it and tightened it just enough to cause slight discomfort. She moved to the other side and did the same with the right leg. I could only imagine the view she was getting with my legs spread wide and my genitals swinging in the breeze. Before I knew it, my wrists were shackled to the front of the sawhorse.

For good measure, she drew a strap from one end of the sawhorse to the other, pulling it tightly over my back, ensuring that movement was all but impossible.

Before she left, she placed a blindfold over my eyes so I was left in almost total darkness.

Then Jennifer was gone, leaving me naked and alone.

Miranda deliberately left me naked and alone like this to ponder my fate. I knew I was about to be whipped for the first time in my life, but I had no idea what else might be in store for me.

The minutes passed.

I was getting worried here.

The door opened.

I had no idea if it was Jennifer or Miranda who moved behind me. Whoever it was moved so quietly I could hardly hear movement. I strained to listen in the darkness.

Then, without warning, I heard a slight whistling sound, followed by a loud crack of leather against flesh.

Her leather.

My flesh.

My cry reverberated throughout the room.

'My dear Mr Morton,' came the voice through the pain.

It was Miranda. Wickedly beautiful Miranda who was also wickedly painful Miranda.

'If you are going to be a baby about this we are going to have to gag you. Please try to be a bit more quiet.'

I braced myself for the next stroke. Instead, I felt a few light taps from the tip of whatever she was using. Then she reached back. I braced again, clenching my ass cheeks tightly.

'The more you clench like that, Mr Morton, the more it will hurt. You will need to learn to relax and accept.'

Easy for her to say.

And the second I relaxed she whaled into me with a second stroke that must have left a huge gash. It didn't, of course, but it sure felt like it. My ass felt like it was on fire from just two applications of her merciless whip.

'He is taking it better than I thought, but he has so much to learn,' said Miranda.

'He is streaking nicely already,' said a second voice.

Maid Jennifer.

'His balls look very nice. You did a fine job, Jennifer.'

'Thank you, ma'am.'

'Would you be kind enough to tease them for me?'

186

'Gladly, ma'am.'

A small hand on my newly shaved testicles, weighing the sack in her palm. Gently massaging them. Pushing them and watching them sway to and fro between my well-spread legs. Suddenly she grabbed them, squeezing them tightly, and pulled them sharply down. I winced, then cried out again from the pain. This was more than 'teasing', at least in my book. When she cruelly twisted my beleaguered sack while applying way too much pressure, I cried out even more loudly than I had the first time.

'He didn't listen very well about making noise, did he?' asked an obviously annoyed Miranda.

'No, ma'am, he didn't.'

'A penis gag might help,' said Miranda.

'I'll get one, ma'am.'

Jennifer stood in front of me and shoved a long, rubbery penis-like device into my mouth, over my tongue. She quickly tied it around the back of my head. It was not long enough to force any gag reflexes in my throat, but I knew it would certainly hold back any further screams.

'Good girl. Let's see how well it works. You may tease him some more.'

Jennifer moved behind me again and grasped my still aching balls. This time there was no preliminary gentleness. She grasped them as tightly as she could and seemed to take delight in watching my head shake back and forth and listening to the muffled cries over the penis gag.

187

'Much better,' said Miranda, 'the noise was getting annoying.'

'But he isn't taking well to the pain, ma'am,' said Jennifer as she twisted the sack mercilessly.

'He will learn ... in time. Try teasing his cock a bit.'

Jennifer released her grasp on my testicles and quickly found my woefully flaccid cock. If her grip on my balls was painful, her locked hand around my manhood sent me through the roof in pain. She pulled it down so hard I felt like she was going to rip it from my body. Sweat gushed from my forehead. The penis gag drowned out my screams, leaving incoherent moans and unintelligible noises as the only sounds filling the room.

'Enough,' Miranda said and Jennifer released her grip on my manhood. I never knew such relief in my life. I heard Miranda move in front of me. I couldn't see her behind my blindfold, but her familiar perfume wafted to my nostrils. She moved her index finger to my chin and raised my head.

'You are actually doing better than expected, Mr Morton. There are always rewards for pain, but we are not done with your little initiation. I need to talk with you first.'

I felt Miranda's hand behind my head, undoing the knot, pulling the penis gag out. My mouth was terribly dry. 'Thank you ... Mistress.'

'Listen *very* carefully, Mr Morton. You are free to get up and leave right now. No questions asked. But if you go you will never see me again. If you choose to stay, you will be invited back at times I choose for you. Sometimes the pain will be unbearable. At other times you will be teased to the point of ejaculation, but you may not come without my express permission. If you do, you shall be punished severely.'

She pulled the blindfold from my eyes and let it rest on my forehead. At first the light in the room blinded me, but, as my eyes became accustomed to the light, I gazed upon her beautiful face. I was under her spell. I would endure anything just to be with her.

'Do you wish to leave, Mr Morton?'

'I hurt so much, Miranda. My ass, my balls, my cock ...'

'It is nothing compared to what you can expect each time you return.'

I wondered how I could take even more pain, but out of love I calmly said, 'I accept your desires.'

She smiled. I had pleased her, obviously, and in my heart I was happy to have done so. I looked further down her body.

She knelt on one leg, and in doing so offered me an inviting glimpse all the way up her short black skirt. She was not wearing panties, and her pussy was totally shaved. Her vulva was puffy with a prominent clitoral hood. I thought I saw some moisture inside the delightful slit.

She caught me staring at her goodies and, grasping my hair, pulled my head up sharply so I was now staring into her pretty blue eyes.

'Did you enjoy the view you just had, Mr Morton?'

'Yes, ma'am,' I admitted.

'From this moment on, you will *never* gaze upon any part of my body, even my face, without permission. In my presence, you must always look down at the floor, head bowed, in respect of your Mistress.'

I closed my eyes. 'I understand.'

'The penalty for looking at me is hardly worth the risk, Mr Morton.'

I nodded in agreement.

'Now you will *pay* for looking up my skirt. *Shame on you!* Get me the cat, Jennifer.'

I had no idea what Miranda meant by a cat, but I would soon find out. With my eyes still closed, I sensed her rising and moving behind me once more. Jennifer returned from the side of the room with the cat in her hand.

'Have him kiss it, Jennifer. You may open your eyes, Mr Morton.'

It was Jennifer's turn to kneel in front of me. In the palms of her hands she was holding a wicked-looking multi-stranded black whip. Each of the leather tails of the whip was about a foot long and perhaps a quarter-inch thick. The handle was made of braided leather. I knew this mean-looking sucker would hurt like hell. She held the whip to my lips and I kissed the strands that would soon be the cause of pain.

She arose and handed the cat to Miranda.

'*Why* are you getting whipped, Mr Morton?

I said, 'Because ... because I looked up your skirt, Mistress.'

I thought I heard a faint 'whoosh' in the air, then the loud crack of the twelve leather strands meeting my naked ass. Without the penis gag to hold it back, my scream echoed through the room. In time Miranda would teach me to accept a whipping without screaming, but this time I think she wanted the audio affects.

'Are you ever going to look at me, any part of me, without permission?'

'No, ma'am,' I replied as best as I could, for I had quite a pain in my ass.

The whip swished again with an even louder crack, snapping my head back. I cried out. Hardly pausing, she gave me another one. And yet another. I sucked in my breath and let out a horrendous scream.

My backside was on fire from the three quickly delivered strokes.

My whole body bucked against the cuffs and chains that held my arms and legs.

'That was merely a surface scratch, Mr Morton. If you ever disobey a rule again, you can forget about sitting down normally for a week. *Do* you understand?'

191

I took a deep breath before I could answer. 'Yes, Mistress.'

'Let him loose, Jennifer.'

Jennifer undid each of the cuffs and the strap over my waist, and then helped me rise from the sawhorse.

My body ached from its awkward position. I stood on rubbery legs until Miranda told me to turn and kneel in front of her.

I kept my head lowered, staring at the carpet, as I knelt submissively in front of her.

'Part of your training, Mr Morton, is to show an appreciation of women. *All women*. Not just me, though you will come to love me more than anyone you have ever known. To appreciate a woman, you must know what it is like to be one. When I was in high school, I was raped, anally, by a teacher I thought I could trust. I was only fifteen. The shame and the pain were quite unbearable. You will come to know how I felt that day.'

I nodded. 'Yes, ma'am.'

'Every woman endures a monthly cycle, from puberty to her fifties. It is not pleasant, not at all, but it is part of life. I can't even begin to help you understand its unpleasantness, but I can help you gain a little appreciation for it. Turn around and get on your hands and knees.'

I had no idea what she was planning to do, but I knew not to hesitate in following any of her commands. I knelt, head lowered, eyes closed, my naked ass and newly shaved balls only a foot or so from her head.

'Get me a tampon, Jennifer.'

A *tampon*? I realised what was in store for me.

Jennifer left, returned in seconds and handed the white cloth cylinder with its familiar string to Miranda.

'Open him for me.'

Jennifer straddled my hips and pried my ass cheeks apart with her hands, revealing my anus to both women. I had never felt so exposed in my life.

'Women have to put this damn thing inside them so many times in their lives. It is never pleasant, Mr Morton, as you shall learn. And you will never know all the other discomforts associated with it. Actually, I prefer a pad, and I will even allow you to change it for me when the time comes. But the tampon will give you a better feel for a woman's plight.'

'I am having my period now, ma'am,' said Jennifer.

'And do you need changing?'

'I believe so.'

'Good. A little practice never hurts. But first, let's feminise him a bit.' I felt the somewhat hard cloth cylinder touch the centre of my anus. I braced myself. 'Stretch him wider, Jennifer, the poor baby is still a virgin even to this small a thing.'

I felt my anus being opened wide as Miranda began moving the tampon into me. There was no pain involved, but the humiliation was unbelievable. Slowly but surely several inches of the tube was fully ensconced. Jennifer closed my anus around the string that hung outside my ass. Miranda tugged lightly on the string to add to my embarrassment.

'Do you feel that inside you, Mr Morton?'

'Yes, ma'am,' I softly replied.

'You may take it out tomorrow morning. But not before. Understood?'

'Yes, ma'am.'

'Good. Now you can bestow a favour on Jennifer. Go get a pad, dear.'

Jennifer left the room and returned moments later with a white feminine pad in her hand. I couldn't believe what I was about to be expected to do.

'Kneel in front of her, Mr Morton. You may open your eyes so you can see what you are doing.'

I knelt in front of the young maid, my heart racing.

'Raise your skirt, Jennifer.'

Right in front of my face, Jennifer blithely lifted her black skirt all the way to her waist, revealing a pair of pretty white shiny rayon panties.

The bulge in the panty crotch was obvious.

'Lower her panties, Mr Morton.'

I slowly lowered the dainty undies to her thighs. Jennifer's pubic hair was pure black. The triangular curls were thick. I felt a familiar stirring in my loins as I looked at the forest in front of my eyes. I started to raise the panties, but Miranda interrupted me.

'Kiss it first, Mr Morton. To show your appreciation of womanhood.'

I leaned forward until my nose grazed against the delightful pubic curls. Jennifer put her hand on my head, holding it in place, and opened her legs slightly, in obvious invitation for me to kiss her pussy.

'Very good, Mr Morton. Let's get her back to normal.'

I pulled the panties back up after getting one last look at Jennifer's pretty pussy. She lowered her skirt and I dutifully lowered my eyes, still kneeling in front of her.

'He will make a wonderful student,' Miranda said.

'I do believe so, ma'am,' Jennifer agreed.

'He deserves a reward.'

'He has had a difficult night, ma'am.'

'Turn around, Mr Morton.'

I turned on my knees facing Miranda, head still lowered.

'Get me a chair, Jennifer.'

Jennifer pulled a leather armchair from the side of the room and moved it behind Miranda. Miranda sat in it, facing me.

'You may look at me, Mr Morton.'

I opened my eyes.

Miranda was right in front of me, seated, her gorgeous legs tightly closed. I felt the presence of the tampon in my ass, but I was slowly getting accustomed to the odd feeling.

'You enjoyed looking up my skirt earlier?'

'Yes, ma'am,' I admitted.

'And what you saw there pleased you?'

'Very much so, ma'am.'

'If you were to see it again, would you have a desire to give pleasure to it?'

She was teasing me mercilessly, but just the thought of being asked to pleasure her hairless pussy was suddenly driving me wild.

'I would indeed, ma'am,' I said.

She opened her legs ever so slightly and leaned forward.

'If you don't make me come, Mr Morton, I will beat your worthless ass raw.'

I needed no incentive. If she were to allow me a few moments between her legs I would spend it wisely. She opened her legs just wide enough to afford me a view of the creamy lips of her pussy.

My heart was beating wildly.

My Mistress was showing me her treasure.

She pulled her skirt up, opened her legs as wide as she could and rested the backs of her knees on the arms of the chair. Her slit was opened enough to reveal a good deal of pink, very moist tissue. The sight before me was perhaps the ninth wonder of the world. Her cunt was certainly out of this world.

'Go for it, Mr Morton.'

I didn't care that Jennifer was behind me, watching. I

leaned forward, between the widespread legs, and began kissing the puffy pussy lips. Miranda moaned at the first touch of my lips. Her womanly smell wafted through my nostrils.

Using several fingers of each hand, I boldly pried the lips apart. The slit was filled with clear and copious moisture. It was mine for the taking. With the flat of my tongue I licked her from her vagina to her clit, gathering as much moisture as I could. Her taste was exquisite. She moaned again, this time more loudly.

Then, with my thumbs, I opened her clitoral hood, exposing the tiny nubbin. I touched it lightly with just the tip of my tongue and Miranda raised her hips and shoved her pussy into my mouth. I circled the clit with my tongue over and over, driven by her continuous cries of pleasure. I sucked it into my mouth and flicked my tongue back and forth over it in maddening delight.

Satisfied that I had let her feel my pleasure on her clit, I lowered my head and drove my tongue straight into her pussy, as deeply as I could. She was wet as the sea and I enjoyed every moment.

My cheeks were soaked with her womanly juices. There was no holding back. I fucked her with my tongue, some-times slowly, sometimes so rapidly my tongue became tired. She bucked her hips wildly as she tried to push my tongue further into her.

When her breathing became laboured, I thought she was

close to coming. I was right – she screamed in ecstasy for a few wonderful moments before she slowly came down.

'He needs a reward, Jennifer,' she said after she came back to our world.

'And that would be, ma'am?' asked the maid.

'Your ass.'

'Yes, ma'am.'

'You'd like that.'

'Yes, ma'am.'

Miranda said to me, 'Jennifer is quite the anal slut. Have fun, Mr Morton.'

'Thank you, ma'am.'

Miranda left us alone. Jennifer started to undress. After that taste of my mistress, my cock was very hard and needy.

Jennifer started to apply lubricant between her ass cheeks. I noticed a strange look on her face.

'Is there something wrong?' I asked.

'Will you put it in my pussy instead of my asshole?' she asked. 'I haven't had something nice like that in a while.'

'I would be honoured to fuck your pussy,' I said.

The naked maid came to me, into my arms, and I held her before entering her. A little tenderness after pain – but I loved Miranda, and so did she, and I had a feeling our ma'am was watching us from somewhere. I hoped she would not punish me – both of us – for not engaging in the kind of nasty sex she demanded.

The Belt
Elizabeth Coldwell

I knew before we left the house that morning that by the end of the day I'd find myself in the most compromising of positions, getting my bottom spanked for my bad behaviour. I just didn't know how I'd manoeuvre Simon into giving me the punishment I craved – or that when he finally dished it out I'd be tied up and helpless.

Sometimes I wake with the urge to bring my bad, bratty side out to play, and that Saturday was very much one of those times. For once, Simon didn't have to devote himself to work. I'd grown so used to him shutting himself in his office for most of the week, poring over figures and projections and giving every indication that he shouldn't be disturbed, even if the house was burning down. Not that I minded on those occasions when he handed me his credit cards and told me to treat myself to something nice; meeting up with a couple of my girlfriends for some retail therapy on Bond Street was always fun. But I wanted to spend some quality time with my husband, and I hadn't had much of an opportunity to do that in recent weeks.

So when Simon settled himself at the breakfast table with the *Telegraph* and a second cup of coffee, showing no signs of needing to be anywhere near his computer and office phone for the next few hours, my stomach gave a little flip of anticipation. It was playtime.

'D'you fancy doing a spot of shopping this morning, Samantha?' he asked me over the top of his newspaper.

When I talk about shopping, I mean shoes and handbags and all the girly trinkets that make life that bit more fun and frivolous. What Simon means by shopping is poking around in the overpriced antique shops along Camden Passage, looking for the perfect armoire. I find it boring, and he knows all too well by now how dangerous it is to let a brat get bored, particularly a brat who's not averse to making a scene in public. Maybe that's why he suggested it. Whatever the reason, I agreed enthusiastically, and went to change into something more appropriate for the occasion.

Coming downstairs twenty minutes later, I found Simon standing at the bottom of the stairs, clutching his house keys and looking eager to leave. He's like me in that respect: once he gets an idea into his head, he has to act on it straightaway, and as far as I knew I might already have earned a demerit mark by keeping him waiting. Good.

Alongside the impatience in Simon's expression was something more; something best described as frank admiration. I'd gone for a simple but classic look. A fluffy white angora sweater that left my midriff bare and was Simon's favourite, teamed with a skirt so short I couldn't bend over in it without flashing my underwear. Anyone close enough to catch a glimpse of my panties would notice they were patterned with the sweetest pink daisies, so very girly and feminine. The finishing touches involved white knee-length socks and sensible Mary Jane shoes, and I'd twisted my hair into twin bunches, one each side of my head, secured with hair bobbles in the shape of fat red cherries. You can quite easily make a fool of yourself dressing like an overgrown Japanese schoolgirl in public but, until I reach the age where the glances I'm getting make it obvious I look clownish rather than cute, I am determined to play the part to the full.

'At last,' Simon said peevishly, probably stifling the urge to glance at his watch. I might have taken my time, but I was sure he liked the way I'd dressed. If I knew him even half as well as I thought I did, there'd be a subtle but palpable stiffening in his chinos, and already he'd be wondering how and where I might decide to act up. Just like me, he enjoyed the sense of anticipation, the first steps in our complex routine of misbehaviour and resulting punishment.

The first real spell of fine summer weather had brought the crowds out in force on the streets of Islington, and we negotiated our way through little knots of shoppers dawdling along Upper Street. When Simon strides out, stretching those long legs that help take his height well above the six-foot mark, I have to really scurry to keep up with him. We appear so oddly suited in physical terms, the top of my head barely reaching his shoulders, and his silvery hair making him look even older than he is, and people base all kinds of assumptions on this mismatch that we don't necessarily attempt to correct. All that matters to us is our physical compatibility and our shared love of kinky sex games.

In Camden Passage we bypassed the shops selling silver plate and vintage clothing, Art Deco jewellery and Oriental vases, much as I might have liked to browse there. With his usual single-mindedness, Simon marched over to a display of bookcases and occasional furniture, where he stroked the smooth wood just as lovingly as he caressed my bare bottom in the moments before he commenced a spanking. While he examined the antiques on offer, I looked round, hoping one of the shop owners might be worth indulging in a spot of flirtation with to pass the time, but no one – male or female – caught my eye. And it soon became obvious that none of the furniture was to Simon's liking, as he stomped back to me with a disappointed expression. It seemed today might be a wasted day after all.

'Why don't we go and have lunch?' I suggested, when he'd exhausted all his usual haunts and come no closer to finding a suitable chest of drawers for the second guest bedroom. 'We could always try that new gastropub that's opened up on the other side of the Angel. I hear they do smoked haddock fishcakes.'

Simon conceded it was as good an idea as any; a pint or two of porter and a generous helping of old-style nursery food never failed to brighten his day. And that was how our expedition might have ended, if it hadn't been that, as we walked past the entrance to the newish little shopping centre containing a cinema and concert venue, we noticed a farmers' market had been set up.

'Ooh, can we have a look?' I asked, my voice deliberately more high-pitched and excited than usual. A passing couple turned to look as I tugged at Simon's arm. I could see them struggling to work out the exact nature of the relationship between us. 'Please, please, can we?'

'If you must, Samantha, but make it quick.' Simon had slipped without effort into the role of the world-weary guardian whose young charge was delaying him on the way to his well-earned lunch.

Permission granted, I gave a little squeal of gratitude and trotted off to explore, Simon wandering behind me at his own pace. This, I quickly discovered, was some kind of event promoting French produce. Stalls were heaped high with artisan cheeses, sourdough loaves, flavoured oils and vinegars and all manner of charcuterie. The smell of so much fresh food made my mouth water, but I bypassed it all in favour of something far more attractive. Halfway along the row, the sexiest man I'd seen since I'd left the house this morning, my own dear Simon notwithstanding, was selling leather goods.

Bags in shades of black, brown and oxblood hung from hooks, and wallets and belts were laid out in neat rows. Picking up a thin, supple, honey-coloured belt, I wound it around my hand. I'd just bought the most beautiful pair of cream Capri pants, and this would be the perfect accessory. Not to mention all the other uses Simon and I could put such a belt to, in the privacy of the bedroom …

'All belts are only five pounds today. Special offer.' The stallholder's heavily accented voice cut into my thoughts. From a distance, he'd been cute. Close up, he was the fuel for a thousand filthy fantasies. Stubbled chin, eyes dark as sin and lips that had seemingly been designed for a thin roll-up to droop from them. He had no cigarette in his mouth at the moment; instead, a white paper lollipop stick jutted from between his lips. His eyes never left me as he removed the lolly with an audible pop, and I felt a gush of hot juice flood my daisy-patterned panties. In the presence of such raw sex appeal, my body couldn't help but react in the most primal of ways. And all I was supposed to be doing was buying a belt.

'You like what you see?' he asked, the question so loaded with meaning I swore he'd been reading my mind.

'Oh, very much so,' I answered, and gave the man a pouting smile. All morning I'd been looking for the opportunity to flirt, and now it had been handed to me, I intended to enjoy it to the full. The fact that Simon couldn't be too far away, and would realise exactly what I was doing as soon as he saw me talking to the stall-holder, only added to the naughty thrill coursing through my body.

'Maybe you should try the belt for size, make sure it's not too big for your pretty little waist ...' He stepped out from behind the stall and took the belt from my trembling fingers. Close to, he smelled of sweat and tobacco, and his clothes were as rumpled as if he'd slept in them. My skirt had no belt loops, but I'd suspected the idea of measuring my waist was simply an excuse to touch me, and, as he wrapped the cool leather round my bare flesh, those suspicions were confirmed. As he pressed close to me, claiming to admire the way the belt looked, and how it complemented the honeyed tones of my skin, I felt his cock nudge against my leg. The baggy cut of his jeans hid its outline, but it felt deliciously solid to me. In other circumstances, I might have been tempted to push back against him, making it obvious I wanted to feel that hard length filling my pussy.

But at that moment Simon stepped forward, holding

a carrier bag from which one end of a thick baguette protruded. The similarity to the fat baton in the stallholder's jeans made me giggle aloud.

Simon looked at the stallholder's grubby fingers where they still rested on my hips, then at me. When I didn't immediately pull away from the other man, he snapped, 'Come on, Samantha, it's time to go.'

'Can I get this belt first?' I asked.

'Don't you think you have enough belts?' He sounded weary, fed up. 'You're always buying things you never wear.'

'But I really want this belt,' I told him in a sulky tone, the brat determined to get whatever she wanted. 'Don't you think it looks good on me? Don't you think I deserve it? And it's only five pounds. Please buy it for me.'

'Samantha ...'

'Please, please, please!' I tugged at my husband's arm, threatening to explode into a full-blown tantrum if he refused me. If I hadn't displeased him enough by letting another man chat me up so blatantly in public, this attention-seeking behaviour was guaranteed to compound the offence to a level where Simon would feel compelled to take it out on my bottom.

The stallholder was regarding Simon with an expression of utter contempt, as if he couldn't believe anyone could be so weak-willed. Whether he thought he was dealing with my elderly uncle or some kind of indulgent sugar daddy, I didn't know. Whatever, it didn't stop him taking the five-pound note my husband handed over, and giving my arse a little squeeze as he gave me the belt, stashed in a brown paper bag.

'Just wait till I get you home,' Simon muttered in my ear as he marched me away from the stall.

'Why, have I been bad?' I replied, fixing him with a look of pure butter-wouldn't-melt innocence. When I glanced behind me and caught the stallholder's eye, the man gave me one of those Gallic shrugs that can be interpreted in any of a hundred ways. I assumed he was feeling sorry for me, stuck with a stuffy old stick who didn't let me have any fun. If only he knew.

* * *

Simon, proper to the last, stowed the groceries in the fridge as soon as we got home, apart from a round of evil-smelling cheese that gave the impression it could have crossed the kitchen floor unaided. Only when everything had been put away did he take my new belt out of its bag. When he wrapped it round his fingers, the gesture was so full of promise I felt my pussy go liquid-hot all over again. Nervous as always in the prelude to a spanking, I let out a giggle. He quelled me with a stern look.

'You make it so – difficult for me, Samantha.' He'd almost said 'hard', but he knew that would only have set me off giggling all over again. 'I try to take you out for a nice morning's shopping, and what do you do? As soon as my back's turned, you start making eyes at every Tom, Dick and Harry –'

'Henri,' I interjected.

'I beg your pardon?'

'He was French, so he'd have been Henri. Or maybe Pierre. Or –'

'Samantha, would you still your chatter for just one moment?' Again he wound and rewound that length of new, strong-smelling leather around his fingers, and I had a sudden sharp intuition that he was rehearsing the motion. It wouldn't be the first time he'd wrapped a belt around his hand before using it to beat my unprotected arse.

'I've had just about enough of your bad behaviour, young lady.' Whenever he called me 'young lady' I knew I was really in for it. I hung my head, trying to express a contrition I didn't feel. 'You need to learn how to conduct yourself in public.'

'But I was only being friendly,' I told him. 'And you were far too busy buying that horrible stinky cheese to pay me any attention.'

'So, it's attention you want, is it?' Simon shook his head, as though the workings of my mind were beyond him, even though we both knew I'd been manipulating him towards this point from the moment I'd gone upstairs to change into my sluttiest schoolgirl attire. 'Well, this is where you get it. Or at least, this is where your bottom does.'

With that, he caught hold of my wrists. Still convinced he was going to thrash me with the belt and mentally doing my best to prepare for the feel of it cracking against my backside, I could only gape in surprise as he instead wound the supple leather around my wrists a couple of times before fastening it securely. He allowed me a moment to appreciate the irony of having my new purchase used on me in such an unorthodox way. We don't often incorporate bondage into our spanking games, but the feeling of being restrained as well as beaten always adds an extra level to my feelings of helplessness, and Simon was all too aware of that fact.

I waited for him to pull a chair out from under the kitchen table and haul me over his lap for the inevitable spanking, but the sight of me with my wrists bound by the belt must have sparked something in him. 'Wait there,' he said, and went bounding out of the kitchen. I heard footsteps receding up the stairs, then nothing for a good couple of minutes. Maybe he'd gone to fetch his favourite spanking implement, the plaid slipper with its sole worn almost smooth from years of being applied to my recalcitrant bum cheeks.

When he reappeared, he was indeed holding the slipper, but he'd also been hunting through my closet, for he had with him a selection of belts.

'You see,' he began, dumping them on the kitchen table, 'I was right. You do have too many of these things.'

'But they all go with a different outfit,' I tried to explain, my inner brat not entirely subdued by her unexpected spell in restraint. 'Men just don't understand the concept of accessorising.'

My comments fell on deaf ears. Single-minded Simon was too busy dragging the kitchen stool into the middle of the room. He came over and untied my wrists, but any respite I felt at being free was only temporary. Before I could react, he'd pushed me over the stool and was using the new belt to tie my left wrist to one of its legs. Then he plucked a black patent belt from the table and fastened my right wrist in place with it.

This was getting silly, and I wanted to protest, but a thick, hot excitement pulsed through me at being effectively restrained. With so many belts in the pile, Simon must be intending to use some of them to bind my legs, but instead he just seemed to be standing, contemplating something – bent over as I was, I couldn't really turn my head to see what he was doing. Instead, I had to be guided by sound and touch. He came close behind me and pulled down my skirt in one swift motion. When he hooked his fingers in the waistband of my panties, I squeaked and tried to beg him to stop.

'Be quiet, Samantha,' Simon ordered me. 'How will

you ever learn your lesson if you don't take your spankings on the bare, like a good girl?'

I felt my panties being tugged down my legs. They reached my ankles, and on Simon's command I stepped out of them. I could only imagine how I looked, bare from the waist down, still wearing my silly, girly socks and the fluffy sweater. As Simon took my ankles in turn and tied them to the legs of the stool, the movement spread my legs slightly. My sticky sex lips peeled apart, offering him a perfect view of the wet pink secrets between them. I felt helplessly exposed, fiercely turned on, knowing he could see everything from my cunt hole to the pout of my anus and not being able to do a thing to cover myself up. Every sensation seemed heightened by the fact that I was held securely in place, unable to move, entirely dependent on my husband's whim for pleasure and release.

He'd positioned me so I was able to watch as he walked over to the table and picked up his punishment slipper. Smirking, he flexed it between his hands, the sole bending almost in half. That slipper and I had a love-hate relationship, and he knew it, as he strung my anticipation of the first swat out to the point where I almost begged him to just start spanking me and have done with it.

'Don't worry,' he said, 'I'm only going to give you six.'

Only? Six with the slipper was like a good couple of

dozen with his hand, made worse by the fact that I'd feel the sting of the blows long after a hand-spanking would have faded. But I'd teased and taunted and embarrassed him in front of a stranger; I couldn't say I didn't deserve it.

He caressed my bum absently, no doubt admiring the way my posture thrust it up high, inviting touch, demanding punishment. Then he tapped each cheek lightly, once, with the slipper, just as a little taster of what was to come. Shivering in my bonds, I took a deep breath.

I didn't have to wait any longer for my spanking to begin. The slipper seemed to whistle through the air, announcing its presence in the moment before it cracked down hard on my vulnerable arse. I gave a full-throated yell, knowing no one would be disturbed by my cries.

'For heaven's sake, Samantha, we've barely begun,' Simon pointed out.

'But it hurts,' I retorted.

'Well, you should have thought of that, shouldn't you?' Not prepared to take any more of my nonsense, he set about spanking me in earnest. He dished out the prescribed half-dozen strokes ruthlessly but dispassion-ately, giving me just enough time to recover from one before laying on the next. Fire raged through my arse but, though I wriggled in my bonds, Simon had made sure I couldn't get free. Pain mounted on pain, hot and harsh, but bubbling beneath the surface was a wellspring of pleasure. I fought for that pleasure, drinking it in; I might be bound, but I swore I wouldn't be broken. By the time he'd finished with my beating, I doubted I'd be able to sit down for the rest of the day, but I felt a strange sense of satisfaction at having taken it all.

'Good girl,' Simon murmured, laying down the slipper. Now when he ran his hand over my arse, his touch was pure tenderness. His fingers traced over the sore and no doubt blotchy skin, and when they slipped lower, into the cleft between my cheeks, I didn't object.

'So how did you like it?' he asked, brushing my lips with the pad of his finger before moving down to dip into the well of juice flowing from my cunt. 'Being tied up, unable to stop me doing whatever I wanted to you ...'

Now I wriggled again, no longer wanting to be free, only needing more of his teasing, frustrating touch. 'I loved it,' I told him honestly.

'Even though I used all of your pointless belts?'

'Vital accessories,' I retorted, my bratty side reasserting itself just for a moment. Then one of Simon's slippery fingers jammed itself into my arsehole, filling my tight rear passage, and his thumb began to play lazy circles over my clit. Ripples of pleasure rolled through my belly. 'After all, if I hadn't had so many belts, what would you have used to tie me up?'

Simon just chortled, and increased the speed of his strokes, reaming my arse, stimulating my pleasure button.

The combination was too much to resist, and I gasped and bucked in my bonds. Driven to a point where there was no longer any holding back, I came, creaming all over his steadily wanking hand.

When I'd stopped seeing stars, Simon withdrew his finger, and I heard the sound of him tugging down his zip, and letting his trousers drop to the ground. He didn't bother to untie me, just put the head of his cock to my arsehole and shoved home. Only when he was snugly lodged in place, in the moment before he began to fuck my punished arse, did he give an answer to my earlier question.

'What would I have done if I hadn't been able to fasten you in place with all those belts? Well, really, Samantha. Why do you think a gentleman owns so many neckties?'

Putting on the Dog
Heather Towne

It was the lap of luxury. And I was feeling antsy, uncomfortable in that plush, polished lap, staring across a cup of tea at Livia Chienne. The bone china alone was worth more than I was.

The fiftyish heiress was elegantly attired in a white silk blouse and cream silk skirt, a pearl necklace arranged around her slim, tan neck, golden-blonde hair swept back from her sleek patrician face. I needed a smoke in the worst way, my rumpled brown suit and tired hound-dog countenance woefully out of place in the airless, soundless, flawless white penthouse.

'You wanted to hire me?' I rasped. My voice grated through the perfumed stillness like a chainsaw. I could hardly believe the super-rich widow had a use for the likes of me.

She took a delicate sip of tea, set the cup and saucer

down. 'Yes. This may sound foolish, Mr Barker –' her crystal-clear blue eyes looked downwards, high cheek-bones reddening just a tad under the bronze '– but I want you to find my ... dog – Tom. He's gone missing.'

I blew out my cheeks, then hastily wiped away the spittle. Now it all figured. 'Your dog? Tom?'

'He's an English cocker spaniel. He just turned seven last Friday. He disappeared when I was taking him for his walk last night. He, um, was about to do his business against a wall in the mouth of an alley, so I looked away.' She looked up at me, dazzling eyes suddenly shiny with moisture. 'And when I looked back ... he was gone.'

I put the cup of tea down on the antique coffee table without breaking either and rose up on my hind legs. 'I'd suggest a call to the pound, maybe a few posters around the neighbourhood, a Facebook page. I don't chase runaway pooches, Mrs Chienne.'

She came to her feet as gracefully as a yacht slipping anchor and handed me a piece of paper. My puppy dog-brown eyes popped as I read it, an old-fashioned ransom note sent via email: 'I've got your dog. Leave $100,000 in the wire garbage bin by the yellow fire hydrant at the entrance to Talooley Park at midnight tonight, and Tom will be returned unharmed. 894376152.'

'894376152?'

'That's Tom's ear tattoo number.'

216

'Better than his real ear,' I mumbled. 'A hundred g's is a lot of dog biscuits.'

'I'm willing to pay it, Mr Barker – Ben. You see, Tom's … all I've got, since my husband died.' The blush again, the glittering blue eyes.

'What do you want –'

'I want you to deliver the money, ensure Tom is safely returned to me. Talooley Park is a dog park not far from here. The money is in that duffle bag over there. I'll pay you five thousand dollars.'

It was bigger than a doggy-bag, all right, stuffed with green cabbage of the non-edible kind. 'OK,' I said, zipping the bag back up and hefting it. 'I'll do it.'

What the hell? It wouldn't do my rep any good – gone to the dogs? – but it was the only bone I'd had tossed my way that month.

'But Tom might already be –'

She gasped, a slender hand fluttering up to her mouth. She was cool-as-ice elegance and beauty, but still a caring, loving woman beneath all the sheen. I reached out and touched her shoulder in a gesture of reassurance, and she shivered, stiffened – body and breasts. I was suddenly aware of her nipples indenting that über-expensive top of hers now, pointing in my direction.

Her hand closed over mine on her shoulder, warm and soft and feminine. 'I – I appreciate what you're doing, Ben. It's good having a man …'

I swept her up in my arms and kissed her full on the mouth.

It shocked me, too. But the lovely lady's exquisite appearance, her scent, the surroundings, her needful, noticeable yearning, compelled me to do it. Sure, I was more than twenty years her junior, she three tax brackets my senior, but sometimes a man and a woman are just that, the barriers stripped away, damn the propriety and consequences. Livia threw her lithe arms around my gangly frame and kissed me right back.

Our mouths moved together, urgently, passionately. Her lips were slick and velvety as rose petals. Her tongue darted into my mouth, wet satin, played against my tongue. We entwined our slippery mouth-organs, speaking the same lusty language, on the same level, breathing hotly into each other's faces. My big hairy hands slid down her silken, curved back and onto the soft swells of her bottom. She moaned in my mouth, as I squeezed her lush cheeks.

Then she was out of my arms and hands, dropping down to her knees on the hushed white shag, deftly pulling my belt and zipper open. The sophisticated lady getting down and dirty. I watched in amazement, tremoring at the thrill of her hot, dainty palm on my hard, swollen cock, as she pulled me right out into the open and popped my bulbed hood right into her moist, heated mouth.

'Yeah!' I groaned, hovering my shaking hands over

her perfect hair; then diving my long, blunt-nailed fingers into her coiffed yellow strands, when she took more of my pulsating meat into her mouth.

The contrast of cool wealth and red-hot lust was stunning. Livia took fully two-thirds of my rigid dong into her mouth. She sealed her glossy lips tight around my shaft, her cauldron of a mouth squeezing me, my cap crowding the back of her throat. She kept me locked down in that humid hothouse, staring up at me with brimming eyes until I desperately guided her head back and forth.

She hungrily sucked my cock, vaccing tight and wet and wonderful. I poled out for all I was worth in her mouth, my one man-asset now making up for all of her monetary ones. Her head bobbed in my hands, lips gliding, tongue caressing, mouth tugging – faster, and faster, and faster.

I was about to push her back, for fear of soiling her sultry silver-spoon mouth, when she bobbed her head right off my prick, disgorging my dripping tool. She had experience, had sensed my impending explosion.

Livia went lower, dirtier than I had any right to expect her to go, dropping her golden head down and sucking my hairy, hanging nut sack into her wicked mouth. My knees buckled and I almost folded like my cheap suit as the woman swallowed my pouch whole and pulled on it, jostling my balls around with her tongue. I gaped down at her, my big, ugly, veined dick jutting out over her cameo-perfect face, getting tea-bagged by an expert.

I pulled her to her feet. We stumbled over to the lace-shrouded seventeenth-century dining table, Livia losing her skirt somewhere along the way. I lifted her up onto the table, set her down on the edge, then ripped her modest white cotton panties in half. She rocked back, planted her hands on the table, lifted her legs and spread them. I clutched the slim limbs to my chest, staring at a pussy shaven breathtakingly clean.

I kissed Livia's tapered ankles, caressed her smooth calves. She tore a hand off the table, grabbed my cock and slotted it into her glistening cunt. 'Fuck me, Ben! Fuck me!'

She didn't have to ask twice. I grabbed her taut thighs to my torso and pumped my hips, sawing my cock back and forth in her tunnel. She was tight and juicy as any woman half her age, but mature enough to convulse her cunt muscles so that she sucked on my cock as I fucked her.

'Jesus!' I gulped, pumping in a frenzy, wildly rocking the woman and the table. 'Livia, I'm going to –'

'Come inside of me! Come in my cunt!' she screamed, her hand plunging down onto her clit and frantically buffing just above my pistoning cock swelling her pussy. Then she shuddered and bucked, vibrated in all-out orgasm.

I pounded, exploded. White-hot ecstasy shot out of

my spasming cock and deep into the beautiful lady, my body and brain jolted by wicked joy, over and over.

* * *

I was at Talooley Park at midnight, carrying the duffle bag full of cash. But I'd made a stop beforehand – at a K9 buddy of mine. He'd treated the dough with a special doggy scent and lent me one of his trackers. I'd vowed to treat him to two football and three baseball games in exchange.

I tossed the duffle bag into the wire garbage bin, on top of plastic bags and bags of dog doo-doo. The park was empty, dark, not a mutt stirring or yapping. I walked back to my car, where Police Cadet Bruno was waiting and panting, anxious to make tracks.

We waited another half-hour, then hit the scented trail. The specially trained Belgian Malinois almost tore my arm out of its socket as it made my own dogs do their stuff.

Forty-five minutes later, we were on the outskirts of town. The big black-lettered sign on the large white-washed building just off the industrial park read: Bowsers Obedience & Boarding School. There were steel cages out front for the dogs to run around in during the day. The cages were empty now, the building conspicuously quiet for a doggy dormitory.

Bruno leapt at the red-painted front door, ready to tear strips off. I yanked him back, anxious to let sleeping dogs, and humans, inside lie. Then something round and hard jabbed into my back and someone hissed hard into my ear, 'Hold it right there, buster!'

I held it.

Bruno swivelled and yelped.

'Quiet!'

Bruno's jaws clamped shut, and he hung his head. I wasn't the only one obeying orders.

We left my back-up on the doorstep of the building, tied up to a railing, passive as a Tasered suspect. I was prodded inside, down a hallway lined with staring, kennelled dogs, into a play area carpeted with chew toys. The pooches didn't so much as growl as we passed by. And when the door closed on them, and I was told I could turn around, I saw why.

She was well over six feet tall, whip-thin body sheathed in a gleaming black rubber getup I would've called a catsuit except for the canine surroundings. Her jet-black hair was sheared short and severe, her narrowed eyes just as black and stern, lips slashed with three layers of brilliant red lipstick. Her face was hard and high-planed and handsome, her expression downright imperious. She was probably in her late forties, and had the bearing of someone who'd commanded respect from two- and four-legged animals all her life.

222

'I'm Kay Bowsers,' the woman rapped. 'I own this place. Why were you trying to break in?'

I squared my stooped shoulders and swallowed the lump of fear in my throat. 'You kid-, er, dognapped Livia Chienne's cocker spaniel, Tom. We tracked you and the pay-off here. I want the mutt and the money, in that order.'

She strolled forward on three-inch-high black boot heels, stroking her whip. That's what I'd felt in the small of my back – the handle-end of what looked like an over-sized black riding crop. She stood in front of me, looking down at me. 'Take off your clothes. Then get down on your hands and knees. You need to be taught a lesson.'

'Name's Ben Barker, not Warrindale Fido Von Yorkington, lady. I'm no show dog. If you –'

She cracked the whip across the tombstone-white palm of her hand, her eyes cold as onyx.

I peeled off my duds like I was shedding fur for the summer. There was just something about her – her voice, her posture, her all-powerful presence. Plus, this *was* the play area.

She surveyed my naked body. Then she curled a lip, gestured with the whip. I dropped down onto all fours on the indoor-outdoor carpeting. Kay clamped a studded leather collar around my neck, latched a steel chain leash to it and muzzled my mush with a brown leather-braided muzzle.

Then she strutted away from me in her glistening

black boots, yanking on the leash. I crawled after her, obediently trailing my master all around the room on my hands and knees.

She abruptly stopped. I kept crawling forward. She jerked on the chain and I was pulled up by the collar.

'Let's see your form,' she stated, walking around to the side of my doggy-postured body.

I wasn't exactly sure what she meant.

She meant for me to show my posed form – like in a dog show. That much *did* become clear when she whacked me with her whip of instruction on the small of my back, then up under my dangling dick, pulling my head up by the neck as she did so. I arched my back and neck and thrust out my butt, as rapidly as she snapped out the commands with her crop. I was quickly posed bowser-style, rigid all over and especially at the groin. I could've flushed birds out of the bush with my cock, if I was that kind of dog.

Kay surveyed my form with two very critical eyes, strolling back and forth at my panting side. Then, finally, satisfied to some extent I had no way of guessing, she smacked my rump with her whip. I jumped, body and cock both.

'Let's see how you take commands.'

I'd thought that's what I'd been doing, as obediently as possible. But this was Kay's command performance. I was just the trained animal who did what she said, or suffered the striking consequences. I'd never been lower in my life, or felt higher.

'Sit.'

I sprang up off my front paws and lurched backwards onto my butt. And toppled right over onto my side. The blood had rushed to my head – what little was left from my cock.

Kay yanked my chain and whacked my shoulder. I pushed up and rocked back, splaying my buttocks out on my heels, sitting up on my knees. Anxious to please, I wasn't sure whether to raise my hands into a begging position or what.

Kay studied me, her dark eyes and crimson lips revealing not a trace of emotion. Whether from training or tendency, I wasn't quite sure at that point.

She flicked the flexible leather tip of her whip against one of my nipples, then the other. The pink buds instantly blossomed, hard and buzzing. Being on the other side of the leash was turning me on like I never would've believed. Normally, I like to be the one in control (who doesn't?), but getting ordered around, submitting to an authority figure (with a very attractive figure), was somehow liberating, definitely arousing. Submission was obviously sexually appealing to me. Who knew?

Kay knew. All about command and control, and domination. 'Roll over,' she growled.

I tumbled over onto my side, rolled onto my back. I

instinctively brought my hands and knees up, in a truly supplicating pooch-man gesture. Kay towered over me, looking down at me staring eagerly up at her. Then she smacked the tip of her crop against my balls, and I bayed at the move.

She snorted and smacked my tightened, tingling sack a second time. Then she roughly dragged her crop along the length of my pulsing cock and swatted my bloated cap. My eyes rolled back in my head and I gulped slobber. My stiffened body trembled, my stiffened cock twitching under the stroking, smacking lash of my mistress's whip. She jostled my balls around, painted my shaft with leather, batted my hood back and forth.

'Time to really put you through your paces.'

I blinked my glazed eyes, sucked my swollen tongue back into my mouth. Kay jerked on my chain and I leapt back up onto my hands and knees again. She started jogging, running ahead of me. I bounded forward on all fours to catch up.

It was like the Westminster Dog Show for kinky adults. Kay trotted around the perimeter of the play area with me struggling to keep pace. I watched her taut buttocks clench and shudder in her form-fitting bodysuit, appetising rabbits to my randy racing.

She smacked me on the head, and I kept my head straight. She smacked me on the ass, and I kept my form erect and in line, running along at her high heels in perfect canine rhythm.

226

We made four circuits around the play area. There weren't any judges or spectators to rate my performance, just hard-to-please Kay. She berated my efforts with some hard cracks across my buttocks, begrudgingly rewarded me by stroking between my deliciously stung cheeks, along my sensitive ass crack, with her crop.

The parade finally halted in the middle of the room, leaving me breathless. My cock took a full five seconds to bob back under control and obediently point straight forwards again.

The show was far from over, however.

Ringmaster Kay quickly set up a series of small obstacles for me, by stacking up some of the larger chew toys. Then she dragged me back against the far wall and positioned me for a run and three leaps.

I looked at the three low hurdles evenly spaced down the middle of the room, and grinned confidently up at Kay through my muzzle. Piece of cake for this semi-athletic dawg, I thought. Kay glared grimly down at me, knowing more than I, as usual.

Fact is, it's no easy task jumping over *anything* on your hands and knees. You might be Jesse Owens in the 110-metre hurdles, but put you down on your knees, add your hands to the equation, and you'll find that your limb coordination leaves something to be desired. Unless you're a show-jumping pony girl by nature and training.

I sprayed chew toys all over the carpet with my dragging knees and flopping feet.

Kay slashed my butt cheeks till the red streaks flamed white-hot on my soft back-skin. I was sorely tempted to bark that I bet she didn't inflict this kind of punishment on her real four-legged furry students. But I bit my tongue, because my buttocks and body were actually surging with searing pleasure along with the scorching pain she was cranking out.

Just like I'd never been dominated before, I'd never been punished for pleasure, either. But now I was taking the well-intentioned and well-aimed blows on my backside and thrilling with the sudden sting, the shimmering burn, the internal and external flaming. My cock was jolted with each and every rump-whack, and I was soon leaking pre-come to go along with the tears in my eyes.

It was a raw, rugged new experience for me, and I was revelling in it. Kay with her hard, beautiful face and lithe black body looked good enough to eat to me. I licked my slavering chops.

It took five crossings up and down the room, and many more whippings, but I finally made it – I leapt over the low barriers in rapid succession without so much as jostling a chew toy. I was as proud as a blue-ribbon recipient, my ass and face beaming.

'Good dog,' Kay allowed, pulling me up short at her slut-heels. Then, 'Time to be a bad dawg.'

228

I looked up at her, my tongue hanging out of the muzzle, panting, as she pulled a steel zipper on her body-suit from neck to navel. The rubber garment split open like a blackened banana, and a naked woman stepped out, except for her boots.

Kay's body was white as ivory, just as smooth and shiny, aside from the black bush in between her legs. Her tits were small and taut, tipped by inordinately long, hard, pink nipples. She placed her hands on her hips and spread her legs in a towering power-stance.

'Lick me!' she ordered, jerking on my chain.

I leapt at the woman's pussy, like any male animal would. My paws landed on her lean thighs and my tongue plunged into her downy bush, against the soft, pink petals of her pussy. I lapped like a thirsty mutt at its water dish, jouncing my head up and down, dragging my tongue all through her fur and along her slit. I thrust my sticker as far out and as deep as it would go, though I doubt I rivalled any of her clients in the cages. She glared down at me, teeth set and tits heaving.

I nuzzled her warm cunt, really sinking my nose in, rubbing my face in the woman's wet and woolly sex. Until she snapped my head up with a tug on the chain and tapped the tip of my moist snout with the crop. 'Jump up on my tits.'

I was a show dog for sure now, springing up and landing my paws on Kay's arms, my tongue on a nipple. She shivered

229

slightly, as I swirled my damp licker around and around one of her stiffened, inch-long nipples, then bounced over to her other rubbery bud and gave it the same treatment.

She pointed at the floor, and I climbed down off of her. 'Now you're going to fuck me – doggy-style.'

My tongue lolled out of my mouth, cock jutting at rigid attention from my loins. Kay went down on her hands and knees, leash still wrapped around one fist, riding crop clenched in the other. She stuck her tight, mounded bottom out at me. I sniffed it, probing my nose in between her cheeks. She shuddered.

I dug my tongue in, licked at the woman's soft, silky crack, spun the tip around her pucker. She reached back and whacked my shoulder with the whip, and I mounted her, jumping up onto her buttocks and spearing my cockhead into her fur.

I hit her hole, thrust inside. I arched my back and howled, penetrating my mistress's cold, commanding exterior to the molten hot core. I draped my body over hers and humped like a mad dog.

Kay gasped, gritted her teeth so hard they grated. I grabbed onto her tits and groped them, pounding my cock into her pussy. We banged and burned together, joined at the furry loins. Drool streamed out of my muzzle and sweat off my face, body ablaze, pelvis pumping.

The only indication I had that she came was when she whimpered softly and rippled beneath me.

Then I yowled, bouncing on top of Kay, blowing out my balls inside her in blazing bursts of utter joy.

'You've earned your treat,' she said afterwards, taking Tom out of a pet carrier in her office and handing him to me.

'Why'd you do it?'

The diva of doggy discipline faltered, her eyelashes fluttering and eyes misting. 'I – I was desperate. I need the money to build a no-kill shelter onto this building, but – but I couldn't raise it. People don't care about stray dogs, only *their* dogs. I can't allow any more to die.'

I looked away, embarrassed. What she had was a pipe-dream, but I could sympathise; I was a bit of a stray myself, orphaned at an early age.

Tom barked in my arms and licked my face. 'Don't worry,' I said to Kay. 'I won't tell on you. Livia can afford a measly hundred grand. She'll just be happy to get her Tom back.'

Something like a smile flickered across Kay Bowsers' hard, handsome face.

Tom and I quickly turned tail, before we both got a double dose of discipline to make up for all that unrestrained emotion.

The Unicorn
Kyoko Church

If you were outside the door and heard the uncontrollable giggling emanating from the master bedroom, you might think the people inside were watching the most hilarious movie ever. But then if you stayed and heard the ensuing crying, begging and pleading, you would know otherwise. You might crane your neck, press your ear against the door, to try and hear words to help you figure out this dichotomy. All you would be able to make out, though, would be impassioned pleas of 'Stop!' 'No more!' 'Please!'

What would you see, if you dared to open the door to peek in? Well, wouldn't you like to know! Could you figure it out from what you saw? It would certainly be a confusing scene to stumble across.

You're still here? You still want to know? OK, twist my arm.

You'd see me, a 51-year-old man who should have known better, naked and tied to a chair. You'd see my wife, a woman who, at 44, I still find to be the hottest piece of ass around – save, perhaps, for the other woman in the room, but I'll get to her – naked and tied spread-eagled to our bed. And yes, the other woman. Close in age to my wife. Petite. Brunette. Curvy. Sexy as all hell.

Sounds like a good time, right? That's what I thought too, when I went online to a website catering to couples who want to find a unicorn. You know what that is, right? No? Urban Dictionary defines it thus: 'A bisexual person, usually though not always female, who is willing to join an existing couple, often with the presumption that this person will date and become sexually involved with both members of that couple, and not demand anything or do anything which might cause problems or inconvenience to that couple.'

Considering what happened, that last part would be hilarious if things hadn't gone so madly awry.

So how does a sexy little minx render two grown adults powerless, completely at her mercy? Oh, she's a sly little thing. She made it all seem so harmless at first. There was lots of giggling and wine and oh, won't it be fun if we tie each other up? Except she was the only one doing the tying. Before we knew it our cosy little get-to-know-you threesome soirée turned into something else entirely. By the time we realised exactly who was in charge, well, it was too late.

That's when everything went pear-shaped.

* * *

'Stop!' I rasped, all hoarse and weak. Weak from the hour of teasing handjobs with no release. Weak from watching my wife squirm and struggle and plead at her devious hands. Hoarse from begging on her behalf, on my own. 'Please!'

'Please, Carla. Please, no more,' my wife gasped, her body slumped, her words pathetic.

'Now that isn't what I told you to call me,' Carla said, smiling seductively, trailing her wicked fingers back up my wife's thigh, heading to that spot once again.

'Mistress! Sorry! I mean Mistress!' my wife spluttered, suddenly jolted out of her slump by terror that the torture might continue.

'Hmm, that's better,' our new Mistress said. 'Since you're just learning I'll let it slide. This time.' I could see the relief all over wifey's face as Mistress turned her wicked stare to me. I, in turn, stiffened visibly.

She chuckled. 'You see, I hear him telling me to stop, trying to stick up for you. But it's a little hard to take him seriously, what with that enormous hard-on right in his lap.'

I hung my head in burning shame but nonetheless could feel wifey's accusing stare all the same. Because it's true. My cock was as hard as it'd ever been. It waned slightly when Mistress stopped her tickle torture and I heard my wife's sad, meek little pleas. But only slightly. And when she leaned over and taunted her anew, slowly sliding her delicate but strong fingers with those bright red nails up my wife's smooth pale skin, heading for that spot, those ticklish spots on her hips that Mistress had so deviously discovered, while my sweet girl pleaded and begged her not to, I knew it was wrong, I knew I was a twisted, sick man, but I couldn't help what the sight did to my body. My cock throbbed and twitched in anticipation of seeing my wife's naked, helpless body writhe and twist at the hands of her sexy tormentor.

Mistress reached down into her bag and pulled out a long white feather. Wifey immediately started moaning in anticipatory dread. 'Oh, don't worry, silly!' Mistress said, looking over at my wife consolingly. 'This isn't for you.'

And suddenly her eyes narrowed on me.

If I hadn't already been tied to the chair I would have felt pinned to it nonetheless, by her steely glare alone.

Slinking slowly over to me, brandishing that feather as though she could use it to cut through all the synthetic ties that fastened me to the chair, she said, 'You wanna help the little woman get free?'

I gulped.

'It'll be so easy,' she crooned.

Somehow I didn't believe her.

'All you have to do is hold your little come in your little fucking balls,' she said, all low and dangerous. My breathing hitched at her words. My 'little fucking balls' tightened. 'And I'm only going to use this feather.'

How could I describe the ensuing blissful torture? The soft, silky tendrils of that feather caressing my super-sensitive, rock-hard shaft in slow, lazy strokes. It was madness that it could be so hard to hold back with such limited stimulation. But I felt half out of my mind with it. Somewhere in my addled consciousness I was aware that my wife was watching in embarrassing amazement at just how pathetic her husband was, struggling so hard not to come from a feather on his dick. And that just made it worse.

'Now I'm going to set your alarm clock here for two minutes from now. And if you can last that much more, then I'll tell you what? I'll let the little woman go. How's that?'

Wifey immediately looked awash with relief. But then she looked at my dick. Which was purple. And suddenly she looked fearful again.

'Ready?' Mistress asked. I think I must have nodded. 'This is gonna be fun!' she giggled. And pressed the alarm button.

I fought hard. I really did. As much as it turned me

on to see my wife with our deviously sexy abductor, I could tell wifey really wanted to be untied. So as Mistress stroked me over and over, all over my stiffened prick, I breathed and clenched and did everything I could in my restrained state not to come. I almost made it too. But after a minute and a half she took the end of that feather and wiggled its silkiness in rapid back and forth motions under the sensitive head of my cock. It caught me by surprise. I wasn't prepared. I gasped. And one shot of come erupted onto my bare chest.

'Oh, God!' wifey cried, almost as though *she* had just come, as Mistress cruelly snatched the feather away from my prick, halting all sensation and leaving my hips attempting to thrust up against the restraints while any pleasure from the release was as cruelly snatched away from my body.

I groaned loudly at the frustration of not being able to pump out all of my pent-up seed. Mistress chuckled low again. 'Aww, that's a shame.' Turning back to wifey she murmured, 'Goody. I get to keep you. And it's your turn again.'

* * *

Wifey was whimpering a bit as she watched Mistress walk back to the bed. 'It's OK,' Mistress whispered. 'We're going to try something a bit different this time.'

She adjusted the straps she'd used to secure wifey to the bed so that she was no longer spread-eagled but her knees were bent and her feet were up almost alongside her ass. This way, wifey's pussy was splayed wide open, clearly visible both to me in my chair past the foot of the bed and to Mistress. To my shock, glistening glints of girl goo were visible in the folds of her pretty pink hole.

'Well, well,' Mistress chided. 'What a slutty little mess wifey has made!' She tied another strap across wifey's abdomen that secured her torso to the bed. 'Looks like someone enjoyed our show!' She winked at me and moved back around to the foot of the bed. My wife had put her head back down on the bed so I could no longer see her face, but I could only imagine how it was flushed with embarrassment. We often teased each other in bed. Nothing like this, but I did know how it aroused her to see me struggling to hold my come. Apparently she really liked the feather show.

'We'll have to clean you up,' Mistress purred. And with that she dove between my wife's thighs. And started licking.

If the partial orgasm I'd had – the ruined one that only allowed one spurt of jism to escape my tortured cock – had taken any of the edge off my arousal, the sight of our Mistress busying herself with my favourite task, licking the silvery strands of my wife's excitement from her pussy, and the screams of ecstasy that it elicited from my beloved girl had me ramped right back up again. Knowing what it was doing to me, Mistress made sure she pushed wifey's knees wide and put her own head off to the side just a bit, so that I got a full view of the tongue-lashing. How it made my cock pulse and twitch to watch her lick and suck all of wifey's juices from her cunt, only to reach in with her fingers, pull out more and lick those clean too. On her second dive into wifey's hole, she pulled those girl-come-soaked digits out, reached up and made wifey suck them clean.

'That's a good little slut,' she whispered. Sitting up then, she looked from me, back to wifey and then at me again. You could practically see the wheels turning in her brain. It was terrifying.

'I think turnabout's fair play. Let's see if your stamina is a little better than Mr Quick Come over there.' My cheeks burned bright. I thought I heard wifey stifle a little moan. 'I'll set the clock again. Three minutes this time, since women are stronger than men in this regard. Wouldn't you say so, Quickie?' she said, looking over at me. I could only duck my head down in shame. Turning back to wifey again, she said, 'If you can take three minutes of my tongue and fingers without coming, I'll untie you both and leave you to your own devices.'

That sounded amazing to me! I was so fucking horny at this point, I was ready to fuck my gorgeous wife all fucking night. And she had always been someone who struggled to come via oral. So three minutes would be no problem for her.

'If you don't make it,' Mistress continued, speaking to my wife but with her eyes pinned meaningfully back on me, 'you have to give your husband to me for the night. I have some friends at a little club we have who would like to train him. I mean, meet him.' Her eyes glinted.

Holy shit.

She set the alarm. And then Mistress Carla played my wife's pussy like an instrument, plucking away with her tongue, strumming assuredly with her fingers. Wifey moaned and sighed and occasionally thrust her hips up, then seemed to remember herself, and visibly made herself relax. 'You really like having your pussy eaten, don't you, you greedy little slut?' Carla said, looking up from between wifey's thighs. My wife mumbled an embarrassed assent. 'Does your darling husband do this for you a lot?' A pause. 'Answer me!' she said, and began tonguing her hard.

'Yes! Yes!' wifey called out as her hips bucked. 'He's amazing at it!'

'Is he now?' Carla's eyes narrowed on me momentarily. And then she did something unexpected.

My wife's little clit was a hard, red nub, by now poking out in stiff recrimination from beneath its tiny hood. Mistress gave that sensitive little button a few soft licks, making wifey's body tense and quiver while she gasped out. Then I watched as Mistress puckered her lips in a perfect brass embouchure around that sensitive bit of flesh and blew firmly against it, producing a high, faint buzzing noise.

Wifey cried out. Her body immediately went rigid. I could see her arousal skyrocket instantly. Mistress Carla kept up her buzzy assault on wifey's clit and my poor girl was helpless to control anything. Mistress shoved two fingers inside wifey's cunt in a final attack, shunting them in and out while continuing to be a mouth vibrator on her button. It was useless. My wife came in loud, powerful waves of ecstasy that seemed to go on and on forever, her body contorting and thrashing against the bindings.

When Mistress had rung every last spasm out of my wife's pussy with her mouth, she sat up. Stopping the alarm fourteen seconds before it was due to sound, she turned to me. Licking my wife's come off her lips, she smiled.

'I can't wait for you to meet my friends.'

* * *

If you listened outside the beautiful gilded doors of the exclusive club you would once again hear giggling, mirth-filled laughter. This time however, it wouldn't be one sole female voice.

And if you peeked in? Aw, again! So curious! But this

is a very exclusive club. You have to be a member to know what goes on beyond these doors.

OK, fine, I'll tell you. But I may have to kill you.

You'd see me. The same 51-year-old man, in some ways. And yet totally changed in others.

What would you see to start with? Well, actually not that much at first. They didn't just haul me in, tie me up and start touching me. No, these women were much more devious, their torment infinitely more insidious than that.

When I arrived at the club with Mistress Carla – after being put through a series of ablutions that included washing, trimming, shaving and waxing my most private areas, done by a no-nonsense Asian man dressed in white – I was placed naked in a large room with two other naked men. Our wrists were cuffed behind our backs and we were seated on a padded bench along the wall. Just the room alone was intimidating as it showcased a whole series of toys of all shapes, sizes and colours, as well as instruments of punishment: whips, floggers, paddles, you name it. And then the furniture. Aside from a king-size bed, there was all manner of furniture that at first glance appeared unremarkable until you looked closer and saw the straps and holes in strategically placed areas. I looked at the two men seated down from me. They looked equally stunned and nervous. I wondered if they had been brought here under similar circumstances, if they were 'won' away from their wives or girlfriends for a night.

242

Finally Mistress Carla entered with two other women. Each of them looked mature, their scantily clad bodies lacking the roundness, the softness of youth. Instead it was obvious that these sophisticated women were tight and toned through physical activity, their bodies sculpted at the gym as the gift of youthful splendour receded. But each was different. The brunette Carla was petite with sexy curves, but still slender. The woman beside her was also petite, slightly Asian in appearance and with fuller curves, more voluptuous. The third woman was tall and blonde, statuesque. Together they made for a mouth-watering feast for admirers of feminine allure.

At first they completely ignored us. They put on music, poured each other drinks and started to dance, having a private girl party all their own. They whispered to each other and laughed and kissed, making delectable all-girl sandwiches, taking turns on who got pressed into the middle of the gorgeous sexy trio. Soon their playful kisses turned to full-on make-out sessions. Clothes started to get discarded, hands were on thighs, breasts, tongues flicked, nipples puckered. The giggling and chatter turned to sighing and moaning. I took a sidelong glance at my neighbours on the bench. Like me, each man was shifting around on the seat uncomfortably, watching in stunned amazement and sporting a fast-growing erection.

And still not one of the beautiful creatures looked our way.

Just when I was beginning to think that the torture would be that we were forced to watch this sexy display while unable to touch ourselves and would then be sent home frustrated, the blonde goddess turned a lustful glance in our direction.

'Well, what little treats have we all brought in today?' she said. Her gaze panned over the three of us as though she were surveying cakes in a bakery window. 'Kyomi, which one is yours? You had the winning one last time.' The woman who had had Mistress Carla's nipple in her mouth and had been tonguing it in earnest broke away from her. She smiled slyly and gestured at the man seated beside me. 'That's mine in the middle, Nikki,' she giggled. 'To be honest, I'm not expecting much from this one.'

'Oh?' Nikki asked.

'No,' Kyomi sighed. 'He's a total premature ejaculator.' The shame of the man seated beside me was palpable. I didn't even have to look at him to know how red he was, how sweaty.

'Why did you bring him then?' Nikki's exasperation was plain. 'The last one you brought kept us entertained all night!'

'I know,' Kyomi said. She smiled at the man she brought a bit shyly. 'But you know I have a weakness for the ones who are so cute and helpless! I mean, look at him. Isn't he adorable?'

'Well, might as well get him up here first,' Nikki said, rolling her eyes. 'Sounds like we won't be long with him.'

From experience I can tell you that the only thing more torturous than being in that man's place and enduring the teasing they then put him through was being in the place of one of us left on the bench. Left to watch and listen as the man pleaded and begged, knowing all the while that our turn was coming. Indeed, the man was quick to approach the finish line. But that didn't make his torment any less. Over and over they took turns with their hands, easing him to the brink and then denying him release. Since he was fast to get hard it didn't take long but by the fifteenth time his desperation was palpable and my cock throbbed in aching sympathy for his plight.

'Please!' he intoned. 'Please. Please let me come.' He was barely able to stand, still with his hands cuffed behind him. Finally Kyomi spoke up.

'OK, little boy. I'll let you come.' And she knelt down before him, her face a mere inch from his cock, and stuck out her tongue.

The sight of this exotic beauty before him with her tongue rolled out in invitation before his burgeoning shaft while being flanked by the other two goddesses was too much for the struggling man. You could see his entire body capitulate. He let out a tortured groan and spurted into her mouth.

Mistress Nikki and Mistress Carla each grabbed an arm as he struggled not to collapse. As for Mistress

Kyomi, she never touched the man with her mouth, but caught all of his load on her waiting tongue. Standing up and swallowing she said, 'Mm. Why is it the premature ejaculators are always so sweet?'

* * *

So they did eventually get to me. But not before I was also forced to witness the other man on the bench – a man whom Mistress Nikki referred to as her Pain Slut – strapped to a St Andrew's cross and alternately masturbated by Carla with a Fleshlight and lightly whipped across the back and ass by Nikki with a leather switch. Not being into pain much myself, I watched in amazement as the arousal from the Fleshlight mixed with the pain from the whipping to create a look of torment on his face that was so compelling it made me shudder with what I wasn't sure was dread or excitement.

It was probably both.

Finally the man came, came with strangled, anguished cries into the Fleshlight Carla stroked him with, while Nikki whipped him and chastised him for liking the pain so much and Kyomi looked on, one hand between her legs.

And then they got to me.

At that point I was so aroused by having watched the three nearly naked vixens manipulating helpless men over and over that my cock was twitching and pulsing without anyone even touching it.

I say it changed me, what happened then. Well, it did. How? you ask. What did they do?

Did they masturbate me?

No.

Did they whip me?

No.

Did they let me come?

Not even that.

Mistress Carla went first. She lay back on the bed and beckoned me over with the curl of one finger. Slipping off her skimpy panties she said, 'Now it's your turn. You get to be last. And in some ways, the most special. Because you are here to serve.' She parted her legs as Kyomi came behind me to uncuff my wrists.

Carla's arousal from the evening's events was plain, as her pink folds glistened with moisture, her intoxicating scent rising and reaching my senses. I looked in her eyes and suddenly understood my purpose.

'I have it on reliable authority that you are good with your tongue,' she whispered.

Mistress Nikki and Mistress Kyomi settled on the bed too, one on either side of Carla, as I started my oral worship of her. Normally I like to nuzzle and tease a bit with my lips and tongue on thigh and tummy. But we were both too far gone for that. Her little bud was wet and stiff and I took it between my lips and lapped it the way I was dying for someone to lap the aching tip of my dick. She tipped her head back and moaned out her pleasure, but then looked down again to continue watching me service her with my mouth. I increased my speed a little and pushed a finger inside, then two. Feeling her start to thrust upwards, I kept up the speed for a moment, then backed off a little. Her sigh at that moment made me shift up on the bed a bit, because even the pressure of the bed against my cock while listening to that sigh was too much.

'Oo, yes, girls, he's good,' she moaned. 'Oh, God, wait'll you get your turn. Fuck!' she panted, as I upped the speed again, working her G-spot with my two digits inside her.

That's when I realised I would be their oral slave for the night. I would finish servicing Carla, then move to Nikki, then over to Kyomi, before Nikki decided she needed it again, this time with me strapped to the bed while she rode my face with her cunt, screaming like the wild banshee she was in that moment.

And during all of my service they rarely touched me. But I stayed hard. And not just because serving three gorgeous women orally is the most intoxicating turn-on of my life. But also because they tormented me with comments.

'Aw, look at how stiff his prick is! He must be really frustrated.'

'You have to be a really slutty, naughty little boy to be so turned on by licking pussy.'

'That's it. Hold your little come in your balls. You're here to please us.'

'You exist to give us pleasure. If we decide we want pleasure from your fuck stick we'll let you know. Right now just keep licking.'

In between these comments, one of the two who were not being serviced might stroke my straining shaft quickly, up and down for a few brief, amazingly arousing strokes. I would groan into the pussy I was licking and then hear giggling. 'Hold it in, slave boy!' But that was all.

After Nikki was finished with me, Carla lay down next to where I was restrained on the bed.

'You're in luck, slave,' she said softly, drawing lines down my naked chest, pinching my nipples and making me moan with pent-up lust. 'I'm in the mood to fuck tonight.' She sat up and moved to straddle me. 'Just remember: your purpose is as my fuck stick.' She swung a leg over. 'So don't you dare come.'

Oh, God, the torturous bliss as she eased her tight wet snatch down onto my aching rod. I was not normally so eager, I could usually manage some control, but the teasing, the pussy-licking, all that I had seen all night, plus the words she had just spoken had me close already. I closed my eyes and battled my urges as she began to ride my cock.

'Aw, are you close already?' Carla whispered, no doubt noticing my struggling. 'You're in luck because I'm close tonight myself. Your hard cock feels so good. If you can last just a little bit longer, you'll make me come.'

Oh, how her words did not help the situation! I hovered close, knowing I'd never last watching and feeling her thrash on top of me. But suddenly I felt a sharp, jarring pain on my inner thigh and I yelped out. I looked down to see Mistress Nikki leaning over my legs from the foot of the bed with an evil smile. 'Thought you could use a little helpful pinch,' she said.

The pinch of course didn't slow Carla down. She took advantage of my suddenly decreased arousal and began riding me in earnest, grinding her pussy down hard, fucking herself onto me, over and over. Her orgasm, when it came, was like nothing I'd seen, not soft or ladylike but hard and animalistic. She came, eyes closed, with hard grunts and guttural growls that, I must admit, were way sexier than anything I'd ever seen in porn or real life. At that moment I knew I really was just a pole, a piece of meat with which to assuage her lust. The physical sensation of her pussy contracting around my cock coupled with this feeling of being used as a sex toy made my seed boil in my balls once again.

But Carla was easing herself off of me. 'Phew!' she giggled, looking at the girls. 'That was good.' She yawned. 'I don't know about you girls, but I'm pretty tired. Shall I send this one back now? Call it a night?'

'Maybe,' Mistress Kyomi nodded. 'I have an early Pilates class in the morning.'

'Mistresses!' I said, still tied to the bed. 'Please!' I glanced down at my throbbing shaft.

The three of them sat blinking at me, then looked at each other. Finally Nikki spoke.

'I don't know. Are you in the mood to watch a slave come again?' she asked the other two.

'Not really,' Kyomi said. 'We watched the first two! I thought this one was our winner, our workhorse.'

Oh, God! Were they really planning to leave me like this? Send me home with this aching hard-on, only to dream about the night's events, hold it forever in the spank vault?

'Please, I beg you! I'm desperate!'

'Shhh,' Carla spoke to me then, stroking my hair. 'That really wasn't what you were for, little boy. But I'll tell you what. I'll give you a choice. I will stroke you now and make you spurt your little mess, if that's what you want.' Oh, have mercy, yes, it was. 'Or,' she went on, 'or you can understand that your desire is not relevant here. Here, you exist to please us. And if you understand that and you'd like to choose that option,' she paused a moment and smiled at the two others, then back at me. 'Well then ... you may return.'

* * *

The 51-year-old man you see now may look the same. He may sound the same. He may wear the same clothes and do the same job. But let me assure you, he is not the same. I am not the same. I am changed.

I was not given an orgasm that day. Nor the next time I spent with them, nor the next. I don't know if they'll ever let me come with them, if they'll ever release me in their presence. That is not the point. The point is that I am theirs. When I am there I live to serve them. I put their needs always above my own. I am their toy. Their slave.

And in being their slave ... I am free.